The Browning of the New South

The Browning
of the New South

JENNIFER A. JONES

The University of Chicago Press
Chicago and London

The University of Chicago Press, Chicago 60637
The University of Chicago Press, Ltd., London
© 2019 by The University of Chicago
Published 2019
Printed in the United States of America

28 27 26 25 24 23 22 21 20 19   1 2 3 4 5

ISBN-13: 978-0-226-60084-0   (cloth)
ISBN-13: 978-0-226-60098-7   (paper)
ISBN-13: 978-0-226-60103-8   (e-book)
DOI: https://doi.org/10.7208/chicago/9780226601038.001.0001

Library of Congress Cataloging-in-Publication Data

Names: Jones, Jennifer A., author.
Title: The browning of the new South / Jennifer A. Jones.
Description: Chicago : The University of Chicago Press, 2018. | Includes
    bibliographical references and index.
Identifiers: LCCN 2018024852 | ISBN 9780226600840 (cloth : alk. paper) |
    ISBN 9780226600987 (pbk. : alk. paper) | ISBN 9780226601038 (e-book)
Subjects: LCSH: Winston-Salem (N.C.)—Race relations. | Winston-Salem (N.C.)—
    Emigration and immigration. | Latin Americans—North Carolina—Winston-
    Salem. | African Americans—North Carolina—Winston-Salem.
Classification: LCC F264.W8 J66 2018 | DDC 305.8009756/67—dc23
LC record available at https://lccn.loc.gov/2018024852

♾ This paper meets the requirements of ANSI/NISO Z39.48–1992
(Permanence of Paper).

Contents

Introduction: Race Relations and Demographic Change

In the world in which I travel, I am endlessly creating myself.
FRANTZ FANON

For decades, our understanding of how immigrants acculturate and accumulate social status in the US has been predicated on the presumption that newcomers must distance themselves from blacks. Since the early twentieth century, immigration and race scholars have argued that immigrants quickly learn American racial hierarchies and adopt prevailing social norms. Toni Morrison, in her 1993 *Time* magazine piece, "On the Backs of Blacks," wrote that such distancing has been crucial to the Americanization process.[1] From Italians to West Indians, establishing oneself as nonblack has proven key to accessing the housing, employment, and social status systematically denied to African Americans.[2] Moreover, as a competing low-wage workforce, new immigrant waves are doubly incentivized to engage in interminority conflict.

Today's news indicates that little has changed. Conventional wisdom and recent scholarship suggests that Latinos continue to follow previous immigrant waves, in which they engage, at best, in casual distancing from African Americans, and at worst, in blatant anti-black racism. In the 1980s, a series of riots in Miami was attributed to inherent black-Latino tensions after a black man was killed by a Cuban-born police officer.[3] In the 1990s, we looked to Los Angeles and its purported black-Latino "youth wars" to understand gang warfare and the future of racial conflict. And in 2012, when it was revealed that George Zimmerman, the killer of 17-year-old Trayvon Martin, was half-Peruvian, scholars and pundits hurried to reexamine the shooting as a case of pervasive black-Latino conflict and Latinos' long-held anti-black bias.[4] Researchers report that blacks and Latinos hold overwhelmingly negative stereotypes of one another; see each other as competition for jobs, resources, and social services; and, indeed, commit violence against each other.[5] As the country becomes more and more Latino, we should expect, from these histories, far more open, race-based conflict among minority groups.

The story of white/Latino conflict is just as well-trod. Anti-immigrant sentiment is hardly unusual, especially in periods of crisis, but anti-Latino sentiment is particularly representative of a kind of "foreign invasion" threatening very core of American culture (see the oft-cited Samuel Huntington book *Who Are We: The Challenges to America's National Identity* [2004] for an articulation), and it has been a swelling undercurrent of conservative politics for decades.[6] These arguments often point to structural or economic conflicts with other minorities to broaden their appeal and appearance of reasonability, but in this conception, Latinos are largely constructed as an affront to Anglo-American values, social dominance, and the rule of law. In sum, whether political or academic, these frameworks raise the stakes of demographic change.

And so, the sound of alarm bells, chiming out the "browning" of America, has intensified. Over the past several decades, Census takers and demographers have written and rewritten demographic projections, advising that racial change is happening faster than anticipated and, given current rates of birth and immigration, the US may be a majority-minority nation by 2045.[7] Scholars believe this acceleration is driven not only by rapid growth among new minority groups, particularly Latinos, Asians, and multiracials, but also economic change and reverse migration among African Americans (in which blacks are *leaving* the urban North in significant numbers, reversing the course of the "Great Migration" to move to prosperous neighborhoods in the cities and suburbs of the South and Southwest).[8] Depending on where you live, it may feel like this shift has already happened. Numerous municipalities, from Los Angeles to Charlotte, have already "tipped"; in 2012, for the first time, there were more nonwhites than whites born in the US. Perhaps unsurprisingly, this change is producing panic and political backlash among American whites. As Leo Chavez and Otto Santa Ana have argued, much of their fear hinges on the perception that Latinos in particular are "taking over."[9]

These fears are loosely grounded in social fact: Latinos are now the largest minority group in the US, and more than half of the foreign-born growth in the US population between the 1990s and early 2000s was Latino. Their role in shaping such issues as electoral politics, immigration policy, generational change, and a host of other social concerns is transforming the social landscape. Not only has the Latino share of the population increased dramatically, but Latino populations during this period have also spread out faster than any immigration wave in US history (internal or external), including the Great Migration of African Americans from the South to the North.

While Latinos certainly continued to settle in traditional destinations, such as California, Arizona, and New York, between 1990 and 2000, we have seen shifts in that same period to new destinations like Georgia, North Carolina, Utah, and Colorado. At the same time, the reverse migration of African Americans to places like Atlanta, Raleigh, and Houston ensures that the South (which, as of 2010, was home to 57 percent of African Americans) retains black majorities among its rapidly expanding minority populations.[10] These population shifts raise important questions about racial formation, immigrant incorporation, and intergroup relations. In other words, the US is changing—what will its emerging racial landscape look like? What will be the on-the-ground impact of demographic change on race relations and state politics?

Treating demographic change like a *problem* to be solved, however—often by choosing derisive framing likening expanding Latino populations to an invasion, a tidal wave, and in some cases, a *Reconquista*—not only creates unnecessary political tensions and hostile environments, but also puts new political and social forces, such as the criminalization of Latino immigrants, into motion. These processes, in turn, are also reshaping the Latino population, producing unintended social, political, and economic effects.

This book unravels the tangle of social relations that demographic panics about Latinos have created through an ethnographic account of community change in the southern city of Winston-Salem, North Carolina. Like other cities in the Southeast, Winston-Salem changed rapidly in the 1990s and 2000s, moving from a nearly perfectly biracial middle-class town of blacks and whites, to a tri-racial city.

When I embarked on this project in 2007, I was certain that I might gather insight into how race works among new Mexican immigrants, particularly in places where they encounter blacks and whites in equal numbers. I looked to Winston-Salem as a natural experiment in racial formation and race relations, where large numbers of whites and African Americans were increasingly joined by significant numbers of Mexicans, as well as some Central and South Americans, and Puerto Ricans, including large minorities of Latinos with significant African ancestry.

From my research and discussions with scholars and experts in the US, I knew that many Afro-Mexicans were migrating from the coastal regions of Veracruz, Oaxaca, and Guerrero to settle in North Carolina, as well as in Santa Ana, California, and in Georgia. In my preliminary research, I learned that Winston-Salem was a key destination, and so I embarked on a study that would examine these new settlement patterns.

My thinking at the time paralleled Eduardo Bonilla-Silva's Latin Americanization thesis,[11] in which phenotype would matter most. I expected darker-skinned Latinos to ally with African Americans, while light-skinned Latinos would see themselves more closely aligned with whites. In other words, rather than band together as a single minority group, Latinos would distribute along an existing racial hierarchy, complicating our ideas about Latino integration and race relations, but not necessarily race itself.

I spent four months in coastal Mexico learning about Mexican racial frames, ideas of blackness in Mexico, and the contradictions of racial ideology at the local, national, and transnational levels.[12] I also investigated the causes and motivations for new migration streams, attempting to unpack why so many Mexicans were now departing for the US from all over the country to settle in places not traditionally known as receiving centers for Latinos. When I arrived in Winston-Salem, I fully expected to apply this knowledge to the case city's racialized patterns.

What I found, though, is that Winston-Salem—along with the rest of North Carolina—is more of a natural experiment than I could have anticipated. I overestimated the predictive value of existing intergroup relations theory to explain a particular case and underestimated the importance of the interplay between demographic change, racial politics, and local context in shaping racial identities. Instead, I found, as Brian Behnken argues, black-Latino relations are not a zero-sum game—either conflictual or collaborative.[13] Rather, like all social relations, they are complex and dynamic, mediated by social context and changing over time.[14] Nor are race relations simple dyads. Rather, they are constructed relationally. In the case of Winston-Salem and its surrounding communities, rapid demographic change (often leading the rest of the country) and shifting longstanding black-white dynamics were at work, but the region also experimented with social and political solutions to that change, ranging from integrative policies like translation services to punitive agreements between federal immigrant enforcement agencies and local sheriffs.

Instead of being shaped by shared phenotype, I uncovered that Latinos' ideas about race were largely constructed from their social experiences of discrimination and political shifts, as well as relationally, through both their encounters with, and understandings of, the racialized experiences of blacks and whites.[15] In other words, as decades of racialization research has highlighted, phenotype does not have a linear relationship to race-making. While phenotype certainly matters, race-making is a far more complex set of social and relational processes that allow the assignation and adoption of race at both the individual and social level that can shape intergroup relations in unexpected ways.

In this book, I tell the story of contemporary Winston-Salem through the eyes of its new Latino residents. It has been tumultuous. They have been welcomed, un-welcomed, and then partially re-welcomed, in a relatively short period. I show that, when demographic panics set in among white residents, Latinos experienced a fundamental shift in their racialized minority identity and toward political alignment, rather than conflict, with their southern African American neighbors. The contributions of this book are at least two-fold. First, it uncovers solidarity between Latino immigrants and African Americans based in common experiences of racialization that fly in the face of standing theory. Second, it helps pinpoint the formal mechanisms and informal interactions that engender this positive, collaborative, two-way relationship.

While focused on one community, *The Browning of the New South* also makes the case that this outcome not only is being repeated across cities and states throughout the country, but also is a significant deviation from how we have understood Latino identity and politics, as well as interminority relations, for generations, and has important implications for racial meanings and politics. In other words, I show how fearing a new majority-minority has, in fact, led to it.

*

In the fall of 2008, I drove the 30 minutes down Highway 40 from Winston-Salem to neighboring Greensboro, North Carolina, where a two-day conference was scheduled on black-brown relations in the Piedmont Triad area. Both cities had experienced rapid and recent increases in the number of Latinos residing in their cities and surrounding communities—a six-fold rise since the 1990s. For weeks, civil rights activists, church leaders, educators, students, community members, and union organizers from Greensboro, Winston-Salem, and other surrounding communities had planned this gathering to discuss and organize, with the explicit purpose of forging positive relationships between African Americans and Latinos. Coming together for two days in a local Baptist church and community center, African American and Latino church leaders, organizers, and community representatives spoke to nearly 300 participants about the similar conditions faced by black and Latino communities. They shared, we were told, problems with gangs, poor schools, employment, institutional discrimination, violence, and exploitation, and they would come together as a minority community to resolve these shared challenges.

Throughout the conference, spirits were high and participants were energized. They chatted over sandwiches, listened intently to workshop speakers, and eagerly participated in group exercises. Not once were the motives for the gathering questioned. At the end of the conference, all the participants gathered in the sanctuary. Though this closing exercise marked the end of the long days of meetings, workshops, and lectures, the participants stuck around. They formed a rippling oval around the outer perimeter of the church sanctuary, circling around the pews to make space so that all participants might join hands. The two pastors leading the gathering—one African American and one Latina—asked everyone to cross their arms and join hands. Once each hand held another, participants were asked, one by one, to pledge their commitment to black and brown unity by stating "*esta cadena no se romperá conmigo*" or "this chain won't break with me"—however they felt most comfortable. As the last pledge was spoken, the participants all joined the pastors in a rousing version of "We Shall Overcome," a gentle sway undulating the unbroken circle.

This event was one in an ongoing series of meetings between blacks and Latinos in the Piedmont triad area of North Carolina, and is one of several efforts to cultivate an alliance between them across the state. Black and Latino civic leaders have made a concerted effort to create a discourse about shared minority experiences and mobilize as a coalition. Indeed, it was this same group that played a key role in rallying black and Latino workers in the Smithfield poultry plant strikes two years earlier[16] and in protests at town halls later that year against the Greensboro Sheriff's plans to sign on to the 287(g) program.[17]

The meetings also represented a seemingly counterintuitive process at work in communities across the country. African American and Latino leaders are working diligently and systematically to develop partnerships and coalitions, reaching out to each other as minorities with a shared political agenda, through the lens of their own experiences and a shared commitment to protecting and expanding civil rights. Throughout the South, alliances and coalitions are emerging. In October 2011, the Alabama NAACP (National Association for the Advancement of Colored People) joined the Alabama Coalition for Immigrant Justice to collectively oppose the passage of Alabama's controversial anti-immigrant legislation, HB 56,[18] and worked together to pressure the state to repeal HB 56 alongside restrictions on voters' rights. Wade Henderson, the African American president of the Leadership Conference on Civil and Human Rights, was one of the first to denounce the law, noting that it was designed to "terrorize the state's Latino community."[19] Other local African American leaders have called it a "Juan Crow Law," comparing it to Jim Crow in both letter and spirit. This hardly suggests that interminority relations have been uniformly resolved, but it certainly indicates that black-Latino coalitions are not only plausible, but, in the South, viable. Importantly, these leaders' efforts not only shaped intergroup relations, but also had an impact on Latino identity formation as pan-ethnic, racialized, and part of a shared nonwhite majority.

So why hasn't existing research indicated that such shifts toward a Latino minority consciousness and politics might arise? From what scholars have written, we would expect that, throughout the Southeast and other new immigrant destinations, Latino newcomers, like the generations of immigrants before them, would distance themselves from blacks and seek to identify with and see themselves as closer to *whites*.[20] But in Winston-Salem, I saw immediately that Mexican migrants identified with and saw themselves as closer to *blacks*. Conventional wisdom and academic scholarship tell us that black-brown conflict is pervasive; on the ground, the situation looks a lot different.

The Southeast, long underexamined empirically and overtheorized symbolically in social science literature, has served as a kind of symbolic boundary for the US. Not unlike racial formation practices that situate blacks and whites as racial opposites or position migrant mobility against an invisible, unassimilable black underclass,[21] the South functions as a regional foil. As Zandria Robinson argues, scholars and other commentators frame the region not only as distinct, but also as the *opposite* of the rest of the nation.[22] This framing of the South hinges on a kind of mythical past that is alternately backwards, unsophisticated, provincial, and patently racist, as well as timelessly genteel, warm, and simple. Indeed, Robinson describes how the South has "often served as a repository for national illness, quarantined, sealed off, and punished in order to maintain a national façade of progress and morality."[23]

And yet in the wake of rapid transformation, economic development, and demographic change, social scientists have no choice but to crane their necks away from California and New York, as symbols of progress, and look to the South for signs of what lies ahead. In a context in which both racial terrorism and racial progress have been and continue to be forged, what can we learn about race relations, immigration, politics, and ourselves?

This book approaches race relations from the ground up, investigating the ways in which race is constantly made and remade through day-to-day experiences. In this way, it diverges from much of the work that has queried, in recent years, where the "new color line" will fall in light of shifting immigration patterns, rising interracial marriage, and higher birth rates among nonwhites. First, in framing the kinds of racial formation that lead to a revision of racial hierarchies as part of a single, coherent, national, process, I believe many race and immigration scholars are misguided about racial change. Racial formation is deeply contextual and contingent. In the case of Latinos, for example, how they will come to see themselves racially depends on the local racial political context. And while there are some broad patterns, important differences between the configuration of settlement in Los Angeles and New York, versus Charlotte and Atlanta, should lead us to an analysis that frames racial change as a rapidly shifting patchwork of race relations, rather than a unifying framework. That is, while race continues to constrain and configure intergroup relations, life chances, and political ideologies, how groups relate to one another and access resources is fluid and context dependent. Instead of seeking out a new color line, I posit that locating Latino immigrants within a racial hierarchy requires a lens that views race as locally made. How Latino newcomers are incorporated, and the dynamic nature of incorporation, both play an important role in shaping the racialization process.

Second, as Moon-Kie Jung argues, sociology tends to speak almost exclusively to racial divisions and conflicts, and is nearly silent on what he calls *interracialism*, or the practice of forming political community across racial boundaries.[24] I find that this is especially true when considering interminority relations, despite there being no inherent rationale for division and conflict as social fact. In turn, I upend the understanding of black-Latino relations as always conflictual. I instead replace that universalizing notion with a far more nuanced theorization of black-Latino relations that includes a range of possibilities, including positive relations, that rests on the recognition of a common experience of racialization that manifests in shifted or expanded group boundaries that encompass both groups. I do not argue that African Americans and Latinos consider themselves racially the same, but that, in a more fine-grained and political way, their similar experiences of historical and contemporary racial oppression in North Carolina and various municipalities throughout the South allies them together and cultivates a sense of a new majority-minority through what I call *minority linked fate*.

Race and Immigration

This book aims to address these issues not only by illuminating new local and regional patterns in racial formation and intergroup relations, but also by explicitly linking the two disparate literatures of race and immigration. Although the immigration and race literatures initially began as one core area of sociology, by the mid-twentieth century, they had evolved into two distinct subfields.[25] In this volume, I bring the enormous contributions of these distinct subfields together. Specifically, where immigration scholarship attempts to capture and explain the dynamic interaction between host societies and immigrants, much of the recent work on immigrant incorporation has given little attention to power, inequality, and racism. It has emphasized ethnic formation and the potential for the assimilation of groups understood as "between" black and white.[26] Race scholarship, on the other hand, examines these processes in detail but is overwhelmingly focused on black-white relations, emphasizing the work of maintaining or shifting polar racial categories. This reinforces a de facto division of labor, relegating important theoretical questions about Asians and Latinos as groups to immigration scholarship, while blacks and whites (and less frequently, American Indians) are theorized under the purview of race scholarship. Still, the relationship between these two bodies of work is implicit, particularly in each subfield's attempts to understand the connection between upward mobility and identity.[27]

Nearly a century ago, in an effort to theorize the incorporation of Eastern European immigrants into the white majority in the 1920s and '30s, Milton Gordon, Robert Park, and others elaborated a theory of assimilation in which Europeans lost their ethnic distinctiveness over time through extended contact, adaptation, intermarriage, and reproduction.[28] This process of becoming white Americans was viewed as more or less inevitable, as well as necessary to achieve socioeconomic mobility. Gordon, in particular, provides a comprehensive yet concise social-structural framework in which assimilation becomes possible only through structural assimilation—that is, the acceptance of non-Anglo white Protestants into mainstream institutions.[29]

Whiteness scholars show that acquiring a white identity facilitated immigrants' structural assimilation and that a key piece of this process was to distance oneself from being identified with blacks, as many European groups, including Hungarians, Italians, and Irish initially were in the US.[30] In this framework, new immigrants perceived whiteness as the first asset accrued toward economic mobility. Separation from blackness was a necessary strategy for acquiring access to the privileges of whiteness. This linking of racial identity, distancing, and upward mobility formed an essential mechanism through which immigrant incorporation was achieved and understood.

However, in the post-1965 era of immigration in which the vast majority of migrants to the US (regardless of status) have been non-European, new paradigms for understanding the prospects for assimilation have become a project of immigration scholarship. In taking on contemporary immigrant incorporation, scholars of nonwhite immigration have sought to uncover how migrants assimilate when phenotype makes the strategy of achieving whiteness difficult, if not impossible.[31] Because African Americans are situated in this paradigm, both implicitly and explicitly, as the prototypical "underclass," most immigration scholarship has taken a prescriptive view of the whiteness theory of immigrant incorporation, arguing that non-European immigrants who seek a slice of the pie are best served by avoiding blackness and aspiring toward whiteness and mobility through racial distancing.[32]

While some scholars maintain that straight-line assimilation processes continue to dominate contemporary immigration patterns, even among Latino, Asian, African, and other nonwhite immigrants, segmented assimilation has become the dominant paradigm of contemporary immigration theory. This framework modifies the straight-line assimilation model by paying attention to racial differences and the relative difficulties of being accepted into the mainstream and achieving structural mobility, as well as avoiding downward mobility into the minority underclass.[33] Most notably theorized by Alejandro Portes and Min Zhou,[34] segmented assimilation splits the assimilation process into downward and upward trajectories, in which one "replicates the time-honored portrayal of growing acculturation and parallel integration into the white-middle class; a second leads straight into the opposite direction to permanent poverty and assimilation into the underclass; still a third associates rapid economic advancement with deliberate preservation of the immigrant community's values and tight solidarity."[35]

Such trajectories are understood to apply to all nonwhites, even black immigrants, who presumably face discrimination due to skin color, but desire the paradigmatic upward mobility achieved through migration.[36] As a result, the vast majority of the literature on Afro-Caribbeans, for example, highlights their efforts to maintain ethnic ties over a black identity in order to practice what immigrants, regardless of era, have seemingly known intuitively—being identified as ethnic, and therefore say, Jamaican, rather than racial, and therefore black, makes them preferable for hiring, opens up opportunities for interethnic association, and therefore, offers more pathways to upward mobility.[37] Vilna Bashi Treitler, in particular, highlights the importance of ethnicity versus race in the effort to achieve mobility and integration. She argues that at the heart of the ethnic project lies an attempt to achieve mobility by claiming an ethnic group identity and rejecting a racial one.[38]

This framing in which mobility and access to resources is obtained by distancing from African Americans is prevalent throughout the immigration and whiteness literatures, but it has not gone unchallenged. Scholars including Alejandro Portes and Rubén Rumbaut, and Portes and Alex Stepick, find distancing practices become untenable over time.[39] The prevailing racial inequalities in American life, they find, ultimately compel Afro-descendant immigrants, for example, to identify with African Americans around a shared racial group identity.[40]

Moreover, as Alex Stepick and Carol Stepick argue,[41] there is growing evidence that associating with native minorities as collective nonwhites can actually have positive outcomes, such as access to communities, cultures, and a sense of belonging, as well as strategies for mobility and increased access to structural resources through civil rights policies like affirmative action.[42] There is reason, therefore, to believe that the advantages or disadvantages of identifying and developing close social relations with native-born minorities, particularly blacks, varies depending on the conditions of minorities in local context. Kathryn Neckerman, Prudence Carter, and Jennifer Lee address this variability concretely, arguing that the segmented assimilation paradigm largely ignores the cultural and class heterogeneity of minority communities, and thus overlooks the range of possibilities that may arise from acculturation into minority populations.[43] In particular, they highlight how acculturation into middle-class minority communities that have overcome structural barriers and discrimination to achieve economic and social mobility can benefit immigrants. They propose a "minority culture of mobility" that "draws on available symbols, idioms, and practices to respond to distinctive problems of being middle class and minority."[44] Indeed, Joel Perlmann and Roger Waldinger [45] note that the problem of downward assimilation is that immigrants are frequently incorporated into highly segregated inner-city structures where both resources and attitudes toward mobility are poor. Robert Smith documents this phenomenon, making the case that, for Mexicans in New York in the 1990s, becoming black or claiming blackness actually served as a mobility strategy, producing what he calls "conjectural ethnicity," in which adolescent Mexicans made social and political claims to blackness despite a lack of literal African ancestry.[46]

In challenging the assumption that incorporation into minority communities is always a form of joining the underclass, Smith, Perlmann and Waldinger, and others indicate that the issue of mobility and intergroup relations between new immigrant groups and native-born minorities is shaped by class status, access to the labor market, and community-level resources, in which minority communities may hold mainstream norms and resources as well as critical analyses of discrimination and anti-racist politics.[47] Indeed, in the case of Mexicans and Mexican Americans in Texas, Julie Dowling theorizes racial identity as a continuum, shaped experientially through ascription and discrimination and discursively, depending on how Latinos conceive of their place within a racial hierarchy to construct an identity that aligns with their racial ideology.[48] In her interviews, Dowling uncovers how assertions of whiteness are assimilative, leading Mexican Americans to assert colorblind frames and highlight their own prospects for upward mobility through meritocracy. On the other end of the spectrum are those who assert a strong Mexican American, Latino, or Chicano identity—what I would consider a minority identity. This group believes that racism is pervasive, asserts an anti-racist ideology, and aligns its racialized position with immigrants as well as African Americans.[49] For Dowling and others, whiteness is as much about ideology as it is about cultural and structural assimilation.[50] Therefore, despite an overwhelming emphasis on racial distancing as a key mechanism through which strategic racial and ethnic identities are produced, a smaller body of scholarship unpacks how minority racial affinities and identities may be produced, emphasizing experiences of racial discrimination and perceptions of shared racialization as key explanatory factors.

LATINOS

While this paradigm has been applied to all immigrants, Latinos in particular have been framed as having an unsettled sense of racial identity.[51] In large part, this stems from US relations with Mexico, Puerto Rico, and Cuba in the nineteenth century, in which colonial endeavors and a domestic understanding of whiteness as tied to property rights, modernity, and global democracy underscored the importance of whiteness. For example, while Mexicans throughout US history have seen varying racial designations and experienced varying degrees of exclusion and inclusion,[52] their long fight to assimilate and be considered white Americans (to, for instance, access property rights in the 1950s) has not entirely replaced or been replaced by a Latino identity.[53] Although claims to a white racial status are certainly less pressing in the post-Jim Crow era, when discrimination is no longer explicitly mobilized in the law, and whiteness is no longer the only legitimate path to claim access to resources, scholars show that as recently as the 2000 US census, 48% of Latinos identified as white.[54] Latino identity varies regionally and is signaled by distinct label preferences—Hispanic, Latino, Chicano, Boricua—that indicate US-born of Latin American origin and may sometimes be pan-ethnic, sometimes not. Context has shaped the experiences of, say, Mexicans and Mexican Americans in the Southwest, who often experienced explicit segregation, discrimination, and exclusion from institutions in qualitatively different ways from Puerto Ricans and Boricuas in New York.[55] Moreover, an increasing share of the Mexican population are newcomers who, in some cases, import a preference for whiteness as dictated by Mexican *mestizaje* ideology and a widely held belief that education and wealth are properties of whiteness.

Carrying with them a deference to and aspiration toward whiteness poses a significant challenge to the development of a minority identity, since most newcomers to the US have explicitly immigrated in order to work and achieve upward mobility (even if transnationally). Thus, as in their home country, what many Mexican immigrants are trying to achieve is, essentially, the trappings of whiteness (if not the racial category of whiteness).[56] For decades, scholars have argued that Latinos develop aspirational identities in which they see themselves as more similar to whites.[57] In 2014, the *New York Times* revisited this theme, reporting that while race is "an immutable characteristic" for many, "it's less clear for Americans of Hispanic origins," citing data that more Latinos are identifying as white[58] than in the previously mentioned 2000 census.[59] This not only affects interracial relations, but also suggests an undetermined political alignment. Pollsters frequently consider Latinos an "up for grabs" demographic, neither Democrat nor Republican, in part because it is assumed that Latinos do not necessarily perceive themselves as a minority group, are relatively religious, and feel that voting Republican is an active way to distance themselves from blacks and assert an upwardly mobile white American identity.[60]

Some scholars find that Latinos even assert a white identity when they are well aware that are not recognized as white by mainstream society.[61] Explanatory theories include that this is merely part of a long-term strategy in which "white" will expand into a more multiethnic category that includes Asians and some Latinos, situating most of the American population above blacks and thus maintaining a racial hierarchy even amid changing demographics.[62] Alternatively, Latinos might choose to disassociate from both blacks and whites, developing more insular and distinct ethnic identities. And still others posit that Latinos' frequent choice of an "other" category, or a national identity rather than an ethnoracial one, suggests that they are choosing, en masse, to eschew racial categories altogether.[63] While this literature attempts to parse out the various factors that lead Latinos to identify or not identify with whites or blacks, with notable exceptions the authors rarely take into account that these experiences change across time and context, constraining and expanding the ability of newcomers to assert new identities. Indeed, this question is central to my research: What happens in new destinations, where Latino newcomers are key players in significant regional change?

Twenty-First Century Migration

Latinos have settled in the Southeast for decades, including in Florida, Louisiana, and Mississippi, where, at the turn of the twentieth century, they first replaced African American workers migrating north, then later spread throughout the region as Bracero workers. The late twentieth century, however, marked a more explosive period of Latino population growth nationally,[64] the result of increased migration, high birth rates, and the spreading out of the Latino population from a few key traditional receiving destinations to small towns and suburbs coast to coast. By 2000, Latinos represented 12.5% of the US population, outnumbering all other minority groups. In addition to strong birth rates among their relatively young population, migration from Mexico, Central America, and the Caribbean drove a great deal of the growth in the Southeast. Highlighting the rapidity of this population growth, demographers note that, as of 2010, approximately one-third of the foreign-born had arrived in the US after 1999. At its historic height in 2007,[65] the undocumented population was 12 million—approximately one-third of the foreign-born population in the US—seven million of whom were of Mexican origin.[66]

In this period, both traditional and new receiving destinations in the Midwest and Southeast (where the states with the highest growth are situated) saw significant Latino population growth, primarily of undocumented Mexican migrants. States like Georgia and North Carolina now rank in the top ten highest populations of unauthorized immigrants, despite possessing few Latino residents just two decades ago. Latino immigrants, authorized and unauthorized, now live in every state and are no longer concentrated in urban areas.[67]

While there is clear evidence of a significant national demographic shift, it obscures a patchwork of state and local demographic change. In some states, the shift was clear. As of 2013, 11% of American counties (mostly urban counties) were majority-minority. Texas, California, and New Mexico were majority-minority states, and 11 additional states had majority-minority toddler populations.[68] Understanding "the role that new destinations play in shaping intergroup relations," Mary Waters, Philip Kasinitz, and Asad Asad argue, "is a critical and understudied area of sociological research."[69] But large minority populations are still concentrated in a relatively small fraction of American counties, largely along the West, South, and East coasts, in America's central cities, and Alaska, and Hawaii, leaving many counties untouched by demographic change. This new distribution of minorities suggests both significant variation in how race relations are configured in a given city, county, or state and that such experiences are subject to rapid change.

THE NEW SOUTH

The South now represents a regional manifestation of diversity. It is a part of the country where, at the turn of the twenty-first century, migration really mattered. Population changes are undoubtedly part of a significant national trend, but in the Southeast, Latino population growth has significantly outstripped growth in the rest of the country: North Carolina (394%), Arkansas (337%), Georgia (300%), Tennessee (278%), South Carolina (211%), and Alabama (208%) have all seen incredible minority population growth.[70] They had very few Latinos before 1990, yet "registered the highest rate of increase in their Hispanic populations of any states in the US between 1990 and 2000, except for Nevada (217%)."[71] And the numbers are still rising.

North Carolina is a prime example of this rapid demographic transformation. From 1990 to 2000, North Carolina's immigrant population increased four-fold, including about 300,000 new Latinos.[72] As is the case across the region, much of that growth has resulted from an increase in the Mexican population,[73] both through direct migration streams from Mexico and through an influx of migrants coming from traditional receiving states, like California and Texas, which were experiencing economic decline. The Pew Center estimates that as of 2010, North Carolina was home to approximately 325,000 unauthorized immigrants, just below Arizona in the rankings of undocumented residents, and that between 65% and 75% of these migrants are Mexican.[74]

The Southeast gained a reputation as a welcoming destination through a confluence of factors. In the 1990s, the region saw rapid growth in both wages and employment (with unemployment below national average levels throughout the decade). States throughout the region expanded manufacturing and added service, agricultural, construction, and white-collar jobs just as traditional destinations saw their labor markets hit saturation (and their white population began to express anti-immigrant labor resentments), resulting in widespread population growth including significant numbers of white and African American workers who were flowing into to the region for largely the same reasons.[75] Because the Southeast also has notoriously low rates of unionization, large employers maintained high levels of political and economic leverage in the region, so anti-immigrant pressures in the labor market were low and easily ignored.

From the bulk of New South Studies literature, which aims to analyze race relations in the New South, a particular picture of cities, towns, and institutions bursting at the seams and overwhelmed and underprepared municipal leadership has emerged. Consistent with much of the race and immigration literature, this scholarship highlights interminority conflict and concludes that race relations are largely strained. Tensions between blacks and Latinos are perceived as particularly high, driven by competition over scant resources.[76] As in decades past, scholars argue that such competition incentivizes Latino immigrants to develop a sense of closeness with whites, who are likely to hold status and resources, and conflict with blacks, who lack status and compete with Latinos for housing and work. As a result, our general perception of race relations in newly majority-minority cities like Winston-

Salem bears almost no resemblance to the scene I described at the outset of this chapter. Many scholars describe the contemporary multiracial South as a continuation of a long, ugly history of conflict among minorities, and few would likely expect that my description of a gathering in which blacks and Latinos address shared community concerns and articulate a sense of shared minority status and linked fate could be more than an exceptional anecdote.

In *The Browning of the New South*, I show how contextual-level change shaped Latino racial identities and interracial relations. The rapid influx of newcomers, including Latino immigrants and native-born Latinos, blacks, and whites, has meant that many Southeastern states and municipalities were forced to adjust to managing these new populations. Initially, the migration was a perceived as a win-win. Mexicans who settled in North Carolina, Georgia, and other southeastern states in the early 1990s advised their families and friends in Mexico as well as in traditional receiving areas of the US that work was plentiful, the weather pleasant, and the cost of living low. Many counties were welcoming, providing newcomers with information and support to adjust to their new communities. Community colleges held welcome fairs, city departments printed bilingual brochures, and schools scrambled to hire bilingual administrators who could communicate with parents. By 2005, however, many of these same places were seeing citizen concern about the shifting demographics. The tide began to shift.

In many counties throughout the Southeast, states and municipalities have either passed punitive legislation or looked to the federal government as partners in an enforcement-first strategy. From 2000 to 2004, few immigration laws and ordinances were considered, but in in 2005 alone, 45 immigration laws were passed. In 2008, 206 laws were passed. Nearly every state considered immigration legislation annually after 2008, passing 277 new laws in 2013 (with a slight dip in 2012).[77] Importantly, some scholars caution that local differences within the region play a central role in immigrant incorporation.[78] Thus the variation in how states and cities have addressed immigration over the past decade,[79] with parts of the Southeast emerging as extremely aggressive in enforcement strategies, and others remaining relatively welcoming. (For example, as of early 2018, Mississippi had passed only one anti-immigrant bill, an e-verify bill that was unenforceable because it was unfunded.)

In the case of Winston-Salem and elsewhere, Latino Southerners had previously felt welcomed and had made significant efforts toward becoming members of their communities, and then quickly saw those gains evaporate. Such changes in context have significantly impacted the day-to-day experiences of Latino Southerners. This shift from welcome to unwelcome has begun to reconfigure the local racial context through a process that I call *reverse incorporation* (see chapter 3). Not only did Latino immigrants experience exclusion and downward mobility, but they also experienced an erosion in their understandings of their place in the racial hierarchy. As a result, their racial identity shifted. Because race is made relationally, I use day-to-day experiences to show how Latinos in Winston-Salem came to see their exclusion as orchestrated by white conservatives, and to a lesser extent, moderates and progressives who could not be trusted. Simultaneously, given the presence of a significant black population (including a significant number of politically powerful and economically stable African Americans), Latinos began to look to blacks to help interpret their own newly racialized experiences. That is, I observed how Latino immigrants frequently shaped their identities, networks, and politics through their experiences of shared discrimination with their African American neighbors. Because these neighbors had significantly more political leverage and resources,[80] they were often willing to serve as powerful allies against what they, too, saw as systematic and increasing discrimination against Latinos.

Again, we must recall that conditions are not uniform—how states and municipalities managed immigration, the level of initial welcome, the economic and political power of African Americans in the area, and a host of other factors vary greatly across the Southeast. But patterns emerge: like in Winston-Salem, states and municipalities are increasingly aggressive with regard to immigration and minorities are increasingly likely to live in the suburbs and to comprise a larger share of the middle class. Taken together, these changes suggest that the conventional wisdom regarding black-brown relations may be largely inadequate.

New South studies have taken on the challenge of explaining how the region's "southern distinctiveness" has quickly evaporated in the wake of rapid demographic and economic change.[81] Because Latino newcomers are integrating into communities that are largely African American and white, many with long histories of racial tension, how race and race relations in the New South will unfold remains an open question. Certainly, the racial dynamics that have led Southern whites to characterize Latinos largely in relation to blacks can be as much a force for minority-cooperation as it is for any sense of competition.[82]

Indeed, recent work digs deeper into the role of Latinos in community-level change and race relations throughout the Southeast, demonstrating the importance of context in shaping intergroup dynamics,[83] accounting for how municipal and state immigration enforcement policies are impacting incorporation, racial formation, and race relations.[84] Scholars such as Helen Marrow, who published some of the first comprehensive work on Latino immigrants in the South, capturing a distinct era of pre-enforcement migration settlement prior to 2005, illustrate the importance of distinct economic integration prospects and community-specific attitudes toward immigrants.[85] Likewise, Angela Stuesse, who looks at race and labor relations in the Mississippi poultry industry in the midst of the enforcement shift, finds that race, anti-immigrant sentiment, and the state of the labor market are essential in structuring the integration of newcomers.[86] As organizers elsewhere struggle to build successful alliances between blacks and Latinos, Stuesse writes, African Americans have been central to immigrant rights struggles as major players in Mississippi's labor movement, perhaps as a result of their empathy for Latino immigrants with regard to their similar position in the racial hierarchy and exploitability.[87] Still, many blacks in the area were competing with Latino newcomers for increasingly low-wage work and were frustrated by a shift toward hiring preferences for undocumented Latinos over the native-born. Stuesse goes further to suggest that Latinos failed to see their connections to African Americans as readily as the reverse, in that they saw blacks as relatively more privileged, especially within a given plant, and that immigrants may be unaware of the difficulties blacks have faced contemporarily and historically, including the exclusion of blacks from the poultry industry until the 1960s. Vanesa Ribas, who conducted 16 months of deep ethnographic research of life on the line in a North Carolina hog processing plant where Honduran and African American workers predominated, also considers how critical dimensions of work affect racial formation processes and race relations. Ribas argues that in a context of heightened enforcement, exploitation, and daily interactions that shape ongoing boundary work, race relations are best characterized as a prismatic engagement, in which intergroup relations are refracted *through* whiteness.[88] In her view, while both conflictual and cooperative relationships coexist, they are always structured by white control over resources, the relative social and economic positions of nonwhites, and white views on racial difference. Similarly, Natalia Deeb-Sosa's analysis of the tense interracial dynamics among staff in a North Carolina health care clinic from 2002 to 2003 demonstrates how, alongside rapid demographic change, structural conditions, low pay, and the indifference of higher-status white staff contributed to ongoing tensions between African American and Latina clinic staff.[89]

Other studies, such as those in the carpet factories of Dalton, Georgia, indicate that powerful white employers have sought out cheap immigrant labor to avoid paying higher wages to native-born residents, thus creating tensions between locals, who saw themselves being marginalized from the labor market, and elites, who supported immigrant settlement in order to extract greater profits.[90] African Americans had largely been driven out of the area decades earlier when they were barred from access to better-paying mill jobs. And when elites began recruiting Latino workers in the 1990s, they protected them (for a time) from anti-immigrant activism. Eventually, however, rapid Latino population growth and job losses among local whites gave way to aggressive anti-immigrant sentiment and a variety of anti-immigrant measures throughout the state and county. Jaime Winders' work on Nashville in the mid-2000s demonstrates that local patterns of racialized segregation and local histories devoid of an immigrant history, alongside economic growth, institutional invisibility, and racialized difference, conditioned the integration context.[91] Thus, in Nashville, Winders argues that the newness and geography of Latino immigrant settlement produced a kind of exclusion through history, in which ignorance about the contours of its neighborhoods, institutions, and racial past made integration and social membership difficult for newcomers. There, Winders saw avoidance rather than direct conflict among racial groups.

Indeed, ever-expanding areas of the New South literature highlight the role of Latino entry into labor markets—replacing black *and* white workers in many sectors, producing a great deal of tension between the native-born and newcomers.[92] Elaine Lacy reports tensions between blacks and Latinos due to labor market competition in South Carolina, as well as discrimination against Latinos at the hands of both blacks and whites.[93] Brian Rich and Marta Miranda find a similar sense of escalating tension between the working-class native-born, both white and black, and newcomer Latinos in the Lexington, Kentucky, area, where Latinos have become a major part of the horse-racing industry.[94] As in Laura López-Sanders' work in Greenville, South Carolina[95] and Marrow's in eastern North Carolina,[96] we see time and again that rapid demographic change, resource competition, existing race relations, and increased enforcement, or its absence, all play key roles in shaping the experiences of newcomer Latinos to the South.

Together, these literatures, contrary to my own findings, suggest an overarching incorporation model of Latino newcomers avoiding blacks, either to strategically evade downward mobility or to maintain a national origin–based identity, even as they sometimes experience sympathy from blacks who perceive that Latinos are both exploited and similarly positioned in the racial hierarchy. But, similarly to my analysis of the case of Winston-Salem, in their attention to local context, these studies also reveal that key factors—specifically the labor market and availability of resources, the demographic composition, the turn toward punitive immigration enforcement measures, and the preexisting sense of racial threat and race relations—all shape immigrants' reception by native-born community members and their resulting strategies of assimilation and activism.[97]

For example, although scholars find that competition between groups is pervasive, they also rightly direct our attention to the role of resource access in constructing relations between racial groups. This body of work suggests that we should consider how the absence of competition can facilitate positive intergroup relations; specifically, increasing contemporary integration into suburban and small-town communities where native-born minorities hold a stable position in the labor market, may forestall a sense of economic competition, opening up the possibility for minority cooperation.[98]

Social relations and politics also matter, as heightened anti-immigrant sentiment and local-level immigration enforcement can produce a feeling of exclusion and targeting among Latinos that racializes them as a minority group. And, finally, leaders in both the black and white community vary in the ways in which they encourage or discourage positive race relations and distinct narratives around shared status. Their actions cannot be taken lightly, as they have power to shape political and social relations, locating Latinos on what Julie Dowling calls a *racial ideology continuum*, in which racial identity and labeling are contingent upon an individual's own interpretation of their racialization experience.[99]

Positive Black-Brown Relations

So how are new destination newcomers becoming incorporated? Through an in-depth analysis of racial formation and race relations in Winston-Salem, North Carolina, *The Browning of the New South* gives us new tools to understand the social processes underfoot in Winston-Salem and across the Southeast. How new, nonwhite arrivals to the US will come to identify themselves and be situated within the country's racial hierarchy is, as in generations past, a slippery question. Nevertheless, new Latino Southerners are forging a path toward identity and politics that I show results in a sense of racialization and minority status that is both the result of, and an impetus to, develop both positive relationships and political ties with blacks.

Specifically, for Latinos in Winston-Salem new identity comes as a result of two related processes: a political backlash in the form of "reverse incorporation" for Latinos and on-the-ground relations with native-born community members, whose attitudes and practices shape newcomers' ideas about race. Their sense of minority status is cemented through positive relations with blacks and negative relationships with whites. Together, these processes not only undermine pervasive arguments that black-Latino relations are *always* strained, but also suggest a significant identity shift to what I call *minority linked fate*. And, that linked fate has the potential to produce a powerful, sustainable, and majority-minority political coalition in the New South.

In critically examining the relationship between immigration enforcement and race relations, this book argues that the spread of anti-immigrant policies and the growing relationship between minority interest groups (such as congressional caucus coalitions and collaborations between the NAACP and immigrant rights groups) will reshape US politics. Leveraging state power to maintain control of local and state institutions, the white power elite in Winston-Salem and communities throughout the US have inadvertently galvanized these new minority coalitions in a process that may diminish white conservative power over time—to the extent that it hinges on racialized exclusion. At the same time, black and Latino leaders have capitalized on this political opportunity to forge cooperation among minority groups.

Winston-Salem

The Browning of the New South focuses on the Winston-Salem metro area in Forsyth County, in the northwest quadrant of North Carolina. North Carolina experienced some of the fastest, most dramatic population growth in the Southeast, and Forsyth County experienced some of the fastest growth in the state. It is distinct in that it attracted a significant minority of Afro-descendant migrants from Mexico, but, while this population was the initial impetus for my site selection, I saw through 12 months of ethnographic research that this group actually made little impact on race relations in the city. From 2008 to 2009, I lived, worked, and participated in community life as I conducted 86 interviews with immigrants and community members. I supplemented this extensive field work with an analysis of 20 years of black, mainstream, and Spanish-language press coverage regarding immigration issues in the area to triangulate my understanding of the Winston-Salem community over time. This study design allowed me to examine incorporation at the community level, taking into account both the experiences of newcomers and the attitudes and practices of native-born residents.[100]

ETHNOGRAPHY

This book was built from the ground up, informed most broadly by community-level, inductive ethnographic fieldwork following four months of exploratory fieldwork on racialization and migration processes in Mexico. While many deeply theoretical and empirically informative ethnographies have investigated race relations by looking at the workplace and schools, I center my analysis on the community in an effort to link institutional relationships to the mechanisms that shape neighbor-to-neighbor relations. I also foreground the role of church spaces as key locations of race-making and political activism. In three key church sites with significant Latino populations, I saw that these spiritual centers were somewhat immune to the structural pressures of the economy and the labor market.[101] Because Winston-Salem has a long history of oligarchical leadership and low levels of unionization, churches have emerged as the most important civil society institutions in town.[102]

I developed relationships with these churches by attending services and meeting with outreach personnel, who then facilitated my volunteer work and access through the churches' outreach programs and services for Latino immigrants. Latino immigrants and blacks are highly religious,[103] and therefore likely to seek out churches more than other forms of civic participation, and churches provide many social services for both communities. Church membership is also a low-risk form of incorporation for minorities: congregants are not required to pay money, provide identification, or reveal any information that would put them in danger. Thus, economic fluctuation and changes in immigration enforcement have relatively little impact on church participation; in fact, churches often serve as sanctuaries and safe spaces for the undocumented. Because of the position of churches as longstanding civic institutions, they can also serve as a space for coalition building and organizing civic life. Though they are "positive" spaces, they are also spaces in which political attitudes and identities are debated and challenged.[104]

Recognizing that churches can vary widely by denomination, composition, and engagement in local affairs and politics, I chose three sites with extensive programming for immigrants but different theological orientations and different locations within the city. My strategy was to capture a varied slice of the Latino population in town and account for the possibility that differences between churches might be significant in shaping how Latinos perceived their reception experiences. The first was a Catholic church, which held separate Spanish masses and services and had a chapel to serve its overwhelmingly Mexican immigrant population. Considered the most welcoming of the three Catholic Churches in town, this site had an attached school. Its English masses were predominantly filled by white attendees, but also had significant numbers of blacks and Latinos. The second church was a small, independent Christian church, founded by a South American couple and attended primarily by Latinos. Located near a trailer park, it attracted many Mexican immigrant neighbors and housed after-school and parenting programs run almost exclusively by whites. The third church was a progressive Methodist church with a multiracial congregation and several community outreach programs, including community organizing, food banks, health clinics, and other services for the poor. The volunteers hailed from all races, though most recipients of this church's services were black and Hispanic.

I spent two to four hours a day, three to five days a week, in these three locations. My time was divided between observation (attending church services and church-sponsored community events or simply socializing) and participation as a volunteer in service provision. After establishing relationships with the outreach staff at each site, I also accompanied the staff on visits with church members, attended relevant meetings, and joined the board of a Latino church group organizing a nonprofit to meet the needs of local Latinos. Finally, I served as a regular participant in an interfaith community organization in which two of the three churches participated.

Still, I was aware that not all Mexican newcomers would be interested in or able to participate in religious services.[105] Therefore, I triangulated my access to Latinos in two ways. First, I used snowball sampling techniques to leverage my contacts through the churches and meet with Mexican residents who were not church members. Second, I developed this project as a community-level study, making observations and recruiting interview participants in a variety of nonsectarian institutional sites, including the Winston-Salem human relations department, the local library and community college, ESL (English as a Second Language) courses, after-school programs, the downtown YMCA, and conferences, town halls, events, and festivals. I interviewed city officials, nonprofit managers, immigration lawyers, political campaign volunteers, journalists, and professors. I also visited and attended meetings at the three universities in town. In the end, I captured a heterogeneous group of migrants as well as a holistic picture of the dynamics at work in Winston-Salem's immigrant integration, racial formation, and race relations.

Not all of this was easy or straightforward. Many Mexican immigrants were suspicious of outsiders and reluctant to engage with me. They needed significant assurance from other community members that they trusted. Others were simply difficult to get ahold of: many immigrants had no phone or email address. Again, establishing relationships with trusted community members and becoming, myself, a civically engaged local resident, helped me to access the Latino community.

In collecting my ethnographic data, I observed a variety of community, organizational, and individual-level interactions, both within and between racial groups. I saw how newcomers were perceived and treated by others, as well as the structural barriers and avenues of mobility available to them. The resulting data yielded important information regarding not only the nature of interactions, but also the ways in which groups explained, justified, and understood the ways in which blacks, Latinos, and whites related to one another. These were essential to revealing socioeconomic and racial statuses at work.

INTERVIEWS

In 86 formal and informal interviews, I asked participants to reflect extensively on the experiences of newcomers and on immigration and race relation in their communities over time. Of these, 37 were formal ethnographic interviews with Mexican immigrants, and three were with immigrants of other Latin American origin (29 of the foreign-born in my sample were unauthorized).[106] The remaining 46 formal ethnographic interviews were with black, white, and Latino community members who helped me develop a more holistic account of community perceptions and views on integration. I gained access to my respondents using ethnographic contacts, contacts that I established before entering the site, and flyers.

The majority of foreign-born Mexican respondents in my study reported little formal education beyond high school.[107] This concentration of foreign-born respondents at the lower end of the class and education structure as well as a high number of residents with temporary or no documentation is consistent with the class structure and status of Mexican immigrants in the area, as well as their sending communities, though, as in the broader population, there was significant variation among the respondents.[108] The blacks and whites I interviewed were heavily middle- and upper-class (as was the general population), but I am careful to mind that these were community leaders, not a representative sample of blacks and whites in Winston-Salem. I deliberately oversampled for community leaders in the interview pool because these are visible arbiters of community relations and were more engaged with immigration issues than the average resident. They also provided important insights that helped me put my interview data from Mexican respondents, my ethnographic observation data, and my media analysis in context. In terms of real political and social transformation, I believe this blended interview strategy best captured racial change and the strategic work to build or fail to build community-level change by empirically foregrounding the experiences of Latinos.

Interviews and ethnographic data were examined in tandem: the interview data allowed me to collect community members' stated views and opinions, while ethnographic data allowed me to investigate the extent to which they voiced the same opinions and conducted themselves according to their

TABLE 1. INTERVIEW RESPONDENT CHARACTERISTICS

Respondent characteristics	Foreign-born	Respondent characteristics	Native-born
% of total sample (n)	100% (40)	% of total sample (n)	100% (46)
Age (in years)		**Age (in years)**	
18–30	40% (16)	<18	2% (1)
31–50	50% (20)	18–30	26% (12)
≥51	10% (4)	31–50	22% (10)
		≥51	50% (23)
Gender			
Male	40% (16)	**Gender**	
Female	60% (24)	Male	41% (19)
		Female	59% (27)
Race			
White	3% (1)	**Race**	
Latino	98% (39)	White	54% (25)
		Black	26% (12)
Country of origin		Latino	17% (8)
Mexico	93% (37)	Other race	2% (1)
Other Latin America	5% (2)		
Other	3% (1)	**Highest education level**	
Documentation status		Did not complete high school	2% (1)
Citizen/legal status	28% (11)	Some college	2% (1)
Undocumented	73% (29)	Completed college	96% (44)
Highest education level		**Employment sector**	
Did not complete high school	30% (12)	Government	17% (8)
Completed high school	23% (9)	Nonprofit	50% (23)
Some college	15% (6)	Professional	20% (9)
Completed college	33% (13)	Self-employed/small-business owner	7% (3)
		Work in home/retired	2% (1)
Employment sector		In school	4% (2)
Government	10% (4)		
Nonprofit	8% (3)		
Professional	8% (3)		
Construction	15% (6)		
Service	25% (10)		
Manufacturing	13% (5)		
Unemployed	15% (6)		
Work in home/retired	5% (2)		
In school	3% (1)		

Note: Percentages may not add up to 100 because of rounding. Government: city council, social services, and schools; nonprofit: churches, service agencies, advocacy groups.

stated positions in informal settings. That is, I could see both what they *said* and what they *did* (and sometimes, what they said about what they did). Examining these complementary data helped me determine whether and how respondents' views of intergroup relations changed across time and context.

Formal interviews were conducted in English, Spanish, or both, and they lasted between 45 minutes and 3 hours (see appendix for formal interview schedule). Ethnographic interviews were informal and somewhat shorter, between 30 minutes and 2 hours.

To see whether the trends I observed in field research were mirrored in public discourse, as well as to pinpoint shifts in time within and across group perspectives, I created a database of articles on immigrants and/or Latinos from the *Winston- Salem Journal, Winston Salem Chronicle*, and *Que Pasa Piedmont Edition* spanning from 1989 to 2009. These three newspapers represented the mainstream regional press, the local black press, and the local Spanish-language press. Mentions of immigrants and/or Latinos were tabulated by year, then reviewed and inductively analyzed for emergent themes.[109] I supplemented this analysis with a review of other area newspapers to assess broader state discourses.

Together, these newspapers provided context from three group perspectives. The mainstream press increased its coverage of Latinos and immigrants over time. The Latino press covered all local events pertaining to Latinos and immigration, while the black press also frequently reported on Latinos or immigrants during this period. However, in the black press, relatively little of this reporting was substantive, focusing primarily on shared events and institutions in the Winston community. Moreover, there was a gradual negative shift in the tone in coverage in the mainstream press, and an increasingly alarmist shift in perceptions of anti-immigrant attitudes and practices reported in the Spanish-language press. In the black press, by contrast, reporting remained largely neutral or positive over time, locating Latino immigrants as sharing not only community space, but also status. These data confirmed that media portrayals of Latinos generally, and Latino immigrants specifically, mirrored the reports given by my respondents.

✱

Empirically, this book proceeds chronologically, tracing the increased migration to and economic expansion of the Southeast, with a focus on the three decades from 1980 to 2010. The book opens with a historical overview of the economy and race relations in Winston-Salem, focusing on large-scale economic and demographic change throughout the region in the 1990s. The heart of *The Browning of the New South* is the major turning point for the community: the anti-immigrant backlash shaped by state and municipal leaders and the impact of that backlash on the Latino community in the mid-2000s. Drawing from the media, community leaders, and the reactions of Latino immigrants themselves, I illustrate the lead-up to and aftermath of that shift, highlighting the importance of the rise of anti-immigrant policies in shaping immigrant experiences and the role of community leaders in shaping the meaning of those experiences. I then provide a richly detailed ethnographic analysis of how Mexicans in the Winston-Salem area became "minorities" and how this process is being duplicated in various communities throughout the South.

The Browning of the New South proceeds in six substantive chapters that illustrate the process by which Winston-Salem's Latinos came to see themselves as minorities alongside the community's blacks. Chapter 2 describes the setting and details the early stages of community-level change in Winston-Salem. Linking daily interpersonal interactions with large-scale political and economic shifts that shaped community relations through the 1990s, I provide a historical overview of race relations and economic conditions prior to massive demographic change. I then zoom out to macro-level factors that shaped the area over the next two decades, providing a brief overview of the push-pull factors that brought Mexican migrants to North Carolina. Chapter 2 elucidates a period of both heightened economic prosperity and demographic change, a time of growth, mobility, and opportunity for all residents.

Chapter 3 explores the abrupt shift in immigration policy and social responses to the influx of Latinos into North Carolina and throughout the region. Focusing on state-level legal changes and municipal actions from 1990 to 2010, I show how legal changes beginning in 2005—namely, legislation that denied access to state identification and driver's licenses to undocumented immigrants—were key in changing the immigration experiences of Mexicans arriving in Winston-Salem. As individuals, immigrants experienced the anti-immigrant shift as distinctly local and largely shaped by municipal actors and local bureaucrats. In taking a turn away from labor recruitment and toward racial exclusion and discrimination, Winston-Salem and similar municipalities fundamentally altered incorporation patterns. I explore what I call *reverse incorporation*, in which Latino immigrants who had previously been welcomed were abruptly denied access to both structural resources and welcoming attitudes, underscoring the significant damage it did to Mexicans' prospects for upward mobility.

In chapter 4, I detail the racialization of Mexicans in Winston-Salem after 2005. Latinos in the region experienced a sudden shift that altered their interpretation of their position within the racial hierarchy. Because Mexicans were aware of the discrimination faced by blacks in the region and saw that their interactions with blacks and whites were divergent, they came to interpret their discrimination experiences as akin to those of blacks. This led to a sense of Latino identity that was distinctly racialized.

Chapter 5 considers intergroup relations between Mexicans and African Americans in Winston-Salem. Contrary to previous studies, I found that a sense of shared minority status coupled with an absence of resource competition facilitated a high level of positive intergroup relations and social support between these racial minorities and increased the social distance between both groups and whites. I describe the on-the-ground interactions and institutional efforts that shaped intergroup relations, and make the case that status is key in formulating relationships among blacks, whites, and Latinos, producing what I call *minority linked fate*.

Chapter 6 turns to the broader political landscape. In this chapter, I apply the patterns I observed in Winston-Salem to other sites throughout the region that have experienced similar significant shifts in demographics, economics, and local immigration enforcement, and consider their implications for political change. This situates Winston-Salem squarely within a set of context-specific practices that are becoming increasingly common across the Southeast, such as in places like Georgia, where I take a closer look at similar trajectories of welcoming and closure, alongside increasing support from black activists and political leaders, as well as increased Latino racialization. In looking to the region more broadly, I draw from emergent coalitions in Mississippi and Alabama to make the case that such alliances result from similar processes and may foreshadow a political and social sea change in which the New South may be characterized by majority-minority coalitions on the one hand, and white backlash and political retrenchment on the other.

In chapter 7 I conclude *The Browning of the New South* by applying the mechanisms I uncovered here to other empirical studies of Latino immigration to the New South; highlighting how context-specific attention provides inroads to deeper understandings of how racial formation and race relations unfold. In reiterating some of the major findings of the book, I consider the implications of my findings for the race and immigration literature and the value of qualitative work in theorizing the impact of demographic change.

Open Doors: Race and Immigration
in the Twentieth Century

The city's black neighborhoods and improvement in housing in the first half of the twentieth century reflect the city's development from a small business center to one of the leading manufacturing centers of the South, and contained the residences of many of Winston and Salem's most prominent African-Americans of the period, as well as the working families who constituted the backbone of the city's economic growth. The neighborhoods further represent the city's increasingly urban character and the growing number of African-Americans in middle- and upper-income brackets.

LANGDON OPPERMANN, preservation planner[1]

Reshaping the South

In the past few decades, scholars and pundits have taken to calling the Southeast region of the United States the *New South* or *Nuevo South*. Distinct from the Bible Belt or Dixie, the New South is notable for its cosmopolitanism, economic development, and growing racial diversity. This image of vitality is as a direct counter to the hegemonic construction of the Old South as a black and white region where the roots of an explicit and intense racism run deep; a region defined by rural landscapes and small towns where the past is always present and religion rules; and a place where a certain kind of abject poverty remains common.

In truth, the region has always been complicated. The South was, in fact, the epicenter of slavery and a "tortuous racism that fundamentally and systematically denies black humanity" to African Americans, but as Zandria F. Robinson notes, the South also "has come to embody a racial paradise, one in which black political and economic power trumps racism for which the South is most infamous."[2] Religiosity, too, is common, but so is faith-based action, in which progressive movements for civil rights leverage their moral high ground for political and social change. Poverty exists, but the South is also home to extraordinary wealth and a low cost of living, numerous research institutes and universities, and, in the late twentieth century, a diverse and multifaceted economy that has expanded as economies in the West and Northeast lagged.

Nor has it ever really been *just* black and white. Latin American migrants, especially Mexicans, have been settling in the American South for decades. The first wave of labor migration was the result of an effort by the planter class to replace African Americans following emancipation in the nineteenth century. White landowners wanted to punish manumitted African American laborers and replace them with Mexicans, seen as more pliant workers and less likely to argue (unlike blacks) over the terms of employment.[3] But that effort was piecemeal and short-lived. A few decades later, however, in the mid-twentieth century, African Americans, fed up with a lack of economic opportunity and diminished social and legal status, left the region in droves. Beginning in World War I, this movement initiated the Great Migration of southern blacks to northern receiving cities including Detroit, Oakland, and Chicago that lasted until the civil rights movement. That steady loss of agricultural workers incentivized the recruitment of seasonal workers and culminated in the Bracero Program, the largest foreign worker program in US history. As a result, Latin Americans came, in relatively small numbers, to prop up the agricultural workforce of the South, though they rarely opted for permanent settlement in the region.[4]

The incentives for recruiting immigrants did not change much in subsequent decades, though the structural and contextual arrangements employers made with migrant workers shifted dramatically. New economic agreements, changing immigration and security rules, the end of the Bracero program and a shift to temporary visas and unauthorized labor, and significant economic growth throughout the Southeast coincided with economic stagnation in Mexico and much of the US. This greatly intensified Mexican migration, particularly to the US South.

The 1990s and 2000s marked an extraordinary period of Latino population growth nationally. Latinos certainly continued to settle in traditional destinations, but between 1990 and 2000, the number of Latinos living in the South quadrupled, then grew another 57 percent from 2000 to 2010. By 2010, 36 percent of US Latinos lived in the South. In less than two decades, the racial composition of the South had completely shifted from a black-white binary to the multiethnic region now known as the "New South."[5]

As California had done before, in the 1990s and 2000s, the Southeast served as a beacon to US residents and immigrant newcomers seeking opportunity, a fresh start, a warmer climate, and an escape. For the most part, the region welcomed new arrivals with open arms, providing ample housing and employment, and, until 2005, a political climate of integration for all those who wanted to make a life for themselves in states like Georgia and North Carolina.

In a 2005 Pew Report, "The New Latino South," the authors argue that robust economic growth drew young Latino men with "a greater intensity and across a larger variety of communities—rural, small towns, suburbs and big cities—than in any other part of the country." The report advised: "The South, different in so many ways for so much of its history, now offers lessons to the rest of the country."[6] Using 2000 Census Bureau estimates, Pew reported that six Southern states—North Carolina (394%), Arkansas (337%), Georgia (300%), Tennessee (278%), South Carolina (211%), and Alabama (208%)—registered the highest rates of increase in Latino population of any states in the US between 1990 and 2000, save Nevada (217%).[7]

Moreover, the story of this demographic change is not merely one of newly arrived Latino immigrants. College-educated, job-seeking, and retiring African Americans (a 21% increase) and whites (an 11% increase) were also drawn to these six states in large numbers.[8] This suggests significant regional growth, especially compared to the many other states that saw significant Latino population growth, but alongside drops or stagnation in the white and black populations during this period. Latino settlement was largely foreign-born (though Latinos often engaged in stepwise migration), while black and white migrants moved from urban areas in the Northeast, West, and Midwest. And these trends persisted into the next decade, with population growth in the Southeast outpacing the national average. The region was suddenly being rewritten by new residents with few attachments to local traditions, values, or politics, and they helped open up new political and social opportunities for change. They also, of course, spurred their twin phenomena: political retrenchment and backlash politics.

Within the context of the Southeast, this population shift raises important questions about racial formation, immigrant incorporation, and intergroup relations. The region has a complex racial history, yet it has never *dealt* with immigration in a meaningful way. This shift has also upended much of what we think we know about immigration and the Latino population in the US. States like Georgia and North Carolina now rank in the top ten of states with the highest population of unauthorized immigrants, despite having seen few Latino immigrants before the 1990s. Since immigrants are now also less likely to settle in areas with long histories of immigrant settlement, municipalities must develop policy and civic programming to help them adjust to new populations. Today, Latinos find themselves in a variety of Southern towns and suburbs whose views on immigration have changed significantly, sometimes advancing and at others retreating from the open-arms reception of the late twentieth century.

Becoming the New South: Twentieth-Century Transformations

Winston-Salem is a mid-sized town of approximately 215,000 in the triad region of northwestern North Carolina.[9] It is the largest city in Forsyth County and the fourth largest in the state.[10] When I arrived there in 2008, its draw to blacks and whites from the North and Latinos from the West and south of the border was apparent. At the heart of Winston-Salem's downtown is a thriving arts and business district, and its many local landmarks are a tourist draw on par with its year-long mild temperatures. And while its core is relatively urban and compact, Winston (as the locals call it) is nestled in the foothills of the Blue Ridge Mountains and the wider community is dotted with farmland, golf courses, and expansive parks. Universities, hospitals, and corporate headquarters are distributed throughout the city, ensuring a strong, diverse economy.

Despite this seemingly bucolic setting,[11] Winston-Salem, like many cities, has struggled with its growing diversity. Its robust economic history has always drawn newcomers and fostered relatively broad economic mobility, and that has shaped race relations in a manner that is distinct from its neighbors. In this chapter, I detail the history of Winston-Salem's decades of population influx, how both local and global economic and political forces intensified that process, resulting in a very welcoming context for inflows of Latinos in the 1990s and 2000s.[12] Until the mid-2000s, these factors meant that lacking documentation was a relatively benign position for Latino immigrants in the community.

Winston-Salem

Winston-Salem is a largely prosperous community with little outright conflict, though race is never far from the surface. Unlike the state's rural counties, as highlighted in the opening quote for this chapter, the metro area has a solid black middle and upper class. It is true that in the city, the median income of blacks was still half that of whites in 2000 ($32,277 and $51,016, respectively), but nationally, the medians were $30,439 among blacks and $44,226 among whites, suggesting greater affluence across the board.[13] Poverty rates were similar to the national average, with approximately 15% of all Winston-Salem households below the poverty line, and about 23% of black households, compared to 11.1% of all households and 22.1% of black households nationally.[14] In 2010, however, the cost of living in Winston-Salem was about 7.6% lower than national average, and 10.4% lower in 2005, and many of its wealthier residents have relocated to its neighboring suburbs.[15] Moreover, its lively economy, deep well of social service organizations and nonprofits, and multiple universities and community colleges meant that economic opportunity was accessible and social safety nets in place to support its most vulnerable citizens. Still, many blacks were upfront about persistent segregation. Some of the most prosperous blacks in the region call Winston home, but on average, black people were receiving far fewer resources than whites in the county.

Many black residents told me that they felt uncomfortable trying to talk about race or politics with their white friends and colleagues, and they described the community environment as full of racial slights and other micro-aggressions. Well-to-do black respondents reported, for example, that white colleagues confided in 2008 that they would never vote for a black president. Other times, white acquaintances assured them that they never thought of *them* as black. Dining at the large home of a retired black couple in a tony part of town, I learned that they'd switched dentists after an uncomfortable conversation about Obama and "those blacks." Clearly, many local black residents found it hard to trust whites—even those they might otherwise have considered friends.

Some saw this situation as a failure of the black community to stand up and ask more of the city and county. They told me that area public schools omitted black history from the curriculum and emphasized athletics over academic achievement when it came to counseling black students. Others pointed to serious problems including racial profiling by law enforcement and racial bias problems in the court system. The 2004 exoneration of Darryl Hunt, a black man who was wrongly convicted of the rape and murder of a white woman in 1984, exposed some of the community's deep racial divides; one of Hunt's attorneys reported that his children were ostracized by their schoolmates for *years* because of his involvement in the case. In early 2009, there was a rash of incidents in response to Obama's election (many targeting known Obama supporters in the community), and it was rumored that the Ku Klux Klan was gaining strength in surrounding counties. For all their prosperity, blacks hardly believed that their white neighbors saw them as equals.

Still, blacks and whites, for the most part, have found a sort of peaceful coexistence fostered by mutual prosperity and various forms of segregation, whether in neighborhoods, universities, or Winston's hundreds of churches. As in many cities throughout the South, economic stability and politeness generally preempted political discord or open conflict, giving blacks a sense of relative safety, despite ongoing divides and mistrust.

In large part, this uneasy stasis stems from Winston-Salem's nearly 200-year-long history as a center of manufacturing in which racial tensions

were managed and brokered by powerful business owners. With ample resources and near complete political control, a handful of wealthy business-
men maintained segregation and placated black communities by leveraging
financial support and high wages. The legacy of this strategy—dismantling
social movements by funneling resources into black communities—is still felt
today.

EARLY WINSTON-SALEM

Founded originally as a Moravian community in the late 1700s, Winston-
Salem began as the slave-holding community of Salem, North Carolina.[16] Often considered the "North" of the South, North Carolinians prided themselves
on their relative gentility and tolerance compared to neighboring states during the slavery regime. In Salem in particular, the presence of the Moravians
arguably made for a less violent and terroristic version of slavery, and many
slaves were integrated into Moravian religious traditions, trained to work in
factories, and sometimes allowed to receive wages and run small businesses.

In the 1850s, however, the Moravian theocracy began to lose power. Power
in the town fell to a rising business class, headed by the Reynolds and Hanes
families, and Winston was established next door with the founding of several
tobacco factories, including those owned by Salem's prominent families. By
the 1880s, there were nearly 40 tobacco factories in Winston, and Hanes and
Reynolds would spend the next 25 years absorbing them and fighting for control of the tobacco business. (Hanes finally sold to Reynolds in the early 1900s
and began a new business in textiles.) Until the 1890s, the black population of
Winston was relatively small, but the Reynolds family continued to expand
their empire by recruiting black workers. By 1910 blacks represented 40% of
the population (a proportion that would hold through the end of the twentieth century). As business flourished, poor blacks migrated to the area to work
in tobacco factories and as domestics, while poor whites tended to find employment in the knitting factories. Winston quickly became known as a place
of opportunity for blacks and whites.[17] By this time, Salem's residents were
largely employed in Winston, and the towns began considering a merger.

In the subsequent decades, the Reynolds family would rise to prominence
as titans of the tobacco industry, while the Hanes family flourished in cloth-
ing and hosiery manufacturing. Nearby Salem would continue, for its part,
as a center for religion and culture. The families flourishing, the cities finally
agreed to merge, with Winston-Salem officially incorporating into a single
city in 1913. By the 1920s, the Hanes and Reynolds families controlled city
government, built universities, invested heavily in infrastructure projects,

and sponsored the arts. In effect, these families—this region's Vanderbilts and Rockefellers—*were* Winston-Salem. As a result, along with a handful of other prosperous business owners (including the owners of Wachovia Bank), they controlled and administered for decades in what has been called "a benevolent oligarchy." The Reynolds family particularly shaped the landscape of Winston-Salem, concentrating the operations of the R. J. Reynolds Company, the makers of Camel cigarettes, in Winston-Salem. R. J. Reynolds built the Reynoldstown development to house its workers, and by 1920, the company owned 121 buildings in Winston-Salem. It was, at the time, the largest city in the South, save Atlanta.[18] Its headquarters, the R. J. Reynolds building, was among the first skyscrapers in the south and would serve as a prototype for the Empire State Building.

In addition to these developments, Winston-Salem benefitted from the long-term presence of Salem College, a women's college first established as a girls' academy by the Moravians in 1766 that began granting college degrees in the 1890s.[19] Slater Industrial Academy was founded at about the same time on the black side of town. As Cheryl Streeter Harry notes, "The thriving tobacco industry delivered swift progress for African Americans in the Twin City, placing them on the level of the 'Black Wall Street' cities in the South. Slater Industrial Academy (now Winston-Salem State University) provided the educational foundation."[20] Wake Forest University was, between 1941 and 1956, imported by the Reynolds family from the town of Wake Forest (just outside Raleigh) in an attempt to transform Winston-Salem into a cultural and intellectual hub.[21] Together, these resources allowed for the training and production of a highly skilled work force, albeit one divided by gender and race.

By 1940, Hanes and R. J. Reynolds tobacco employed 60% of the workers in Winston-Salem. R. J. Reynolds alone had approximately 12,000 employees, thousands of seasonal workers, and the largest tobacco manufacturing facility in the world.[22] Importantly, two-thirds of Reynolds workers were African American and one-half were women.[23] At its peak in the late 1940s, after nine weeks of contract negotiation, R.J. Reynolds' overwhelmingly black workforce, members of the Tobacco Workers International Union, went on strike. Despite flourishing businesses and access to higher education, until this point, blacks nevertheless failed to hold any political power. Following the strike, the union worked to increase voter registration, swelling the ranks of black voters from 300 to 3,000, and electing the city's first black alderman.[24] Yet attempts to build a power base quickly evaporated. R. J. Reynolds stymied future organizing by offering higher wages and blacklisting organizers. Panics over communism led to the federal decertification of the International Union in 1951, marking the last of the twentieth century's attempts to organize Winston's tobacco workers. Through the 1950s and '60s, major employers would successfully undercut the organized labor by providing relatively high wages and pensions to black employees.[25] Many also speculate that the companies bribed local clergy to help smooth over racial unrest.[26] As a result, Winston-Salem saw a deliberate, shared affluence between blacks and whites, designed to produce a tacit racial tolerance in which conflict was minimized by the maintenance of prosperous—but separate—lives and communities.[27] The unintended effect was that Winston-Salem appeared to be a racially progressive community, and that appearance resulted in tangible benefits for local African Americans. Historian Robert Korstad notes,

> Winston-Salem power brokers ameliorated some aspects of racial discrimination while keeping the larger system of racial capitalism in place. Local officials reluctantly extended voting rights, built low-income housing, and formed biracial committees on community relations. They brought in selected members of the black middle class to sit on governmental boards and on the board of the local black college. They increased spending on social services and philanthropy to the black community.[28]

By the late 1950s, blacks won seats on the city council. African Americans continued to make socioeconomic gains, as studies consistently ranked Winston-Salem as having one of the most prosperous, well-educated black populations in the South. All this blunted the civil rights movement in Winston-Salem, which saw only limited unrest during integration and just one small riot in 1967 (no one was hurt, despite significant property damage). Black integration into the power structure was incremental and came largely with (and only with) the blessing of the Hanes and Reynolds families.

Still, throughout the 1950s, many of Winston's African Americans became quite prosperous. Long-term tobacco workers received Reynolds stock and generous wages, and black businesses like The Safe Bus Company (which ferried black residents throughout the city, employed hundreds of black workers, and was purchased by the city transit district in the 1970s) flourished alongside black hospitals, universities, and churches. Over time, blacks moved out of the company-built neighborhoods and into East Winston. One of these neighborhoods, Alta Vista, was among the first black suburbs in the nation, and wealthy business owners built their homes near the university, along East 14th Street.[29]

In 1959, a so-called revitalization of the city, undertaken to accommodate expansion of the R. J. Reynolds Company and Winston Salem State University (WSSU), destroyed entire neighborhoods. Black neighborhoods bore the brunt; in the 1960s, 600 acres were seized and 4,000 black families moved in the name of progress. East Winston, Happy Hills, and Kimberly Park, all historically black neighborhoods, were redeveloped, and black businesses were destroyed. A majority of the remaining black families relocated to the east side of town, shoring up an invisible racial dividing line that coincides with the very visible US Hwy 52 (built in 1934). The divide persists to this day, with white families predominantly in the west and black families in the east.[30]

Though segregated, many black residents were satisfied with stable, productive lives. As neighboring Greensboro became known as the site of the first Woolworth's sit-ins and substantial civil rights activity, the Winston-Salem oligarchy successfully limited protest and keep open turmoil at bay. Nevertheless, its large population of relatively prosperous blacks could not be ignored. A small but influential black elite, connected to the city's religious

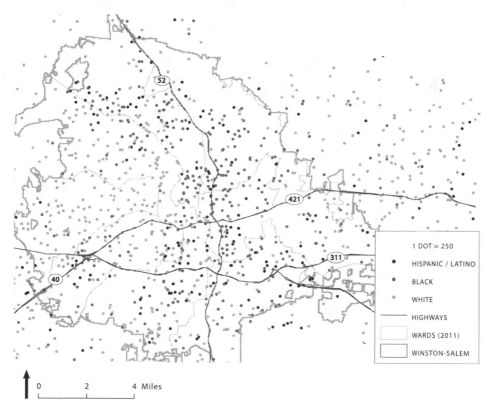

0   2   4 Miles

FIGURE 1. Distribution of population by race and ethnicity, Winston-Salem, 2010.
Source: Census Redistricting Data SF, Table P2. Minnesota Population Center. National Historic Geographic Information System: Pre-Release Version 0.1. Minneapolis: University of Minnesota, 2004.

hub and deeply embedded in Winston's financially stable and respectable black communities, slowly integrated into the city's post–civil rights power structures.

In the 1970s and '80s, as white flight, with affluent white families heading for the suburbs, became the norm, the economic tides shifted. Much of Winston-Salem's manufacturing center was bought out, merged, or bankrupt. In 1979, Hanes was bought out by Sara Lee and, in 1983, Phillip Morris superseded R. J. Reynolds as the largest tobacco manufacturer in the country.[31] In 1987, R. J. Reynolds, now RJR Nabisco, left for Atlanta. Winston-Salem scrambled to attract new companies to replace the 13,000 manufacturing jobs lost in the county, and service and retail jobs soon filled the gap, while Sara Lee expanded local operations. As a result, Winston-Salem's economy bounced back, finally shifting away from its religious-oligarchic roots. By the early 1990s, when much of the country was economically stagnant or experiencing a mild recession, Winston-Salem saw another economic growth spurt—the result of its aggressive efforts to recruit corporations and medical centers. Alongside big tobacco, corporate headquarters in the financial, airline, and manufacturing industries arrived, as did a center for medical research.[32] By 1990, Winston-Salem had more jobs and employers than a decade prior.[33] Moreover, this economic diversification meant that there was a dramatic increase in the number of white-collar jobs available in the area, and many blacks, particularly those educated at WSSU, moved into managerial and professional occupations. The black middle class continued to expand and gain a foothold in local governance. Still, Winston-Salem, by 1990, was ranked as the most segregated large city in the South.[34]

Economic growth in the 1990s was a boon to those of all races, but it came faster than locals could accommodate, particularly in low and moderately skilled positions. As African Americans moved up in economic and educational status, fewer were interested in such low-paying, semiskilled and unskilled work. Winston-Salem began to attract migrants of all backgrounds, quickly becoming an ideal destination for new Latino migrants.

NEW LATINO MIGRATION

In the 1990s, massive economic growth pulled thousands of white and black Americans to the South; an unskilled and semiskilled labor force was needed to handle increasing manufacturing needs as well as massive construction projects and service work. Throughout the Southeast, this demographic shift occurred alongside general population growth.[35] Despite rapid population growth, the unemployment rate in North Carolina remained below the national average until 2004.[36] The influx of Latinos to the region did not mean job losses for non-Latino residents; rather than economic competition, new *and* established Winston residents had little difficulty finding work.

Mexican migrants came to the region in astonishing numbers pulled by employment opportunities, but also pushed because the North American Free Trade Agreement (NAFTA) was shrinking employment options in Mexico.[37] NAFTA completely restructured the Mexican economy[38]: the Mexican government sold off state-owned enterprises, rolled back social safety net programs, ended farm subsidies, completed a process of agrarian privatization, and opened up the Mexican economy to more foreign trade and investment, but it did little to protect workers or facilitate labor mobility between countries.[39] Mexico soon fell into a recession. Since the Immigration Reform and Control Act (IRCA) in 1986, however, migration had become more difficult: there was greater enforcement at the border as well as increased penalties for unauthorized crossing. This heightened risk incentivized migrants to remain in the US for longer periods, or permanently, rather than crossing back and forth on a seasonal basis. Anti-immigrant settlement swelled in historic immigrant destinations in the US, reducing incentives to settle in these areas.[40] As a result, new migrants were recruited to fill a labor need—right alongside previously settled migrants from California and elsewhere (regardless of documentation status) who sought steady work and a less anti-immigrant climate. North Carolina's relative abundance of semi-skilled and unskilled work throughout and its low cost of living made it an attractive and important destination for immigrant laborers.[41] In the 1990s and early 2000s, plant owners recruited heavily in Mexico and other parts of Latin America[42]; sometimes, entire communities migrated across the border from regions that had never before been represented in the US in large numbers.[43]

The South was also attractive because, at the time, there were zero immigration enforcement measures on the books. Particularly in North Carolina, documentation status did not matter much. The state experienced nearly 400% growth in its Latino population from 1990 to 2000,[44] the highest growth of Latinos in the US over the past two decades.

The impact was felt most keenly in North Carolina's urban and metropolitan areas. As of 2004, 33% of the state's Hispanic population was concentrated in four counties along the I-40/I-85 corridor: Mecklenburg (12.8%), Wake (9.8%), Forsyth (5.6%), and Durham (4.8 %). Between 1990 and 2004, these four counties accounted for one-third of the state's Latino population increase.[45] In sum, urban and suburban North Carolina quickly became the preeminent site of the "New South."[46]

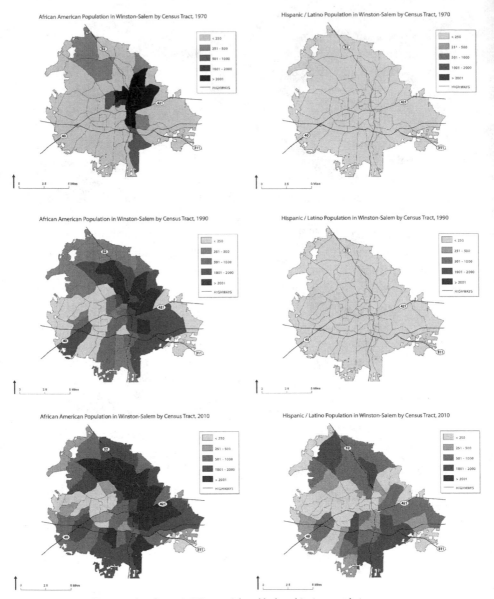

FIGURE 2. Demographic change in Winston-Salem, black and Latino populations, 1970–2010. *Source:* 1970 Census of Population and Housing, File CNTP4, Tables NT105; 1990 Census of Population and Housing, File SF1, Tables NP6; 2010 Census Redistricting Data SF, Table P2. Minnesota Population Center. National Historic Geographic Information System: Pre-Release Version 0.1. Minneapolis: University of Minnesota, 2004.

FOLLOWING THE NORTH CAROLINA MIGRATION TRAIL

While most North Carolina counties experienced significant growth as part of a trend in expanding immigrant settlement throughout the Southeast, this concentration was due in large part to the economic expansion in metro areas where various white-collar businesses set up headquarters. The growth in these sectors not only created new jobs, but also created opportunities for native-born workers to move out of difficult and lower-paid manufacturing work. These labor market shifts opened up numerous job opportunities in construction, service, agricultural work, and manufacturing, and Mexican immigrants and other Latin Americans were recruited to fill those positions.

The rapid recruitment of largely undocumented Latino workers was made possible, in part, by the simple fact that North Carolina was the least unionized state (with a 3.9% unionization rate as of 2007).[47] By the late 2000s, there were no unionized state, city, or county employees in North Carolina.[48]

With limited federal, state, and union oversight, employers were deeply incentivized to recruit immigrant labor. At a meeting I attended on the rights of the undocumented in North Carolina, a Latino man in front of me noted, "Most people here come from Guerrero, you know Acapulco, Cuaji [Cuajinicuilapa], etc., at least the people that I work with in the church. They told me that about 10 years ago, there was a sign posted in the town [Cuaji] that stated there was work in Kernersville, NC."[49] While it is difficult to find evidence of direct recruitment, several of my respondents corroborated his account of advertisements. In most cases, however, people told me they arrived following family members. In some instances, they continued the migration chain, calling family members who had settled in other parts of the US to Winston-Salem. Studies indicate that this is consistent with larger state dynamics in which the majority of migrants came to North Carolina through industrial recruiters, family, and community networks, most arriving directly and without documentation.[50]

Miriam, an African American councilwoman, said that the welcome mat had been laid out to Mexican labor for some time:

> We've always had migrant workers . . . the farms are out in Surry and Stokes and, and some parts of Forsyth, and Yadkin County. And really and truly, Mexican labor was available to the state of North Carolina because of one powerful senator in the United States Senate who was Jesse Helms, from down east where the farmers needed help. . . . And of course the farmers in North Carolina, for the thirty years that he was in the Congress, were desperate for farm labor because the, you know, those were almost like tenant farmers and sharecropper places. . . . Yes. And so, Virginia Foxx and Jesse Helms were good

friends. You know, Jesse Helms was in charge of the Senate Foreign Relations committee, and so our borders were open on welcome hinges for that migrant labor that lived in wretched conditions on a lot of farms. Blueberries, tobacco, those two big crops down east I know, and tobacco all over the state, so nobody should be shocked that we have Mexicans in North Carolina.

As North Carolina had some of the lowest levels of union participation, low labor law enforcement, and a very high concentration of big business reliant on low and semiskilled work, it is unsurprising at the time that Republican legislators worked to ensure a steady stream of labor. As the economy expanded, the recruitment of Mexicans expanded. In fact, Mexicans accounted for 21 percent of growth in the population in the state from 1990 to 2000.[51] This massive migration not only was due to economic and political practices in North Carolina, but also was the result of broader international trends in immigration. Latinos would eventually reshape the American South.

MEXICAN MIGRATION

Employment opportunities, a low cost of living, and nonexistent immigration enforcement are among the "pull" factors drawing Latinos to the Southeast in the 1990s and 2000s. But like migration chains elsewhere, while Winston-Salem certainly drew migrants from all over Mexico, as well as Guatemala, Venezuela, and El Salvador, migration was particularly steady from the Guerrero, Guanajuato, Oaxaca, and Veracruz regions of Mexico. A combination of shifting push and pull factors prompted new population streams out of these states.[52]

Mexicans have been arriving in the US steadily since the mid-1800s, following the Treaty of Guadalupe Hidalgo. The patterns of out-migration have remained largely stable, with the majority of migrants coming from the Western states of Mexico.[53] Only since the late 1980s have migration patterns shifted away from traditional "sending" Western Mexican states of Guanajuato, Jalisco, Michoacán, and to a lesser extent, Durango, San Luis Potosi, and Zacatecas (together, these had accounted for over half of migrants' sending states between 1926 and 1992).[54] In the late twentieth century, however, migrants began arriving from states throughout Mexico, leading to a major shift in the regional, class, and racial experiences of newly arrived Mexicans in the US.

The 1990s marked another uptick in the spread of migration due in large part to NAFTA, the trilateral trade agreement signed in 1994 by the US, Canada, and Mexico. One of its consequences was a shrinking market for Mexican-produced corn and sugar. At the same time, US corn exports flooded the Mexican market, crowding out Mexican corn producers and sparking the use of corn syrup for local products.[55] This was coupled with a severe curtailment in government-sponsored loans for small Mexican farmers, particularly those who grew corn and raised cattle.

The Mexican government's failure to buffer against NAFTA meant that many farmers who were previously able to subsist on small-scale production now saw temporary migration to *El Norte* as the only option to obtain the necessary funds for the growing season. In many cases, opportunities for self-sufficiency dried up permanently, forcing towns to empty of able-bodied men. The situation in many of these small towns deteriorated even more quickly for families, who need to find a way to pay for education and health care.

In my sample, the migrants who had settled in the US for more than 10 years by the time of our 2008 interviews said that they believed more and more migrants were coming from Mexico because its economy was in decline. They blamed the situation on NAFTA-related work shortages and said that for many Mexicans, particularly those from the countryside, there no choice but to migrate.[56] Most, they told me, intended to return to Mexico eventually, but border crossings were becoming more difficult. Moreover, because most migrants were young adults who either brought young children to the US or subsequently had children while in the US, the incentive to return had diminished.

The imprint of this massive out-migration is readily apparent at the border between the Mexican states of Oaxaca and Guerrero. It is a three-hour coach bus ride on a hot, dusty two-lane road from Acapulco (and its nearby villages) to Cuajinicuilapa, and the road is lined with pick-up trucks with North Carolina plates. Young men wearing baseball caps in the signature "Tar Heel Blue" of the University of North Carolina nod to each other from the trucks' cabs, saying "What's up?" It's the only English they know. Cuajinicuilapa's bodegas have names like "Mercado Carolina," and market stalls sell CDs with popular *chilenas* about going "North to Carolina." At the local post office, 90% of the mail coming in is postmarked from Raleigh, Durham, Charlotte, Winston-Salem, Greensboro, and elsewhere in North Carolina. Teenagers sit in the shade under the trees in the town square, discussing their plans to leave for Carolina soon. They are unable to locate North Carolina on a map, but they have cousins, uncles, brothers, and fathers there who will help them find their way.[57]

Shifts in the push-and-pull dynamic between Mexico and the US are significant not only because of the increasing diversity in the class and educational backgrounds of migrants, but also because Mexicans everywhere are feeling the pressure to migrate if they hope to sustain a reasonable quality of life.[58] The coastal regions in particular, which rarely sent migrants before the 1980s, are losing the small farmers who now have little alternative but to migrate. Mexican policies intensified this process, offering little economic support to those who would have preferred to stay.

INTERNAL MIGRATION

As mentioned earlier, Mexicans and other Latino migrants were leaving not only *Mexico* in droves, but also traditional receiving areas of the US, particularly California, Arizona, and Texas. Through employer recruiters and family networks, they found their way to North Carolina. "Between 1995 and 2004, 38.2% of North Carolina's Hispanics migrated from abroad, 40.2% migrated from another US jurisdiction, and 21.6% were born in North Carolina."[59] As Emmanuel from Guerrero put it:

> Well, when people go, and there's no work, they move somewhere else. So, lots of people, they went to California, but then when people got there. . . . they moved on, because it was expensive. There's not much work there now.

Indeed, for many of the Latinos I met in Winston, North Carolina was not their initial destination. The majority had originally settled in California, though a few came from Texas, Arizona, and the Northeast, with the earliest arriving in the early 1990s. While the primary motivation was to leave the service labor market in favor of better opportunities, for those Mexicans who had families with children, the political and economic situation in California and other Southwestern states was becoming difficult. California had reached a kind of saturation point, and so job opportunities had dried up while a political backlash gained steam. North Carolina offered better job prospects and a lower cost of living, as well as a more welcoming atmosphere for Latino immigrants (particularly the undocumented).

Contrary to our notions about California as a progressive vanguard, in the 1990s, the Golden State took the lead in anti-immigrant policy. In 1993, it cut off undocumented immigrants' access to institutional benefits like driver's licenses and, in 1994, it passed proposition 187, a ballot measure also known as the Save Our State Initiative. It was promoted as a way to deal with fiscal pressures, but was quickly revealed as a way for voters to "send a message" to the numerous immigrants in "their" state. The initiative was extremely popular among conservatives and garnered support from Governor Pete Wilson, winning by a significant margin—59% to 41%. Every California county, excepting the liberal counties surrounding the San Francisco Bay Area, voted in favor of the law.

Prop 187 even sought to ban undocumented immigrants from the use of public services, including hospitals and schools. The measure was quickly rendered unconstitutional, but voters were engaged in a symbolic politics whose message to Latinos was clear—"*We* don't want *you* here." In one exit poll, that was, in fact, exactly the reason people said they voted for the measure.[60]

Despite the legal challenges in California, other US states with large immigrant populations would soon come to propose similar legislation, presumably with a similar intent—to register dislike and opposition to the immigrant population. These economic and social pressures did little to halt the flow of new immigrants to California and other traditional receiving destinations, but the pervasive sense of racial threat created significant pressure for already settled immigrants to try their luck elsewhere. Though migration into the US from Mexico increased throughout the 1990s and 2000s, migrants who had been in the US long enough to establish networks elsewhere in the country were the first to explore interstate migration.

In 2008, I attended a meeting for immigrants at the Winston-Salem public library. When discussing migration patterns with regard to immigrants' rights, the facilitator, Sara, asked why people were coming to North Carolina from other states. A young woman answered that her friend from Arizona had moved because the law was *fuerte* there, and they can't do anything there anymore. Sara nodded, saying that she'd heard "that people are coming from the border states because it's less violent here, it's calmer here, better weather, it's cheaper, and there's more work." This pull to North Carolina promised better quality of life, not only in terms of economic opportunity, but also the low cost of living and freedom from increasingly restrictive immigration policies.[61]

The phenomena of push factors in Mexico and traditional receiving states like California, alongside pull dynamics in North Carolina where the economy was robust, the cost of living low, and enforcement nonexistent created a new Southeast region, drawing new immigrants at breakneck speed and sparking the largest dispersion of internal migrants since the Great Migration.

BECOMING THE NEW SOUTH

By 2000, the Southeast had officially become tri-racial. From 1990 to 2000, the North Carolina population of immigrants increased four-fold, with about 300,000 new Latinos, most of whom were Mexican.[62] Census data indicates that this is evidence of a significant shift in immigration patterns. In 2000, 55.6% of foreign-born residents in North Carolina were Latino, while only 2.8% of native-born residents are Latino.[63] The Pew Center estimates that, as of 2010, North Carolina had approximately 325,000 unauthorized immigrants,[64] putting it just below Arizona in its number of undocumented residents.[65]

The Piedmont Triad area, consisting of Greensboro, Winston-Salem, and High Point, experienced massive economic expansion and population growth. From 1970 to 1980, its Latino population grew 17%. From 1980 to 1990, it grew by 809%, and from 1990 to 2000, 962%.[66] The 2008 state migration estimates indicate that about half of persons moving to North Carolina at that time were Latinos, and over 75% of those Latinos were Mexican.[67] In Forsyth County, where Winston-Salem is located, the Latino population in 2008 was estimated at 12.2%.[68]

By the mid-2000s, communities such as the historically black, but largely abandoned, Waughtown district had transformed. On the Southeast side of Winston-Salem, this area was, in the 1980s and 1990s, blighted with unoccupied apartment buildings and empty retail space. By mid-decade, it was a thriving Latino district. Que Pasa Media, Compare Foods, Disco Rodeo (a Norteño nightclub), clinics, retail shops, taquerias, and small businesses, such as the Botánica Costa Chica, and Arely's Nutrición Natural, filled strip malls like the Southeast Plaza, while Mexican families moved into cheap rental housing nearby.

For the quarter-century prior to 2005, Winston-Salem was a welcoming community for Mexican immigrants, who quickly acquired jobs and property, increased wages, improved their educational status, accessed native-born social networks, participated in civic institutions, and experienced widespread acceptance. This match of welcoming community attitudes, an expansion of city services, and available housing and employment made incorporation relatively easy and accessible for most Mexican immigrants, regardless of immigration status. Understanding this warm welcome is important for understanding its reversal.

WINSTON-SALEM: THE WARM WELCOME

While community lore holds that Highway 52 still segregates black and white communities, census data indicate that blacks are now segregated somewhat differently, clustered around the center of the city, then fanning out, primarily to the north and then throughout the city over time.[69] As more managerial and white-collar positions became available to African Americans in the '90s, blacks began to move out of lower-cost, lower-quality housing near the downtown area, and into more expensive homes away from the city center, largely to the north and west. As in the Waughtown district, blacks' departure created an easy pocket of available housing stock for new Latinos to settle into.

This kind of settlement in black communities is typical, historically, as formal and informal mechanisms of racial exclusion and segregation limited housing options to existing minority communities or racially mixed working-class developments.[70] In those cases, however, white flight would quickly turnover entire neighborhoods, resulting in a longstanding history of nonwhites of different racial and ethnic backgrounds settling side by side, devoid of all but a handful of white residents. This was true not only in the South, but all over the US.[71] While such high levels of contact and constrained resource access can instigate conflict, shared experiences of housing discrimination, exploitation in the labor market, and shared institutions have more frequently led to solidarity and intimate social relations.

In the case of Winston-Salem, Latinos frequently moved to the black side of town, living alongside wealthier African American neighbors, racially mixed neighborhoods close to downtown, or in predominantly Latino trailer parks and apartment complexes. Housing developments on the South side of town, for example, now populated by Latinos were considered revitalized.

> The Southside has a record for getting dumped on. But it also has a proud heritage of gracefully accommodating all sorts of people. That didn't happen without cooperation all across that community. The Southside remains the only part of the city where blacks and whites live together in proportions that reflect the city's population. In the early 20th century, mill owners and mill workers often lived within blocks of each other. These days, a growing Hispanic population has brought new vitality to the area.[72]

In 1970, most African Americans were concentrated in the city center, where the tobacco processing plants were located. In the 1980s and 1990s, they spread out across the east side of the city. Blacks are now represented across the city, with the exception of a cluster of exclusively white northeast neighborhoods. This pattern indicates that in contemporary Winston-Salem, while most whites reside in predominantly or exclusively white neighborhoods, blacks and Latinos tend to live together or in diverse neighborhoods, populated by all three groups.

Although the black and increasingly Latino neighborhoods are less opulent than those that are predominantly white, the cost of living in Winston-Salem is low and home ownership rates among African Americans are high. Rental housing is spacious and usually features shared outdoor areas—looking more like the desirable middle-class apartment complexes we might find in urban cities to the north than the run-down complexes that often plague poor urban neighborhoods. Because there was no competition for housing, the transition of Latinos into the black neighborhoods of Winston-Salem was relatively smooth.[73]

Latino newcomers found safe, inexpensive housing with hospitable neighbors. Retail establishments and service providers soon cropped up to respond to their needs. Until the mid-2000s, Latinos, regardless of documentation status, had no trouble accessing employment, housing, goods, and services. To many, Winston-Salem embodied the *tranquilo* atmosphere they sought.[74] This openness to undocumented migrants was common throughout the region, but in North Carolina, access to institutions, legal documents, and services was particularly unfettered. For example, until 2005, North Carolina was one of 10 states that issued driver's licenses to applicants without verification of citizenship status. Antonio, a Mexican reporter for the Spanish language newspaper, noted:

> One of the reasons that [migration increased] was because you could get a driver's license. North Carolina was probably one of the last states in the United States, and that changed in 2006, that would give you a driver's license. For several years–seven, eight, nine years—would not ask for more than passing the examination. You know, the driving examination, the written examination and a number. You didn't have to prove anything else. They required two addresses, and that's it! That's part of the reason. I understand that people from Georgia, from South Carolina, from Florida, you know, neighboring places, started to come here to get driver's licenses.

Throughout the 1990s and early 2000s, it seemed that this new Latino migration was a win-win. Mexicans who settled in North Carolina in the early 1990s advised their families and friends in Mexico as well as in traditional receiving areas of the US to come to North Carolina, a good place to find work and live without fear. In Winston-Salem in particular, as many African Americans rose into the middle class and moved away from the city center to the suburbs or to larger, higher quality housing nearby, empty housing stock was available at reasonable prices. Mexicans did relatively well in the New South, purchasing cars, establishing small independent businesses, generally doing as they pleased. They largely flew under the radar of the state, too: not only were there no mechanisms to count Latinos (until the late 2000s, official forms only included blacks, whites, and "others"), but there were no mechanisms to exclude them from a kind of social citizenship, in which they experienced a sense of both institutional and interpersonal belonging.

Such belonging was not inconsequential. For example, with the benefit of driver's licenses and state identification cards, it was easy for newcomers to apply for work, open bank accounts, receive small loans, and purchase trailers, homes, and vehicles. Essentially, through this recognition, even undocumented Latinos gained access to the American Dream. Further, since undocumented migrants living in North Carolina could legally purchase a car in their own name, along with insurance and registration, it became relatively easy to live a more transnational lifestyle, driving across the border to visit family, check on investments such as small farms and retirement homes, bring gifts and money for friends and family, and check on children and elderly parents.

This also meant that integration efforts were left to municipal leaders, rather than the state and federal government, who were generally more concerned with creating welcoming neighborhoods and institutions, appeasing local businesses, and maintaining safety and security than issues surrounding documentation status. At least at first, concerns over immigration status were beyond the scope of interest of area city councils, mayors, and managers. Like the bureaucrats in Helen Marrow's rural North Carolina, local bureaucrats and service providers were motivated by a desire to serve residents, particularly in those institutions and city agencies with strong client services missions.[75] Like other periods of policy formation, in the absence of robust national and state-level discourses that portrayed Mexican immigrants as a drain on social services as job stealers, as criminals, and as illegal, city bureaucrats and service-providers were free to construct Mexican newcomers as they saw fit.[76] In this period of economic expansion and growth, most bureaucrats saw newcomers as future North Carolinians, capable of integrating into Winston-Salem's communities and contributing to the well-being of the state. In particular, because Winston-Salem was, historically, governed by business leaders, there was little incentive to treat Mexican workers in a manner that was at odds with the needs of the economy. Because local institutional responses preceded state and national ones, government workers, nonprofits, and businesses alike worked hard to provide accessible services to Mexican newcomers, highlighting their potential as workers, taxpayers, and consumers, as well as family-oriented, religious folks who brought much-desired diversity.[77]

In this sense, Latino immigrants in Winston-Salem and throughout much of North Carolina appeared to briefly experience the best of the immigrant experience: retaining family ties while accessing upward mobility. To be sure, the region was not free of racism and xenophobia.[78] In 2000, ex-Klansman David Duke led rallies to protest immigrant settlement in the state.[79] Still such incidents were few and far between. In fact, in the 1990s, most residents didn't *realize* that Latinos were settling in large numbers, possibly because local bureaucrats made it their business to accommodate newcomers and help them integrate into the community as quickly as possible. From 1990 to 2000, then, local and state policy toward immigrants, as well as the community-level reception, was largely positive and accommodating.[80]

Most important was the match between immigrants looking for work and an expanding, diversifying economy that needed all sorts of workers. Abundant opportunity facilitated mobility as the 1990s saw the state's unemployment level dip to 3% and as low as 1.7% in several urban counties—the lowest level in decades.[81] In counties where working-class whites and African Americans were upwardly mobile, Latinos filled an economic void.[82] Unemployment was so low that, in 1998, a local newspaper's staff writers reported on employers' desperation and an aggressively promoted job fair to which only three applicants responded:

> From the high-tech companies in Research Triangle Park to the region's schools, just about every industry is begging for help. But the labor shortage is most acute when it comes to hourly workers in low-paying jobs. Thousands of newcomers moving to the Triangle each year looking for places to live, eat and shop have created a demand for service, retail, construction and maintenance workers. . . . A large and growing number of illegal immigrants have also found employers who offer steady work and ask few questions.[83]

Like other states in the region, North Carolina offered abundant employment opportunities, and some immigrants were able to accumulate enough resources to start small businesses, including construction crews, restaurants, food trucks, and markets. Local institutions helped to facilitate upward mobility by employing Latinos and providing access to capital through bank and credit union loans and community education. Some small banks and cooperatives targeted services to Latino immigrants seeking small business loans, including the Southern Community Bank and Trust, which opened in 1996, and the Latino Cooperative Credit Union, which opened its first North Carolina branch in 2000, then expanded across the state.[84] In fact, reaching out to area Latinos to provide banking services was a major growth strategy for local area banks. In late 2002, the *Winston-Salem Journal* reported:

> Winston-Salem's Southern Community Financial Corp., which owns Southern Community Bank and Trust, is beginning to make a name for itself among the area's swelling population of Hispanic immigrants. The bank is closely tracking the evolution of the market and placing bilingual employees in pivotal customer-service roles. All employees are encouraged to go the extra mile for Hispanics, most of whom are unfamiliar with banking systems. South-

ern Community has also taken to the streets. Its outreach began two years ago when the bank hired Maria Sanchez-Boudy, a bilingual consultant and founder of Latin Connection in Colfax, to take an up-close-and-personal approach to the target population. "Maria took the ball and ran with it," said Jeff Clark, the bank's president. "She's very aggressive and does a good job of keeping us on target" . . . In the community, she speaks to church and social service groups and knocks on doors in Hispanic neighborhoods. It is a job that has taken her to the parking lot at Wal-Mart, into ESL (English as a Second Language) classes and to the doorsteps of residents at trailer parks. "I don't miss an opportunity to give out information," she said . . . As an example, she said, a few Sundays ago, Southern Community's Peters Creek branch opened for regular business specifically to cater to Hispanics. "We helped them open accounts and do wire transfers. But we also did a cookout, had a DJ and invited agencies which serve the Latino community, so that it would not be all about the bank. This is not your average marketing campaign," she said.[85]

This credit union was one of the fastest growing institutions in the state and provided numerous services to Latino immigrants. A vice-president noted that clients wanted "mostly auto loans, but we are seeing a rise in mortgages, and then personal loans. Then there are the basic financial services, and then we have wire transfers, which allows them to set up an account here, and an account in Mexico and transfer between them, for a very low cost" to its nearly 50,000 members. In 2002, Bank of America embarked on a major advertising initiative aimed at Latinos in the state, and many banks accepted the *matricula consular* to access bank services, in addition to a driver's license or state ID, which undocumented immigrants could, at the time, obtain.[86]

From 1990 to 2000, local and state policy toward immigrants and the community-level reception were largely positive, reflecting market needs. As the economy expanded, recruitment of Mexican laborers increased, and Mexicans immigrated to the state because of its openness and its economic opportunities. These immigrants were able to work through a robust temporary H2B visa guest worker program and through the nonenforcement of laws preventing undocumented labor.

Janet, an unauthorized immigrant from Guerrero who came to Winston-Salem in 1995, explained: In the 1990s, "he [my husband] had plenty of work. He worked five or six days. And so, things were good. We both worked, and he earned good money. And well, we just didn't have any worries then." A stable income and access to transportation meant that, despite their legal status, Mexicans felt they were doing well, building a life, and becoming a part of the Winston-Salem community.

To understand the institutional reception these immigrants received, we can look to local newspaper reports. Few newspapers even mentioned immigrants until 2001. At that time, even in the midst of a growing national anti-immigrant sentiment, local institutions worked against the broader sentiment, seeking to build welcoming institutions and structures that would help integrate Latino newcomers into the community. On January 1, 2002, an extended report on the post-9/11 climate noted:

> That backlash has hit Hispanic immigrants as well, said Miriam Hernandez, who leads the Hispanic Action Plan Office for Neighbors in Ministry. "The majority of them are here to seek the American Dream as each and every one of us has done, and for a better education for their children," she said. . . . Some local residents said that arguments over religion and ethnicity that flared after the attacks underscore the long-standing need for people to cross lines and work together. Hernandez plans to encourage such cooperation in the New Year by opening the Hispanic International Action Center. The center will draw together leaders from throughout the county to help Hispanic and other immigrants with a wide range of services. Beyond helping with basics such as health care, Hernandez said that the center would also help immigrants "understand what our country is going through, and what our responsibilities are as individuals living in this country."[87]

Throughout the early part of the decade, local organizations and institutions continued to reach out to Latinos in order to improve their access to local businesses and services. Indeed, in 2003, the *Winston-Salem Journal* reported, "the average Hispanic household in the Triad makes more than $31,000 in income, said Maria Sanchez-Boudy, a diversity consultant with Latin Connection. Sanchez-Boudy assists Southern Community Bank & Trust with its grass-roots effort to reach Hispanic customers."[88] At the time, the number of Latino residents in the county was estimated at over 32,000, according to a report by Faith Action International House, a Greensboro advocacy group, only a third of whom used conventional banking services. News reports highlighted that increased wealth and therefore large cash reserves among Latinos made them particularly vulnerable to property crime, a major concern for local police.[89] Together, these reports suggest that in the early 2000s, Latinos were experiencing rapid upward mobility alongside efforts at community integration, and law enforcement concerns centered mainly on *protecting* Latino immigrants from predatory property crime, not immigrants as criminals themselves.

The depth of this welcoming context was most evident when even unemployed Latinos were treated sympathetically in the press:

In better times, Carlos Marin would never be out fishing on a weekday afternoon. But Marin was laid off from his construction job at the end of December. "This is one of the worst economic times I've seen since I arrived in North Carolina two years ago," Marin said as he pulled his fishing line through the water at Lake Thom-A-Lex. In December, the state's unemployment rate rose to 6.3 percent—its highest point since 1984—and the economic downturn is hitting Hispanic workers hard. . . . Employer worries about immigration laws have also contributed to the jobless rate among undocumented Hispanics, said Lisa Alexander, a caseworker at Casa Guadalupe, a Hispanic outreach program of Catholic Social Services. "We've had a lot of people come to us because they're out of work, but that has a lot to do with immigration law. A lot of companies are getting a lot stricter," Alexander said. "The biggest problem is that employers are verifying documents, and because of that people are unemployed." Casa Guadalupe has been inundated with requests for financial help, she said. Alexander said that the agency has been getting about five calls a day from people inquiring about job leads, compared with five calls a week in better economic times. "Six people called for food yesterday, and we have a very small food bank, so it wiped us out," she said.[90]

Empathy was evident even in cases where it was widely known that undocumented immigrants were being recruited and employed; news reports in the early 2000s were largely sympathetic to undocumented workers, critiquing employers for potential exploitation. More remarkably, news outlets positioned North Carolina residents as *against* federal enforcement, criticizing the government for acting on post 9/11 anti-immigrant sentiment. When Tyson Foods in nearby Wilkes County faced federal indictment for conspiracy to smuggle illegal aliens, the *Winston-Salem Journal* reported:

For Jose, a 72-year-old Mexican immigrant, and hundreds of other Hispanic immigrants, the chance to work at Tyson Foods' poultry-processing complex is a good opportunity for steady work and a reliable income that most did not have at home. The work is hard—Jose washes out the chickens and removes gizzards, often standing in water as he works—but it's a big improvement over farm labor. Jobs at Tyson Foods pay at least seven times what many Hispanic immigrants could make in their native lands. "Work is better at Tyson. It's always the same temperature—neither hot nor cold," said Jose, who like other Hispanic workers, did not want to give his last name. . . . The indictment came after two key events, the Sept. 11 attacks and the slumping economy, and that has some experts questioning the government's motives for cracking down on illegal immigration. Jim Johnson, a sociologist and an immigration expert who teaches in the Kenan-Flagler Business School at the University of North Carolina at Chapel Hill, said he thinks that the indictment is interesting not because of its scope but because of the government's timing in pushing the issue. "What Sept. 11 did was demonstrate to the public exactly how pervasive the presence of undocumented immigrants is in our country," Johnson said. "What strikes me now is that people who are central to our country's economy are being treated as scapegoats."[91]

According to Grusky and Weeden's measure of economic mobility as a package of investments (e.g., education, savings); endowments (e.g., skills, networks); working conditions (e.g., safe, engaging); and rewards (e.g., wages, benefits), Latino immigrants were upwardly mobile.[92] This mobility was visible in both the retrospective accounts of my interviewees and in newspaper reports. Latino families acquired endowments and investments in terms of new skills and education. For example, Latino immigrant youth attended and completed primary and secondary school in large numbers, with approximately 101,000 Latinos enrolled in North Carolina schools in the 2004–2005 school year (approximately 7.5% of the school-going population), positioning them to outperform their parents in terms of educational attainment.[93] New residents also took advantage of free ESL courses provided by a partnership between the community college and library.

Latino migrants were also upwardly mobile in terms of investments and rewards: they were able to garner steady employment, earn reasonably high wages for their skill levels, and build up modest savings. Newspaper reports and interviewees noted high levels of employment, savings, and asset accrual. Several respondents started their own businesses, mostly in basic construction services, such as house painting and drywall installation, but also in retail services and restaurants. All indicated that these businesses were relatively successful, providing them with enough capital to expand, hire workers, save money, and/or send funds to relatives in Mexico. Many immigrant entrepreneurs and workers also benefited from institutional support. Diego, who migrated in 1999, told me, "Before, it was easy. There were many Latinos inside of the [employment] agencies, and they helped us. We didn't have problems." I met Diego, an immigrant from Acapulco who arrived in North Carolina to meet up with his wife and sister, through a contact at the small white and Latino church. He'd had plenty of disposable income before 2005. He had purchased, by his estimation, ten different cars during his decade in Winston-Salem, paying in cash each time.

A 1995 story in the Greensboro *News and Record* noted the relative ease with which immigrants were able to find work in the Piedmont Triad[94] area:

Unlike the recession that has plagued California, the Triad economy is healthy, with a low unemployment rate and no shortage of work for anyone willing to

take the hardest jobs, such as construction and agriculture. Where the Hispanic community once consisted mostly of young men who moved here in
search of work, living Spartan lives and wiring most of their money back to
relatives in their native countries, today the community is taking shape with
families who mean to stay. Sandra and Rodolfo Guevara are a good example.
Rodolfo, a painting contractor, came here from Texas on a job that stretched
to 18 months. Rather than be without her husband, Sandra Guevara moved
north and put their two children in school. As the husband pursued his business, the wife opened a thriving combination video and grocery store, stock-
ing thousands of Latin movie titles and whatever else it took to help the customers feel at home: white straw cowboy hats piled high, devotional candles
and religious art, dried chili peppers, fresh tamarind and cold nonalcoholic
sangria for workers coming in out of the hot sun.[95]

By and large, the 1990s and early 2000s typified ideal migration conditions,
setting the Southeast region apart from many more-traditional gateway states.

Current research suggests that immigrants consider a locale's institutional
openness and economic opportunity in their migration decisions. Much of
the dispersion of immigrants from the Southwest and California to new destinations in the Midwest and Southeast is attributed to increasingly restrictive
policies and economic decline in the West alongside openness and economic
opportunity in these new destinations.[96] In Europe, studies suggest that state-
level integration policies influence immigrant economic performance and
level of integration.[97] Given North Carolina's institutional structure before
2005, it is no wonder that Mexican immigrants described this period as one
of relative prosperity.

RECEPTIVE COMMUNITY VIEWS AND IMMIGRANT PERCEPTIONS

In the period before 2005, Latinos faced relatively little surveillance in North
Carolina, few mechanisms counted Latinos, and few efforts excluded them
from social and civic life. Newspaper data corroborate the lack of controversy or concern over immigration during this time. For example, in 1994,
the *Winston-Salem Journal* referenced Latinos, immigration, or Mexicans
in the state in only 21 articles, despite the significant influx over the course of
the 1990s. It was not until 1998 that the number of relevant articles exceeded
100 annually.[98] Moreover, many of the stories published on Latinos by local
papers during the pre-2005 period reported positively on Latino leaders' efforts to integrate immigrants into the community, rather than the associa-
tions with crime and illegality that came later.

Reflecting on the pre-2005 period, none of my respondents recalled feeling hostility from native-born community members at that time. Though the community lacked resource-rich ethnic enclaves and networks due to the recent arrival of most Latinos, access to American cultural norms and institutions enabled upward mobility. Unauthorized immigrants faced more obstacles, but they too were able to achieve structural and social mobility.

During this period, Latino immigrants were treated as members of the community and locals worked toward integration. For example, in 1998, a local university hosted a family day for immigrants, designed to teach immigrant families about the university and its programs. The event was advertised as an explicit effort to help "immigrants assimilate into the community" and to "teach newcomers about college."[99] The program's chairwoman was quoted saying that university officials wanted immigrants to know "campuses are friendly places, and they belong to everyone."[100]

The few stories published in other local papers reported positively on Latino leaders' efforts to integrate immigrants into the community or how their growth in the state led to the founding of new institutions, such as a new million-dollar Hispanic center in neighboring Yadkin County (2002).[101] One series featured "Persons of the Week", including a feature on Frank Gonzales, a Cuban immigrant profiled along with his wife about their successful chain of grocery stores catering to Latinos, and their work to help Latinos negotiate city life. Frank and his wife would do whatever they could to help Latino immigrants, including,

> driv[ing] migrant workers to the Division of Motor Vehicles for driver's licenses; help them obtain car insurance; help them plow through the paperwork involved with buying and registering a car . . . take people to banks and help them fill out forms for obtaining tax identification numbers, [and] make calls to area landlords, helping new families find a place to live.[102]

In the piece, the local police chief attests to Gonzales' outstanding character: "'He's just a great guy,' said Angier police Chief Mike Aponte.[103] 'He's done a lot here to make Hispanics aware that the police aren't out to hurt them. He's a good man. It's just a lot of little things. He goes out of his way to do the little things.'"[104] Not only were concerns over demographic change and immigration enforcement nearly absent, but efforts to integrate immigrants both officially and unofficially were praised by both local officials and the media. Access to and the support of key individuals and institutions created an essential, if informal, welcoming policy, even for the undocumented.

A thorough analysis of *Winston-Salem Journal* reporting that mentioned Latinos or immigrants from 1989 to 2005 found that the chief editorial critique of Latino immigrants during this period centered on the problem of littering. In fact, in 2002 and 2003, two major Latino immigrant issues arose in the Winston-Salem area: higher rates of death from carbon monoxide poisoning from the use of space heaters, charcoal, and stoves as heating elements in closed homes; and, in 2003, the conditions of the Lakeside apartments, where many new Latino immigrants lived, were perceived to have lowered the quality of life by littering. A few letters to the editor began to debate the use of Spanish in the community, though there were also letters countering that the provision of services in Spanish was simply the hospitable way for the community to receive its new members.

Other news reports recognized efforts by native-born community members to help Latino newcomers navigate local bureaucracies, noting a desire to build goodwill between Latinos and local institutions.

> When Jeff Broome saw a problem a few years ago, he didn't just shake his head or complain about newcomers. He's done something about it, and his solution provides solid assistance to recent arrivals who need to get acclimated to U.S., state and local laws and policies. Broome's radio call-in program, which airs at 10 a.m. Fridays on the frequency 1030 AM, answers callers' questions about a variety of traffic-related issues. Broome is a city police officer.
>
> In 1999, while handling school bus stop-arm violations, he said he noticed that many of the Hispanic drivers were violating the bus and child safety seat laws. He started clinics, then asked for a little air time to promote them. Next thing he knew, he had himself a call-in show, answering questions about everything from how to change court dates to whether you need a nice car to take a driver's license test. The program is doing more than just answering questions, however. It's building goodwill and helping melt suspicion about law enforcement. Residents originally from Latino countries may need some adjustment to understand differences between officers there and officers here.
>
> Too often, tragedies involving citizens and police occur because of miscommunication, misinterpretation or misunderstanding. Anything that can help solidify citizen-police relationships is good for everyone. The call-in radio show led by Broome, who's just been named city employee of the year, is even more astonishing because of the language barrier. Broome doesn't speak much Spanish. A radio-station employee does the interpreting. It's a good bet that Broome is picking the language up as he goes. Maybe his next project could be clinics and seminars for his fellow police officers on understanding Hispanic residents.[105]

Similarly, government leaders in the western part of the state planned trips to Michoacán, Mexico, in order to facilitate cultural understanding and improve policymaking.[106] Winston-Salem's leaders took their own trip to Guanajuato:

Community leaders and elected officials from Forsyth and Guilford counties
are to travel to Mexico in May to gain a deeper understanding of the culture of
Mexican immigrants. The Forsyth contingent includes Allen Joines, Winston-
Salem's mayor; Joycelyn Johnson, a city alderman; Dave Plyler, a Forsyth
County commissioner; and Gayle Anderson, the president of the Winston-
Salem Chamber of Commerce. During their six-day trip to the central Mexican state of Guanajuato, they will visit community-development centers,
museums, public schools and families with relatives who have moved to the
United States. Forsyth and Guilford officials were invited on the trip because
the counties' Hispanic populations are among the fastest-growing in the state,
said Winifred Ernst, the Hispanic initiative coordinator with the N.C. Center
for International Understanding. The center, which is part of the University
of North Carolina, is organizing the trip. Several other counties will also be
represented.[107]

Just one letter to the editor decried the trip; others, and an editorial board
statement, expressed approval:

> A better understanding of our Hispanic residents is an important first step to
> assimilating this segment of the population into our society. There are good
> reasons to do that, welcoming them rather than suggesting they go home. Im-
> migrants built the United States into the strongest country in the world. The
> influx of Hispanic people is part of a long and rich tradition. Despite what
> some isolationists would have you believe, Hispanic immigrants are net con-
> tributors to the nation's wealth, not a strain on its resources. To the extent that
> those on this trip understand who these people are and why they have come
> here, the trip will be rewarding and should help us to know what our new
> residents need to become even more productive citizens. That seems worth a
> week of local officials' time.[108]

Accompanying the city-leadership to Guanajuato, *Journal* reporters filed stories detailing the life Mexican migrants left behind and their reasons for migrating to North Carolina. Such reports touched on all types of institutions
and services, especially health care and education, where new immigrant
residents were most visible.

For example, Winston-Salem's Community Care Center opened in 2000
to provide medical services to the uninsured, free of charge. Its clients were
overwhelmingly Latino. In 2004, "United Way organizations from five local
counties are sponsoring a new Spanish-language telephone-assistance service
to better serve the area's growing Hispanic population."[109] The organization
expanded its 2-1-1 help-line service toward helping callers find community
assistance agencies in six counties, including Spanish representatives. United

Way also partnered with the owner of Que Pasa Media on an information campaign so that Latino residents would be aware of the service.

Unauthorized status came, of course, with problems, but proved to be a relatively minor obstacle to structural and social mobility. Local institutions hired additional interpreters for police and hospitals, offered ESL classes through Forsyth Tech (a local community college), targeted public transportation advertisements and services to Latinos, and integrated services for immigrants into local banks and retail businesses.[110] Such efforts existed in both the public and private sector, and were, at the time, even bipartisan.

> Southern Community Bank is considering whether to accept the Mexican-issued cards as documentation for the purpose of setting up bank accounts. Bank of America, based in Charlotte, recently announced plans to begin accepting the cards. While the Mexican consulate can provide many services to Mexican citizens, Flores said, one thing it can't do is give illegal migrants the documents needed to work legally in the United States. That kind of action would take legislation by the U.S. Congress, Flores said. At the same time, she said, Mexicans who are here illegally deserve basic human rights. "They are human beings who are working the fields and working in the service area, and they are helping the economy of the U.S," she said. "They have rights as human beings. They are undocumented, but they have rights." State Sen. Ham Horton, R-Forsyth, said that something should be done to give Hispanics more access to higher education. The lack of a Social Security number creates a barrier for many Hispanics who want training to better their lives. "You have people who are ambitious and very much want to improve their marketability and skills, and they can't get admission," Horton said. "Has there ever been this number of people who have come into our county that have been so easily assimilated? They've got family values and the work ethic and all the values that we like to think we ought to have."[111]

Likewise, in 2003, Cazacasa Services Inc. opened for business. A strong indicator of the perceived integration and economic potential of the Latino community, Cazacasa Services was a residential real-estate company in Winston-Salem aimed at serving the Triad's potential Hispanic homebuyers, providing bilingual real-estate professional services, including working as a buyers' agent and leading clients through the home-buying process.[112]

Where these services were aimed at getting monolingual Spanish speakers, recent immigrants, and low-skilled immigrants necessary services, other programs encouraged upward mobility and integration among Latino youth.

> The YMCA of Greater Winston-Salem's Community Outreach Services branch has been awarded a three-year grant totaling $147,000 from the U.S.

Department of Education. The money will be used to create a mentoring program called Hispanic Achievers. Modeled on the YMCA's Black Achievers
Program that targets black teen-agers, the focus will be on providing motivation to Hispanic youth in grades 4 through 8 to succeed at school and to avoid
risky behaviors such as inappropriate sexual activity, drug abuse and crime.
The program goals include matching each student with an adult mentor who
will serve as a positive role model and friend; helping Hispanic youth develop
a positive sense of self; encouraging youth to set goals; exposing youth to a
variety of career options; and meeting the needs of participants' families by
providing them with pertinent information about community resources.[113]

This program emphasized career goals, requiring Achievers to choose a career
cluster (options included health care, law and government, and engineering)
in which they would receive exposure and mentorship. Similar efforts were
made to recruit Latino families into the county's free early childhood education program, targeting Hispanic-serving businesses and neighborhoods for
advertising.

Notably, the absence of hostility toward Latinos during this period was not
a function of a conciliatory tone toward minority populations in general. For
example, *Journal* reports on African American issues, efforts to make Martin
Luther King day an official holiday, speeches by local clergy and civil rights
leaders on the persistence of racial inequality, and even positive reports on
multicultural events such as the annual interfaith prayer breakfast were met
with swift rebuke by readers who claimed any reporting on race was "anti-
American," "playing the race card," and, in the case of a statue commemorat-
ing the efforts of firefighters in New York on 9/11 that represented the men as
white, Latino, and black (though the statue was inspired by an event in which
all three firefighters were white) "misguided." Such distinct characterizations
indicate that at the time, Latino immigrants were, by and large, perceived
as assimilable. As Julie Weise points out, stereotypes of blacks, not Latinos,
set the tone for immigration debates in the 1990s. Implicit comparisons that
highlighted Latinos as "not lazy," "family oriented, loyal, patriots, and people who don't expect the government to give them money" were explicit attempts to drum up support for Latino migrants by juxtaposing them against
a set of anti-black stereotypes. Latinos were appreciated, partly, due to their
perceived social distance from African Americans.[114]

So distant was the discourse on Latino immigrants from being racialized
or xenophobic that the growing Hispanic population was often referenced
not as a liability but as an untapped market for economic growth[115]:

Furniture-makers looking for the greatest potential for new business in a slow
economy should consider the growing Hispanic market, Terry Laughlin, the

vice president of sales and marketing for Univision National Sales in Chicago, said yesterday. . . . Laughlin said that Hispanic spending will increase more than twice the rate of non-Hispanic spending between 2000 and 2020, especially in such areas as furniture and consumer electronics.[116]

Equally important to Latinos' integration prospects was the prevailing view that Latino immigrants were community members. Media stories highlighted Latino successes and entrepreneurs, including the fast-growing Sunday soccer league and the newly surging fleet of *paleta* vendors. Longer profiles included stories on individuals such as restaurant entrepreneur Jesus Ruiz, who owned a local chain of popular Mi Pueblo Mexican restaurants in Winston-Salem and neighboring counties. A profile on Ruiz, who emigrated from Michoacán in the 1970s, highlighted his positive characteristics as a family man and employer, noting that:

> Ruiz's friends talk about him with respect. "He's very demanding," said Eugene Rossitch, a retired group executive for Wachovia Corp. and a friend of Ruiz, "but he will not demand from anyone anything he's not willing to do. At the same time, he's very understanding." Ruiz is a "wonderful" father and husband and an "excellent businessman," he said. Olga A. Soetermans, the office manager for Mi Pueblo, has worked for Ruiz for two years. "He's a good boss," she said. "He demands, of course, that the job be done, but he's very easy to work with, very nice and easy going." Miguel Trejo, the manager of the Mi Pueblo restaurant in Clemmons, described Ruiz as a "very simple person." "That's what makes him a great person," Trejo said. "He's like a friend. It's not like, 'Watch out, there's the boss coming.'" Mi Pueblo is a company that welcomes anybody who wants to do a good job and improve his or her life, Trejo said.[117]

During this time, the acculturation trajectory for Latinos followed traditional assimilation paradigms. Recent immigrants retained ties to their country of origin, even as they highlighted their commitment to the US and their desire to become true members of the community through English language training, long-term employment, and home ownership. The welcoming atmosphere and upward mobility suggest that Mexican immigrants may have been well poised to adapt the kind of aspirational whiteness and distancing practices highlighted by Alba, Waters, and others, who argue that acculturation trajectories and strategies for mobility are accompanied by movement into the mainstream.[118] Without large, longstanding Latino populations, selective acculturation would not have served as a meaningful pathway to mobility. Instead, though no respondents reported on this retrospectively, immigrants were mostly likely at this time to see themselves as closer to, and socially aligned with, whiteness. Their constant portrayal as welcome newcomers would have supported this perception. Despite their recent arrival to the community, Latino immigrants were largely represented as they desired to be seen—as good neighbors and residents.

In one particularly poignant example, a local resident who died of leukemia at 29 was memorialized in the *Winston-Salem Journal*:

> Octavanio "O.G." Gomez, 29, battled leukemia for nearly two years before he died. But Gomez, a Mexican-born immigrant, fought other odds and won. . . . Gomez was born in Guanajuato, Mexico—a city notable for its wealth of silver and its stark poverty. Gomez came to the United States with his father and siblings in the early 1980s when he 9. Gomez grew up in Yadkin County. He helped his father work on local farms, and dropped out of high school to help his family when he was a freshman, said his wife Patricia Gomez. Octavanio Gomez was both American and Mexican, she said. "I don't think he was either kind. He was just Octavanio," she said.
>
> He became well-known in the Hispanic community for his willingness and ability to bridge the gap. Family friends said that Gomez went out of his way to help other Hispanics. Gomez would interpret for those who didn't speak English, going to the N.C. Division of Motor Vehicles to help them get a driver's license, or to the hospital or courtroom. "Sometimes at night, he would get four calls from the hospital," said Patricia Gomez. "Sometimes he would be at the hospital from 1 a.m. to 4 a.m. in the morning, to be sure the person got home." Gomez worked at local factories, first working at Tyson Foods, where he cut the wings off chickens, and later at Unifi Inc. But he wanted something more out of his life, Patricia Gomez said. He wanted to become a lawyer to help the Hispanic community. "He always said, 'I'm going to make sure that everybody is treated equally,'" Patricia Gomez said. He had started attending Surry Community College when the first signs of his illness struck."[119]

Indeed, news reports more frequently linked Latinos in the area to positive stereotypes, such as a cultural emphasis on family, than negative ones. In a report on Mother's Day, the *Winston-Salem Journal* profiled a group of local Latino teenagers:

> They spent more than 12 hours Friday night and early yesterday honoring their mothers, and members of the Hispanic youth group at Our Lady of Mercy Catholic Church say it was worth their time. . . . To recognize Mother's Day, youth-group members from Our Lady of Mercy and St. Benedict the Moor churches spent the night in Winston-Salem driving from house to house, serenading happy mothers and giving them roses. It was the fourth year they have done it here. Hispanics traditionally consider Mother's Day one of the most important holidays. "To us, Mother's Day is like Christmas, so special,"

said Luis Garcia, the youth-group leader. "On that day, we always try to have a dinner and be together as a family."[120]

In constructing a portrait of Winston's Latinos as family oriented, church-going, and neighborly, local newspapers helped to create a context in which the dream to integrate children and family members as Americans and North Carolinians seemed achievable.

A January 2003 editorial, "Changing Face of America," embodies the Winston-Salem area's prevailing attitude toward Latino immigrants at the time:

> Anyone who's been paying attention has witnessed this remarkable change in the population here in Piedmont North Carolina. The Hispanic presence and influence are evident nearly anywhere you look or listen—schools, churches, businesses, factories, stores, restaurants, playing fields and throughout the fabric of everyday life. Our society is the richer for it . . .
>
> This is an increasingly diverse nation, and that diversity can be a great strength. The more society works to help all people—black, Hispanic or whatever race or ethnicity—become full participants in American life, with all its opportunities and responsibilities, the better off we all will be.[121]

SHIFTING TIDES AND DEMOGRAPHIC EXPANSION

For its new Latino residents, Winston-Salem seemed somewhat isolating, but nevertheless the picture of opportunity. Many of the migrants who came as children remember that, as students, they had often been the only Latino person in their class; now, they said proudly, they made up a significant proportion of the public school system, increasing from less than 1% of the school enrollment population in 1990, to 7.5% in 2004.[122] Roberto from Oaxaca told me:

> Yes, because before, we were very few. When I arrived, there were very few Hispanics. You would find one or two in a factory. And they treated us well. And after, there were many more, but I think the population really grew a lot here in 2005 or 2004, something like that. But I arrived in '98, I think. Yes '98, I arrived. And no, there weren't many. There was only one Hispanic store when I got here.

Many of my informants who had lived in Winston-Salem for ten years or longer verified the impact of such rapid demographic change on the community. When they arrived, it had been unusual to see another Latino person while out and about. Now, you could overhear Spanish being spoken in lots of places. Jorge, a Mexican resident who had lived in Winston-Salem for several years, recalled in our conversation:

JORGE: Back then it wasn't, it wasn't like a big crowd. It was, it was rare, you know, to see a Hispanic guy like in a store, or at the mall . . . I mean back then . . . you were happy when you saw them. . . . You'd go like, "Oh, hola!" You know? But now it's just like, there are a lot of us, you know?

JJ: Yeah.

JORGE: We're like invading.

JJ: What changed? Why did so many people come over?

JORGE: Yeah, it's jobs, you know? People were telling people that we've got a lot of jobs in the area. I used to own my own company. I used to do drywall. And I used to travel a lot. And it used to be good. [For] like five or six years. If you were self-employed you would get a lot of money. You would probably send some of the money [to Mexico]. You would get paid good. But now it's like, you got so many of us, you know, that we, every time we ask, or bid for a job, it's not even worth it, you know?

Inez, an unauthorized woman who arrived from Oaxaca in 1998, reported that when she got to Winston-Salem, she was easily able to acquire a driver's license. She noted that "back then, it was much, much easier. But right now, it's not like it was then . . . Because the laws now aren't the same as they were previously."

In reflecting on the growing number of Latinos, many respondents reported that their fortunes had reversed. Before 2005, Latino immigrants believed that Winston-Salem provided the context for their social integration and economic mobility. In the coming years, however, a shift in context would dramatically alter this perspective. Much like California in the 1990s, North Carolina reached a tipping point. The economy was no longer expanding. It could not absorb new workers or provide opportunities to move up. The Latino population had reached what Ivan Light calls a saturation point, approaching double digits.[123] In January 2004, President Bush proposed a new set of immigration reform policies, putting the issue of immigration back on the national agenda. In February 2004, federal initiatives to restrict the acceptable documents to receive state IDs and driver's licenses would be made to eliminate the acceptance of such documentation as expired licenses, individual tax-identification numbers, and licenses and other ID cards issued by the Mexican government.[124]

In addition to these demographic, economic, and political changes, by 2006, local policies and attitudes toward immigrants would decline precipitously, despite immigrants' ongoing efforts to integrate socially and economically. By 2006, Mexicans and other Latinos in Winston-Salem would not suffer discrimination as a result of simply being undocumented. Rather, they began to experience a *new* status: unwelcome. In chapter 3, I trace this shift in public opinion and show how the backlash affected migrant Mexicans, fundamentally shifting the context of incorporation in distinctly racialized ways.

Closed Gates: The Rise of Local Enforcement

It is in cities like Winston-Salem, as well as smaller communities, that the presence of criminals who have illegally entered the country is most keenly felt. In many cases, such elements come together to form classic street gangs, staking out territories and dedicating themselves to controlling the local drug trade. . . . Additionally, illegal immigration is straining government at all levels throughout the country as schools, hospitals and welfare agencies, as well as law enforcement, are pressed to respond to the needs of new populations that are consuming far more in tax revenue than they pay. Few states have had to struggle with this burden as much as North Carolina.

REP. MARK SOUDER, Hearing before the House of Representatives, April 12, 2006[1]

Yesenia had been in Winston-Salem for only six years. She was pregnant when she walked across the border from Guerrero, and after a few months in California, she had joined relatives in North Carolina. They exploited her, preventing her from leaving the house, forcing her to serve as a kind of household servant. To escape, she quickly married a man, a Central American with legal permanent residency status. He, too, proved abusive; she had moved from one bad situation to another. When we met in 2008, Yesenia spoke little English and had few contacts outside of the church programs staffed by fellow Latina and white women volunteers at Nueva Esperanza. She worked outside the home briefly and regularly volunteered at the church, but had been unable to secure employment for a few years. She was shy but warmed to me quickly, offering, in a comfortable Spanglish, to teach me to cook some of her specialties and agreeing readily to a formal interview.

When we sat down in one of the offices and I closed the door, she smiled nervously, eager to be helpful. I started with the warm-up questions in my interview protocol, asking how she ended up in Winston and what life was like for her here. She promptly burst into tears. Sobbing, she told me:

We are not free. We are afraid to—we don't have the power to leave. We cannot drive with any confidence because we are always thinking that the police are going to stop us. We don't have licenses—they don't give us licenses. And it's worrying because if the police stop you, you get a ticket or have to go to court. Sometimes they will take away your car. And we don't know if we go someplace, if we will be able to return home. We are fearful when we leave

to go to Wal-Mart and [im]migration comes, that they will take you, so we
always go in fear.

Gripping wadded up tissues in her hands, Yesenia repeated, "We are not free
here." Daily life, for her, was plagued with fear and paranoia.

Given the integrative context of the 1990s and early 2000s, integration processes in Winston-Salem seemed consistent with traditional straight-line and
segmented assimilation theories, which would predict Yesenia would tell me
about how Winston-Salem came to feel more and more like home. After all, as
we saw in chapter 2, there was significant support available to immigrants at
the local level. Local leaders had paid careful attention to interpreting Title VI
of the Civil Rights Act mandates at the city level and had provided a staffed
city information hotline with interpretation services in multiple languages,
city-wide cultural diversity festivals, and a new bilingual initiative to enhance
communication. Moreover, unlike other municipalities in North Carolina,
minorities were serving in Winston's local leadership positions in Winston,
spearheading many of these initiatives (and, as I show in chapters 4 and 5,
these leaders would come to serve as important brokers of interminority relations and counterpoints to broad anti-immigrant sentiment).

And yet, the more I observed and spoke with other Latinos and community members, the more ubiquitous Yesenia's experience seemed. At Nueva
Esperanza's after school program, a middle-schooler lamented as he doodled
in the margins of his homework that his mother didn't let him go anywhere
because she couldn't drive to pick him up. The church's director of outreach
services sighed that they were having trouble with youth soccer participation
because even though they had secured a van and a coach who was willing to
pick up team members for practice, parents worried that the van might be
stopped by police. They decided that their children were safer at home than
playing sports. Week after week, the local Spanish-language weekly *Que Pasa*
reinforced these fears with headline after headline of checkpoints, raids, new
restrictive bills proposed in the state legislature, and the latest county to sign
up for 287(g), a policy that allowed for partnerships between ICE and municipal governments.[2]

In 2008, to be Mexican and undocumented in North Carolina meant a
life of risk. If you left the house, the police might show up. If you went shopping, the police might give you a citation regardless of whether you are doing
anything illegal or suspicious. If you went out, you might not return home.
Legal status rarely spared you from being targeted, as you still were subject
to harassment and profiling. Moreover, because most Latino immigrants in
the state are from mixed status families and communities, it was common to

come home to the news of a detained coworker, friend, or family member. Yesenia's constant anxiety was shared widely. It was as though a whole swath of civilians was living in a state of war or under a repressive dictatorship.

Though all these fears were true, they were also *new* in Winston-Salem. Familiar with the difficulties faced by undocumented immigrants in North Carolina, I thought that Winston's Latino newcomers had knowingly chosen to enter a less than ideal set of circumstances that was nevertheless better than where they were coming from: state surveillance versus poverty and joblessness. Instead, as described in chapter 2, Winston's newcomers had joined the community under one set of conditions, and within the decade, were living in another. What happened?

Closing the Gates

The shift in Winston-Salem's reception of immigrants is as much a political story as a personal one. In many ways, North Carolina is a barometer for immigration debates throughout the United States. As Hannah Gill notes, along with the rest of the Southeast, the state has become a "frontier for Latin American Migration to the United States."[3] Since the early 2000s, Americans have witnessed a macrostructural shift toward the securitization of immigration enforcement. The newly intensified deportation regime has important consequences for long-term mobility and incorporation, even in immigrant-dense contexts such as Los Angeles and San Diego.[4] Recent research suggests that *intragenerational* changes are particularly important for those wishing to understand why some immigrants are blocked from mobility even as they work hard to accumulate financial, social, and human capital.[5] For example, scholars Roberto Gonzales, Cecilia Menjívar, and Leisy Abrego highlight the role of illegality in creating constraints on behavior and practices at key points in the life course, truncating ambition and producing long-term marginalization.[6] These scholars specifically focus on the stigmatization that comes with the criminalization of unauthorized immigrant status. Their findings are consistent with what I have called a *reverse incorporation* trajectory in which macrostructural shifts produce local-level institutional changes that create long-term obstacles to mobility across the life course.[7] For example, Gonzales finds that as minors in the 1990s and early 2000s, undocumented youth worked diligently to acquire human capital and were largely able to acculturate. However, as securitization and institutional closure blocked access to institutions such as higher education and denied privileges such as driver's licenses, these gains were halted or reversed when children came to adulthood.[8]

Rafael Alarcón, Luis Escala, and Olga Odgers argue that, when it comes to distinctions between citizen and alien, the "brightest boundaries are not imported and have nothing to do with ethnicity; rather, they are fundamentally political, made in and by receiving states, exercising long-term consequences at the individual level and beyond. . . . While immigrants may integrate *into* a society by learning its language or gaining new competencies, the societal integration *of* immigrants—or lack thereof—involves political decisions about rights and access to citizenship, decisions largely made by the nationals and their leaders" [italics in original].[9]

Under the conditions of reverse incorporation, the immigrant's receiving context shifts, resulting in marginalization, exclusion, and downward mobility. Residents experience a shift from tolerance to criminalization through processes of racialization. Among first, 1.5, and second-generation immigrants, integration and intergenerational progress now has less to do with the presence of co-ethnics and acculturation—which, as Tomás Jiménez has argued, are so essential in later-generation integration practices—and more to do with open and closed gates.[10] While Jiménez' insights are useful in making sense of immigrant integration under receptive conditions, they may no longer apply to the current climate of closure and racial marginalization.[11] As Jiménez notes, race matters in that "nativism is often couched in a racialized language that ties discontent about immigration to all people of Mexican descent, not just Mexican immigrants. This nativism activates immigration as a core event defining the Mexican American experience, leading respondents to identify with the experiences of their immigrant co-ethnics."[12] Such racialized boundaries became so pronounced in terms of policy and discourse at mid-decade that Mexican-origin populations as well as other Latinos, regardless of immigration status, saw not only their life chances, but also their identities conditioned by the politics of immigration.

Reverse incorporation happens in two ways. First, through institutional closure, in which state and community institutions and resources are no longer available to immigrant Latinos. They can be removed through formal means, such as institutional, structural, or political measures, or informal means, such as the use of bureaucratic discretion to deny services.[13] Institutional closure fundamentally alters the context of reception for all immigrants, whether established residents who have made economic and social gains or new arrivals. Second, institutional closure occurs in a mutually constitutive relationship with souring public attitudes toward and perceptions of immigrants. While attitude reversals do not have the same direct effect as institutional closure, they create a hostile environment, closing off access to local social networks, and reinforce informal practices of exclusion. Reverse incorporation fundamentally changes not only the context in which immigrants live, but also their ideas about themselves.

Policy changes culminating in the passage of the Real ID Act in 2005 and the simultaneous spread of local and federal partnerships that target immigrants, such as 287(g), produced a fundamentally distinct political context for undocumented Latino immigrants. The primary impact of 287(g), in particular, was to instill systematic fear, particularly among Latinos living in the South and Southwest. Racial profiling, wage theft, raids, and mass deportation existed well before 287(g), but this program codified the practices as both tacitly legal and public. Individual citizens came to see themselves as border protectors, and Latinos in North Carolina and elsewhere saw their status decline rapidly from valued worker, volunteer, parent, and neighbor to highly vulnerable positions as unwanted and deportable subjects. Now denied courtesies and basic rights previously afforded to them, immigrants, particularly Latino immigrants, have been forced to rethink their perceptions of the Latino experience in the US. To understand this shift in status and the ways in which Latinos perceived it as sudden and life altering, we must look to the broader political changes that made the localized shifts possible.

Making the Undocumented

Much of the literature on Mexican immigration presumes that the contemporary sense of outsiderness is a fixed, rather than mutable, characteristic of the Mexican experience.[14] Indeed, the US expressed political anxiety about the Mexican population as early as the signing of the Treaty of Guadalupe Hidalgo, in which the US reluctantly extended white status to Mexicans living in what became US territory so that they might access the full benefits of citizenship and property ownership. In practice, Mexican-origin peoples were often discriminated against, and frequently served as the target of immigration policy concerns. Race, as David FitzGerald and David Cook-Martín argue, was always at the center of immigration policy, in which migrant selection was, and arguably continues to be, considered *only* in light of racialized ideology.[15] As the formal immigration policy regime emerged in the twentieth century, Mexicans were at the center. For example, the concept of systematic deportation emerged under the 1917 Immigration Act, which added excludable categories and extended deportability beyond the sick and criminal.[16] In 1924, all forms of entry without visa or inspection were made illegal, and a land border patrol was created.[17] Visas quickly replaced medical inspection, and deportation and enforcement became key activities of the immigration service. The Johnson-Reed Immigration Act of 1924 was the first comprehensive restriction law, creating both quotas and a racial and ethnic hierarchy of favoritism in admittance.[18] Over the next few decades, Mexicans quickly became associated with illegal immigration because of their status as temporary visitors or laborers. By the 1950s, Mexicans were systematically and consistently symbolized as the racialized, illegal alien.[19] The year 1954 marked the apex of this transition, in which Operation Wetback was initiated to repatriate Mexican immigrants into Mexico. Over the course of this program that involved both border and interior removals, over one million Mexicans were apprehended. Thousands were in the US legally, but that mattered little. Many deportees were deprived of the right to recover property or, worse, were left in the desert or other rural areas under harsh conditions with few resources.

Following the 1965 immigration reforms that abolished immigration quotas and ended the Bracero program, the number of Mexicans allowed into the US via legal channels greatly decreased. Thousands used extralegal channels to migrate. In the 1970s and 1980s, immigration reforms included increased policing at the border, as well as amnesty for undocumented migrants residing in the US, as a mechanism to resolve this ongoing political issue. Still, it was not until 1986 that undocumented immigration became a significant political phenomenon; the Immigration Reform and Control Act served to militarize the border and further restrict federal immigration policy.[20]

In the 1990s, the focus of federal efforts to manage immigration from Mexico permanently shifted to enforcement and militarization at the border, with some small concessions, including a visa lottery. New immigration policies included sanctions on employers who would hire illegal immigrants and the elimination of some social services aimed at immigrants. State and local governments began to propose punitive anti-immigration policies, largely in connection with demands for welfare reform and the contraction of social services. The last comprehensive immigration reform bill of the twentieth century was passed in 1996: the Illegal Immigration Reform and Immigrant Responsibility Act (IIRIRA). The law was heavy on enforcement and security, with new provisions mandating jail time for some immigration violations, increasing the budget for enforcement, reorganizing asylum, encouraging legal immigrants to become citizens, and creating provisions for greater cooperation across federal agencies, states, and local agencies.

9/11 STATE

From the mid-1990s until 2001, a robust economy kept anti-immigrant discourse and activity relatively subdued in the Southeast,[21] while economic stagnation in California stimulated the first state-level anti-immigrant policies, pushing Latino immigrants to more hospitable cities with better job opportunities. As the unintended consequences of NAFTA pushed them out of Mexico, economic expansion pulled them toward specific US states.[22]

Local and state officials in the US became increasingly involved in immigration policy, proposing and adopting punitive anti-immigration policies, though the federal government remained relatively uninterested.[23] Throughout the decade, the zeal for immigration enforcement remained confined to parts of the Southwest (here including southern California), where draconian policing strategies stimulated an underground economy of human trafficking and violence.

Still, the localized efforts raised the bar of entry into the mainstream for nonwhite immigrants who had long-since been acculturated and economically stable—status-markers that Richard Alba and Victor Nee argue had been supported by institutions shaped by the civil rights movement.[24] And after 9/11, when the fear of terrorism was tied so explicitly to undocumented immigration, the issue was forced back onto the national stage. As David Hernández puts it, "Much like other national crises in U.S. history, fighting a war against terrorism came to mean fighting immigrants, even though empirical data on the criminality of immigrants has consistently reflected noncitizens' lawfulness."[25]

Tying national-level security to border policy dramatically altered the discourse on immigration all over the country. Now Latinos, primarily Mexicans, were not only racialized minorities, but also potential threats to the state.[26] Politically, it not only instigated a general sense of anti-immigrant sentiment, but also inspired a key enforcement change from the 1996 laws. As analyzed by Carrie Arnold, the move toward securitization reversed the federal government's position on the role of states in immigration policy. No longer would immigration enforcement fall only to the federal government; now it was an all-levels, all hands-on-deck situation.

> After the tragic attacks of September 11, 2001, the lack of communication and cooperation among local, state, and federal law enforcement became the subject of intense criticism. Under pressure to deal with illegal immigration, the Department of Justice ("DOJ") began to consider extending immigration enforcement responsibilities to state and local agencies. In 1996, the DOJ had asserted that state and local officers do not have the power to enforce civil immigration violations, such as overstaying one's visa, but have the power only to enforce criminal immigration violations, such as illegal entry into the country. In a 2002 Memorandum for the Attorney General, the Office of Legal Counsel ("OLC") *withdrew the 1996 position* and instead included that "[s]tates have

inherent power, subject to federal preemption, to make arrests for violation of federal [civil and criminal immigration] law." [italics mine][27]

That is, in 2002, the Department of Justice broadly authorized states to enforce federal immigration law. New guidelines gave states the ability to request agreements with Immigration and Customs Enforcement (ICE) using section 287(g) to identify unauthorized immigrants for detention.[28] An array of additional interior enforcement strategies involving federal/local partnerships followed as states and municipalities were urged to take on the task of immigration enforcement.[29] Still, most localities, including throughout much of the South, waited for federal immigration reform, preferring to use the standard channels to deal with an issue that was both controversial and complex. As part of the changes initiated by the Office of Legal Council and the creation of Immigration and Customs Enforcement (ICE), the earliest 287(g) partnerships were entered into by Alabama and Florida in 2002 and 2003, respectively, and these remained the only two agreements between municipalities or states and the federal government until 2005.[30] By 2009, there were 67 partnerships in 23 states.

Perhaps unsurprisingly, at the federal, state, and local agency levels, this created a great deal of controversy; very real concerns were raised about the potential erosion of trust between the police and community. What would happen if immigrants could not report crime victimization for fear that calling the police was tantamount to calling ICE? The DOJ also came under fire for expanding the potential for civil rights violations and concern that enforcement cooperation agreements were part of an effort to deliver resources and assistance to local agents without providing adequate training. The use of a Memorandum of Agreement formalized these partnerships as a way of stemming some of these criticisms, but they kept coming.[31]

While the federal government was restructuring security operations to include the regulation of immigration, more and more undocumented immigrants were arriving in the US. Advocates on all sides were demanding a federal plan for immigration reform. Conservatives called for increased enforcement, while liberals called for a more efficient and viable pathway to legal residency and citizenship. State and municipal governments argued that they bore the brunt of dealing with new populations: static budgets strained to provide social services, let alone immigration enforcement. Ultimately, despite both executive and congressional efforts, including significant bipartisan bills, all efforts at federal immigration reform over the course of the decade failed. The stalemate seemed indefinite.

As authority on immigration issues devolved to the states, it produced massive policy divergence. While the legal order is always pluralistic rather than monolithic,[32] immigration law became the target of wildly different strategies of legal-social practice. States not only began to contest piecemeal federal legislation, such as refusing to comply with regulations including Real ID, but also were emboldened to pursue their own immigration agendas. Building on the lessons of California's proposition 187 (a ballot initiative that would have prohibited unauthorized immigrants from using non-emergency health care, public education, and other services) and growing opportunities in the newly formed Department of Homeland Security to partner with federal agencies and access their resources, states, especially in the South, but also in the Midwest and Northeast, began to pursue punitive policy actions.[33]

At the federal level, a handful of congressional leaders continued to join together security and immigration. Most notably, Jim Sensenbrenner (R-WI)[34] linked the regulation of undocumented immigrants with national security in the Real ID Act of 2005. Real ID federally mandated that individuals provide a social security number and other evidence of legal status in order to procure legal documents including driver's licenses and set guidelines for state-level enforcement. For the first time, persons without legal status would not be able to get state identification or even drive legally. The policy's enactment was repeatedly suspended at the federal level, however. Over the course of a decade, some states protested and stalled in adopting the new regulations (fearing its impact on minorities, immigrants, and the elderly) while other states, including North Carolina, signed on and promptly instituted the requirements.[35] In locations where Real ID took effect, federal and local partnerships expanded and strengthened; traffic stops were an important first-line of enforcement and a primary means for identifying the undocumented.

By 2006, many municipalities began signing up for these 287(g) partnerships in which they would refer immigrants to ICE on suspicion of having no driver's license (or an invalidly attained license).[36] In 2007, at the height of unauthorized immigration and the beginning of a nationwide economic crisis, various cities and counties throughout the Southeast enacted laws and ordinances to restrict immigrant access to social, educational, and medical institutions and benefits.[37] Access to ICE enforcement was widespread, even in counties that did not have 287(g) agreements, because sheriffs used a "wheel-and-spoke method" of delivering immigrants to neighboring counties with 287(g) agreements for processing. At the same time, other states rejected such measures, further fragmenting state and municipal contexts of reception.

North Carolina and the Shifting Political Terrain

The devolution of immigration policy meant that immigrants—even those with similar levels of human capital—encountered very different enforcement regimes and therefore had very different experiences depending on where they lived.[38] Researchers typically think of undocumented status as a fixed disadvantage, but the increasing involvement of local officials and bureaucrats in immigration enforcement calls this into question. Lacking a clear set of federal guidelines and procedures for the treatment of immigrants, local governments have substantial discretion in determining which institutions, benefits, and services will be made available to immigrants, documented or undocumented, and under what circumstances. Moreover, as Michael Lipsky and others have highlighted, street-level bureaucrats, who have "wide discretion over the dispensation of benefits or the allocation of public sanctions," experienced even greater latitude and autonomy in dealing with immigrants under these conditions. They could, in effect, "make" immigration policy.[39] As a result, unauthorized immigrants who were previously detectable only under specific circumstances now experienced substantial diversity in treatment. A robust body of scholarship shows that this variation in policy initiatives has particularly significant consequences for undocumented immigrants and their families.[40]

In sum, by the mid-2000s, state and municipal governments were increasingly concerned about security, and by extension, immigration issues. As a result, after a decade of open and integrative policies, North Carolina was well poised to take advantage of federal changes, seizing on alternative strategies to manage immigration and beginning the process of rolling back its welcome to its Mexican newcomers.[41]

INSTITUTIONAL CLOSURE

Macro-level shifts including the massive demographic spread of Latino immigrants in the 1990s and intensive securitization around immigration issues following 9/11 were underway at the national level, but in Winston-Salem, local institutional closure reached its critical juncture in 2005. Like other states and municipalities, North Carolina's governments were frequently pivoting away from efforts at integration in favor of exclusion.[42] Archival analysis of the *Winston-Salem Journal* indicates that North Carolina residents began to express anti-Latino anxieties by the mid-2000s. As highlighted by Mat Coleman, Hannah Gill, Helen Marrow, Jaime Winders, Julie Weise, and others, it wasn't just discursive hostility; the state became a pioneer and an enthusiastic adopter of municipal-level enforcement policies and state regulations on immigrant access to government resources.[43]

In 2003, the North Carolina General Assembly proposed a bill to allow some undocumented immigrants to pay in-state tuition and the state Senate passed a resolution to study issues relating to immigration (with a report due in 2005). When the tuition bill received significant public backlash, one state Senator capitalized on public resentment and introduced a bill that would deny state services to unauthorized immigrants.[44] Both bills died in the committee, but touched off an intensified focus on Latino immigrants, and, in 2005, in accelerated compliance with new federal regulations, the governor signed the Technical Corrections Act,[45] determining that social security numbers would be the only acceptable documentation for driver's licenses.[46] In 2004, North Carolina had been among just 10 states still issuing driver's licenses to applicants without verification of citizenship status.[47] The year-to-year change had two major effects. First, the loss of a driver's license was extremely consequential to Latino immigrants.[48] Nadine, a white adult ESL teacher and manager of programs for undocumented migrants, explained:

> First, anyone could get licenses. Then, they switched to I-10s or social security numbers only, then they stopped accepting foreign birth certificates, or *matrícula*, as they call it in Mexico, then they switched to only American government issued documents. Now they can't have a license without a social security number. Then, then couldn't get plates without a social security number. People have to help them buy and register cars. At that point, people had insurance, and now they don't, so it's dangerous, too.

Without access to a driver's license, license plates, or insurance, Latinos were stumped; losing the ability to drive presents a significant hardship in a state where public transportation is limited. According to the Brookings Institute, Winston-Salem ranked 15th among the 20 worst metropolitan areas for public transportation access and the Winston-Salem-Greensboro-High Point metro area was ranked in the bottom quartile of the top 100 metro areas in terms of transit accessibility.[49] Immigrants' primary means of getting to and from work was cut off, as was transport for school, church, appointments, and other services. As a result, the new regulation limited access to networks and organizations that might also provide access to resources and mobility.[50]

The second major effect was that driving, which most were obligated to do out of necessity, became dangerous. Immigrants now faced criminal arrest and deportation for driving without a license. This was true not merely because most immigrants now lacked proper driving instruction and insurance, but also because driving violations became explicitly linked to immigration enforcement.[51]

From 2005 to 2007, nearly 60 counties nationally signed 287(g) agreements with ICE; North Carolina was the most enthusiastic of these new partners, with eight agreements.[52] The only states with more agreements were Arizona and Virginia, with nine each.[53] The proliferation of agreements, the use of wheel-and-spoke methods, and the Technical Corrections Act all allowed ICE to expand its presence in North Carolina through training local police and sheriffs and using local jail-based technologies. By 2007, any local law enforcement officer could find a way to check the status of any person (though in practice, this was applied almost exclusively to Latinos) and potentially ask ICE to issue a detainer for deportation. Many sheriffs denied that 287(g) intended to get rid of undocumented migrants, insisting that the focus fell squarely on serious criminals,[54] yet a report by the North Carolina ACLU and the Immigration and Human Rights Policy Clinic at UNC Chapel Hill retorted that a majority of individuals arrested by 287(g) officers in Gaston, Mecklenburg, and Alamance Counties were arrested for traffic offenses.[55] By 2007, North Carolina had six jail enforcement programs (meaning ICE systems were accessed once an arrestee was processed in the jails) and two targeted programs (meaning that officers could engage in targeted street-level enforcement), all with universal mandates. Rather than target specific criminal actors, authorities had the bureaucratic autonomy to treat *any* crime as a possible opportunity for detainment, even if, as in jail-based programs, officers had not been trained by ICE.[56] The 287(g) agreements all but guaranteed that pre-textual arrests and racial profiling would become commonplace.

All 40 of the immigrant respondents I interviewed in this study were aware of this policy change. Many reported other forms of institutional closure, including increased policing, diminished access to social services and higher education, and an increased ICE presence. They all reported that institutional shifts created personal challenges, including a sense of fear that diminished their mobility, vulnerability to the police, and difficulty obtaining and maintaining employment. Institutional closure had a direct and negative impact on mobility in every sense.

Andres was a citizen and urban professional who arrived in the US in 1968. He was a long-time resident of Winston-Salem's suburbs and was involved in the area's oldest Hispanic organization. He noted:

> They're making it extremely complicated if you're illegal to get a license. And what I've always found interesting, is that they will make it very difficult to get a license, very difficult to go to school, go to college . . . which in essence, is

going to create a second-class citizen. . . . They'll put other laws in place that
prevent you from really moving up. . . . That, I think, is a pretty big injustice,
what's going on.

In this context of hostile enforcement and diminished access to resources,
many immigrants found their previous gains evaporating unexpectedly, suggesting a significant intragenerational shift. That is, not only would immigration experiences differ across accounts of, say, parents and their children, but
within the parents' own experience. Jessica, from Guerrero, was unauthorized
and had lived in New York City for 11 years before coming to Winston-Salem
in 2002. When we spoke about the shift toward criminalization later in the
decade, she said: "I would never think such a thing would happen. One thinks
that it's always going to be the way it is, or that North Carolina law is going
to be same."

After negotiations toward a federal immigration reform bill came to a
halt in 2007, some Winston-Salem city council members and Forsyth County
commissioners pressured law enforcement to seek a 287(g) agreement and
participation in various enforcement programs, arguing that immigrants
were a drain on economic resources at a time when the entire nation was
entering fiscal crisis.[57] Despite evidence that immigrants produced no net
costs for most counties,[58] state and local lawmakers completely overhauled
the state's enforcement policies. In particular, North Carolina became a significant contributor to national immigrant enforcement numbers, accounting for a quarter of the nation's deportation requests by 2008.[59] Many of
Winston-Salem's neighboring counties participated in 287(g), providing ample opportunities to process Latinos through the ICE database. As elsewhere
in the state, sheriffs claimed in public forums and the press that 287(g) was
a law enforcement tool, but a majority of 287(g) arrestees in western North
Carolina were for traffic offenses, not serious crimes.[60] None of these 287(g)
agreements appeared to target other ethnoracial groups, suggesting that area
sheriffs intentionally targeted Latino immigrants.[61]

In Gaston County, for example, 83% of the persons arrested and referred
for deportation by deputized officers had been charged with traffic offenses.
In Mecklenburg County, over 2,000 undocumented immigrants were put
into removal proceedings in 2007, with fewer than 5% charged with felonies
and over 16% with traffic violations.[62] Nationally, in 2010, nine Southeastern counties accounted for fully a third of the detainers issued for traffic
violations.

Contrary to expectation, there were few financial incentives for communities to participate in these programs. Counties remained legally liable for

rights violations complaints, and while there was a reimbursement from the federal government and some jails can make a profit, these funds rarely make up for the additional personnel costs needed for immigration enforcement. Studies even suggest that participating in such programs drained community resources without any obvious returns, whether measured in reductions in crime or the alleviating of institutional pressures.

Locally, sheriffs and community leaders sometimes claimed that such policies were a necessary part of enforcing federal law. That is, yes, it was an added expense, but they had no choice. Others were more brazen in making the call to get rid of Latino immigrants explicit. Mecklenburg County's Sheriff Jim Pendergraph (whose jurisdiction includes Charlotte) stated publicly, "We've got millions of illegal immigrants that have no business being here" and "This is about homeland security. This is about the sovereignty of our country."[63] Unsurprisingly, in 2006, Sheriff Pendergraph's jail population was over 90% Latino. Every year, his programs have cost the county in excess of one million dollars.

For a brief period, 287(g) was later streamlined and many agreements were phased out.[64] North Carolina became an early adopter of Secure Communities, a program that is identical to the jail-based version of 287(g) and first piloted under the Bush administration in 2008. Several counties volunteered as pilot sites, with Wake, Buncombe, Gaston, and Henderson Counties signing on in November 2008.[65] By 2011, *every* North Carolina county was participating in the program.[66]

In addition to these wide-reaching federal-local partnerships that North Carolina adopted so quickly and enthusiastically, state-level anti-immigrant measures were proposed following the 2005 legislative session. In 2006, North Carolina passed a bill to study the impact of immigration on the state, followed by the passage of North Carolina HR 2692, which, in addition to calling for the establishment of an immigration court in the state, urged Congress to make DWI convictions deportable offenses. It also called for the expansion of a Department of Homeland Security program permitting local officers to identify persons not legally present in the country, those who have previously been deported, and those wanted on outstanding felony charges to immigration officials.[67]

In 2007, the state legislature passed a law requiring jails to ascertain whether those charged with a felony or DUI were in the country legally. In 2008, it restricted access to the North Carolina Kids Care program, a newly implemented, reduced-cost health insurance program for impoverished families, to those meeting federal citizenship requirements. The adoption of such varied tools quickly expanded the reach of bureaucratic discretion in immigration enforcement. They empowered not only police officers, but also service providers to distribute the privileges and punishments accorded to noncitizens.

In the same period, North Carolina created a sort of roller-coaster regarding the inclusion of undocumented immigrants in the state community college system. In 2001, they were banned entirely. In 2004, colleges were instructed to use their own discretion. In 2007, the state board of regents required that undocumented students be admitted, only to ban them again in 2008. In 2009, North Carolina reversed its policy again, allowing admission, and then, in 2011, proposed an outright ban that ultimately failed in the legislature.[68] Even without a ban, the UNC system treated undocumented students as out-of-state students, often rendering tuition prohibitively expensive. Further, because the state community college system changed its policy on unauthorized immigrants five times in 8 years,[69] youth received the message that their ability to acquire new skills and degrees was precarious. The lack of clear guidelines encouraged further bureaucratic discretion in the form of school counselors and administrators left to determine for themselves whether to support Latino students' efforts to pursue higher education.[70] Judging by race, class, and other key social markers (such as perceptions of immigration status), bureaucrats are more likely to discriminate against clients who are different from themselves.[71] So, as wider attitudes toward immigrants soured, undocumented immigrants and Latinos were more and more likely to be counseled out of college.[72]

Beatriz recounted her experience with this kind of institutional closure as early as 2003:

> I tried really hard to get into [community college], but they didn't let me because they, they were very honest with me. They told me I wasn't legal in this country and even if I finished my education, my college and everything, nobody will hire me in any company because I wasn't going have any legal papers to show them who I was. And, and they told me I had to pay like five or six times more than Americans do, so—I mean, I thought it was really expensive, so I didn't go to college. Yeah, and I was so depressed because all my friends from Mexico have careers. . . . And, I didn't, so I got really, really depressed after I finished high school because they had good jobs now, and when I talk to them and they ask me, "Are you working or [trails off]." I mean, something, something about my education, I just don't know what to tell them. Well, I tell them the truth, but then, I didn't. I kind of changed the conversation. Yeah, because I was embarrassed. Yeah but, that was really, really hard. . . . And all my friends, like, probably we graduated like five or six Hispanics so just one got into college because she had papers. And the other five, are working in factories [now] and things like that.

Beatriz was discouraged from enrolling in college initially due to the absence of an in-state tuition policy for unauthorized immigrants and the perception that hiring opportunities were truncated for the undocumented. Those attitudes persisted and intensified over time. When I asked if she wanted to try to go back for her degree now, Beatriz replied:

> Uh, probably two years ago I took a class. Data entry class at [community college]. Well, it was in Goodwill and yeah, I got this certificate for taking this class but they told me, "You have to take like four more classes to get the diploma. But if you get the diploma, nobody will hire you because they want to have someone with a good record, with a social security number and, and you don't have one. So, it will be like a waste of time if you keep taking those classes." Plus, the books are really expensive, and, I quit.

These policy reversals were complicated, discouraging, and restrictive. Hannah Gill reports similar findings in Alamance County, where undocumented youth have become frustrated by the new barriers to opportunity, resulting in disillusionment and obstacles to belonging.[73] The barriers also spurred an attitude change among local bureaucrats and service providers, who internalized the message that it was not worthwhile to provide undocumented immigrants with an advanced education, further marginalizing Latino students. Marco told me:

> Basically, you're putting a whole population of kids who are graduating high school with no opportunity to pursue the American dream. . . . Now, the other colleges, they never accepted undocumented students with the in-state tuition, but at least they did have the community college. Now they don't have it. And that's basically what creates the problem with the creation of gangs. That's a huge problem. As soon as you close the door to higher education to these guys, that is really troubling.

For Marco, the progressive restriction of opportunities for immigrant youth created new social problems. Unable to access higher education or vocational training, youth, he argued, would become disaffected and closed off from opportunities of upward mobility. In his view, delinquency and gangs would fill the void, steering entire generations of youth into crime rather than higher education. In North Carolina, where, in 2010, nearly 75 percent of Latinos were under the age of 34, not providing an avenue for mobility is a big gamble.[74]

Closing off access to the tools of mobility and education were hardly the only forms of closure to affect Latino immigrants. Many reported increased policing, diminished access to social services and higher education, white flight from some neighborhoods, an increased ICE presence in neighbor-

hoods, a souring of native-born attitudes toward Latinos, and a general, pervasive sense that many Americans would prefer that Latino immigrants leave.
Together, such changes created a sense of fear among immigrants, diminished their mobility, made them vulnerable to the police, and made it more
difficult to obtain and maintain employment. Worse, they were sudden, making the unanticipated shifts feel more clearly discriminatory and unjustified.
Diego, who came from Guerrero in 1999, shared these sentiments, noting that
acquiring job opportunities before was quite easy.

> But now, after the attack on the Twin Towers, it's been a bit more difficult. . . .
> With the war, they already had the rules to check on the people more and
> more. Then the [Smithfield] raids. Now the economy. So, yes, it's a lot more
> difficult now.[75]

Life became more challenging for Mexicans and other Latinos both in Winston and across the state.[76] Local officials and experts agreed that enforcement had little to do with actual criminal threats. Rather, as UNC Law pro-
fessor Deborah Weissman noted, by 2009, when Forsyth County began to
pursue a 287(g) agreement in earnest, arrests of Latino immigrants were
rarely for serious offenses. Rather than use the law to address serious criminals and thwart terrorism, "what's happened instead is that, after Sept. 11, the
program began to be used to deal with worries about illegal immigration,"
she said. "Instead of going after people committing felonies, the largest category of people passing through the program in several counties have been
people arrested on traffic violations, not counting DWIs. It's been more of a
political football."[77]

In a short period, many of Winston's leaders went from promoting active
efforts at integration, to direct calls for punitive policy. This was also true at
the state level; consider that only one representative of Latino descent served
in the state general assembly and was a Republican.[78] There was little political pressure to pursue alternative policy strategies or even to resist the punitive turn.[79] Soon, Latino community leaders in Winston-Salem indicated that
Latinos who were legal residents and citizens were also being profiled and
detained by law enforcement, right alongside unauthorized migrants.

The net result of these shifts was that over the course of a few short years,
North Carolina's undocumented Latino immigrants, who in 2010 represented
an estimated 45% of Latinos in the state,[80] not only became the target of political and legislative scrutiny, but also saw their access to important institutions
and resources such as education, health care, and driver's licenses, restricted.
Even authorized community members were impacted by this shift, whether
through profiling and harassment, or collateral damage through family and

community members. With a quickly deteriorating economy and increasing pressures to refuse to hire unauthorized immigrants, Mexican immigrants found their mobility quickly truncated.

Just the fear of law enforcement reorganized daily life, closing off avenues of social integration. For instance, on days when there were rumors of police checkpoints, respondents reported that church attendance fell. More than one respondent reported losing a job after police set up checkpoints on their routes to work. In 2011, Winston-Salem officials held a town hall meeting to discuss the use of checkpoints (after an ACLU complaint that such checks were disproportionately conducted in minority neighborhoods). Latino residents were forced to improvise and take significant risks. Spanish-language radio broadcasts reported checkpoints, and after-school programs provided transportation to ensure that Latino children could participate even when their parents were afraid to drive. This heightened sense of risk produced a significant change in Latino immigrants' daily lives and integration into their communities.

SOURING PERCEPTIONS

In the 1990s, Latinos were largely invisible to the white majority in North Carolina. Most resided in rural areas, on the property of farm owners, or embedded in deeply segregated minority communities in urban areas. In 2005, however, public discourse began to shift dramatically to explicit denigration of Latinos. Political leaders who had previously been receptive to immigrant labor now publicly maligned those laborers. Virginia Foxx, Forsyth County's Republican representative in Congress, promoted neutral policies on immigration (in line with the agricultural and business interests of the region) until 2005, then changed her stance to strongly anti-immigrant, supporting 287(g), sponsoring a bill to declare the country "English-only," and advocating the abolition of birthright citizenship.[81] Capitalizing on a broad national anti-immigrant backlash and growing anti-Latino sentiment, Foxx said, "This wave of illegal immigration is a threat to our entire way of life." She quoted a section of the US Constitution that says one of the federal government's primary functions is to protect the citizenry from "threat of invasion." "We may be destroyed from within before we're destroyed from without," she said.[82] Elsewhere, "Debra Conrad, a Forsyth County commissioner who has spoken out against illegal immigration," picked up on the effort to revoke birthright citizenship, noting that many Hispanic children in North Carolina might be "anchor babies" (a term some use for US-born children of unauthorized immigrants who may help parents gain a toehold in the US).[83]

Attorney Deborah Weissman testified before the United States House of Representatives that Sheriff Steve Bizzell, former president of the North Carolina Sheriffs' Association:

> Described an incident of drunk driving that resulted in the death of a young boy by saying that the child paid the ultimate price for *another drunk Mexican* [emphasis added]. Bizzell further vocalized his hostility toward immigrants. He stated that "they are breeding like rabbits," and that they "rape, rob, and murder American citizens." He classified Mexicans as "trashy" and said that he thinks "all they do is work and make love."[84]

The ACLU testified that in Alamance County, Sheriff Terry Johnson stated, "[Mexicans'] values are a lot different—their morals—than what we have here. In Mexico, there's nothing wrong with having sex with a 12, 13-year-old girl. . . . They do a lot of drinking down in Mexico."[85] These were the public officials determining the course of immigration policy, and they had minimal federal oversight as they provided a legitimating discursive framework for anti-immigrant public discourse and bureaucratic action.

Statewide profiling and anti-immigrant discourse were, as highlighted above, accompanied by municipal efforts to restrict or deny access to social services. Despite the wide variety of tools available to local bureaucrats to limit immigrants' access to social institutions, many officials went so far as to engage in extra-legal practices, risking not only fines and sanctions, but also the possibility of excluding Spanish-speaking citizens or immigrants with legal status. Marco, an editor at the local Spanish-language newspaper who had arrived a few years earlier from Mexico on a work visa, told me:

> The other sort of responses that people received, that Hispanics received in this area, is the attempts to deny them social services. Those attempts have been ruled illegal by either state legislation or the state programs . . . but [there] have been attempts, for example, in . . . Beaufort. . . . They tried to pass an ordinance banning [telephone recordings in Spanish], and basically they received a notification from the state health department, saying, "You cannot do that. If you do that, you lose funding for programs."

In 2008, nearly 50% of Latino workers in the southeastern US reported knowing someone who had been treated unfairly by police, and over two-thirds reported regularly facing discrimination and hostility.[86] National data from 2007 showed that 78% of unauthorized immigrants felt that discrimination against Latinos was a major problem.[87] And in 2010, according to the Pew Hispanic Center, most Latinos felt that Americans were less accepting of Latinos than they were five years ago, and that this was due largely to status and skin color.[88] In other words, Latino immigrants reported a growing sense of systematic and arbitrary racial discrimination. Racialization, in turn, would serve to reconstruct their personal identities and their political attitudes.

In March 2009, I spoke to Marco, the newspaper editor, about how Mexicans were faring. He said, "In general terms, in North Carolina, the responses from the authorities and society haven't been good in the last four or five years." Marco explained that 287(g) and the measure depriving unauthorized immigrants of driver's licenses created a dragnet to "profile immigrants by the color of their skin." These programs were supposed to help root out crime and potential terrorist activity, but Marco said they seemed to exist only where there were high rates of Latino immigration.

When I spoke with Antonio, a reporter for *Que Pasa* who had arrived in the US from Michoacán in 2006, he assessed the native-born community's shifting feelings toward Mexicans in Winston-Salem:

> People that have been here even longer [than I] used to say that back in the 1990s when someone saw a Hispanic, the first reaction was curiosity. "Hey, how are you?" You know? It was, "Good! Hey! So strange to see anyone here!" The treatment was different. . . . Hispanic . . . has a negative connotation now. Hispanic is illegal, unauthorized, poor, nothing to offer to the society, criminal, gangster. All sort of negative connotations are together with that phrase "Hispanic." I remember sometimes, and especially when it comes to Hispanic and drunk drivers, Hispanic and illegal, Hispanic and gangs, I think that's what's in the people's mind when they talk about Hispanic.

Though Latinos occupied a lower socioeconomic status than whites and African Americans in North Carolina, there is no evidence that Latinos were responsible for an increase in crime or disproportionately participated in delinquent behaviors in Winston-Salem or any other municipality in the US. Instead, scholars have repeatedly found that immigration is associated with declines in criminal activity, despite their higher than average concentrations in low-resourced communities.[89] Still, the argument that Latinos are associated with increases in crime became a common justification for enforcement. Sheriffs insisted that immigration enforcement was necessary to remove felons, drunk drivers, and gang members from its streets.[90] Like African Americans, who have been criminalized in the US in the process of justifying punitive policies promoting their social control and alienation,[91] Latinos, particularly immigrants, became prey to totalizing frames.[92]

In 1996, the *Winston-Salem Journal* published 58 articles pertaining to immigration or Latinos. By 2006, I counted 299 (a peak-level for local immigration coverage). These articles were no longer profiles of residents who supported immigrant integration; instead, reports of DUIs, car accidents, theft, and violent crime were increasingly accompanied by information regarding the arrestee's ethnicity and citizenship status.[93] Stories with leads like "Illegal immigrant convicted in pregnant woman's death" were becoming common.[94] And this was *before* economic collapse.

In more neutral reports, the media highlighted the impact of immigration on local institutions. Schools were hit hard by Latino population growth; not only did more students need education, but more students required specialized services such as ESL classes and bilingual staff.[95] Some articles still suggested that the community should provide better services and additional resources to integrate the immigrant population, but others framed the immigrant population as a source of social and cultural conflict, even as a potential threat to the county, state, and the region.[96] One article in 2006 read:

> An Elon University poll released yesterday indicates that North Carolinians feel more negative about the effect of Hispanic immigration on the state than they did just seven months ago. A little more than 56 percent of the people polled said that the immigration of Hispanics has been bad for the state, up from 44.2 percent in April. About 18 percent said it has been good for the state, compared to 26.2 percent in April. Elon polled 533 adults between Nov. 13 and 16. The poll has a margin of error of plus or minus 4.3 percentage points. Elon conducted a similar poll of 677 adults about several issues, including immigration, in April. Hunter Bacot, the poll's director and a political-science professor at Elon, said that the results reflect the value North Carolinians see Hispanic immigrants contributing or taking away, particularly in areas such as jobs and the economy. "They are perceived as a burden on the state," Bacot said. "It looks like the popular perception among the public is that they are taking more than they are giving back." Bacot said that the increase, about 12 percent, is notable, and might be traced to the election season and negative campaigning about illegal immigration. "When you see a double-digit movement, something happens," Bacot said.[97]

These discourses were also highlighted as the basis for institutional closure.

> Two Forsyth County commissioners raised questions yesterday about the number of Hispanic children coming into the school system, after educators said they would need $405 million for new schools and renovations over the next 10 years. Commissioner Beaufort Bailey first raised the issue by asking for an ethnic breakdown of the student population. He then asked Superintendent Don Martin whether immigration laws might help stem an increasing student population. His comments came after he had said earlier this year during a forum on the issue of homelessness that efforts to help the homeless should not focus too much on Hispanics. At the time, Bailey said he had nothing against Hispanics but believes they are too often singled out as needing more help. Meanwhile, Debra Conrad-Shrader, the vice chairwoman of the

commissioners, said at yesterday's meeting that she has been told that 80 percent of Hispanics living in Forsyth County are undocumented workers. She acknowledged that she has not independently verified that figure.[98]

At a conference panel on immigration, Rebecca, a staff civil rights attorney for the ACLU, spoke of the widespread use of enforcement measures to manage Latino populations. She gave one example of a student who was sent out of class for being disruptive. Instead of calling school security or suspending her, the teacher called ICE. It was becoming more common for native-born residents to think of immigrants as, if not criminals, a real drain on local resources.[99] In the mid-2000s, Latino immigrants who had made significant efforts to incorporate socially and economically into the community were rendered by political and institutional shifts unwelcome. Efforts to expunge immigrants from North Carolina communities were explicit. As the *Winston-Salem Journal* reported in 2006:

> The Minuteman movement is expanding to the Triad, and its leaders are pledging to shine their watchdog spotlight on employers that hire undocumented workers. . . . The Minuteman Project and the Minuteman Civil Defense Corps Inc., which are not affiliated with each other, are best known for their controversial monitoring of the U.S.-Mexico border for illegal-immigrant crossings. The Minuteman Project is planning a chapter in High Point; Minuteman Civil Defense is establishing a Greensboro chapter. The groups said that targeting employers of illegal workers is aimed at reducing the job incentive for both employers and workers and spurring public demand for the enforcement of immigration laws. "We've been saying for years that North Carolina would be hit by the next tsunami of illegal workers in the country, and it's happening now," said Jim Gilchrist, the founder of Minuteman Project and a retired accountant from Laguna Hills, Calif.[100]

As Julie Weise points out, "In the twenty-first century, middle-class white residents of the region's least Southern spaces—exurbs that developed more than a decade after the fall of Jim Crow—took their lead from the West's exurban anti-immigrant movements as they mounted the South's first major anti-immigrant movement targeted at Latinos."[101] Despite their initial welcome compared to California in the 1990s, by the mid-2000s, cities with sprawling metro areas like Charlotte, Winston-Salem, Raleigh, and Durham saw growing hostility foment in their suburbs and exurbs.[102] Resentment flared toward Latinos. Weise writes that the early stages of anti-immigrant sentiment in the state were shaped by white entitlement in the suburban Charlotte area, "because white families did not see Mexicans as one of 'us,' they targeted 'them' as unworthy consumers of private and public goods."[103] In addition to peddling rhetoric that framed immigrants as illegal, as criminal, as a drain on public resources, and in some cases, as culturally inferior, white voters also supported a number of anti-immigrant local ordinances across the state, designed formalize anti-immigrant hostility and push Latinos out of their neighborhoods.[104] Such practices were also at work in Forsyth County, where, in December of 2007, the *Winston-Salem Journal* reported: "Several Forsyth County commissioners are praising a new internal study that shows that illegal Hispanic immigrants will use $11.2 million in county services this fiscal year. They say that the new data will help the county lobby state and federal officials for more stringent immigration laws."[105]

I asked Cecelia, a legal resident who had lived in Winston-Salem since childhood, about her feelings regarding the legal changes in North Carolina. She responded furiously:

> My name is Cecelia Ramos. Do you think they—that they're not gonna arrest me? Or if they question that I'm driving with my friends—if my license is legit? Seriously. . . . And you can't even get an ID. And it's gotten to the point where people are so paranoid they get IDs for their small children. You know? Because there are people in this state whose parents are in court, and then they don't come back. Is that humane? How do you do that to people? And their children are left with the babysitter or whoever. How is that even legal?

Though unauthorized immigrants were the explicit target of institutional closure, all Latinos felt its effects. At the national level, of the approximately 11.3 million undocumented immigrants in 2015, 52 percent were of Mexican origin.[106] Some 5.2 million children in the US have at least one undocumented parent, and the vast majority of those children—4.5 million—are US-born citizens.[107] The fear of deportation is constant and well founded. In addition to the fact that the most Latino citizens in Winston come from mixed-status families, many Latinos who were authorized or were citizens also reported being profiled by law enforcement, bureaucrats, and area residents.

As Milton Gordon observed in the 1950s and 1960s, discrimination and marginalization create formidable obstacles to integration for immigrant newcomers and racial minorities.[108] In his view, not only does prejudice prevent full social and civic inclusion, but it is also the basis of barriers to key integrating institutions such as education and health care. We see evidence of the importance of social exclusion in recent memory, too. In emboldening white nationalists and the broadly xenophobic, racist right in the 2016 presidential election, immigrants and African Americans were targeted with hate speech, violence, and general exclusion in a way that instilled fear and undermined access to social and institutional resources.[109]

The Shifting Terrain: Immigrants' Perceptions of Institutional Closure

Such shifts culminated in reverse incorporation, a process by which political change and social backlash rapidly changed the landscape for Mexicans, reversing the integration gains they had made and permanently altering their sense of belonging. Policy shifts meant broad bureaucratic discretion within an atmosphere in which anti-Latino attitudes were both acceptable and actionable. Gates that were open were now slammed shut.

A few short years before, these were workers who made contributions to local economies, bought cars and homes, participated in the community, and raised families. By 2006, many were literally afraid to leave the house. Identity scholars note how the swift shoring up of citizenship boundaries and sweeping generalizations about the foreignness of all Latinos has "uniquely positioned Latinos as permanently foreign immigrants in the imagination of Anglo Americans."[110] Ultimately, the goal of these policies was not mere exclusion, but expulsion.

Elisa, an unauthorized single mother from San Nicolas, Guerrero, who arrived in 1991, described the fear instilled by ICE. Her brothers had already been deported, and she feared that she was next.

ELISA: I feel afraid. I have a lot of fear for my children, well, because if they take me, my children, where are they going to stay? I have my son here, and I think about this a lot. . . . I have to drive because I have to go to work. Or take my children to the doctor, or to do my errands. I have to drive.
JJ: But you are always afraid?
ELISA: Yes, I am so afraid. When I see an officer go by or something, I feel sick. I pray to God. I tell him, please God, take care of me.

Both the authorized and unauthorized immigrants in Winston-Salem experienced what Cecilia Menjívar and Leisy Abrego call *legal violence*, the harmful effects of the "increasingly fragmented and arbitrary field of immigration law gradually intertwined with criminal law."[111] As highlighted by Elisa, immigrants' everyday lives were highly structured by the enforcement of immigration policy in their communities. Immigrants also saw unwarranted social closure. Diego sighed:

They try to intimidate us, to close the doors to us; they don't want to help us much. Along with the fact that they don't give us licenses, they've damaged a lot of people. A lot of us don't have problems. We don't have accidents. We don't drink and drive. We only want to go to work. With this situation, if someone is authorized to give you a ticket—just imagine it. It's 70 dollars that

I have to pay if I don't have my license. And if I'm not working, how will I pay
it? And if I don't pay them, or I don't go to court, they are going to give me
an arrest warrant. And if they arrest me, my family, then, well, there are a lot
of ways that they hurt us. Why? Why do they do this? Why? Because, well,
because they don't want us. Right? They don't want to help us.

Diego's sense was that the broader community and local authorities were
engaging in practices intended to punish a largely law-abiding, productive
group of people. Others expressed confusion over the shift in tone toward
immigrants. Beatriz noticed that Mexicans were now perceived as job-takers:

I mean, how are we taking their jobs? I mean, most of the Hispanic men work
in construction, factories. . . . They don't have really good jobs. Not like Americans. . . . In a way, the immigration thing started with George Bush, when he
didn't want to give any legal papers to Hispanics. But since this started, we've
seen a lot of differences. Like Americans treating Hispanics really bad.

These experiences of closure not only impacted immigrants' sense of reception and well-being, but also had tangible effects in terms of mobility.

DOWNWARD MOBILITY

As migration increased and the economy stagnated in 2008, immigrants
in the Winston-Salem area began to feel a strain in the labor market that
matched the chill in their community.[112] Ultimately, shifts in the local context created both direct and indirect intragenerational declines in mobility.
Without a license, many unauthorized immigrants lost their jobs, could not
find new employment, and could not build the credit to obtain small business
loans. They were unable to invest in assets such as vehicles or homes or in the
building of cultural capital through education and degree programs.

Public policies that target undocumented immigrants can foreclose access
to insurance, loans, property, and other services that facilitate mobility.[113] Efforts to restrict access to education and training truncate the ability of both
youth and adults to acquire the package of investments, endowments, working conditions, and rewards that facilitate upward mobility.[114]

Of the 40 Latino immigrants I interviewed in-depth, six reported that
they or someone in their household did not enroll in school or dropped out
due to changes in state policy. Sixteen reported that someone in their household experienced a wage decline or reduced hours at work, seven reported
that someone in their household experienced job loss, and every unauthorized immigrant in my study lost their access to a driver's license. Since most
Latinos in the area lived in mixed-status families, in practice, many citizens

and legal residents also lost ground. This change in economic trajectories and political context was a decisive shift from the integration patterns experienced just a few years earlier. Community closure, as scholars have shown, was common throughout the region.[115]

I met with Mayra, a Puerto Rican job placement officer, to discuss the situation for Latino job seekers. Mayra explained that she had only two companies that would hire people without papers. I asked whether she thought it was this was related to economic decline. With a wave of her hand, she dismissed the idea:

> It's not the economy. It's the new 287(g) laws that are causing problems. . . . Some people I know are returning to California and Texas because there is nothing here and the laws are getting very dangerous. Recently, a friend's whole family was taken back to Veracruz. You know things started getting worse in 9-1-1[9/11], and after that, the focus shifted to immigrants. Hispanics are not the only immigrants, and they had nothing to do with 9-1-1! They are not here to hurt anyone. . . . I also know a woman with six kids whose husband is going to be deported. And she can't find work, so I got together a collection for Christmas to get the kids toys so they would have something at Christmas.

Respondents reported that the recession magnified the effect of institutional closure on contracting employment opportunities for Latinos. For example, Marco told me:

> In the beginning, Hispanics here were a novelty. They just were required. Nobody here was willing to take those jobs in manufacturing companies, and also the sort of jobs in construction and the service sector. But it hasn't been positive in the last years basically because Hispanics are very new to the area. And in the South, and in North Carolina, people have become very intolerant. The responses to immigration have been putting up barriers that basically aim to identify who came here without authorization. . . . As I told you, though it depends county by county, I can say in general terms, in North Carolina, the responses from the authorities and society haven't been good in the last four or five years.

Mexican immigrants largely attributed their downward mobility to punitive immigration policies and growing hostility toward immigrants. I accompanied the Hispanic Outreach Coordinator at the Catholic Church on a visit to her parishioner Linda, a Latina immigrant who arrived from Guerrero in 1996. Linda told us that being a migrant means always being afraid. She'd had a job at a factory in Clemmons, but a few months after she was hired, "it was raided, and lots of people were arrested and sent back." At the factory, she was earning enough to support herself and attend school (she was studying to be an accountant). Following the raids, she found it difficult to find steady work and had to leave school.

Losses due to political change were magnified by bureaucratic closure. Many employers, officials, and service providers stopped assisting immigrants, stopped hiring undocumented residents, and actively discouraged Latinos from seeking benefits and services. Latinos reported that they were disproportionately targeted for firings, wage cuts, and hour reductions. Companies that had never before asked about legal status suddenly required it for hiring or asked their current workers for social security numbers. One respondent told me that her employer cut the wages of all his Latino workers by $2 per hour. They told her if she didn't like it, she could find a job somewhere else.

The disproportionate impact of labor market contraction on Latinos is in line with countless studies showing that in times of economic downturn, African Americans and Latinos have higher levels of unemployment, are more likely to lose their homes, and take significantly longer to find new employment.[116] While many unemployed Americans use periods of unemployment to seek out additional education and skills training, these avenues were not open to unauthorized immigrants. After the recession, construction work dried up. Even if it hadn't, institutional closure blocked these migrants from obtaining loans, licensing, insurance, and materials for their businesses.

Paola arrived in North Carolina from Mexico City in 1996. She and her husband bought a trailer in a suburb. He was able to get good work, and she worked part-time and attended school. Paola liked Winston-Salem, recalling it as "such a peaceful place." Though both Paola and her husband were unauthorized immigrants, they made significant gains in education, property ownership, and income. By all measures, they were upwardly mobile. But in 2007, Paola's husband was detained for using false documents to work. They lost his full-time income. In 2008, Paola told me that without "a social security number, many doors are closed to me now." Paola's children were citizens, but she was unable to obtain the Supplemental Nutrition Assistance Program (SNAP) and Supplemental Program for Women Infants and Children (WIC) they were entitled to because a caseworker was unwilling to process her claim due to her unauthorized status.[117] Paola now worked two part-time jobs, and her family struggled to make ends meet. According to research, the recession that began in 2008 did not necessarily create new categories of poverty; instead, it plunged marginal or already poor groups into deeper poverty.[118]

This chapter shows that in place of ethnic attachments or human capital levels, migrants' mobility was conditioned on institutional closure and attitudinal reversals. To the extent that macro-level shifts such as economic recessions shape mobility trajectories, they do so in large part through resource-control mechanisms. Despite consistency in immigrant attributes and persistent, pro-integration attitudes, changes in local conditions can and do result in downward mobility.

In the fall of 2008, I spoke with Catherine, a manager at a cooperative bank that targeted immigrant clients. The bank had recently opened a branch in Winston-Salem. She told me:

> We have a lot of people who are interested in buying a home, that want to create stability in their families, who want to be a part of the mainstream. But the political atmosphere makes that very difficult. People want their children to get an education, but these families are definitely going against the grain. . . . Things are much more difficult now; particularly the driver's license issue makes things very difficult. People can't get to work or take their kids to school, it's very hard. We hear of people afraid to leave their homes, and are doing the best they can, they still need to work, to live, but it's definitely much more hostile.

Contrary to studies that suggest upward mobility is hampered largely by a poor match between the immigrant and context, or the failure to accumulate human capital, in this case, it was the changing context of reception that made achieving milestones newly difficult.[119]

MARGINALIZED STATUS AND INTERNALIZATION

Of course, Latinos did not experience the Southeast as free of discrimination prior to 2006.[120] However, changes in context intensified both the tenor and regularity of anti-Latino and anti-immigrant settlement.[121] Stereotypes connecting immigrant status and criminal behavior—which, as discussed above, were often unfounded—became key features of the negative shift in attitudes toward Latino immigrants.

At a 2011 Winston-Salem town hall meeting on license checkpoints, a local weekly newspaper reported:

> A number of residents spoke during the town hall meeting, including Gabriela Melo. A 12-year resident of Winston-Salem, Melo described a recent incident where she was stopped at a driver's license checkpoint near the Waughtown Street exit off US Highway 52. Melo said she was stopped by a police officer and asked to show her driver's license, but a Caucasian driver in a vehicle behind her was waved through the checkpoint. "I felt so discriminated

[against]," Melo said. "Because maybe I look Mexican, you ask for my license, but you looked at him, he's white and you don't ask him for his license. That's so unfair. If you're checking licenses, you're checking mine, you're checking his—you're checking everybody's."[122]

A report in the Greensboro *News and Observer* confirmed:

> Immigrant advocates, religious leaders and doctors who work with immigrants said they have gotten calls this week from people all over the state who fear a massive immigration roundup. "People are scared to death and going underground," said Dr. Luke Smith, a child psychiatrist from Hillsborough who works with Hispanic patients. "People are afraid to get health care. They're staying home from their jobs. Their kids are missing days of school."[123]

The impact of the use of checkpoints and other measures to profile Latinos was not lost on the Winston-Salem police chief, who stated publicly that he opposed the tactics because they resulted in lower Latino cooperation with police.

Juan, a Mexican man who had lived in Winston-Salem since 1995, told me that a friend who was a Latino US citizen was sitting on his own porch when the police came and asked him for identification. The friend said his documents were in his house. The police followed him inside to wait for him to produce the documents, which he did. Juan continued:

> If I can't get health care, if I can't go to community college and get an education, it's a problem. You know, for example, if someone robs your house, *you* can report it, the police will come. But if I am robbed, *I* can't report it, because the police will want my ID, and they might deport me. I can't protect my human rights. . . . If you don't feel free, you can't do anything.

Juan's sense that he was being deprived of basic rights was echoed by many other respondents. Anti-immigrant attitudes, policies, and behaviors created the sense among Winston-Salem Latinos that they were now an excluded minority. When I asked Yesenia, whom I described as wracked by fear, if she had any worries about her status, she burst into tears:

> These are the worries you have with the licenses because it adds up. *There are times when for no other reason than being Hispanic, they stop you* . . . but the police, many police they stop me for nothing. I am in my car—it's registered, because I don't have it in my name, but it's registered. It has insurance. My car is fine, it's perfect, everything, the lights, everything. And the police, for no reason, I don't know. They see that I'm Hispanic . . . Only because I'm Hispanic, because I'm not documented, they do this. . . . They stopped me for no reason except to check and see if I was carrying my license. . . . The laws are tough right now. Why? I do not know. I do not know.

Rapid institutional closures and attitude shifts racialized Latinos immigrants at significant emotional and psychological cost.

Immigrants who face marginalization internalize these effects, in which they perceive a collective and systemic state of marginalization, provoking a sense of reactive ethnicity.[124] I build on Dina Okamoto and Kim Ebert's findings that when external conditions brighten group boundaries, a new sense of status and self emerges to highlight the impact of closure on racialization and politicization.[125] The literature on pan-ethnicity shows that collective identity formation occurs in response to structural discrimination and in relation to hostilities directed against the group.[126] In this way, contextual changes are part of the racial formation process.

Further, recent academic studies and policy reports indicate that this perception of profiling is widespread among Latinos in communities with ICE programs. As in Winston-Salem, reports indicate that across the Southeast immigrants have retreated from public places, interacting less frequently with schools, churches, local businesses, and other local institutions, and even changing their driving patterns to remain out of sight.[127] My Latino respondents adopted this new strategy of invisibility out of a sense of mistrust of officials. They came to see themselves as racialized Latinos who were subject to surveillance, victims of discrimination, increasingly denied access to institutions and services, and commonly disparaged by white residents. Whereas theories of segmented assimilation see downward mobility as exposure to, and adoption of, "underclass" behaviors, in the case of reverse incorporation, it is shaped by institutional barriers and contextual mechanisms. That is, marginalization and exclusion are ascriptive processes. In other words, race is not merely a barrier or a cause of integrative challenges, but the *result* of them.

Immigrants' political identities also shifted. Migrants came to develop resistive identities, reflected in their speech. In one town hall meeting, immigrant participants framed the need for political action as an issue of shared minority rights, shared civil rights, and shared human rights, not simply as an issue of immigration reform. Many of my respondents also explicitly reported that Latinos were becoming more political, paying closer attention to elections and weighing candidates' positions on immigration reform. Some cited demographic change as a reason for political engagement—they saw Latinos as the wave of the future. Others thought Latinos were beginning to channel their fear into action. Maritza, who arrived from Guerrero in 2006, noted:

> Because now you can see that, you can see that there have been groups, large
> groups that want something better for the Latinos. And before, this wasn't

the case. Or I imagine it wasn't before, not much happened then. Like before, people had more fear. And now, there are lot of people who are afraid.
A lot of people. But there are also many people who are fighting, doing
something, thinking about something. You know? Yes, that's what I think is
happening now.

Paola, too, who came from Mexico City in 1999, connected the politicization of Latinos directly to changes in the law: "Now, because right now we
are suffering, because we don't have licenses, we can't move. So, now things
are getting more political for us." And Camila, who arrived from Sonora in
2008, thought that people were politicized because of the current legal and
economic conditions:

> If you listen to us, you would know the only thing we want here is to work.
> Because I don't feel that, that we are taking anyone's job, because each one
> gets what they deserve . . . the job comes to a person who works or not. Each
> person has to do what they have to do and has what they deserve. And nobody
> has to be above anyone. I, I would like that, they would help us with licenses.
> And so, everything that they are doing with their strikes, and many youth,
> many children are left alone without their father or mother. Why? Because
> they take them to Mexico. And so, I feel that the strikes are good. But who
> knows if they will listen?

Camila critically makes the point that Latinos are a population with a voice.
They want to work, and they are looking for specific political concessions
to meet their basic needs—to have access to driver's licenses, to prevent the
deportation of adults with children, to travel to and from work and school
without fear. She argues that strikes and marches are necessary to make these
views heard, and is supportive of these efforts, regardless of their immediate efficacy. This kind of call and support for direct political engagement as
Latinos, even if, as immigrants, they lack voting rights, suggests a heightened
sense of political engagement triggered in part by the new forms of exclusion
they experienced.

Before the shift in immigration policy and attitudes in the broader community, Latino-focused organizations in the city largely involved business
leaders and focused on creating cultural events. Later, these organizations
began to engage in advocacy work. New groups emerged, including small
interfaith groups and small nonprofits organized by Latino community members. The presence of outspoken Latino advocates was also felt at community
events and in the Winston-Salem media, paralleling national-level actions. In
2006, Latino organizations and media outlets across the country organized a
march for immigrant rights in response to the proposed Sensenbrenner Bill,
an extremely punitive proposal that would have criminalized violations of

immigration law.[128] This series of marches was, at the time, frequently referred to as a "twenty-first century civil rights movement" whose leaders emerged out of a sense of collective marginalization. As in Winston-Salem, such politicization was strengthened as stigmatization and marginalization persisted, altering Latino migrant identities in significant ways.

A CHANGE HAS COME

Certainly, while there are always exceptions to the rule, upward mobility became extraordinarily difficult under these circumstances, and many, if not most, Latinos saw gains in some dimension reversed. Such outcomes are especially important to understand, as new legal research suggests that institutional closure against Latino immigrants is likely to increase and to spread because emerging forms of immigration enforcement overwhelmingly target Latinos, including citizens and lawful residents.[129]

Reverse incorporation occurs when macro-level changes or crises alter attitudes towards immigrants, spurring new large-scale institutional regimes that scapegoat immigrants and recast them in a negative light. Under these new conditions, local-level actors respond by either resisting or embracing shifts. Few changes occur in contexts where local actors resist these shifts. When they embrace them, however, major contextual-level changes occur.

Reverse incorporation is the result of the mutually constitutive processes of institutional closure and the transformation of native attitudes, which together lead to the internalization of this marginalization and exclusion among immigrants. It posits that changes in the institutions and attitudes of the context of reception can undo incorporation gains in three ways. First, the decline in economic investments and rewards results in individual losses in income, skills, and assets that are difficult to recover, even if circumstances shift. Second, the losses produce individual-level declines and impact households, producing cohort effects over time. Third, persistent marginalization intensifies the racialization of immigrants, a process they internalize, reshaping ethnoracial identities (and challenging their fixity) and instigating political activation and integration.[130]

The intragenerational reverse incorporation process unfolds when policymakers and bureaucrats block structural or public forms of integration through institutional closure: restricting access to employment, housing, education, services, and physical mobility. These restrictions transform the context of reception from open to closed. Where institutional openness plays an essential role in facilitating access to resources and social membership, institutional closure seals off access to resources and social membership.

Because there is great variation in how US municipalities treat undocumented immigrants, enforce laws, pursue punitive or protective policies, and use status as a determining factor in accessing city resources and protections, there is also significant variation in the level of disadvantage experienced as a result of undocumented status. Moreover, the intensity and specificity of these disadvantages change over time and across locations. Lacking a clear set of federal guidelines and procedures for the treatment of immigrants, local bureaucrats have substantial discretion in determining which institutions, benefits, and services will be made available to immigrants and under what circumstances.[131] For undocumented immigrants and their families, then, institutional access can be an especially volatile driver of mobility.

These reversals are intragenerational in nature, but have long-term, even intergenerational effects. In particular, the kind of racialization and downward mobility experienced by Latino immigrants and second-generation Latinos has been shown to have a significant negative impact on Latino health outcomes.[132] Stigmatization, diminished institutional access, and limited support especially in the realm of education appear to impact long-term mobility trajectories not only in the first generation, but in the *third* generation,[133] indicating that the processes and practices at work in the Winston-Salem context may have multigenerational consequences.

Reverse incorporation is not particular to new destinations—immigrants anywhere and everywhere are vulnerable to various changes in the context of reception. Yet recent efforts to exclude and marginalize immigrants in the US indicate that Latinos are especially vulnerable in new destinations. In places where elected officials feel threatened by rapid demographic change, or where economic recessions (one form of macro-structural change) may motivate job protection, institutional closure may be spurred in that local officials may be more willing to take an experimental, if not extreme, approach to dealing with population shifts.[134] Indeed, stratification scholars suggest that recent declines in Latino wages and wealth and increases in Latino poverty rates and residential isolation can be attributed in part to immigration enforcement policies.[135]

In light of federal guidelines that replace top-down immigration enforcement mechanisms with local law enforcement, new research must consider reverse incorporation processes to make sense of new patterns of immigrant mobility and intergroup relations. In terms of policy, comprehensive immigration reform intended to help immigrants manage their legal status in the US will fail to support positive incorporation unless it also reforms the role of states and municipalities in defining and enforcing immigration regulations. Defining policy at the local level creates the potential for conflict, particularly in small towns and suburbs where service providers and law enforcement agents are also neighbors. Local-level institutional closure also fosters an acute sense of *social* exclusion.

More importantly, these immigrants' internalized experience of racialization and discrimination is likely to persist, even if experiences of discrimination become rare. Though native-born attitudes may once again become receptive, immigrants are unlikely to forget their previous negative experiences or to revise their political attitudes and racialized identities. In this sense, reverse incorporation involves macro changes with a unidirectional effect—once they are internalized, they are very difficult to purge.

Similarly, once intragenerational reverse incorporation results in downward economic mobility or stagnation, it is difficult for immigrants to recover economic losses, even if they experience some upward mobility over the life course. Though macro-structural conditions may change, studies of adults who grew up during recessions show that they never recover their initial upward trajectories.[136] Carola Suárez-Orozco and Marcelo Suárez-Orozco suggest that institutional closures and increased anti-immigrant sentiment are likely to affect recently arrived immigrant youth and the children of immigrants, shaping their experiences of place.[137] Similarly, Frank Bean, Susan Brown, and James Bachmeier argue that undocumented immigration status, especially fear of deportation, lack of access to civil rights and experiences of exclusion, and limited access to high quality employment, is a transmitted disadvantage that hinders upward mobility in the second generation.[138] In addition, Alejandro Portes and Rubén Rumbaut show that among second-generation immigrants, experiences of discrimination have direct effects on racial identity and long-term perceptions of self.[139]

In the next chapter, I detail the specific ways in which Latino immigrants came to understand their identities as racialized and the importance of that shift both for their understanding of themselves as Latinos and for their relations with the two other major racial groups in town—blacks and whites. For the Latino residents of Winston-Salem, reverse incorporation highlighted marginalization and discrimination that looked and felt very similar to the experiences of blacks in their communities. Moreover, they interpreted efforts at exclusion as direct efforts by whites to shore up their status and shunt Latinos to the bottom of the racial hierarchy. African Americans, for their part, supported and even cultivated these interpretations by engaging in systemic efforts to build bridges with the Latino community through a sense of shared status. These dual processes of intragroup formation and meaning-making and intergroup relationship-building reveal more nuance in the relational nature of race and racial formation.

Racializing Mexicans: New Latinos

Because they [African Americans] have suffered in a sense. They have also had their leader, Martin Luther King, who also fought for their rights. So, I believe they identify more with us, because they also lived in a situation like us.

D I E G O , undocumented, from Guerrero, lived in US for 10 years

In March of 2009, near the peak of interest in the 287(g) program, Guilford County's sheriff announced that he was pursuing a jail-based program with ICE, allowing sheriffs to search for the names of all arrestees in ICE's database and process any who were undocumented for deportation. Guilford County is in the middle of the Piedmont Triad, and the prospect of a Triad 287(g) program spurred activists and community members to action. On April 1, a Latino church in Greensboro held a town-hall meeting to at least create some transparency around the program and get the sheriff on record regarding its rationale. The meeting was so crowded that parking attendants were needed and the church hall was packed. The crowd included mostly Latino families, but also a slew of organizers I recognized from other community forums: African Americans, including many from area church groups, members of the ACLU and the Southern Christian Leadership Conference (SCLC), a smattering of South Asian and Pakistani residents, members of the Spanish language and mainstream press, and various other concerned neighbors.

The moderators were a Latina community member and a black woman who served as a nurse in the local jails. The women explained how they brought together the panel to create awareness and facilitate dialogue between officers and the community. They called for civility. Simultaneous translation was provided, and the panel included the county sheriff, a portly white man, the Greensboro chief of police, a trim black man, and a panel of respondents from agencies and organizations representing and serving Latino populations in the Triad.

During his time, the sheriff made clear that he was pursuing the program because it was "the law." To enforce the law, he explained, his officers would ask residents about their status to determine whether they were in the US illegally. By contrast, Greensboro's police chief made it clear that he had no interest in participating in the program, but had to send the people he arrested to the county jail, where the program would be enforced regardless of his preferences. The invited respondents asked a variety of questions about the intent and nature of Guilford County's participation in the program before opening up the conversation to the audience. Immediately, a mid-30s Latino man stepped to the microphone. It appeared that he did not feel entirely comfortable speaking in English, and so he had written down the remarks he directed to the sheriff:

> I am happy to be here and am enjoying the opportunity to see you in the hot seat. You noted that there were 68 Hispanics in the jail and 43 illegals. What was their crime? My second question is that if I tell you I'm illegal, would you take me to jail? You say you have to enforce the law, but when I read history, in the '60s and '70s, and about Martin Luther King and the civil rights movement, he was talking about laws, but he stood up to those laws, because those laws were wrong.

Amid sustained applause, I overheard a Latina woman whisper that the man had voiced what she was too afraid to say.

*

Diego, quoted at the outset of this chapter, and this young man shared the perception that Latinos were being targeted, maligned, and persecuted in North Carolina. Given the dramatic shift in political and community context they saw in just about a decade, their feelings are unsurprising. More notably, though, the men framed their experiences as spurs to a call for the defense of civil rights. They made explicit ties to the experiences of African Americans in their communities—a lens through which many others had come to understand the Latino experience in North Carolina.

When I first met my respondents in Winston-Salem, I asked, as a matter of course, what race they belonged to in the United States. All of the Latin Americans identified themselves as Latino or Hispanic.[1] Upon further probing, they revealed that not only was Latino a race in their estimation, but that white and American were races they could *not* choose. This kind of identity framing is not a given. In this study, however, I found that they asserted a newly racialized sense of *Latinidad*, marked by discrimination, profiling, and exclusion, as well as what I call a sense of *minority linked fate*—that their race that was not merely about the social and cultural experiences of Latinidad, but a sense of shared status with blacks.[2]

As highlighted in chapter 3, in just a few short years, Latino immigrants in Winston-Salem and across North Carolina felt a sudden shift: the once-welcoming community was now closing its doors. Where municipal and state-level policy once facilitated their integration, it came to offer only restriction and exclusion. For new Latinos, this shift had structural and psychological consequences. Not only did formerly upwardly mobile immigrants see their trajectories truncated or reversed, but they also began to internalize what they perceived as discrimination. They were, effectively, racialized.[3] The speed of these changes fundamentally altered the way that Latino newcomers experienced their community, interpreted their position within the racial hierarchy, and thought about themselves as Latinos.

Latinos didn't simply understand this process as mere backlash, nor did they perceive that, somehow, *they* had changed in a way that might trigger a change in how neighbors, representatives, and institutions saw them. Rather, they experienced reverse incorporation, a distinctly racializing process, in which they were being maligned and discriminated against in a manner that felt arbitrary, unfair, and attributable primarily to their physical characteristics, rather than their behavior. The shift from an integrative community context to a punitive one meant that Latinos were suddenly and negatively reconfigured in the collective imaginary of the community.

Exclusionary behaviors are not experienced in isolation, and the Latinos in my study demonstrate how race is configured and experienced relationally. That is, race only makes sense within a racial system. And, as Claire Kim argues, rather than form autonomously, the racialization process is mutually constitutive.[4] Thus for Latinos to see themselves as racialized necessitates an explanation that accounts for the relationship between their experiences and that of others. In this way, racialization is not merely something that happens *to* groups, but is also produced *by* them, in dialogue with their day-to-day experiences.

Historically, scholars have frequently argued that the experiences of Latin American migrants suggested a strong identification with whites, due in part to the phenotypic appearance of many Latinos and to the ways in which they have been portrayed as hard-working, entrepreneurial, and upwardly mobile, as well as pious and family-oriented.[5] For many Latinos, accepting and performing this shared status meant asserting whiteness and distancing themselves from blacks to avoid denigration and downward mobility.[6]

This framing in which mobility and access to resources, regardless of phenotype, is obtained by establishing distance from African Americans is prevalent throughout the immigration and whiteness literatures. Still, scholars including Alejandro Portes and Rubén Rumbaut, Alejandro Portes and

Alex Stepick, and Reuel Rogers find distancing practices to be untenable over time.[7] The prevailing racial inequalities of American life ultimately compel Haitian and West Indian immigrants, for example, to identify with African Americans around a shared minority racial group identity.[8] Rogers, in particular, finds that those Caribbean blacks with collectivist beliefs are more likely to routinely interact with African Americans in civil and social networks.[9] They adopt black group consciousness as a source of identification. It is worth noting that this form of identity appears to have an empowering, eye-opening effect on Rogers' Afro-Caribbean respondents, with none of the demoralizing consequences typically associated with race-based oppositional consciousness among immigrants in other studies.[10] This smaller body of scholarship suggests that racial affinities may be produced through experience, particularly racial threat and discrimination, rather than through assimilation and acculturation into whiteness. It also more effectively captures what Victoria Hattam argues is lost in much of the literature—attention to relations *between* groups as instrumental in producing racializing experiences and identities— and captures the roles of inequality, power, and racism in producing racial outcomes.[11]

Indeed, how Latinos would identify and whether they would assert collective identities or meanings has been the subject of much debate and scholarly investigation. In considering how Latino identity is shaped, scholars such as Gilda Ochoa, G. Cristina Mora, and Julie Dowling have demonstrated the complex dynamics of intragroup relations between immigrants and citizens, between national origin groups, and among those of disparate phenotype and class backgrounds.[12] Rather than a natural progression toward the collective, these scholars show that identity formation is both relational and contingent, shaped by individual and group perceptions about their position relative to other racial groups, especially blacks, and by their competing desires and strategies to be upwardly mobile, obtain resources and political power, and develop strong community bonds and solidarity. Nevertheless, each argues, to varying degrees, that the need for solidarity in the face of racialized discrimination and denigration plays a significant role in the identity formation process.

Of course, Mexican racialization is nothing new. Overwhelmingly concentrated in Texas and California until the mid-twentieth century, Mexicans long served as a cheap agricultural labor source. Particularly in Texas after the Civil War and the Great Migration, Mexicans replaced slaves and free blacks as sharecroppers or seasonal wage-workers to harvest and plant cotton. Even earlier, Paul Taylor writes, in Nueces, Texas, Mexicans were considered cheap and exploitable alternatives to slaves. Still, despite being perceived as "excellent and subservient labor," Mexicans were also seen as a threat to the institution of slavery. They were complicit in supporting and assisting fugitive slaves escaping to Mexico,[13] and white Texans believed, when it came to the drivers of the Civil War, that "Mexicans were involved, either from sympathy with and by extending aid to the slaves, or from the fact that it was their border which offered freedom and barred pursuit."[14]

Mexicans were, in many ways, distinct from blacks, yet racialization was produced through extra-legal discrimination in schools and restaurants, where they were segregated despite their legal standing as whites. Texans frequently justified discrimination by situating Mexicans as parallel to blacks. As Taylor quotes, "The Mexican has his place about the same as a nigger,"[15] while others suggested that although perceived as unequivocally inferior to Anglo Texans, Mexicans were nevertheless "a good grade above [blacks]."[16]

The resulting complexity of intergroup relations appeared to linger in intermarriage patterns with both blacks and whites and some continued resentment among blacks that Mexicans were not strictly considered "colored," and therefore afforded some legal privileges not available to blacks. There were, too, moments of potential solidarity.[17] At the start of the twentieth century, some Mexicans adopted and asserted "white attitudes," while others maintained good relations with blacks (a purported holdover from the Civil War period).[18] The variance in both the socio-legal racial positioning of Mexicans relative to blacks and Anglo Texans, as shown by Taylor, and its influence on intergroup relations and self-perceptions highlights the importance of context in understanding racial formation practices.

Similarly, Tomás Almaguer wrote of nineteenth-century California, "racial categories are historically contingent and fluid in their specific meaning."[19] Mexicans in California were extended the legal privileges of whiteness, but not necessarily social ones. The racial project in California, Almaguer argues, was formed through a dialectical struggle between Anglos, Mexicans, Asian immigrants, blacks, and Native Americans over land and labor market position.[20] In Almaguer's view, the specificities of state context undoubtedly shaped the specific racialization of each group, but the process nevertheless extended white supremacy into the American Southwest. In other words, while racialization is context-specific and deeply relational, it is, at core, a struggle within, against, or for, white supremacy.[21] In California, contestations over racial meanings were fiercely debated political struggles, in which racialized meanings as conferred by the California state constitution in 1850 would determine who would access land rights, citizenship, resources, and other essential privileges of critical importance.[22]

In this context, Mexicans were extended citizenship and "whiteness," while Asians, blacks, and American Indians were not. Still, class and phenotype mattered, as darker-skinned Mestizos and lower-class Mexicans were locked out of the social privileges of the Californian elite. Mexicans' relatively privileged status would evaporate almost entirely by the end of the nineteenth century, when the massive dispossession of their land would tie with the increased immigration of working-class Mexicans to reposition Mexican Americans at the bottom of the social structure—unskilled laborers alongside other racial and ethnic minorities.[23]

It was this kind of relational construction of Mexicanness that was at the heart of the construction of early twentieth-century immigration law. As Natalia Molina explains, the period between the Johnson-Reed Immigration Act of 1924 and the 1965 Immigration and Nationality Act was one of considerable racial anxiety. Fear and periods of resource scarcity served to shape the parameters of race in America.[24] For Mexicans, who had long been considered temporary workers, this period cemented their position as racialized nonwhites and noncitizens, perpetually equated with illegality. This held even as they maintained a relatively *valued* status relative to Asians and blacks and as necessary workers. Such "racial scripts," Molina argues, laid the groundwork for struggles over Mexican belonging, racial status, and access to citizenship in the contemporary era.

Indeed, as Julie Dowling and others show in contemporary Texas, assertions of whiteness among Mexicans and Mexican Americans were expressions of a desire to be seen as "fully American," even if such identities were not entirely available to them.[25] Such assertions were not based in class background or even skin color, but in an ideological positioning that internalized the view that American equals white, and that by calling attention to racial barriers, those barriers are reinforced. These views, Dowling contends, exist on a continuum, in which white identity constructions that are color-blind are at one end of the continuum, and anti-racist racial "other" or minority identities are at the other. Mexicans and Mexican Americans who highlight racial barriers and prejudice are far more likely, however, to assert a shared racial status with blacks and affirming that status through social relations and solidarity.

Alternatively, Ian Haney López and others have shown that, historically, when Latinos, primarily Mexican Americans, could not access white privilege, they turned inward, producing a new form of ethnic identity. This identity was rooted in racial hybridity and foregrounded the role of the border in creating the Latino experience through an Americanized ideology of *mestizaje* that was distinct from both whites and blacks. In spaces like Texas and

California, where Latinos have had a multigenerational presence, the civil rights movement provided an important lesson in how racialized mobilization could be an effective and transformative force.[26] Nevertheless, for these groups, blackness was highlighted as a temporary reference point, in which Chicanidad or Latinidad was configured as racialized, but emphatically not black.[27]

In the Southeast today, where privileges have failed to materialize and mobility was reversed, Mexican newcomers quickly discard any notion of aspirational whiteness as useful or attainable. In recognizing, as G. Cristina Mora and Michael Rodríguez-Muñiz note, "that in the U.S. ethnoracial order, entrenched privileges and opportunities are afforded to some and not to others," belonging, or becoming American, was no longer available to them.[28] Under these circumstances, Latinos have had to make sense of a set of experiences defined by discrimination rather than success. At the same time, they reside in a new destination area—the Southeast—which has a relatively limited history of Latino settlement but a long history of black organizing around labor and civil rights. The idea of an internally coherent Latino identity distinct from blackness, as was constructed in Texas and California, seemed neither accessible nor prudent. Jaime Winders and Barbara Ellen Smith write:

> In the southern states that are home to the new immigrant destinations we discuss here (that is, the "traditional" South), the history of African–American enslavement and the strong presence of Black labor in southern agriculture, as well as postbellum labor practices such as hostility to unionism and an overall absence of industrialization, historically made them inhospitable for immigrants, especially in comparison with gateways such as New York. This fact, along with these southern states' colonial histories that largely differ from those in Florida and Texas, yielded a binary racial configuration that, while clearly present in parts of Texas and Florida, differs from racial formations in these locales.[29]

For Latinos in the Southeast, experiencing new discrimination and living among African Americans with similar complaints, the frame of comparison shifted. This process situated them as minorities most similar to, and best understood by, blacks. Without a longstanding co-ethnic population, other Latinos could not serve as a reference for understanding discrimination and political mobilization. Instead, it was the black community that served that role, creating an opening for a sense of interminority solidarity.

In this chapter, I show how Latinos described and understood their experiences as Latinos to be distinctly racialized, and how they came to interpret their experiences of discrimination and marginalization as akin to those of blacks, and distinct from that of whites. As a result, they came to view themselves as sharing a minority identity. For both newcomers and long-time residents, it fundamentally shifted the way they understood their ethnoracial identity—from one based primarily in national identities, culture, language, and the experience of being a newcomer, to seemingly arbitrary but increasingly harmful labeling as outsiders and criminals, excluded, and discriminated against by skin color.

Making Minority Identities

Experiences of discrimination have long been linked to important social outcomes for marginalized groups. Some of these are negative, including social psychological outcomes, disconnection from core institutions and practices that are linked to mobility and the middle class, and isolation and violence.[30] Others find that discrimination perversely builds resiliency and can strengthen identity, encourage solidarity, and activate political consciousness.[31] Rapid and radical marginalization is important not only in terms of its relationship to structural outcomes, but also in the ways in which it can reshape the marginalized group.

So, while discrimination is undoubtedly harmful, it also serves as a resource for group formation, reinforcing or reconstructing boundaries in order to shore up solidarity and mobilization. As Yen Le Espiritu notes, "External threats intensify group cohesion as members band together in defensive solidarities."[32] Broad-based national research corroborates this assertion, suggesting that punitive immigration laws intensify feelings of linked fate among Latinos in the United States. Such findings may be deeply consequential: a 2014 survey by Latino Decisions found that 78 percent of Latino immigrant respondents believe that there is an anti-immigrant/Hispanic climate in the US.[33] For the Latinos of Winston-Salem, the contextual changes experienced by Mexican newcomers and the broader Latino community between 2005 and 2009 were experienced as discrimination and sparked a dialectical process in which racialization began to fundamentally alter the ways in which they thought about themselves.[34]

In Winston-Salem, it was readily apparent that such a transformation of identity and perceived group position was underway. At the same town hall meeting described at the outset of this chapter, a young Latina woman in the audience directed her question to the sheriff: "287(g) supposedly is for all undocumented persons, but we know that this is being applied only to Latinos when we know others come illegally—Haitians, Pakistanis, etc. Why

are Latinos targeted?" When the sheriff responded that he doesn't intentionally look for any one race, she retorted that "she had not yet seen any raids on
Asians yet." She received sustained applause. Most of the Latinos I encountered agreed that it was Latinos who were being targeted.

These experiences were widespread among Latinos in Winston-Salem.
Many respondents reported feeling newly criminalized, too—a distinctly racializing experience. Diego, for example, reported a shift that left whites in his
community to assume he was a criminal. Asked to describe his relationship
with blacks and whites, Diego said he got along well with blacks, but with
whites, things were strained.

> An example is if I ask them for something and, or I ask them something, they
> don't answer me. They look at me and turn around. Well, there are some white
> people who if I park my car next to them, they turn on the security alarm in
> their car. They think I'm going to rob them [chuckles]. This is what I've no-
> ticed many times, many, many times.

This criminalization of minorities in order to alienate them and justify social
control is, of course, not new; it has been applied to African Americans for
generations.[35] However, while Latinos, particularly immigrants, have been
subject to such framing, it is only recently that states and municipalities have
had the freedom to construct extensive webs of social policy around these
stereotypes.

Documented, naturalized, and native-born Latinos, too, reported feelings
of surveillance, instances of discrimination, and general frustration and mal-
aise. Emmanuel, a Presbyterian pastor who arrived in 2000 and had a green
card, noted how all this made him feel closer to the experiences of African
Americans:

> Because now the Hispanics are like the African American people fifty years
> ago. Discrimination and at the end of the line. And for the color of the skin.
> One day I went to leave my car at the dealer, for service, and they were going
> to give me a ride. The driver said, "Hey, hello, in what restaurant you work?"
> He asked me. Because of my color, no? "Why do you say a restaurant?" I asked.
> "Oh, all the Hispanics work in the restaurant."

For Emmanuel, whose personal, day-to-day perceptions of racism and discrimination were shaped more by microaggressions than by overt hostility,
there was, nonetheless, a palpable shift in the context of reception.

Maria, a Puerto Rican long-time resident in North Carolina, explained
that when she was the director of a Hispanic center in a neighboring town
in the 1980s and 1990s, Latinos rarely faced the type of discrimination they

experience today. She remembered, "People felt welcomed," and lamented, "it's a shame that racism is getting worse." Maria said that a lot of people are trying to help, "but there are more people coming and a change in the laws that have made things really difficult." Across the board, anti-immigrant attitudes, policies, and behaviors were creating a broad sense of groupness among Latinos. They were now an excluded minority.

Feeling Similar to Blacks

Importantly, this process of marginalization was not racializing merely because it was perceived as arbitrary and severe. As highlighted above, Latinos also widely reported that their experiences of racialization were similar to that of African Americans. Such perceptions are not altogether unique, as Sylvia Zamora finds that Mexican immigrants and Mexican Americans in Southern California also perceive that blacks are the targets of white racism.[36] However, in Southern California, sustained, regular encounters with African Americans were uncommon; in Winston-Salem, immigrant Latinos interacted with African Americans on a regular basis—in their neighborhoods, workplaces, and local institutions, such as schools, hospitals, and grocery stores. Within this context, local Mexicans drew heavily on the experiences of blacks to make sense of their own new experiences of exclusion. This process occurred partially through osmosis—by interacting with community members, noting important landmarks and celebrations, or learning from their neighbors and children. But it was also intentional, cultivated by black leaders who wanted to make the case for similarity and solidarity.

By 2006, the shift in Latino representation as excludable, criminalized minorities was palpable. Spurious linkage between immigrant status and criminal behavior, as reflected in the media analysis in chapter 3, was a key feature of the negative shift in attitudes toward immigrants, particularly Latino immigrants. That blacks also experienced a broad sense of diminished political and social status resonated with many of my respondents in the context of this anti-Latino sentiment. That such experiences were being written into law further cemented their views.

June 2005 marked the first in a Winston "Soul and Salsa" series, initiated by the City of Winston Human Relations Commission (led by Tracy, a black woman) to improve relations between Latinos and blacks. The community forums aimed to bring together minority leaders, officials, and residents and, as early as the second meeting in 2006, they began to address topics such as relations with the police, getting involved in elections, and community activism. These small neighborhood forums grew into one of the commission's most successful community-wide efforts. At the 2006 forum, a Latina woman in the audience remarked to the police captain:

> Hispanics are more and more receiving the kind of treatment that African Americans are getting on the street from police, and I speak from personal experience, but it was frightening and I was terrified. What is frightening, is that both communities are identifiable by color, most of the time, and that makes them targetable. And the difference between the two is that Hispanics are perceived to be from a different country.

For many of the respondents in my study, blacks were not only a neighboring group that often expressed empathy for their recently racialized status, but a lens through which they could make sense of their own newly marginalized identities. Sometimes they didn't feel that they occupied the bottom rung of society alongside blacks, but were instead slotted below their black neighbors. Juan, who had learned English and lived in the area for over 15 years, was particularly disillusioned with the status of Latinos in the community:

> For Latinos, they are thinking about today, not tomorrow, because they just need to get through the day. It's probably better that not everyone thinks the way I do, because we might have a suicide problem. You know, the President [George W. Bush] is always saying that it's a country of laws, of family values. I don't see that. The impact of immigration is that the idea of human rights doesn't mean anything. The UN can say we are human beings, the church can talk about that, and our voices, but it doesn't matter if we don't have any rights. But it's not the heart of the problem. The "bottom line," as they say. If we can't speak as equals, then we can't really change anything. We really need immigration reform. Some people tell me I'm wanting a pink elephant, but I think it's the only real solution. We have no rights in this country, under this government without it. For Afro-Americans, it's true that many times their rights are violated. But they can't send them away.

Juan's pessimism was countered by Ramón's extraordinary optimism regarding the election of Barack Obama:

> I think things will be different. I believe it. To start, he's black. He knows black people's problems and Hispanic people's problems. He has his own past, his history, and his experience with these problems. He knows what worries us and I believe that he is going to help. Because before, all of the [past presidents] were Americans [whites], and they had no interest in Hispanics or blacks. They—well that's why they were worried when they said the president would be black. How will there be a black president when there's always been whites? But now everything is going to change. Imagine it. . . . Now the world is changing. Soon, there will be a Hispanic president. . . . It's changing right

now. It's not the same as it always was because before there was always a white
president who made laws for his own people. And now, with this black president, I believe things will change a lot. I believe in the next election he will be
reelected. I believe and hope so.

That both men closely tied together politics, race, and immigrants' rights
was not unique. Many of my respondents shared similar views, highlighting
Obama's blackness to note their shared status with the president, and therefore the potential for radical change in the position of both blacks and Latinos
in the US hierarchy.

In North Carolina, 67% of the Hispanic vote went to Obama in 2008.[37]
Such support was reflected nationally as well. In polls conducted by Latino
Decisions, when asked, "Which party do you think has more concern for the
Latino community?" 61% of respondents answered Democratic. Moreover,
71% of respondents believed that things in America would get better with
Obama as President, and 69% believed "that things would get better for the
Latino community in particular with Obama in office."[38] These views per-
sisted throughout Obama's tenure, with approval ratings among Latinos na-
tionally spiking as high as 81% in 2009 and only as low as 61.4% in 2010.[39]
This plurality of political support from Latinos suggests a significant shift in
self-perception in the political landscape, markedly different from the up-
for-grabs demographic Latinos have been perceived as in previous elections.
Racialization and experiences of discrimination may be driving this shift.
Eliana, who felt that Latinos experienced more discrimination in school, described the similarities she saw between Latinos and African Americans:

> I think—Hispanics and African Americans are more close than other races
> because of, of—African Americans were like slaves before and then Latinos
> they are sometimes not treated right either, so they're kind of closer together
> because of that, more than anything else.

How groups understand themselves in relation to the dominant group matters. In the case of shared minority status, a sense of shared racial alienation
(as opposed to a sense of aspirational whiteness) is essential to forming cross-
group racial solidarity, distinct from whites and whiteness and the benefits
that so often accompany those designations.[40]

Such views are not specific to the Winston-Salem context. Julie Dowling
finds that among Mexican Americans in Texas who assert strong racial minority identities, they too highlight parallels between blacks and Latinos.
For example, Dowling reports that Juliana, who grew up in a working-class
neighborhood with a mixture of "Mexicans and African Americans who
lived 'all poor, all together,'" credits "African Americans with 'opening a lot of

doors' for Mexican Americans," and says, "Our situation is just like the blacks, that we have struggled against discrimination. We should work with them and with immigrants, all together."[41] For a number of Dowling's respondents, as with mine, discrimination and cross-minority solidarity were important features of their racialized worldview as Mexicans and Mexican Americans.[42]

I met Maritza, an undocumented Mexican immigrant, through a contact who attended ESL classes at the Catholic Church. She and her siblings crossed the border together and originally settled in California. Then Maritza and one of her sisters made their way to North Carolina. When asked whether she felt she had more in common with whites or blacks here, she didn't hesitate: "blacks." I asked why. "Because well, they are like us. They [whites] don't want us here, and they wanted them [blacks] gone. Or rather, they [blacks] felt the same as we feel now." Diego not only felt more akin to African Americans than to whites, but he admired them, too:

DIEGO: Well, I have more respect for the African Americans. I've respected them more. I feel less rejected from them than from whites. Yes . . . on the TV, I've noted that they fight for some common causes, more often the Latinos with African Americans . . . it's more similar between us. We are closer than with the whites. I've seen more [African Americans and Latinos] on television them fighting for a cause. . . . But whites, almost never. They don't mix much.

JJ: Not whites?

DIEGO: No, I haven't seen it much. The majority are always against the things they they've done—sometimes they are against the African Americans and sometimes the Hispanics.

Later, we discussed the future. I wondered if Diego thought that relations between blacks and Latinos might become politically powerful:

I think so. I imagine so, and I would like it if it were true because they, they have suffered in a sense. They have also had their leader, Martin Luther King, that also fought for their rights. I believe they identify more with us because they also lived in a situation like us. It can happen some time, in some moment. But now the president is something new. It's never happened before. And he is helping not just the African Americans. He is not only making a difference for them. Or for Hispanics. He is doing something for all of the nation. And there are presidents who have come before, I imagine, at best, they didn't do much for the African Americans. Less for the Hispanics. Right? And in what he [Obama] is, his cabinet, his group of people, they haven't often had many African Americans inside of the government. They are now making changes. But it's been difficult.

Among my respondents, a few exceptions still felt closest, race-wise, to whites. Isabel, a woman from Michoacán, had arrived in Arizona, smuggled by an American Indian tribe who then transferred her to a family member in Phoenix before she reunited with her husband in Winston-Salem. She was a member of Nueva Esperanza church, and she said she didn't feel kinship with her black neighbors:

> Because for whatever reason, blacks cannot be trusted. Basically, because we have, how do I say it? Because they, the African Americans, they almost never work. They just live off the government that helps them with their rent, with their food, and almost, there are a lot of people who don't work, that do nothing more than find evil things to do, find houses to rob, and I, I feel that the whites are the ones that put forth more effort and there are fewer whites doing bad things than African Americans.

Isabel asserted well-worn, derogatory stereotypes about blacks, yet she felt strongly that President Obama was especially equipped to help Latinos precisely *because* he was black. She explained, "We have hope in him. Because we know that he—they also have had difficult things and for many years, it's true, that they also had bad experiences like that. I think that Obama understands us more than the other presidents that there have been." When I asked her to clarify:

> Because he is black. Because they also suffered a lot of discrimination and they [whites] already killed their [black] people, right? And I think that he is, he is moved to do something for us. And he, the fact that before in his campaign he said that he would do something for us. Now he still stands. That's what he said in his campaigns. Because other presidents when they gain power, they've already forgotten their promises that they've made and they don't mention them again. And this president continues to say the same thing.

I asked whether Isabel thought this was true of other blacks:

> I think so, yes, I think that they understand more, in that aspect. Because, well, they had been slaves and someone came and saved them from slavery. And now, we have created this hope that someone will come also, and save us from slavery. We don't know when. We don't know how . . . but we know that God has his hand in it, and it's going to happen. Something is going to happen. Something good for us.

This idea that Latinos as undocumented workers were a kind of slave, experiencing massive labor exploitation and a lack of rights, was a common parallel drawn by many Latinos in my study, especially those who asserted a strong sense of commonality with African Americans. Isabel's views, though they lead her to a different conclusion in terms of her own racialization and view of race relations, nonetheless suggest that racialized status and citizenship are deeply entwined in their perception of self and status in their everyday experiences. Her ideas about whether whites could sympathize in the same way were more complex:

> Because you see, basically, when in Obama's campaigns or—all the rumors that they said, well, we see discrimination sometimes. And, I have heard, well, in the news. I haven't had the experience of discrimination directly, but what you hear is that there are people that like us, and those that don't. There are people that say, "You come to my country and invade my country. Go back where you came from." And others say, "My country is your country." We've had a marvelous experience two weeks ago here. Here, this church, is composed by Americans. They are the ones that provide the money for it to exist. And two weeks ago, we had a dinner. Everyone that came brought dinner for them. There were maybe 60 Americans that came. And it was so nice that we felt that that we could stay there, that the Pastor he is in charge of all the Presbyterian churches, he said, "Thank God for the food that was delicious. Everything was very good, and one thing I want to say is: My country is your country."

Isabel, who has had notably positive experiences with whites and perceived blacks to be lazy, nevertheless believed that a black President would more seriously consider her interests as a Latina. Moreover, while she aspired to whiteness, she argued that blacks and Latinos faced a similar form of discrimination and would likely benefit from the same political leadership to eradicate those barriers. Such complicated views most frequently emerged among Mexicans who, like Isabel, who attended a church in which there were ample opportunities to meet sympathetic whites and reported very positive experiences with them. Still, Isabel made important distinctions between the ability of blacks and whites to sympathize with Latino marginalization and do something about it.

A third group of respondents felt hesitant to relate to *either* blacks or whites. Some had no formative experiences or only negative experiences with people of other races. Armando, a Mexican from Oaxaca, had lived in California for eight months before moving to Winston-Salem in 2003. He was unsure whether he had more in common with whites or blacks: "There are black people who are good, and there are white people that are good also. So, I can't say one." A few minutes later, he amended this, saying he had "more [in common] with blacks." When I pressed, he indicated:

> Well, because well, because the blacks, or, because I think, I'm not saying it's this way, but I think that what's happened to the blacks is more of what's happened to us [Latinos]. Even [those who are] from here. I think that the black

person has also had what's happened to us with whites, because he is black, not white. At best, they also discriminate against the blacks, although they are from here.

Despite his ambivalence, Armando expressed a kind of *minority linked fate*, explaining that things were likely better for Latinos because blacks had fought for their rights as minorities earlier:

Things have changed a little because, well, they say that before, a black person could not enter where he wanted, or go to a restaurant. And now, well, now I believe a lot has changed. So, in that way, a lot has changed. . . . And that's why, why there has been a bit more opportunity for the Latinos, for us Latinos.

Thus, for most of the Latinos in my study, the idea that they could be on the verge of honorary whiteness—even if they wanted to be—and that such whiteness is what creates opportunities for mobility, simply didn't ring true.[43]

Feeling Distinct from Whites

In the immigration and racial formation literatures, few scholars theorize Latino racial formation as a minority identity developed in relation to the experience of African Americans. And yet, this is precisely how Mexicans in Winston-Salem described their experiences: closer to blacks, further from whites. Because race is formed relationally, this triangulated affirmation by Mexican residents of their position as at, or near, the bottom of the racial hierarchy, is extremely consequential in our broader understanding of the Latino racialization process.[44]

Yesenia described her thoughts on North Carolinians this way:

Well, there are all types here. Here there are all kinds of Americans. There is the type of "redneck" American that will inculcate their children with this racism against Hispanics, against African Americans. They inculcate them this way and because of this, there is a lot of violence between students, between young people that attack Hispanics. Because their parents inculcate them. That's what I think.

Yesenia's sense that there is a white racist community and her knowledge of the term *redneck* surprised me, since she knew very little English. And the sense that a subset of white Americans was responsible for training their children to hold racist views against both blacks and Latinos, and in some cases, engage in violence, was extremely consequential for her understanding of race. In other words, discriminatory practices were essential to making sense of the Latino experience in North Carolina.

Tanya Golash-Boza sums it up nicely: discrimination "plays a fundamental role in determining not only one's racial attitudes, but also one's racial or ethnic identification."[45] In other words, to recognize race and status is to recognize discrimination. While Latinos of various backgrounds are subject to discriminatory practices, Mexicans are uniquely positioned in the US context to suffer the brunt of anti-Latino and anti-immigrant attitudes. Because of their historical positioning as the "illegal immigrant," the position of Mexicans in the US immigration policy framework and numerical size makes them especially likely to be targeted by anti-immigration politics.[46] This positioning, for many respondents, meant for them, whites were the ones doing the targeting.

Eliana, for example, pointed out how she felt the state government differentiated between whites and minority groups: "They treat whites better than African Americans and Latinos." When I asked why she thought that, she replied, "I know most of the people in the governor's office are white. Some people don't think that we're equal and they want . . . they think that whites are better than Hispanics and African Americans."

Pedro noted that while he thought some African Americans believed that they were losing jobs to Latinos, whites simply believed that "Latinos were below them." Which is to say, Pedro saw how individuals and groups worked to protect white supremacy. Cristian, who arrived in the states in 1998, said, "Well, also, it's that I believe that a white person feels superior to a black person, even though in reality, blacks, whites, we are the same. I don't know why they feel there is a difference." He went on to argue that many Latinos are, status-wise, below both groups because they are not citizens.

Without exception, my Latino respondents believed that whites held most of the political and economic power in their city, the state, and the country. Whites were, from what they could see, hoarding opportunities, actively looking out only for themselves, and preventing Latinos (and, to some extent, blacks) from sharing the wealth.

In this way, the racialization of Latinos occurred at the intersection of two processes. The first was a form of marginalization that shaped the rights and opportunities available to Latinos and other minorities. The second came in the form of interpersonal relations. In relation to blacks, Latinos perceived that blacks were subject to the same types of marginalizing treatment, and they felt greater solidarity with blacks on those grounds. Moreover, most Latinos described blacks as having positive attitudes toward them, free of anti-immigrant sentiment and racial prejudice. Many of the African American church, city, and civil rights leaders I spoke with encouraged this view. In contrast, Latinos reflected on whites' negative attitudes, treatment, and behavior toward Latinos, regardless of whether they were able to exercise power in those exchanges.

Even as some highlighted good experiences with white neighbors, co-workers, and co-parishioners or stated that they saw no difference between the behaviors and attitudes of racial groups, many in my study underscored what they perceived to be persistent negative anti-Latino attitudes held by whites. Ramón, an immigrant from Mexico City, clearly felt that whites looked down on him, and was defiant when I asked about it. He said that whites saw him:

As a person who does not give up . . . The Americans that don't like the way I am . . . If an American is doing something wrong, I will tell you. And if I'm doing something right, and he says it's wrong . . . I do not quit. I do not let some American tell me what is wrong. And that's what they do not like, a Hispanic to answer them. And I've always said this. They say, "The worst thing we find is a Mexican with, with attitude. With attitude." I always say, "I will not leave. I do not leave for any American. For no one." And this bothers them . . . They don't like it. Because of this, I think they don't want us. [Laughter] And black people, they are calmer. They are more relaxed. So, for that, almost no Americans want us here. And [they want] me, even less.

Ramón was just as clear with his view on racial stratification when I described how race relations in Winston-Salem had positioned whites above blacks and asked how Latinos fit in now:

Eh, for me it's no more than two [groups]. So how I see it, is that the whites always want to be better, and below is always everyone else . . . below is everyone, Chinese, Mexicans, blacks, everyone. But whites always want to be above. For them, it's the way they see. For them it doesn't matter if you're brown, white, yellow, blue. They are white, and because of that, they feel good. Or, they believe in nothing more than two races, and they want to treat you bad forever. . . . But the Americans, they only think of themselves. I don't know how they think, but they only think of themselves.

I asked Ramón if ever felt more discriminated against by whites:

Yes. They say to Hispanics—and because of it, Hispanics are always afraid of Americans—because they always say it. "I'm going to call immigration." Or, "You are illegal." And all of that. Yes, because to me, they've never said anything. But I have seen that is what they do. Yes, I know that is what they do.

Ramón dismissed the fear he thought many undocumented Mexicans had about whites, committing himself to defiance. He would not be intimidated or run out of town. In highlighting his "attitude," he called to mind the experiences of African Americans, from being reminded to "remain in their place" in the Jim Crow South, to being characterized as having poor "attitudes" and therefore subject to greater disciplinary scrutiny in schools and workplaces.

Even when respondents had not directly experienced any discrimination from whites, they spoke as if it were only a matter of time. When asked how she thought Latinos were treated on the job compared to blacks or whites, Adrianna from Guerrero told me, "I think there is some of everything, truthfully. Because there are some whites who are also racist, even though, thank God, the majority that I have encountered have been good people. The people that I know, have welcomed me, but the majority, well, no." And when I asked Diego how he thought African Americans perceived him, he said:

> Them? I believe that they too have suffered a little discrimination on the part of whites, because the whites believe they are superior to everyone. They too have suffered a lot. Because I have talked with some, and they are closer with Hispanics than with whites. So, there are people of color that think that—that they are closer to us. A lot. Others no. But I have better experiences with these people. With people of color because they have told me, that the whites always think they are better than us or them.

This idea that whites positioned themselves differently than blacks and Hispanics in the racial hierarchy was widespread among Latinos in my study, who also perceived that this sense of superiority was often linked to racist or discriminatory behaviors and attitudes.

Still others felt that their experiences in Winston-Salem—in schools, social service institutions, public spaces, and shops, and with authority figures—highlighted their distinct position from that of whites. Armando noted that not only did whites persistently discriminate against him, strangers yelled at him on the street that he is illegal and should return to his country, and that police treated him and other Latinos differently. He told me that his neighbor had been the victim of a home invasion; the home-owner caught the white perpetrator and they got into a fight. Yet when the police arrived, they arrested the Latino man. His incredulous neighbors stood by shouting that the *gabacho* [non-Hispanic] was the guilty one.

Amaya, who lived in the States for 12 years, noticed a similar pattern when she went to a free clinic for a prenatal check-up:

> For example, I remember when I was pregnant, maybe more than three years ago, and I was going for a check-up, there was . . . one white woman and maybe three black women and five Hispanic women. That is, there were more of us [nonwhite] pregnant women than white women. And when I realized that the clinics were, well, sometimes they attended to the white women more quickly even though we had arrived first . . . and I think that's where, where

the [white] Americans go in and, and yes, they are upset and say, then, "You are giving this to people who have no papers. They are giving benefits to them and we don't have any." And that's where . . . you do see the difference, and you see it when you go to such places such as clinics and public aid.

Their status in the racial hierarchy, in my Latino respondents' view, was not because of their failure to acquire human capital and achieve upward mobility, but because they faced real structural and social barriers and persistent discrimination. This reshaped not only their sense of status in the racial order, but also their sense of self and relation to others. They came to see Latinos as a distinct group of various Latin Americans whose experience was shaped not only by immigration and language heritage, but also by phenotype and day-to-day treatment.

Douglas Massey argues that Mexicans are being racialized further as they are increasingly exploited and excluded.[47] Drawing from Barth,[48] Massey argues that groups become the targets of exclusion and discrimination and that individuals within that group contest, give meaning to, and accept the meanings attributed to them in various ways. He notes that both the in-group and out-group participate in the construction of the boundaries and identities that create a system of racial stratification.[49] In the post-9/11 era, Massey posits, the framing and boundary work around Mexican immigration plays a central role in their exclusion as a group. Further, he shows that in real terms, the class status of Latinos has dropped below that of African Americans, accompanied by a parallel shift in discrimination against Latinos on a variety of stratification measures.

As of 2000, for example, studies suggest that Latinos are more likely to experience discrimination in the housing market than African Americans, with one out of five African Americans and one out of four Latinos experiencing some form of housing discrimination.[50] In fact, 2012 reports from the Department of Housing and Urban Development show that while discrimination on balance has declined, Latinos are still slightly more likely to experience discrimination in the rental market.[51] Edward Telles and Vilma Ortiz make a similar argument about the exclusion and racialization of Mexicans into the formation of an underclass, though they are hesitant to argue that Mexicans are being unilaterally racialized.[52] Here, it is clear that the term racialization is used to understand a parallel status with African Americans as excluded and discriminated against, with a very low status within the social hierarchy. The alternative would be assimilation into a status similar to that of European whites. In their study, Telles and Ortiz find that neither assimilation nor racialization completely fits the Mexican case. Yet they note:

American society often stigmatizes those of Mexican origin, regardless of
whether Mexicans are considered or consider themselves white, whether they
are physically distinct, or whether they speak Spanish or have a Spanish sur-
name or accent. This racialization also creates shared personal and political
identities, which often become the basis for collective political action.[53]

Importantly, Mexicans themselves refer to this sense of discrimination as
anti-Latino (rather than only anti-Mexican). Moreover, to the extent that
there is spill-over in which other Latinos are negatively framed along with
Mexicans, these processes of Latino racialization apply to them as well. In
this way, I argue that Latinos' attention to discrimination suggests that Latino
exclusion has expanded beyond nationality and citizenship status, to include
other, more classic forms of denigration, such as perceptions of criminality.

These findings regarding the role of discrimination in shaping Latino
identities are not unique, as scholars like Jessica Vasquez have found that
discrimination, particularly in educational settings, plays an important role
in shaping racial identities and integration patterns across generations.[54]
Golash-Boza argues that becoming Latino *is* a form of racialized assimilation, arguing that experiences of discrimination diminish the likelihood that
Latinos will identify as unhyphenated Americans and instead help them to
become Latino group-members.[55] What is often missing from this analysis,
however, is the relational aspect of creating these identities. For Latinos in
Winston-Salem, North Carolina, discrimination matters not only in terms
of how it shapes their day-to-day experiences, but also in how it forms their
relational sense of racial positioning in terms of both whites and blacks.

Making Minorities: A New Latino Identity

Race is a socially constructed and relational concept. Minority status further requires a sense of commonality—similarity and affinity—with other
nonwhites. Thus, we see the Mexicans in this chapter making sense of their
own feelings of discrimination through African Americans' experience with
discrimination. As a result, a specific aspect of their Latino identity is made
meaningful, in part, by its similarity to the black experience.[56]

Gabriel Sánchez's work, in which he finds that experiences of discrimination and expressions of internal Latino group consciousness are contributors of perceptions of commonality with African Americans, reinforces the
idea that the perception of pervasive discrimination increases perceptions
of Latino internal cohesion and groupness.[57] I show how this transformation
increases perceived commonality with blacks, suggesting that Latino identity

is not merely about internal cohesion, but the development of a new racialized identity based in a strong sense of minority status. Such findings are
also consistent with recent scholarship by José Padín, who suggests racialization occurs through the "juxtaposition of normative antipathies between
Americans (read, whites) and Latinos, and by extension, normative affinities
between the latter and blacks. This mode of racialization is defined around a
white/nonwhite axis of distinction. Latinos, like blacks, are symbolically on
the wrong side of the tracks."[58] Again, it is not only their positioning as distinct from whites, but similarities and affinities with blacks.

In G. Cristina Mora's *Hispanic Panethnicity*, she chronicles the deliberate and painstaking process by which social movement organizations, scholars, government agencies, media companies, and corporate entities collabo-
rated and compromised to make "Hispanic" exist as a category between the
1960s and 1990s. Indeed, until the successes of the civil rights movement, few
ethnoracial groups were perceived as both a category and a people. In particular, groups that were largely perceived as immigrant newcomers (despite
their often lengthy history in the US) were designated primarily by national
origin—Cubans, Mexicans, or Chinese and Japanese. When it became clear
that groups denigrated by their ethnoracial status could nevertheless act in
their own interests, groups began the type of consciousness-raising work that
had become de rigueur in the run-up to the civil rights movement. The rules of
peoplehood needed to be established.

For Latinos, Mora argues, consensus deradicalized identity in favor of
foregrounding broadly neutral shared characteristics that were perceived as
positive—an orientation toward family, religion, the Spanish language, and
a vaguely *mestizo* look. Certainly, this framing cordoned Latinidad off from
many who advocated for a rights-based identity, as well as those of African
descent who did not fit the *mestizaje* norm. And yet, this framing was consistent with a scholarly and political shift that sought to claim the Latin American *mestizaje* ideal of a fluid, biracial national ideal for the US, adding to it a
sense of liminality and border crossing—a duality gained from the immigration experience. By the 1980s and 1990s, scholars and writers such as Gloria
Anzaldúa became the voices of a Latino identity politics that was distinct in
its in-betweenness, and yet firmly not black in its orientation.

The Mexican immigrants I spoke with and observed in North Carolina
suggest that Latino identity is once again transforming, at least in the Southern context, this time with a shift away from the *mestizaje* ideal. In their view,
what makes Latinos *Latinos* is not their differences from blackness, but their
similarities to it. Latinidad is not defined primarily by cultural distinctive-

ness, but by social marginalization. In this way, the Latinos in my study have circled back to a Civil Rights Era minority identity, in which, in light of racialized ascription and marginalization, red, black, yellow, and brown were conceived of as distinct groups with a shared status, as minorities who staked their claims in opposition to whiteness, not in aspiration to it.

Discrimination is without a doubt the hallmark of a "raced" experience, and therefore plays an essential role in shaping identities. Portes and Rumbaut find that second-generation youth who define their race either nationally or pan-nationally more frequently report discrimination. "Experiences of discrimination are powerfully associated with subsequent racial identification either as a potential determinant or as an integral component of a racial minority status. All but the white-identified respondents had significantly endured these experiences by an early age."[59] For example, when I asked Maritza how she thought Latinos were treated and, later, how blacks were treated in Winston-Salem, she replied that they were the same. When I asked her to clarify, she said, "Well the difference is that one group speaks English and the other Spanish. But they are the same. At least, that's what they say." Again, I asked her to elaborate:

> Well, how to explain it? Well, I don't know it well, but I have heard and some have told me. A woman—she is Colombian. She was going to teach me English. And she gave me a book about Martin Luther King so I could read it, and according to it, well, he liberated the *morenos*, the *negros*. They were slaves, as they say, like us, who don't have any rights to anything, and just because we are from another country, just like they were. . . . And this is the way they want to treat us. But, I say, as long as you don't bow your head, everything will be fine . . . we came here to find a better life, and to live better. We didn't come to rob people. You know? Or for them to treat us badly. Well, they are free to go wherever. That's great. But why not us? But, well, it's ok. You know, one day this is going to end.

While drawing so explicitly on the civil rights movement may strike some as perhaps more consistent with assertions of a Chicano or perhaps even Boricua identity, these migrants, like many Latinos who came to the US in the 1990s and 2000s, have settled in places where those Latino histories are invisible. There are few long-standing communities of Latinos who are citizens, have lived in these places for generations, or have made claims to the space as their own. The only people they see making such claims are the longstanding African American community, whose history as Southerners they are more likely to be directly engaged with. Thus, Latino newcomers are constructing and reinforcing a parallel, rather than a distinctive, identity.[60]

Thus, while Gabriel Sánchez and Natalie Masuoka find very cautionary support for the long-term development of Latino group consciousness,[61] I draw on this literature to argue that for Mexicans in Winston-Salem in particular, whose immigration experiences are becoming increasingly exclusionary, marginalization drives group consciousness and the development of linked fate to produce a racialized Latino identity. For the Mexicans of Winston-Salem then, *Latinidad* is defined as a race-based minority identity.

Making Minorities and *Minority Linked Fate*

In historicizing the sense of racial group interests among African Americans, despite class cleavages, Michael Dawson describes "linked fate" as a unique concept that "explicitly links perceptions of self-interest to perceptions of racial group interests."[62] Dawson claims that "the historical experiences of African Americans have resulted in a situation in which group interests have served as a useful proxy for self-interest."[63] This shared set of interests that becomes a proxy for one's own self-interests is a useful tool for understanding the extent to which a group is raced by outsiders and articulates a sense of collectivity from within.

More specifically, Dawson presents a framework in which African Americans come to understand their success or failure as tied together by virtue of their collective experiences of discrimination and socio-economic hardships, as well as a sense of shared interests.

The concept of linked fate, however, has only recently been applied to Latinos and, to a lesser extent, Asian Americas and Native Americans.[64] For some scholars, Latinos are strong candidates for developing a linked fate. Others, however, argue that those who intend to assimilate are more likely to view themselves as white or that the identities they bring with them, as well as the various racial categories in their home countries, trouble any possibility for collective consciousness.[65] And yet, the respondents in this study suggest that, under certain conditions, pan-ethnic consciousness and linked fate for these groups is possible.[66]

Further, scholars of Latino identity dispute the level of collectivity among Latinos, but recent work indicates that there is potential for "Latino" to become a salient category for some, particularly as persistent, structural, and interpersonal discrimination is on the rise. Those Latinos who believe that they are the primary targets of that discrimination are much more likely to identify as Latinos. There is significant evidence that Mexicans, particularly first-generation Mexican Americans, are rapidly moving from a "group" to an "identity," no longer simply outwardly defined via a set of shared characteristics, but also beginning to define themselves in relation to others as Latinos and minorities.[67] Reinforcing messages and feedback from other nonwhites can facilitate a sense of minority status as well. Indeed, some of the work that employs a linked fate concept points to the correlation among Latinos between a sense of pan-ethnic identity and a strong sense of linked fate with blacks, suggesting that group interests are correlated with a sense of shared discrimination and hardship.[68] Moreover, this scholarship indicates that shared hardship can catalyze closeness both within, and across, minority groups.

Studies also suggest that first-generation migrants are the least likely to identify with pan-ethnic labels, preferring national-origin ones in large part because scholars assume that it takes a significant period of time to adapt a perspective that fully incorporates them into a United States framework. In previous generations, too, Mexican-origin immigrants were far more transnational, making frequent trips home to visit family and check on small-scale investments such as farms and homes—practices now made difficult by increased border and interior enforcement. Still, in my own research, first-generation Mexicans were highly likely to use the terms Hispanic or Latino. It would seem that certain forms of structural discrimination, stigmatization, and low levels of receptivity can speed up the racialization process, particularly when they are accompanied by reinforcing actors in the local social and political context. Thus, I extend Dawson's claim that solidarity is produced among blacks through racial hostility and reinforced through social networks to the experience of Latinos in the Winston-Salem area into a broader sense of *minority linked fate*.

When groups perceive a shared minority status that is distinct from whites, there is also significant evidence that they perceive other minority groups positively.[69] Where within-group identity and solidarity are forged from marginalization,[70] it is a vital piece of the development of cross-group solidarity. Gabriel Sánchez and Natalie Masuoka see marginalization as a catalyst of black-Latino solidarity, theorizing that strong internal Latino identity is correlated with a sense of minority "group consciousness" and should motivate a greater sense of common status with and positive attitudes toward blacks.[71] Similarly, Sophia Wallace and Chris Zepeda-Millán, in their work on 2006 marches, draw from the social psychological literature to suggest that common perceptions of discrimination can produce a superordinate bridging identity that politicized Latino identity and commonality with blacks.[72] The data presented here support this hypothesis: the activation of a minority group-consciousness is a key mechanism through which shared minority status is established.

According to Dawson's linked fate concept,[73] for that group to develop a sense of we-ness, as a group *for* itself rather than *in* itself, it must also have reinforcing mechanisms. For African Americans, this would come from institutions such as the black church. For Latinos, I find that these reinforcing mechanisms can come from outside of the group—or *be* another group. In this case, African Americans, as a reference group as well as a peer group, engage Latinos in a discourse of shared minority status and contribute to their racial formation processes. In the next chapter, I elaborate, considering how African Americans are engaging in the process of reinforcing the new sense of Latinidad among Winston-Salem's Mexicans and producing a strong sense of *minority linked fate*.

5

Making Minorities: The African American Embrace and *Minority Linked Fate*

Because supposedly, supposedly they say that blacks and Hispanics don't get along . . . it's just much easier to call a black person a friend than an American. Me with the Americans, I don't know why . . . we collide a lot. As if they do not like what I do, and I do not like what they do. I don't know why. I get along with black people, yes, because they've gone through what we are going through. You know the problems that they've had for years, from slavery and all that. . . . The Americans have treated black people badly to this day. They have the same problem that we have: racism. And because of this, we get along better. At least, that's true for me. Because we know how we are treated.

R A M Ó N , undocumented, from Mexico City, lived in the US for 13 years

Ramón began our conversation by marveling at a common trope, "that blacks and Hispanics don't get along," that bore no resemblance to his own experience. In scholarly literature and popular discourse, black-Latino conflict has been theorized as the normative condition of relations between the two groups. But where much of the literature argues that minority groups see each other as a permanent threat, my research subjects largely expressed interracial solidarity.[1]

Throughout my time in Winston-Salem, I was puzzled to find that regardless of phenotype, region of origin, occupation, or time in the US, Latino migrants overwhelmingly (though not exclusively) reported that they got along better with black people than white.[2] Time and time again, Latinos reported counting African Americans amongst their friendliest neighbors and coworkers. More importantly, they reported strong feelings of closeness, even describing African Americans as natural allies in the struggle against discrimination. African Americans, for their part, reinforced this harmonious message through official messaging and political engagement from church leaders, activists, city bureaucrats, and service providers as well as the informal actions of generous neighbors, friendly parents, jovial coworkers, and thoughtful teachers. In contrast, many Latinos perceived white Americans as discriminatory and distant. Puzzlingly, here, Latinidad was not being folded into whiteness; instead, black and brown community members were coming together, undercutting the notion that they were locked in an age-old competition over resources.[3]

Ramón, who was instrumental in unraveling this mystery, was from Mexico City. He had arrived in the US in 1996 and was undocumented when we met through my contacts in the Nueva Esperanza congregation. Ramón grew up middle-class and in the city, far from the rural farming communities or coastal areas where Afro-Mexicans resided or regions where circular migration was common. He was very light-skinned, with blue eyes and a good command of English. Knowing all these facts, I assumed he would hold conventionally anti-black, or at least, neutral attitudes toward African Americans.[4] Instead, he revealed that most of his coworkers were black and "American" (by which he meant white),[5] and he was friendly with all of them. However, he described his interactions with blacks as more positive than with whites:

> Listen . . . with the Americans, I get along well, but by chance I get along better with blacks. . . . Well, I've never had any problem with anyone, not with Americans, not blacks, but I have better relationships with blacks.

Ramón and I talked for some time, nearly two hours. He emphasized not only his preference for associating with African Americans, but also that most of his friendships were with blacks and emphatically not with whites. He was sure that his friendships came out of common, racialized minority status.

> Since I left school . . . I worked in construction and worked in factories. My friends have always been black people and I began to count on them more. I learned to talk like them and everything. My best—I have more black friends than Americans [whites]. To this day, I work more with them, on the weekends they talk to me, just to see how I'm doing. Sometimes they come over to my house. There is one black guy who is maybe 45, who looks very young, and he always says that my mom is his mom. He has always been a good friend of the family. . . . I think in some places, there are those [white Americans] who look at you as less. And in my way of thinking, if an American can do it, I can do it too, and better. Nobody is going to put me down. And for this reason, I think it's easier to get along with black people because in some places, Americans don't like a person, simply because they are Hispanic.

Over the course of our conversation, I came to realize that Ramón was emblematic of a different kind of story emerging in Winston-Salem and communities throughout the region. As with many of the Latinos I interviewed and observed, blacks were friends and allies, while whites were, at best, distant outsiders, and, at worst, a threat. Moreover, being marginalized was formative to their construction of what it meant to be Latino, including in relation to other minorities.

Recognizing their shared experiences of discrimination, Latinos turned to

African Americans for clarity and support. Blacks largely accepted the challenge, embracing Latinos as neighbors, coworkers, friends, and allies. Collectively, they saw themselves as minorities of a similar status, living in the same communities and facing similar struggles. This unexpected emergence of what I call *minority linked fate*, sheds new light on the relationship between immigrant enforcement and race relations, detailing how legal and social exclusion can inspire shifts in identity formation, as well as intergroup solidarity and political action.

Minority Linked Fate

In their analysis of racialization and racial solidarity projects, legal scholars Lani Guinier and Gerald Torres note that we often fail to consider the fullness of racialization projects. That is, we emphasize racial boundaries, the significance of phenotype, and the privileges and penalties associated with racial identity and ascription to the exclusion of nuance in the experience of group membership and racial politics. We analyze race largely as a fixed category, from which, Guinier notes, "many would prefer to escape."[6] Even when we highlight the fluid and constructed nature of race, emphasizing the malleability of boundaries, we nevertheless tend toward seeing race as a constellation of groups, paying little attention to the important power dynamics that race and racial meanings can both reproduce and undermine.[7] Guinier and Torres note, however, that race also contains emancipatory possibilities through what they call "political race." In sum, because race is not merely historical or cultural, but political, political projects that undermine the power structures that distribute privileges to some and punishments to others along racial lines will require political racial projects. In calling for a politics that asks, "with whom do you link your fate," they argue, cross-racial political projects are the key to achieving social change.[8]

Through my fieldwork, I found that positive relations between blacks and Mexicans emerged in three key ways: a sense of physical and social closeness; a sense of shared status and discrimination or consciousness; and an emergent sense of *minority linked fate*. This sense of shared status and solidarity among nonwhites is perhaps presumed, but insufficiently examined in the literature. While I make no prescriptive claims in this book, the idea of political race as a "democratic social movement aimed at bringing about constructive change within the larger community" relies on the actualization of *minority linked fate*.[9] For Guinier and Torres, cross-racial politics happen when "they see that their fate is linked to others who are like them. They see that what happens to one happens to many others, if not to most others, who are similarly situated. Race becomes political in the sense of generating collective action only when it motivates people to connect their individual experiences of other and then to act collectively in response to those experiences."[10] It is *minority linked fate* that links together not only black people, as Dawson finds, but also various marginalized nonwhites who come to think, behave, and practice *minority linked fate* in ways that can lead to political racial projects.

Moreover, the import of linked fate for our understanding of race is not merely its implications for racial politics. While cooperation, collaboration, and coalition building between minority groups are infrequently examined outcomes of intergroup relations, I argue that such efforts are, in fact, far from rare, and have a great deal to tell us about how race works. Indeed, as data from the 2006 Latino National Survey indicate, a nascent sense of *minority linked fate* appears to be increasingly widespread. When Latino respondents were asked whether they believed that their ability to succeed economically was tied to how well African Americans were doing, approximately 66 percent of first-generation Latinos believed this was true "a lot" or "some," as did about 52 percent of the second generation.[11] Linked fate also plays an important role in shaping race relations and racial identities, resulting in a dialectic set of relations in which perceptions about shared status also shape perceptions about self. Most notably, the pan-ethnic literature has revealed how distinct national origin groups collaborate and build coalitions on the grounds of shared interests and for the explicit purpose of producing in-group solidarity and shared identity.[12] Scholars who examine efforts to cultivate pan-ethnic identity reject that they might be based on a taken-for-granted groupness, instead treating pan-ethnic processes as intentional, iterative, contingent, and deeply political.[13]

As pan-ethnicity scholars show, bounded groupness based on racialization and discrimination from the state and community can produce a sense of group solidarity and shared interests among heretofore disparate groups in a way that economic status, for example, rarely does.[14] For instance, studies of pan-ethnic formation and coalition building among Puerto Ricans, Mexicans, and Cubans highlight the ways in which disparate groups have not only consolidated in terms of shared language, colonialism, and anti-discrimination efforts; but also engaged in cross-solidarity movements, such as efforts by Puerto Rican activists in Chicago to participate in immigrant rights demonstrations in an explicit effort to shore up a politicized Latinidad.[15] These processes of pan-ethnic group formation also shape intergroup relations; a sense of across-group solidarity, particularly between blacks and Latinos, influences in-group solidarity, strengthening ethnoracial identity among individuals, as well as the group. In other words, the production of linked fate is an essential component of racialization.[16]

Even these insightful frameworks are rarely extended beyond the examination of a single ethno-racial group.[17] These group-based and temporal limitations hinder the extension of these insights to other group formation processes. Yet similarly, for Winston-Salem's Latinos, the activation of a minority group-consciousness is a key mechanism through which shared racial status is established. In this chapter, I show that one's sense of racial status, one's perception of how and whether other groups share a similar position in the racial hierarchy, and the quality of interaction with community structures and institutions are important determinants of the quality of social relations.[18] In Winston, this process was facilitated not merely by social closeness, but by deliberate and protracted efforts by black leaders to break down stereotypes, establish a sense of shared status and issues, and build solidarity. Black council members, police chiefs, human rights commission members, and other key city personnel helped create visible welcoming policies and community dialogue with Latino immigrants. By contrast, much of the backlash experienced by Latinos was promoted by white bureaucrats and residents. This perceived bifurcation was essential in cementing a sense of shared status and social support among minorities and underscored their distrust of whites, even when white bureaucrats and municipal leaders acted in Latinos' interests. Together, these processes cultivated not only a sense of racialized minority status among Latinos, but also a sense of *minority linked fate* with African Americans.

Interpersonal Relations

POSITIVE BLACK-LATINO CONTACT AND SOCIAL CLOSENESS

The economic expansion of the 1990s changed the geography of Winston-Salem in ways that made it remarkably welcoming for new Latino arrivals. As highlighted in chapter 2, not only were new jobs available to Latino newcomers, but the economy had expanded to include more white-collar positions available to blacks. Increased wages and improved job stability allowed blacks to move out of the rental and lower-quality housing units near the downtown area and into owner-occupied homes on the outer edges of the city center, as well across its north and west quadrants.[19] The now-vacant housing downtown, and in rental complexes in the north and west, created pockets of available housing stock for Latino newcomers to move into, settling into the rental units located within or near stable, middle-class black communities.[20]

Such close proximity provided important opportunities for black-Latino contact, a key mechanism through which intergroup relations form.[21] However, unlike in, say, Los Angeles, where scholars argue ethnic replacement created significant interminority tension, as was also evident in newspaper reports, many of my respondents referred to their neighborhood transition from predominantly black to increasingly Latino, and from empty to occupied, as "revitalization."[22] Human Relations officers that I spoke with confirmed there was little housing competition between blacks and Latinos in the 1990s and early 2000s. The press, too, published few stories of interminority conflict. That Latinos came to settle alongside blacks in traditionally black neighborhoods meant frequent contact juxtaposed against a dearth of interpersonal relationships with whites (more likely to be segregated from both groups).

Brenda, an African American woman who works at a local church, told me a story about black and Latino neighbors who became friends as a result of this proximity:

> This child was the cause, because she was always asking, "What's cooking? What's the food?" You know? And she had [the child] taste it. So, she started to tell her mama what was being cooked and Mrs. James said, "Well, you know, it smells mighty good across the street." So, they just . . . swapped recipes and, and then ultimately decided that everybody would eat supper together one day a week. A Mexican meal and a soul food meal. . . . People find ways to connect with each other when they have shared values. . . . That little girl was the catalyst that caused that whole relationship to develop. That's exactly right. I don't know how many other situations exist that way but, you know, I know they're living together. I know they're living on the same streets.

Similarly, my Mexican respondents spoke of frequent civil interaction with black families in their neighborhoods and cited it as a source of positive relations. Juan, a Mexican migrant who had been living and working in Winston for over 10 years, was surprised, like Ramón, at narratives that insisted there was a lot of black-Latino conflict:

> I have heard . . . that there is a lot of tension, but that's not been my experience. I live in a black neighborhood, and I've never had any problems with my neighbors. People are very nice, and we get along well. . . . I haven't had any problems. My children attend a mostly black school, and they don't have any problems. . . . I think some of this comes from the problem of language, that they don't speak the same language, and in any place where you have two groups that are different, with different values or cultures you will have some kind of clash, but I haven't had any problems. Sometimes people fight, and sometimes the black kids fight amongst themselves. It's often the same kids.

But, I think that's just something that happens when you have young people together, it's not any kind of racial tension.[23]

Other respondents indicated that despite language barriers, blacks and Latinos in their neighborhoods often greeted each other in the mornings, having brief, but pleasant conversations and behaving in a manner that Latinos described as generally neighborly. Another respondent, Linda, who arrived in 1996, a shy young Mexican woman who was unemployed and spoke no English, told me during a home visit with a church outreach coordinator that she had a black neighbor who stopped by regularly to check on her, sometimes bringing a treat for her children. Such small efforts suggested that African Americans were willing to make a point of connecting with Latinos, reinforcing the type of amicable and regular forms of contact that are effective in alleviating prejudice and fostering good relations between groups.[24] Moreover, many of my respondents who lived outside of the historically majority black and Latino neighborhood on the southeast side of the city reported a kind of white flight that was transforming their communities—indicating that when Latinos began moving into their apartment complex or trailer park, whites began to leave. For example, when I asked Blanca about her neighborhood, she described it as very calm and peaceful, but that it had changed since she moved in five years ago—nearly all the white families had left. When I asked Blanca when they started leaving she responded:

They were already doing it. Look, I was there and asking about the trailer, and I suppose we were there about three months before the [neighbors] in front left. That trailer was already sold. Some Hispanics bought it. And after that, maybe six months or so, another American went. They sold and other Hispanics arrived. And little by little they went running—all of the Americans.

As whites fled, the proximity of blacks and Latinos continued to facilitate more amicable ties. Eliana, a 19-year-old Mexican woman who had come directly to Winston from Guerrero when she was 12, described neighborhood relations as positive as well:

At my middle school there were more African American people and Hispanics. There were like almost no white people in there, so—and they all get along, so that wasn't a problem in there. High school, same thing. It's most African Americans and Hispanics and like 5% white people. And Hispanics and African Americans they get along very well. . . . I have a lot of friends that are African Americans at school. We're like, we have a pretty good friendship.

I inquired about the quality of the contact between the two groups—whether students actually have relationships with one another. She nodded and said, "Yeah, they're talking, like, they actually go out together, they like go to parties together or something like that, go to the movies." And when I asked her about similar relationships elsewhere, she noted, "In church, they work together. African Americans help . . . I know a lot of African Americans, who want the Latinos who are here illegally to become legal, and they try to do something to help them." Eliana, Brenda, and Juan found contact between blacks and Latinos largely warm and social, occurring both in and out of shared institutions.[25] By contrast, when I asked about her relationships with whites, Eliana demurred, "Um, I don't think there's actually a relationship. . . . No relations. It's like you don't ever see each other."

Racial avoidance precludes social solidarity, whether between Latinos and whites or any other cross-racial permutation. Social space is largely constructed so that contact between groups is minimal, but where the contact is increased, as in majority-minority neighborhoods, social solidarity can grow. I asked Jorge about his relationships with black and white people in Winston-Salem:

> It depends. It depends on the family. But I'm more comfortable around—with black people. . . . 'Cause where I used to live when we first moved, my community was black. I didn't have any white people around me. And my dad, he was nice to [our black neighbors]. He would make me do stuff for them, especially if they were old people.

Elisa noted that she felt she had more in common with African Americans because she had a neighbor who is African American and that where she worked, there were more African Americans than whites. She loved her neighborhood, which she found safe and filled with good people. And the African Americans at her work were "very, very good people. They help you more." Camila, who also lived and worked with African Americans, agreed, saying that she got along very well with her coworkers and neighbors. She noted that she greets her neighbors with a, "Hi, good morning" and that everything "is very calm." She hadn't known many African Americans in California, but now that she works and lives near many, and she finds them to be "very kind to her." Notably, English-speaking respondents like Eliana, Jorge, Juan, and Camila had more opportunities to meet and develop ties with both blacks and whites. Still, even though English facilitated contact to both racial groups, English-speaking Latino respondents consistently reported closer ties to blacks.

Some of my respondents, especially (but not always) those who were Afro-descendant, described a sort of familial connection to African Americans, professing that they shared more similar social and cultural styles with African Americans than with their own northern Mexican counterparts.

Alma, who arrived in 1999, said, "Well, I think that black people cohabit more with Hispanics. The truth is, they just live together more. I think, and it's not because I favor them, but I think that sometimes black people say that they are like us, us Hispanics, and there are certain characteristics that they have, it's true." When I asked for an example, Alma referred to cuisine: "Well, in terms of food. I know they like spicy food. Sometimes we are eating, and they are like, 'Ooh, give me some.' And I give them a taco. They eat like we do. But white people, no way. They don't like spicy food at all. They say 'no,' and that's it. Black people say 'yes,' about this and other things. There is just more living together . . . that's the truth." Jorge told me that all of his friends were African American because "that felt like home."

SHARED RACIAL STATUS

The literature on immigrant incorporation suggests that even in cases where blacks seek to build alliances with Latinos, Latinos rebuff these attempts in an effort to distance themselves from blacks and what they perceive as lower racial status.[26] I found, however, that distancing only happens absent the factors that *promote* shared racial status. For Latinos, the perception of increased local-level immigration enforcement and whites' increasingly negative attitudes toward them as systemic and racially motivated discrimination spurred Latinos' sense of shared racial status with blacks through what both groups perceived as the racializing experience of discrimination. For example, Jessica noted:

> I feel like, between African Americans and Hispanics, they are basically at the same level, whites are at a higher level than us. I think blacks and Latinos are more similar because they want to be together. They want to unite. To have more relations with Hispanics. Well, that's what I see.

Moreover, local Mexicans drew heavily on the experiences of blacks to make sense of their own new experiences of exclusion in Winston, further shoring up a sense of shared racial status. As they felt the immediate effects of widespread anti-Latino backlash, many of my respondents felt a linked fate with blacks, especially as laws came to target them. Emmanuel, a local pastor, recalled feeling discrimination cropping up:

> I once went to the country to meet with some people on a farm. . . . Someone asked me where I was from. When I said Mexico, the person asked me where my *sombrero* was. I wasn't really insulted by it, I just feel like people are sometimes ignorant. There are some white people who won't respond to me, who are not cordial and support Virginia Foxx or something.[27]

The pervasive sense of discrimination felt by Latinos in my study, more extensively discussed in chapter 4, was not simply a broad sense of oppression. Many located these experiences and views in the white community and power structure. As Mexicans embraced the idea that Latinos and blacks shared a similar racial status vis-à-vis treatment from whites and had more positive relationships with each other, these views were welcomed and applauded by black community leaders. Because checkpoints, raids, and other forms of targeted policing against Latinos took place in heavily black neighborhoods, African Americans such as Dr. Johnson, a local teacher and church leader, expressed to me that they, too, were being caught up in a dragnet of racial profiling and discriminatory policing.[28]

Discrimination can come piecemeal from individuals or structurally through policy. The group formation literature, however, theorizes that it is the identification of a specific threat source that catalyzes group identity formation and mobilization.[29] In this case, a shared view that whites are not only interpersonally hostile, but drive punitive policies and discriminatory policing, plays an important role in shaping both a strong sense of Latino among Latinos and a sense of *minority linked fate* with blacks. Data from the 2006 Latino National Survey also supports this assertion empirically, indicating that discrimination plays a significant role in Latinos developing a sense of group identity.[30] Indeed, research on interracial coalitions indicates that understandings of "one's own disadvantaged status *and* their committedness to other minority groups" leads to stronger intergroup relationships.[31] In the late 2000s, actions on the ground from both blacks and whites played important roles in reinforcing Mexican immigrants' sense of shared racial status and black-Latino solidarity. African Americans, particularly those in leadership positions in government, churches, and local nonprofits, emphasized the need to see commonalities and build solidarity between the two groups.

Other African Americans expressed frustration with racism directed at Latino immigrants and thought Latinos needed to be educated about the history of racism both in the United States and in their home countries. Brenda, like many of the African Americans and Latinos I spoke with, noted:

> We definitely have got to do more marketing so we can get people to want to come and help Latinos—it has kind of shifted a bit now—but helping Latinos build up confidence around understanding the history around racism as it relates to where they came from. Going back to Spain and all that historical stuff. The caste systems. How they're named. That will help bridge the divide between them and the people of color, you know, African Americans. I think that's important because it'll say, you know, you come out of an oppression—

you're an oppressed people, and we're an oppressed people. And it all goes back to Europe.

Brenda also gave a contemporary example of the kind of discrimination and oppression she felt that Latinos experienced in the US that other immigrants did not: the command to "learn English."

> So, why are you pressing them that they need to learn how to speak English? They're going to learn. They're going to learn over time. And I guess the ones who don't learn are no different than Russian Jews who came here, who migrated in Coney Island in New York. Did they rush to learn how to speak English? No. They were—now don't get me started. It's only certain people that people home in on and say, "Oh they don't know how to speak English." You got Chinese people that you, who I don't know, they're probably millionaires, we'll never know it. But I'm just saying, there are Chinese people here and all over the United States, and nobody says they need to learn how to speak English. They just point, help you point to what you want to get and then they say it in Chinese and then they fix it. And they figure out how to give you your money. Have you heard anybody say, "Those Chinese need to learn how to speak English"?

Structural and Political Forces

Certainly, day-to-day contact, perceptions of similarity, views of a shared racial status, and discrimination mattered in providing a strong basis on which to build unity and solidarity. Throughout North Carolina, municipal leaders, particularly African American politicians and bureaucrats, demonstrated support for immigrant newcomers, often working alongside other progressive Democrats. In Winston, significant numbers of minorities in leadership positions took the lead in extending an embrace through community engagement, positive rhetoric, and the extension of services, such as staffing of an information hotline in multiple languages, city-wide cultural festivals, initiatives to enhance communication with Spanish speakers in the city, and careful attention to enforcing Title VI of the Civil Rights Act, which prohibits discrimination. Together, these efforts set the tone for interminority relations in the city.[32]

African Americans in the community were also motivated to build a multiracial coalition of progressive voters and preserve gains made through the civil rights movement. Because anti-immigrant activists and politicians who sought punitive policies engaged in many of the techniques used to marginalize African Americans in the community—racializing immigrant Latinos as criminals exploiting civic resources, heavy-handed policing, stereotyping, and restricting access to voter registration and education—it wasn't hard to link the ideological shift against Latinos to systemic racism against black people. Locally, these connections were reinforced publicly by advocates such as Councilwoman Burke, a long-time African American representative of the Northeast Ward, who at more than one city council meeting in 2008, made calls for equitable treatment of Latinos and African Americans in Winston-Salem, raising the issue of shared minority status and the contributions made by minorities to the Winston-Salem community.[33] She noted "that a study done in 2006 indicated that Hispanics contribute more than $9 billion to the State, African Americans contribute more than $44.5 billion, and spending by Asians exceeded $156 million. She noted that City Hall belongs to taxpayers and the way in which minorities consume, they should be treated equally and fairly, and City staff should do a better job in addressing unfair treatment of minorities by City government as well as in the community."[34] Interactions with local institutions and efforts by community leaders to capitalize on these connections and engage in advocacy work reinforced those connections.

In the wider political landscape in 2008, Barack Obama's candidacy meant that the election in Forsyth County was marked by contradictions around race and immigration. The significance of an electable African American candidate for president in North Carolina cannot be understated. Efforts to turn out the black vote, increase voter participation among Democrats, and convince moderates of the historic importance of the election meant that every political moment in this swing state was shaped by race. Many Republican candidates doubled down on the "Southern Strategy" not only by seeking to undermine Obama's appeal to white voters, but also by scapegoating Latino immigrants in addressing North Carolina's recent economic decline. Republicans campaigned hard on promises to pass extraordinarily punitive immigration legislation aimed squarely at Latinos across the state. The long election season was marked by vitriolic, often hateful discourse against Latino immigrants on the one hand, and hopeful rhetoric regarding the rise of a populist African American leader on the other. On balance, the election rhetoric only served to reinforce perceptions among both blacks and Latinos that their political fates were linked; examples at every level substantiated Mexican perceptions that black leaders would stand with undocumented migrants as whites actively sought to discriminate against them.

For their part, African American leaders emerged as an important counterweight to anti-immigrant discourse, while white sheriffs, political figures, and conservative media pundits were perceived as the key promoters of enforcement policies like 287(g) and Secure Communities. Locally, the African American police chiefs in Winston-Salem and neighboring Greensboro refused to endorse any local-federal enforcement partnerships,[35] and black council members spoke out against any enhanced policing that targeted Latinos in their districts on the grounds that it would impact *all* minorities in the district.

Thus, despite white liberals' immigrant advocacy, the political Right often dominated discourse, facilitating the perception that discriminatory practices were divided along racial lines. Indeed, 2006 National Latino Survey data indicate that among Latinos who reported experiences of discrimination, the vast majority of perpetrators were white: 58.77% among first-generation respondents and 49.22% among second-generation respondents. This was compared to 15.86% of first-generation respondents and 7.87 percent of second-generation respondents who reported discrimination perpetrated by other Latinos, and 11.37% among first-generation respondents and 5.45% who reported discrimination perpetrated by blacks.[36] By looking to race as the basis for their solidarity, Latinos and blacks made stark the failure of whites, regardless of their progressive or liberal orientation, to connect with minorities within the community.

Eliana said, of the teachers at her high school:

ELIANA: Sometimes like when the teachers, they're like treat—they don't treat Hispanics the way they treat, um, the other students. They're treated more harshly.

JJ: Why do you think that is? Are your teachers black, or Hispanic, or white?

ELIANA: [Laughter] There's no Hispanic teachers in my school.

JJ: There aren't any?

ELIANA: No. They're only black and white. Yeah, there are no Hispanic [teachers] in my school.

JJ: Do you think there's a difference between how the white teachers are with the students and how the black teachers are with the students?

ELIANA: Well, black teachers are nicer to all the students than white ones.

This lack of connection with whites, coupled with blacks' efforts to link their experiences, helped Latinos concretize the idea of shared racial status and marginalization. Immigrant Latinos also signaled that they felt African Americans were more likely to be looking out for them. For instance, in a "know your rights" meeting at the public library, the Latino immigrants in attendance were advised on how to proceed if they were approached by police or ICE. The Latina facilitator told attendees: They cannot ask for your papers. Don't answer questions. Don't show fake documents, because if you are detained, they will check everything. One audience member, Silvia, nodded enthusiastically and added that she had met a black woman at the DMV one day when she was getting a license and brought a check to prove her address. The woman warned Silvia not to use her check, because if it had a fake social security number on it or did not match her other IDs, they would take her identification and they could "turn her in." Silvia expressed relief that she was warned before making such a fatal mistake. By highlighting the race of the woman who had looked out for her interests in this predominantly Latino forum, Silvia gave a striking example of trust for black neighbors relative to broad perceptions about whites in the community.

Throughout the region, the Latino perception of white threat was made starker in comparison to relations with blacks. As the level of public anti-immigrant rhetoric and enforcement increased, so did the level of black leaders' involvement on Latino and immigration issues. At the national level, the National Black Police Association (NBPA) signed on to a 2009 letter to President Obama demanding an end to the 287(g) program. The letter and NBPA's endorsement was reported in the Spanish language media, including by Univision, suggesting that many in the community were aware of this work.[37] Circumstantially and intentionally, political and identity shifts increased *minority linked fate* in the Winston-Salem community. For example, in 2006, the *Winston-Salem Journal* reported, "The Congressional Black Caucus has formally entered the debate on illegal immigration by outlining a series of steps needed to ensure immigration reform, according to a two-page document. . . . Watt said he believes that the two minorities can work together and that they do share similar interests."[38] Even early in the anti-Latino shift at the national and local levels, black leaders were reaching out and tying their fate to that of their Latino community members.

CHURCHES AND COMMUNITY LEADERS: ADVOCACY

As early as 2004, there were efforts to make these connections, but they were piecemeal. As the negative public rhetoric around immigration increased, however, black leaders sensed that Latinos were entering a realm of discrimination similar to what they battled during the civil rights movement, and they instigated a call for a collaborative, anti-racist responses. There was also a concrete drive to counter negative stereotypes and respond to questions that emerged among black residents in their districts, all in the service of channeling community concerns into positive cross-racial relations.

June 2005 marked the first of Winston's "Soul and Salsa" series. The Winston-Salem Journal reported on the first meeting, highlighting the potential not just for the development of positive relations between groups, but also for solidarity:

To get to a meeting last night about how the black and Hispanic communities can learn from each other, Idania Lezcano needed something simple: directions. Lezcano, a journalist originally from Cuba, was leaving her home in Ardmore and spotted a neighbor, who is black and she knows only by her first name, Wella. In her broken but improving English, Lezcano asked her how to get to El Cordero de Dios Moravian Church in Waughtown. Lezcano said she couldn't understand Wella's explanation. So Wella got in her car and drove to the church on Peachtree Street, with Lezcano following. And that, Lezcano said at the meeting, is exactly what Winston-Salem's black and Hispanic communities need to offer each other: "A little bit of understanding, dialogue and solidarity," she said. About 50 people came to "Beyond Soul and Salsa: A Dialogue Between Two Communities," organized by the local chapter of the NAACP and the city's Human Relations Commission. Most of the questions and comments in the two-hour session focused on better understanding of the Hispanic population in Winston-Salem, and on common threads between the blacks and Hispanics.[39]

These small neighborhood forums grew into one of the human relations commission's most successful community-wide events, and over time became important venues in which blacks and Latinos might articulate a shared racial position on community issues such as education, housing, and policy. Both groups benefitted from political collaboration: Latinos had yet to develop a strong basis for within-group organizing and had few state and local representatives, while African Americans were deeply embedded in political institutions, but only as a small minority block. They lacked the votes and support needed to push their own progressive agenda. By building a coalition with Latinos, black leaders built political possibility.[40] At the 2006 forum, an older black woman in the audience asked:

> I am a community activist, and I want to know, can a license of my people [of color] be renewed? (Someone in the audience answers that you used to get licenses but now you can't.) Will you allow renewal?[41]

The police chief responded:

POLICE CHIEF: That's not decided by the policy, that was determined a few years ago to change the process, and that is determined by the DMV. You need to meet with them. I believe if you don't have the proper forms, you can't reapply. You need to address the DMV on that matter.

BLACK WOMAN: That's my reason—all these systems, ICE, DMV, there are so many who are just as concerned as you are, and I've been hosting workshops on undoing racism. I mention this because it gives you a better perception of systems and how they put road blocks in front of you. You need to understand that to organize against the 287gs that disrupt our lives—we have upcoming workshops, and if we keep learning, we keep doing this, keep educating yourself. It's not these people who make the laws, who say they are doing their jobs. We need to work together as a family and stick together as a family and learn about gatekeepers. And I thank you for allowing me this time.

By the eighth forum, in May 2009, the Soul and Salsa events were major community town halls, drawing numerous city representatives and citizens, and the series took on the pending 287(g) partnership between the county sheriff's office and Immigration and Customs Enforcement (ICE). When I arrived about 30 minutes early at what appeared to be a new YWCA building just off of Waughtown, people were coming and going, and the rain was just letting up. I met the Hispanic Outreach coordinator from the local Catholic Church, and we went down the hall, remarking on the nice facilities. The new building was over 90,000 square feet. I went upstairs and toward the event room, finding it empty except for human relations staff setting up the chairs, info table, and dais.

Over the next 30 minutes, residents began to trickle in. Most of the people arriving were African American and Latino families, although there were several white people as well. In addition to the forum, there were classes, meetings, and workouts. Childcare was provided, pizza was being served, and people were milling around, talking to the Mayor and other officials. As I took out my notepad, Tracy, an organizer of the series and leader of the Human Relations Commission, welcomed the crowd and turned over the microphone to the Mayor.[42] Few chairs were left empty, the room full of guests from city government, various city services, and community members of various races and ages. More chairs were brought in throughout the evening, and attendees lined the walls and filled the back of the hall.

The panel consisted of representatives from housing development, the IRS, a Latino community liaison, the YWCA, the police chief, and the county sheriff (both of whom were white). In consistently bringing together key community representatives, service providers, and community members, the forums created and sustained important opportunities for African American and Latino residents to think of themselves as part of a shared community.[43] At this meeting, the Mayor turned over the microphone to the vice-president of the YWCA, who said that, because the mission of the YWCA is to eliminate racism and empower women, this event was a natural fit for their organization. The emcee, Tracy, returned to the mic to introduce herself, call out city officials in the audience, introduce forum panelists, and explain the forum's format, which would prioritize the sheriff and chief of police. Videographers from TV-13 would record the event, and the moderators and audience could ask questions of anyone on the panel.[44] Tracy noted that,

> Soul and Salsa was the brainchild of an African American and Latino human relations officer on our staff, and the goal of this event, which is now in its 8th iteration, is to unite African Americans and the Hispanic communities, and to educate the communities about each other. A lot goes on that's germane to both communities, and this is an opportunity to learn from one another, and to break down the myths and misconceptions people have about each other.

Tracy introduced two senior activists in the Latino and black communities as the moderators, and they noted that the idea of the forum was to *begin* a dialogue. It was, they said, a process, not an event.

The moderators began with a question directed to the police chief: How does the 287(g) program apply to the city? Noting his pleasure at being included in the dialogue, the chief said that 287(g) was "not an issue" for the Winston-Salem police:

> We are not actively involved in the program, [officers] are not certified for it, and, as far as the police are concerned, I know that we need to have an open relationship with all members of the community, and if we can't communicate, we can't serve. Fear interacts with our ability to serve. Also, this program has a lot of issues nationally, but we need to look at what's here, what's the local involvement. We are not involved in this program. We believe that any program can be a benefit if it's done properly or perceived properly. But if it's not perceived well, it's not going to benefit.

The chief continued by explaining that 287(g) means that local law enforcement *can* be certified as ICE officers, but, as for his officers:

> We are not interested in how people got here . . . if part of the community doesn't trust us, we can't serve. If you are here to work, live, or visit, we are here to serve you. We are concerned with how people are working to improve our community. So, immigration is a non-issue. The only time is when people are arrested and during a normal system check, they have warrants or a status detainer on them. In those cases, we will notify the proper authorities, just as if they had a warrant in another state. We don't check for it, but we can be made aware of an issue if it's already there.

The co-moderator, a former president of the local NAACP chapter named in the flyer as an African American community activist who had been part of the forums since the beginning, said that people used to come to him with all sort of complaints and myths about Hispanics. He wanted to be sure that the NAACP was acknowledged for its early involvement in coalition building. He asked another question about the efforts of the police department with regard to 287(g). The Chief answered:

> We only use the computer system—but if someone is involved in serious crimes like drugs, robbery, murder, gangs, human trafficking, we'll do whatever we can to remove those people from society, either with charges or an ICE retainer. It doesn't matter their race, creed, nationality, or whatever, it's what they've done. I went to a conference on law enforcement and how we should deal with immigration, and a lot of people are concerned about these issues. But our first priority is the community. This isn't our main issue.

The police chief's policy was consistent with that of many local police agencies. In particular, the Chief, who was recently appointed, emphasized his desire to continue the policies of his predecessor, a black woman, and focus on cooperating with the community. Next the sheriff was asked about his department's plan to use Tasers. A report from Wake Forest had said they were safe, but the moderator had also read an Amnesty International report calling them dangerous weapons only suitable as an alternative to deadly force. So why, the sheriff was asked, were Tasers reportedly used to break up fights? The sheriff answered that the Taser was just one instrument in a continuum of force:

> It's really a judgment call on when it's appropriate to use. It is for a situation that's beyond the officer's control. The weapons an officer has at his disposal is hands, chemical spray, the baton, the Taser, and deadly force. Part of the training for every officer is to be tased, and it does what it's supposed to do. Now I am not familiar with the Amnesty report, but I do work with a trauma doctor. He has evaluated the use of Tasers, and in favor of this because it protects the officer and the community. Getting Tasers is expensive, the equipment costs about a thousand apiece, and they have videos and audio attached the equipment and officers will be held to review for each use. We've had Taser technology in courts, schools and jails, and prevented many officers and citizens from being hurt.

With this question addressed, the sheriff stood up. He wanted to address 287(g). He grabbed a paper and read:

> 287(g) is a program in the 1996 IIRIRA act to train jail employees to be immigration officers in order to deal with immigrants. In this county, we don't have that training available. It is offered to sheriff's department to get training for sheriffs in jails to make an alien inquiry to determine their status. Now, these are *self-detected* individuals—they have committed a crime and are in jail—and it's only when in processing for violation of a state or federal law. The INS database program is not in place in Forsyth. It's in seven counties, and 25 more have asked for training. Forsyth asked for training in 2007, and we have

not yet been offered the training. We have not had that training but we are on the list. There are less than 100 counties nationwide that have the program. It's not an investigatory technique. Law enforcement suffers and the community suffers when people are afraid to come forward. We have fought to get people of minorities to come forward. It impacts less than one percent of the Latino undocumented community. It would only come into play when someone is arrested. It can be anything from driving without a license to murder. They are self-detected. These are people who have violated the law. We do now have an intake procedure and talk to everyone to inquire using standard interrogation for criminal alien processing and make an inquiry with ICE. In the future, we will probably have a 287(g) program, but it depends on funding and staff.

During the question and answer period, both black and Latino community members posed a variety of objections about this policy to both officers, but zeroed in on the sheriff in response to his extensive remarks on the 287(g) program. They voiced disdain for checkpoints in their shared neighborhoods, plans for the implementation of 287(g), and in particular, the sheriff's motivations. Without exception, audience members opposed efforts to bring the program to Forsyth county, and framed it as another policy aimed at punishing minority communities, much to the sheriff's frustration. For audience members, this was not merely a Latino issue. It was a minority issue.

Forums like Soul and Salsa reinforced what Latinos increasingly surmised from their day-to-day experiences—their lives were being shaped by discrimination. Moreover, they were not the only targets of discrimination—they were being situated alongside African Americans in the local racial hierarchy. By engaging in a discourse of shared legal and social marginalization, blacks and Latinos built on their shared racial minority status. Because traditional intergroup relations theory relies on conflict or domination to understand the formation of group boundaries, it often fails to account for situations like these, in which being subject to the same structures of marginalization can blur boundaries among groups who are similarly positioned, even as it brightens boundaries between dominant and subordinate groups.[45] Community contacts also reinforced Latinos' positive views of blacks as friends and allies, elevating good or neutral experiences with neighbors and coworkers to a sense of solidarity.

Certainly, such efforts would likely fail to gain traction if they were seen as a one-way street (that is, beneficial only to the political needs of blacks or Latinos, rather than both groups). Mutuality and reciprocity were necessary for solidarity. Among my respondents, Marco, in particular, argued that the black community provided an important base of support for the Latinos in Winston and throughout the state. He said, "I think that, for example, black leaders are being really, really wonderful with the Hispanic community. They're always fighting for us. You see it in Congress, you see it in marches, you see it in speeches, you see it in demonstrations. And I think this has been an interesting alliance between black leaders and Hispanic leaders, in this state." Such work to integrate Latinos into African American institutions were part of a long-standing effort in Winston. As early as the 1990s, the *Winston-Salem Chronicle*, the city's black newspaper, reported on blacks and Latinos as minorities of a shared racial status facing discrimination. For example, in 1997, a regular column on civil rights by Bernice Powell Jackson highlighted the ways in which blacks and Latinos faced similar barriers, relaying issues faces by parents in New York. In November of that year, she reported on the need for parents of color to teach their children—both black and Latinos—survival skills in dealing with police. "One African-American parent, a banker, had to strategize with his son prior to buying him a new car. They planned what to do when a police officer stopped the son because he was driving a nice car. They decided that the son would carry his father's business card and offer to let the police office call his father. A Hispanic parent told how her child, despite much coaching from his parents, had already been stopped three times at gunpoint by the police. Each time he was in a car that the police suspected of carrying drugs, but no charges were ever brought."[46] Community institutions also began to engage in inclusive work. In 2002, for instance, the North Carolina Black Repertory Theatre, based in Winston-Salem, added a Hispanic/Latino Division to its company. The company's director described the move as an effort of "really reaching out and trying to build a bridge. This has to be a project of trust. We're trying to create and build from partnership within the Spanish-speaking community as well as the African American community and the Caucasian community."[47] And in 2003, the Quality Education School, a mostly black and Latino elementary school, instituted Latin American Culture day to both celebrate and learn about the culture of this fast-growing demographic. "Simon Johnson, executive director of Quality Education Schools said: 'We have a rather sizeable Latino population. We are so proud of the relationship we have here with the parents and of course the students. It is one of harmony and respect.'"[48]

Such efforts, which began well ahead of the broader backlash, also helped to reframe the experiences of Latinos and blacks as a part of a shared identity. Winston was by no means unique in this regard. In the case of Charlotte, while research suggests a somewhat ambivalent initial reception toward Latinos by black politicians in North Carolina, they would come to embrace Latinos through coalition politics, defending Latinos against hostile legislation locally. At the same time, by the 2000s, previously pro-immigrant politicians such as Pat McCrory, Sue Migrich, and Elizabeth Dole would adopt the *opposite* approach—embracing anti-Latino politics.[49] As we have learned, before 2005, few exclusionary policies were on the books, and discriminatory practices against Mexicans in the Southeast were relatively uncommon. But as the negative public rhetoric around immigration increased, so did the sense among African American leaders that Latinos were seeing their civil rights threatened, and that they should step up on their behalf. In 2005, the *Winston-Salem Chronicle*, ran a series of articles calling on African Americans to dispel their stereotypes of Latinos, dispense with misplaced perceptions of competition, and use shared experiences of discrimination as grounds for solidarity. The local NAACP, the Human Relations Commission, and local black and Latino churches held forums and shared grievances that were covered extensively in the black press. Juan Suarez of the Human Relations Commission stated, "'Hopefully we will be able to communicate, educate, and break down some false barriers and walls that have been brought up as a result of a lack of knowledge and plain ignorance.' Local NAACP President Stephen Hairston said he 'doesn't want local blacks to repeat the vicious racist cycle that has been perpetuated by whites."[50] By explicitly building *minority linked fate*, blacks and Latinos in Winston not only rearticulated their sense of groupness and racial identity, but also began to develop a shared politics based in both experiences of discrimination and its coalitional potential.

By asserting a minority status, Latinos rejected long-standing immigrant practices including distancing from blacks and desired closeness to whites. They also adopted an important relational identity with implications for race relations and eventual political mobilization. Luis Fraga and colleagues note that "for group identities to serve to mobilize people politically, two preconditions must be met: individuals must recognize themselves as members of the group, and individuals must be conscious of the political value of acting as a group."[51] In addition to cultivating this viewpoint, blacks' additional efforts to articulate a sense of shared status and solidarity translated into a perspective that evaluated anti-immigrant policies as part of a broad anti-minority stance, concretizing their shared political position.

As noted at the outset of this book, in the fall of 2008, a two-day conference was held in neighboring Greensboro. It included civil rights activists, church leaders, and union organizers from Greensboro, Winston-Salem, and other surrounding communities to forge black-brown relationships. Gathering in a local Baptist church and community center, various pastors and community representatives, African American and Latino, spoke to the similar structural conditions their communities faced. They rattled off shared problems: gangs, poor schools, employment, institutional discrimination, violence, and exploitation. A Latino reverend said, in Spanish (with translation):

> I have a passion to unite black and Latino communities. Whenever we see black or Latino youth on the corner we assume they are doing or selling drugs, and that hurts my heart. . . . I got a deportation order in 1984, and didn't know it until we tried to get our papers together. I've shared the pain and experiences in church, of people who've lost jobs, licenses, lots of people don't understand these situations. My wife lost her license and cannot get it renewed, and she can't leave to go anywhere. When the black community in my church realized this, they went to the house and said that they didn't know that I was illegal.
>
> I live in an Afro-American community, and they got together 100 signatures asking the department of immigration not to deport me. They spoke with lawyers and the police chief not to work with ICE. Latinos can't do this, they can't ask for that, but blacks can. The office of human relations includes a black pastor who is open to seeing the experience of Hispanos. We have the potential and capacity to work together to create a difference in our communities. I'm happy with the support of the black community, and the church is a good place for this, to understand the story of what's happened. . . . In the Afro community, leaders have emerged to talk and work with us. They don't speak Spanish, but they are there with us, working to bring our communities together.

Mr. Muhammad spoke next, telling the crowd:

> The fierce urgency of now is underscored by attacks on the jobs that will occur due to the bailout. This will create cuts, mergers, remove jobs and service. It's also important to have young people at this conference. The desire for unity gets discouraged when there are no instant results—if we don't unite, it means genocide to both communities. Many activists came out of the gangs in the 1960s, who recognized that if they were to be soldiers, they need to fight against those who oppress.

Mr. Muhammad acknowledged divisions, but asserted that

> we need to understand [the divisions'] origins; tensions are cited as cultural, giving the impression that we don't like each other because of our differences. This is a strategy. It was the strategy among slaves to keep different Africans separate. They would have to look for points of unity in history, such as the Underground Railroad. It's taught that that railroad was also in Mexico and Native American villages. It's hidden that other oppressed brothers and sisters helped. I notice that the translation here between blacks and Latinos is done through a white person. I don't mean this as a criticism, but it gives the impression it needs to go through whites, that there's no basis for a direct relationship, racism has made something wrong with that. It creates a distortion.

So, there is a need for a frank discussion, the role of slavery in shaping society throughout the hemisphere and globally, the institution of racism, institutionalized racism in Mexico and Venezuela by Spain, we have to understand what went on inside those countries. We need to identify the battlegrounds and not allow ourselves to be divided.

This sense of not only empathy, but an active desire to connect communities and underscore their shared status from African American neighbors and fellow church members served to concretize Latinos' sense of *minority linked fate*. A Puerto Rican woman in the audience noted that the issues were nothing new, but that "we need to unify blacks and browns in the South. In New York, blacks and Puerto Ricans are always together, we need to know the history of how civil rights opened those doors. It's a lie that blacks will not do the work that Latinos will do, and those rumors just end up chipping away at our rights and benefits."

These public expressions of concern and shared discrimination were not isolated incidents, but part of an ongoing effort to build coalitions. Many black leaders argued from the pulpit and elsewhere that, as civil rights leaders, they must speak out on behalf of Latinos who were experiencing what their community had faced less than a generation earlier.

Mr. Phillips, the lunchtime keynote speaker, began by stating his commitment to ending abuse and to immigration reform. He continued:

> There is a very low union density in the state, that it's the least organized in the country, though sometimes we trade for last place with South Carolina, and occasionally Mississippi. I call you to action! The AFL-CIO has been reorganized so that workers centers can now join. There are 55,000 new union members organized in NC, state workers joined SEIU which has 165,000. There is a need for collective action, for us to organize and take what we want. We need to go to Reynolds and demand them to be responsible as farmers. We need to go to Mt. Olive and Smithfield, which butchers 30,000 hogs a day. That's a lot of hogs!

As if they were in a church service, the audience exclaimed "hmm" and "mmhmm" in response to his words. He continued, talking about the Employee Free Choice Act, and anti-union legislation, and said that black, white, or brown, these were *human* rights he was trying to protect.

> Moncure, at a strike here, turned a hose on the strike line saying that people were on company property. There are some sick folks in this world. There were of course, primarily black and Latino workers on this line. If we are to grow our black/brown coalition, we need to call on people who happen to be white;

we need to ally with those who say this is not right. Labor movements and workers' rights and the faith community create opportunity for labor folks to join hands with black and brown. . . .

This coalition has to be a two-way street. If you are a worker, you should be in a union. The AFL-CIO has an immigrant policy. The system leaves immigrants vulnerable and hurts all workers, benefitting unscrupulous employers. The system is broken. Now, the federation is a little slow. Our policy: Treat all workers as workers and build solidarity to combat exploration and raise standards for all workers. We need to look after all workers. The history of immigrants forming unions is strong. The Irish steelworkers and the German bricklayers started this union. Employers divide workers along race, gender, and immigration status. That is the history.

Mr. Phillips' call to unite as workers rather than acquiesce to divide-and-conquer tactics provided an important counterpoint to the belief that immigrants undermine native-born workers. Reminding workers of their linked fate, he called for a kind of solidarity that was rarely heard among white progressive allies in the community.

It bugs me when I see black folks talking about "them folks." Them folks. Them folks, having them benefits, riding up to the office in a Cadillac—you were in his position three years ago, don't forget we're not going to let employers do that to us this time. Divide and conquer. "Immigrants can't participate. Oughta just pack 'em up and send 'em back." Well, that's a whole lot of packing to do, and it makes no sense. The Department of Labor estimates that it would cost $41.2 billion to pack 'em up and send 'em back. That wasn't the program four years ago or 50 years ago. Why now? Mass deportation has a massive impact on all families. 85% of immigrant families are of mixed status. Where will they go? Sit on the curb? To cousins already struggling, but legal. . . .

We need to change the laws. We need reform. During the freedom ride, membership complained, what were you doing in Siler City with all those Hispanics? . . . Some members think I'm crazy when I propose resolutions on immigration rights—"this will divide employers." "There will be an uproar; you'll lose your seat." Well, I can't afford not to. Let me lose it, I'd rather be on the right side. Delegates need to see a labor camp. See migrant workers. . . . We must be a voice for immigration reform—as a human being we need to do this. We are connected! . . . Some want expanded guest worker programs. Well, if you are a guest, you need to be treated like kings. If you are workers, you need to be treated as workers with all benefits of the work place; you need a path to citizenship. To keep people and not give them citizenship is a ploy of corporations making billions. They want wages to compete with the Third World while CEO wages are sky high. Give people rights and wages to work

in industry by what is needed. . . . In 2008, we are only getting started. This is
a call to action!

Mr. Phillips tied together immigrants, union labor, and civil rights, and he
received a rousing round of applause. Together, they chanted "Not this time!"
Latino participants came forward and testified to experiences of discrimination, exploitation, and deportation. While certainly this conference cannot
be taken as representative of everyday speech, the rhetoric I saw there was
part and parcel of a concerted effort. African American leaders in the community aimed to achieve what Tatcho Mindola Jr., Yolanda Niemann, and
Néstor Rodríguez prescribe as necessary for intergroup solidarity: a focus on
"perceived group commonalities to shape common-group identities among
African Americans and Hispanics. This new merged identity would be in addition to individual ethnic-race identities . . . [and used to] forge group unity,
reduce conflict, enhance relations, and move toward political progress beneficial to both groups."[52]

Ongoing and effective, the solidarity building successfully convinced
many blacks and Latinos of the importance of *minority linked fate* and the
power of political alliances.[53] Such efforts are far from rare, as Natalia Molina
finds, similarly, that African Americans recognized mutual experiences of
disenfranchisement and marginalization with Latinos in 1950s Los Angeles.
Quoting black workers at the Elysian Park detention center who witnessed
detentions saying, "How can they call those Mexican people foreigners? This
country was originally theirs. Wonder if those immigration cops realize how it
makes us Negro people feel when they start kicking the Mexicans around?"[54]
More recently, the African American political leadership in the South has
been consistently found to be pro-immigration, and nationally, nonwhites are
generally more supportive of immigrants than are whites.[55]

Still, interpersonal relations are complicated and messy. Conflict and solidarity can exist simultaneously between individuals, as well as within and
between groups. In Winston-Salem, as is the as is the case everywhere, some
African Americans expressed resentment toward Latinos, some Latinos reported poor interpersonal experiences with blacks, and some whites worked
very hard to build progressive ties of solidarity with both blacks and Latinos.
Nevertheless, these undercurrents were articulated among a small minority and were largely ineffective in shaping the larger discourse. I argue that
these exceptions demonstrate the centrality of perceptions of shared status in
shaping both solidarity and conflict, and can account for the failure of these
undercurrents to take hold.

Whites and Whiteness: The Racial Divide

SEGREGATION AND THREAT

Their shared segregation from white neighborhoods helped facilitate the robust reinforcement of minority ties between black and Latino communities. Few members of either group frequently found themselves in close contact with whites, and we know that high-quality contact is an essential component in building a sense of equal racial status (alongside other drivers, like a sense of shared discrimination and outside threat). Without intimate, regular, and positive interactions at the individual and group level, sustained positive intergroup relations are unlikely to materialize. In Winston, Mexican respondents reported greater quality contact, affinity with, and closeness to blacks than to whites. They saw blacks as friendlier, more likely to know and talk to their Latino neighbors than whites. In fact, many of the Mexicans in my study did not seem to know any whites at all. Their children did not encounter them in significant numbers in school, and, unless they were Catholic and attended the English masses, were unlikely to see them at church. This absence of contact not only makes it difficult to actively promote good relations, but, as Pettigrew suggests, may also encourage intergroup prejudice.[56] With few exceptions, even Latinos who had no negative interpersonal experiences with whites, were challenged to think of positive relationships between Latinos and whites.

Faith, a young white woman working in a local nonprofit, argued that race relations were a matter not merely of residence, but also of social habits. Segregation between whites and nonwhites was nearly ubiquitous in Winston. She said: "I mean, unless you go pretty far out of your way there's not a whole lot of reason that you would, bump into folks. I mean, the sense that, I'm sure that you have some perception of like consumer habits here. But, different populations go to different grocery stores. You're not even going to stand in line with folks. It's hard to know how you would ever even know that they existed." Faith continued,

FAITH: And I actually think that, in Winston-Salem—I know that you're focusing on the Latino population but I think that racially, in general, Winston-Salem is one of the weirdest cities about not integrating that I know of. And it seems that everyone, for the most part, is pretty polite about it. I'm sure it would take you ten seconds to find someone who would very explicitly be racist, but in general, folks tend to be relatively nice about it, but, um, have just created these separate spheres that never bump into each other. I think Winston-Salem still has a lot of black-white racial stuff to deal with, and are you familiar with the Darryl Hunt case?[57]

JJ: Yes.

FAITH: Ok. So, I think the fact that, like, that conversation was still going on in 2003 and 2004, um, with the very last set of legal proceedings, is just a symptom of how much a lot of African American and white racial relationships haven't been dealt with, and so in some ways I think the mentality is almost like, "We don't even have the mind space to get to dealing with the Latinos yet, and integrating them into the society."

Similarly, when discussing whether Winston-Salem was a "progressive county," Robert, a white community organizer, sighed. He sat back in his chair and said:

> This is the most segregated place I've ever been in. Here, there is a black side of town and a white side of town. Segregation is accepted on both sides. That's changing a bit as the younger, more post-modern generation takes over, and is starting to reject what I think is a very modern construction of a black agenda and a white agenda, but it is still very segregated. When I was helping a democratic candidate hold fundraisers for a new candidate that was running against a very conservative person who had held their seat for awhile, we basically had to hold two fundraisers, one for the white establishment, and one for the black establishment. And people from both sides told me that they appreciated what I was doing, and the work to bring people together, but they basically didn't want to upset the balance of things and risk losing their representation.

In a city in which the black and white communities were largely separate spheres, public efforts to bring Latinos and African Americans into dialogue were particularly meaningful signals.

Exclusionary practices and poor quality contact with the white majority also created a sense of fear and distrust among Latinos that progressive whites found difficult to overcome. Despite the fact that many whites in Winston held receptive positions on immigration and Latinos, conservative leaders' hostile actions situated whites as a collective threat to minority well-being. As a result, most of the Mexicans in my study consistently and overwhelmingly characterized whites as people to be feared and mistrusted. This idea was perpetuated at many levels of social discourse and interaction. For example, local congressional representative Virginia Foxx hosted a special session entitled "Gangs, Fraud, and Sexual Predators: Struggling with the Consequences of Illegal Immigration" in 2006.[58] As highlighted in chapters 3 and 4, such alienating actions were pervasive during election season; campaign speeches and robo-calls from local candidates decried the presence of Latinos in the community. Thus, despite the important roles played by white liberals in advocating for immigrants, they were frequently overshadowed by the political Right. Further, the relatively small proportion of white liberals in the area (compared to many traditional receiving destinations like Los Angeles, Chicago, and New York) meant that liberal voices failed to produce the kind of dominant counter-discourse or political leverage that could undermine the highly visible claims of the Right. As in exurban Charlotte, the failure of pro-immigrant evangelical activism to trump what Julie Weise calls "middle-class white entitlement" allowed widespread anti-immigrant discourse and politics to flourish in the state.[59] Hostility from the right served to facilitate connections between African Americans and Latinos, but it did not allow for a broad, multiracial liberal political agenda.

FAILURE TO CONNECT

To be clear, significant numbers of progressive whites tried to reach out to Latinos and advocate for tolerance and immigrant rights and were responsible for providing outreach services in many nonprofit organizations in the community. They failed, however, to build connections on the basis of a shared racial status. For example, two of the church sites' outreach programs were staffed primarily by white volunteers, but even in these situations where Mexicans and whites were in regular contact, they neglected to build connections with Latinos. Whites failed, however, to develop strategies of connectedness and shared experiences. Even in cases where Mexicans and whites came into regular contact, positive relations did not often result.

In a local church with a growing Latino population, a white volunteer confided that she had been working with the outreach programs for 10 years, but hadn't known any of the Latino participants' names until recently. When I asked why, she shrugged and said, "I felt too uncomfortable to build a relationship." She didn't seem to think they had anything in common beyond church, so she didn't reach out. Thus, even in cases where commonality *should* be forged, it seemed that, in Winston, dissimilar racial status was reinforced, rather than bridged between progressive whites and Latinos.

Latinos' interpretation of whites as a threat was so pervasive that even in cases where whites attempted to facilitate better contact, their intentions were often deemed suspect. At the library's "know your rights" event where Sylvia shared how a black woman prevented her from incriminating herself, a Mexican woman informed me that I "needed to be careful" because many whites learn Spanish so that they could use it against Latinos. She told me, "They say they are friends, but they are really racist." Such high levels of distrust are indicative of the strong perception that whites posed a systematic threat to Latino well-being.

The comparison to blacks, who were visibly engaged in supporting Latinos, with whites, who often engaged in anti-Latino statements and actions, not only cemented a shared sense of discrimination between blacks and Latinos, but also coalesced into a sense of threat from whites as an out-group. Consistent with social science research that suggests that an external threat conditions a stronger sense of in-group commonality, under conditions of external threat Latinos saw themselves as even more similar to blacks and dissimilar from whites.[60] In other words, whites' reactive efforts to exclude Latinos were an inadvertent unifier, bolstered by the inclusive actions of key African American and Latino leaders.

Positive relations are unlikely to materialize absent perceptions of racial commonality and contact. While this may seem specific to interminority relations, various studies have shown that Latinos are more likely to build close relations with and see themselves as holding a shared racial position with *whites*, rather than blacks.[61] Such views are theorized as a key mechanism through which immigrant Latinos, among others, acculturate into American society.[62] In the case of Winston, however, barriers to this sense of shared position prevented such outcomes from unfolding.

JJ: What do you feel the relationship is with whites; between whites and Latinos?

MARCO: There are many whites that have the understanding, especially the liberal ones, and the Democrat ones, of the immigration process, they have the understanding of the legacy of migration in this country, and what migration has produced in this country. They understand general tolerance. What is the relationship in states like North Carolina between Hispanics and whites? Mostly it's a working relationship, the white guys hire the Hispanics, and they get paid for that. Aside from that, I don't see much interaction.

In late 2008, an inter-church leadership gathering took place in Winston. It aimed to discuss community responses to the community's unprecedented levels of immigration. James, who appeared to be the coordinator of the project, started by asking everyone to briefly introduce themselves and their affiliations. There were about 35 people present, and the crowd was overwhelmingly white and made up of volunteers from the youth mentoring program affiliated with Nueva Esperanza, teachers, social workers, and retired pastors.

Neither the two black people or the three Latinos present were asked to share their perspectives. When William and Dr. Evergreen arrived later, the total of black people rose to four.

Dr. Miller, a white pastor and director of liturgical studies at a local university, opened by giving a speech about how people of faith should respond to immigration by highlighting the passages on immigration in the bible. She asked people to raise their hands if they were born in Winston-Salem (only one person raised their hand), and then asked people to reflect on the experience of being a stranger. As church leaders, she believed, the goal, regardless of policy debates, must be to welcome the stranger in our midst: "The church leadership has to get involved. In some way, we are all migrants; we all have stories of migration. Please refer to the handout, which highlights various passages on the experience of being a migrating people." Dr. Miller read a passage on being "at home in the role of the wanderer" (the title of her handout), and said that the Bible calls for compassion and hospitality in both the New Testament and the Hebrew texts. "To welcome the stranger is to welcome and love Jesus. I ask you to reflect on the experience of moving and being a stranger in a new community. The Bible points to people of faith as a migrating people, that we are wanderers. And our story is a migration story." Dr. Miller stepped to the side of her podium to more emphatically drive home the idea of welcoming the stranger. Her message was well received, and the speaker that followed demurred he could hardly match such a speech. A second round of applause arose from the clergy and volunteers in the room. While admirable, though, Dr. Miller's framing contrasted significantly with remarks made by black leaders. In referring to immigrants as strangers, rather than say, as fellow potential citizens, residents with similar dreams and values, or ultimately assimilable, whites failed to invite immigrant Latinos or their descendants into the dominant majority. This call to welcome, not at all inconsistent with religious doctrine, nevertheless underscored the distinction between "us" and "them." For many blacks, by contrast, the call to action was not about tolerance or a general moral duty, but a personal sense of justice, solidarity, and identification with the experiences of the Latinos—fellow racial minorities in their community.

Dr. Miller's comments called to mind a contrast with those made by Mr. Phillips at black-brown unity conference. Mr. Phillip's speech, drawing from the writing of Dr. Martin Luther King Jr., specifically admonished blacks who couldn't see the connections between the struggles of African Americans and Latino immigrants. He drew on stereotypes about black welfare recipients in the 1980s, making pointed connections between the civil rights movement and immigration reform. He even encouraged Latinos in the audience to testify, coming forward to share their experiences of discrimination and abuse. Rather than call for tolerance, Mr. Phillips had made a call for solidarity.[63]

As these meetings and conferences were reported in the Spanish-language newspaper, their distinct approaches came to shape Latino views of intergroup attitudes.[64] In failing to establish a sense of shared racial status with Latinos, progressive white organizations failed to situate themselves as reliable allies. Coupled with a relative lack of contact between individual whites and Latinos, white organizations and public officials easily came to *represent all whites*. And whites maintained their distance, "welcoming the stranger in their midst," but not considering that "stranger" one of their own. As "save our communities" politics and racialized rhetoric targeted Latinos as "strange others," calls to welcome strangers did little but reinforce the idea of Latinos as a threat to white hegemony.[65]

Rethinking the Competition Frame: When Relations Sour

Despite broad perceptions of civility and cooperation among blacks and Latinos, as well as significant cross-racial engagement, the conventional wisdom in Winston-Salem (and elsewhere) holds that relations between blacks and Latinos are dominated by hostility and conflict. And, despite significant evidence that relations are far more positive and cooperative, there *is* some underlying conflict. Traditionally theorized perceptions of resource competition and beliefs in racial stereotypes drove some persistent negative views and, at the individual level, the relationships that were positive in aggregate could, in fact, be contentious.[66]

The resource competition and racial threat literature extends Blumer's theory that prejudice results from feelings of competitive threat.[67] Two groups' relative status positions (their access to resources, social standing, and success in the labor market) determine the extent of competition between them.[68] This literature, however, is a blunt instrument for understanding intergroup relations, generally using quantitative methods to examine demographic concentrations and attitudes, while the mechanisms that shape intergroup relations are likely more complex.[69] Findings from these studies reflect the widespread assumption that blacks and Latinos hold a relatively equal position at the bottom of the social structure, and that this low position drives conflict[70] in the labor market,[71] in conflicts over institutional resources,[72] and in debates about political representation.[73] Perhaps unsurprisingly, much of the research on new immigrant destinations finds evidence of actual or perceived competition between minority groups for work, housing, health care, and education.[74]

So, evidence of interminority conflict is substantial, but in-depth studies on the quality of intergroup relations when minority groups hold substantially distinct socioeconomic statuses[75] and/or when resources are so plentiful that competition is unlikely, remain scarce.[76] Such contexts might include affluent minority suburbs or enclaves or periods of overemployment, and these are far from unique.[77] An analysis of 2010 five-year American Community Survey data indicates that in 42.66 percent of census tracts across the US, at least 30 percent of black households had an income above the median (approximately $50,000). In 26.92 percent of census tracts, at least 10 percent of black households had incomes of over $100,000, approximately twice the national median.[78] Such data suggest that a significant proportion of black households are middle-class. We also know that middle-class minorities are likely to live in communities alongside other minorities of various class backgrounds.[79] Therefore, in terms of assuming resource deficits, resource competition models have overestimated the empirical extent to which blacks and Latinos confront each other within zero-sum labor markets[80] and fail to account for interracial relations within contexts of economic stability, which are widespread. Indeed, Waters, Kasinitz, and Asad argue "that research has found little support for the labor market competition hypothesis."[81]

Empirical economic status may also be less important than *perceived* socioeconomic and political competition in shaping hostile attitudes,[82] suggesting cooperation depends not only on the existence of shared interests but the perception of them.[83] Some protracted and intentional efforts to segment labor markets and workplaces along racial lines—like those the black leaders threatened for union building—may do more to shape conflict than unemployment levels.[84] If perceptions drive intergroup relations, deeper qualitative research on community and workplace dynamics and perceptions, rather than a reliance on quantitative reports on socioeconomic status differences, may be needed to overcome a glaring limitation: the literature conflates race and class.

Importantly, this conflation can hide important interactive effects, as scholars have shown that economic interests or socioeconomic status can modify racial perceptions, shaping the extent to which in-group members perceive a sense of linked fate or used shared identity labels.[85] Such work suggests that the characteristics shaping intergroup relations are dynamic and mutable, rather than fixed.[86] When race and class are theorized and analyzed as dynamic and interactive, scholars find significant complexity in the way that socioeconomic status intersects with race and class in shaping intergroup attitudes.[87] Angela Stuesse's analysis of black-Latino relations in a Mississippi poultry plant provides one good case of such complexity: some black workers express resentment because they believe that Latinos are taking their jobs, but also because they believe Latino workers downgrade job quality because they are more susceptible to exploitation. Some of the workers see this as the result of a broader status hierarchy, in which white owners and managers leverage Latino workers to usurp black mobility for their own gains.[88] But while the situation instigated some resentment, Stuesse also found that it motivated empathy and a recognition of a shared status that paralleled African Americans' status before the civil rights movement.[89]

According to much of the threat literature, a growing proportion of minorities in a given community cultivates a sense of threat, rooted in a belief that blacks and other nonwhites will begin to compete for political power and economic resources.[90] But threat studies tend to fuse resource competition with prejudice, extrapolating perceptions of competition from absolute group size when, in fact, the two may not be correlated.[91] This kind of operationalization can essentialize race by reducing it to internally homogenous fixed categories, rather than collectives that both are reacting to ascriptive processes and engaged in ongoing struggle to construct boundaries and make meaning.[92]

In Winston, most white and African American residents were economically stable, and many were affluent, depressing the likelihood that black residents would, in general, frame Latinos as an economic threat. However, some Winston blacks did see Latinos as a source of competition. Tracy suggested, for example, that perhaps there was a feeling of resentment that Latinos were receiving attention for their issues while little had improved for African Americans. I didn't see this kind of zero-sum thinking in my research often, but it came up in my conversations in the ways Tracy suggested, with some African Americans who felt they had tried and failed to leverage political or economic power for years. The fear that the resources and attention Latinos would receive would be siphoned off from the what was available to blacks was not unwarranted, but it relied on the idea that there was only so much to go around.

In more concrete terms, while there was little competition for jobs and housing, population growth did strain local school systems and other municipal services. While infrequent, some African Americans I encountered during my ethnographic observations complained about the increased resources being provided to Latino children. The manager of a small black bookstore put it this way:

> I am not happy at how Latinos are taking over. The test scores, for example, of black children in the 3rd grade at my school have remained flat, while Latino children are improving, because they are getting more resources. . . . And you know the doctor's office nearby was closed, and a clinic for Latinos was

opened in its place. I just don't think it's fair. I have nothing against Latinos personally, but it just isn't fair.

In this case, competition for resources did not emerge from a shared position in the labor market, but from a zero-sum perception of limited institutional resources. It was widely known that the public schools and health care facilities that served minority neighborhoods were of lower quality than those in predominantly white neighborhoods. So, the manager makes a valid claim: resources should be increased for minorities. But she attributed further reductions in services to growth in the Latino population, relative to blacks, who had begun to out-migrate to inner-ring suburbs in greater numbers. In this way, not unlike theories of ethnic replacement in Los Angeles, in which housing, school access, and political representation are occasionally sites of interminority conflict, resource competition frames can undermine feelings of cooperation and solidarity. Later in our conversation, the bookstore manager expressed admiration for Latinos, saying that migration is a difficult choice, and one she might choose if it was necessary to provide for her family. While it was not a clear statement of shared racial status or *minority linked fate*, it did suggest a more complex understanding of the positioning of Latinos relative to blacks within the Winston community, an important nuance to how intergroup attitudes are shaped.

The relatively smaller population of working-class African Americans sometimes also used a competition frame to understand the position of Latinos, shaped largely by their standing in the labor market. For example, an African American clerk at a UPS store lamented that her son, who lacked a college education, was having trouble finding work. She thought his troubles were due to the influx of Latino workers in the area, and she speculated that her son would have to move to another county to find employment. As I waited alongside another customer, the African American clerk and a small white woman with short hair told me they hoped I was "Jones," a customer picking up a large package that was taking up space. I told them sorry, it wasn't mine, and I probably couldn't carry it anyway. When the black woman looked at my ID, she asked what brought me to Winston from California. I explained that I was a visiting scholar, and she said "good for you!" She asked what I was studying, and I told her race and immigration. She responded, "Oh, it's been a problem because they are taking jobs." This was when she explained that her son had tried to get work as a day-laborer at a factory in Rural Hall, but they only picked the Hispanics, sending the black people home. She said, "if it was just him, I might not believe it, but his friends say the same thing, and everyone else says it, too." She asked if I was Hispanic, and I said no. She said that I should go anyway, because I look Hispanic, so I would get work. I nodded and thanked her, telling her it sounded interesting. She nodded and wished me luck.

These expressions of interminority resource competition were not the norm, but they cannot be ignored when considering how a range of intergroup relations may emerge. When competition is sensed in the labor market, political representation, housing, or institutional resources, positive relations are less likely to emerge. Still, perceptions of resource competition are often mediated by other relationships. Indeed, working-class blacks often explained resource competition using a collective external threat frame, pointing to racism from whites as the culprit for limited minority resources. Where resource competition *could* lead to resentment and undermine positive relations, it still did not unilaterally result in the type of hostility or backlash that so often seems preordained in the conflict literature. It appeared that structural economic changes, rather than a given sense of conflict, were more likely to initiate shifts in intergroup relations in Winston.

In my conversation with Olivia, the president of the black chamber of commerce, she reported:

OLIVIA: Salaries were very good here, with tobacco, and I'll say some technology, with the AT&T and Lucent Technologies, the salaries were good here. So, those type industries are very downsized or no longer here, and so we really don't have the jobs that pay well. So that's the displacement, really, because high school dropouts were working for these companies and making, I mean, living like this [she gestured to her large living room], and better. If the husband and wife were working for certain companies, they could live in a place like this as high school dropouts, and live very well. And that was my generation. So, then—that's the displacement, it's not the migrants have come in. It's that those jobs don't exist any more.

JJ: So, would you say now there are very few jobs that are low-skilled but still middle-class wages?

OLIVIA: Yeah. Well, as a matter of fact, a company, I heard this, and I don't know. I don't want to exaggerate. Twenty years ago, a janitor, and I'll just go ahead and say the company, R. J. Reynolds, was making, they said, pushing a broom, making $50,000 a year, twenty years ago. But then Reynolds got rid of permanent employees and brought in temps. And I hear they're working for nine and ten dollars an hour now. That was unheard of because I worked for them, and, say thirty years ago, I don't even think *I* made [as little as] nine or ten dollars an hour, with them *thirty years ago,* I don't think. And I was out of high school, I had not, um, gone to college yet, and it was office setting, but it was unskilled job that I was doing. So, for that to have happened, it's almost like; the young people don't have any hope. [Laughs]. For that to happen, that, you know, not that the Reynolds, that was paying, you know, crazy money back then, and because they could get the cheap labor, and maybe the migrants are in there, now, I—but they got the temps in. No benefits, and nine and ten dollars an hour. Unbelievable. Unbelievable. So, you know, they're, they're kinda fighting for the jobs now.

In Olivia's view, when resource competition existed, it was not a function of immigration, but a restructuring of the local economy and the kinds of wages that had been available to minority workers in previous years. To the extent that African Americans saw immigrants as part of the wage problem, they saw competition. But for those who saw restructuring as a strategy to displace minority workers and a failure to provide resources and quality employment for their communities, such issues created an opportunity for solidarity building. In other words, while dissimilar economic positions are most likely to prevent perceptions of resource competition, how resource distribution is framed can also shape how groups see one another, even if they share a position in the labor market.

Latinos were aware of the resource competition perspective, even if that's not what they would have called it. Juan, who lived in a black community, mentioned that he believed whites thought that Latinos were "below them." When I asked whether this was also true of African Americans, he said, "No, but lots think that Latinos are taking away their opportunities, their jobs, and their benefits. Though the part about benefits isn't true, we don't get any benefits when we are undocumented. No unemployment, health care, they can't go to college, so that's just not true. So, there is a need for better understanding."

So, was *minority linked fate* actually widespread? There are two important caveats to consider. First, as noted in this chapter, interpersonal relations are complex, fluid, and sometimes contradictory. This is true when we consider relations between individuals as individuals, as well as within group relations. For example, the theory of linked fate emerged precisely because it was difficult to explain the high levels of shared voting positions and political support expressed among African Americans despite vast differences in class and social experience. In other words, high levels of within-group political solidarity are neither universal nor common. African Americans are considered the prototypical example, but that is because they provide a glaring exception.

And even among African Americans, sizeable minorities defect to other political parties or take opposing positions, usually motivated by class status, resource competition, or a rejection of shared racial status. Second, among Latinos and Asians, divergence is more widespread, with only recent elections suggesting a sense of growing linked fate (which commentators speculate is due in part to heightened anti-immigrant, anti-Latino, and anti-Asian sentiment). In terms of resources, scholars have also shown that intragroup discrimination and economic competition are common within groups, particularly Latinos.[93] In the context of *minority linked fate*, we should expect those same issues to persist, even as an emergent sense of solidarity dominates.

Still, these competitive reactions to Latinos highlight the importance of socioeconomic status in shaping intergroup relations. Widespread feelings of resource competition can create important stumbling blocks to civility and cooperation in the aggregate. This was largely the case in Helen Marrow's Bedford and Wilcox counties, where similar economic status and shared perceptions that Latinos were vaulting ahead of African Americans sowed mutual perceptions of threat and competition. In Ribas' poultry plant, economic status was similar, but a shared perception that African Americans held a higher status than the exploited Latinos sowed perceptions of threat and competition.[94] In Winston-Salem, where only a small fraction of the group perceived resource competition, the impact of such views was minimal.[95] Rather, to the extent that competitive attitudes were expressed, the city's black leadership used their belief in a shared minority status to *reject* competition, choosing instead to leverage their higher socioeconomic status and access to resources in support of Mexican immigrants.[96] In a context in which resource competition between minorities, perceived or objective, did not dominate, *minority linked fate* was more easily forged.

STEREOTYPES AND RACIAL IDEOLOGIES

Anti-black stereotypes and beliefs are embedded in the fabric of US institutions, and they underpin racial ideologies throughout the Western Hemisphere. As a result, anti-black prejudices and stereotypes also persist among some Latinos.[97] As Mindola Jr., Neimann, and Rodríguez argue, these stereotypes justify racism and inhibit cross-group solidarity.[98] In my study, Isabel (as noted earlier in the book) reported that she felt closer to whites because,

> for whatever reason, blacks cannot be trusted. Basically, because we have, how do I say it? Because they, the African Americans, they almost never work.

They just live off the government that helps them with their rent, with their food, and almost, there are a lot of people who don't work, that do nothing more than find evil things to do, find houses to rob, and I, I feel that the whites are the ones that put forth more effort and there are fewer whites doing bad things than African Americans.

Still, her perception of black-Latino relations was not monolithic. When asked how blacks and Latinos got along in her view, she noted: "In my experience, I say, there are many African-Americans who get angry because they say that you take away their work, and there are others who get along with you and say, 'You do your job well. You work very well. You come early.' So, there are different ways of thinking."

Moreover, Isabel professed faith in Obama's ability to change Latinos' situation for the better: "I think that Obama understands us more than other Presidents before him. . . . Because he is black. Because they have suffered a lot of discrimination also and they've killed his people, right? And I think that this will move him to do something for us."

The juxtaposition of Isabel's anti-black stereotypes, her understanding of different perspectives of competition, and her articulation of shared minority status and linked fate are, I believe, essential to theorizing contemporary race relations and understanding its potential political implications. To the extent that we rely on one dimension of interracial relations, a belief in resource competition or stereotypes without inquiries regarding closeness and linked fate and the complexities and contradictions of identity and racial beliefs, we fail to understand exactly how intergroup relations are formed.

Those respondents who held poor attitudes toward blacks were just 10% of the Mexican subset of my sample, and they reported particularly bad experiences with African Americans. Alma, for example, is a Mexican immigrant from Guerrero, who had been in the US for ten years. She first migrated to California, then came to Winston-Salem, returning to Mexico with her children briefly (but finding no work there). When we spoke, she was thirty and worked in a local factory. She was an active member in the white and Latino church, and Alma was among the few in my study who reported only negative experiences with blacks and only positive experiences with whites. She explained:

Because I saw a black woman that was very . . . you see that someone is racist because they make faces at you, and how they whisper. They say things and because one doesn't know English they think that—they look at you with mean eyes. . . . One time I went into the bathroom and a black woman was leaving and almost ran into me. And she said to me, "Stupid, can't you see?"

And then my friend said, "Don't talk to her that way. She didn't see that you were in the bathroom. Why didn't you put down the lock? When you enter, you lock it." And she started swearing at us.

Alma later reported that, when she was leaving work, the husband of the woman saw her and her friend in the parking lot and began swearing at them. She said he threatened to destroy her car, but she was afraid and intimidated because he could call immigration on them. She almost did not return to work, but the white manager intervened, saying that if anything happened, he'd call the police. The manager also spoke to the husband and diffused the tension. Alma then noted:

> Yes, the blacks are more, more racist than not, as you can see. And Americans [whites] are too, they say, but from my experience, I've never met an American like that. Never. For me the Americans are very amiable, very good people and because honestly, I've never been bothered by an American man or woman. So, I feel fine. I know an American woman named Tania. Every five months, because she has a daughter the age of mine daughter, she always brings me clothes. Always. And because of this, I say that I don't have anything to say about the Americans. Them no. They are good people. But the blacks, yes, they are bad.

Among those individuals who experienced what they believed to be discrimination directly from blacks *and* failed to experience similar types of interactions with whites, their perceptions of closeness and similarity to blacks were the exceptions that proved the rule. The vast majority of Latinos in my study reported negative experiences with both groups, minimal interactions with either group, or more positive interactions with blacks than with whites and framed conflict with whites and blacks accordingly. The first segment, who had negative experiences with both whites and blacks, saw conflict with blacks as an interpersonal issue, while conflict with whites was race-based. Those who reported minimal interactions with either groups or who had more positive experiences with black Americans than with whites developed their perceptions of race relations through broader social and political issues. Among African Americans, some perceived competition with Latinos in the labor market or for resources, but most expressed beliefs of shared status and a desire for solidarity to obtain more collective resources, rather than compete for them. These findings are consistent with Ted Brader and colleagues, who, in national data, find that blacks are more permissive on immigration policies than whites and that group attitudes and symbolic understandings of race and identity matter more than material interests in shaping differences in attitudes about discrimination.[99]

A New Minority Politics: The Importance of *Minority Linked Fate*

While each group's relative socioeconomic status conditions intergroup relations, racial status is essential. In this chapter, I contend that ascription and identity formation proceed relationally and dialectically,[100] and that local context provides the raw materials through which such relations are built. To that end, we must treat racial status as malleable and shifting in order to understand race appropriately.[101]

Racial groups form relationally, often in response to external treatment, constructing and reconstructing allies and adversaries while building group consciousness.[102] Through this process, racial status shapes intergroup relations. That is, despite distinct histories, cultures, and phenotypes, each comes to articulate their individual, and group, identities as shaped by sharing a similar status or marginalized position within the racial hierarchy through a process of racialized ascription.[103] In this way, their position as minorities and the meaning of that status not only become amplified, but also become an important set of meanings and reconstructed identities through which they construct intergroup relations.

The literature on social movements reminds us that collective identities are necessary precursors to collective political action. Hostile environments can increase collective identities' salience.[104] Chris Zepeda-Millán argues that, in the case of Latinos, group consciousness increases when they perceive group discrimination, as do feelings of commonality with other racialized groups. Nativist policies and public sentiments thus have important spillover effects among Latinos regardless of status who are positioned as the "other."[105]

While positive interminority relations are by no means new,[106] the more amicable relations between blacks and Latinos examined at length in this study may be made possible in part by a change in historical context. Black-brown solidarity movements emerged most forcefully in the civil rights era, when a sense of shared status was established and the stakes for rights and resources were high.[107] In the post–civil rights era, blacks have demonstrably and successfully mobilized to attain rights, opportunities, and political power, demonstrating what Kathryn Neckerman, Prudence Carter, and Jennifer Lee call a minority culture of mobility.[108] In this way, the Southern context is particularly likely to produce conditions leading to civility and cooperation between blacks and Latinos; not only are there significant concentrations of middle-class blacks throughout the region but that resonance and relevance of the civil rights movement in attention to minority rights is particularly strong. Blacks, for their part, are likely aware they are living in a period of shifting demographics, in which alliances with Latinos may prove fruitful in the long-term as cities tip to majority-minority. Indeed, the impact of Latinos on politics is likely to come primarily as a voting block, since so few Latinos serve in public office.[109] As a result, black politicians are well served by attending to Latino constituents and laying the groundwork for long-term coalitions. Black leaders have taken this imperative seriously. Representative Marcus Brandon (D-Guilford), for instance, sponsored a North Carolina bill that would allow in-state tuition for undocumented youth, and has called on the Democratic party for greater outreach.[110] And Latinos, through experiences of persistent and public anti-immigrant sentiment, are increasingly *unlikely* to aspire to whiteness; instead, they are building their racialized identities up from an experience of marginalization and denigration. Together, these processes create new opportunities for the production of *minority linked fate.*

In some key ways, *minority linked fated* between blacks and Latino has become apparent in emerging political and attitude polls as well. Even national figures such as Al Sharpton are now claiming immigration politics as a core issue of concern, and immigration rights activists are reaching out to form intergroup coalitions to support voting rights legislation, access to education, and reductions in racial profiling, all issues that both blacks and Latinos face and all of which fall under the general purview of civil rights.[111] As Hannah Gill notes, "Organizations that have historically advocated for African American civil rights have alleviated some of these barriers to access by expanding their efforts to include immigrants."[112] I argue that as Latinos face greater legislative scrutiny and hostility, greater contestation over belonging may ignite the conditions under which a sense of collective racial status between blacks and Latinos can be forged, particularly when conditions for conflict or interminority racial alienation are suppressed.[113]

Throughout the country, the socioeconomic conditions creating resource competition among minority groups are shifting. Now, social relations between blacks and Latinos around the country, especially in large and medium-sized cities, are increasingly looking like the conditions in Winston, where substantial numbers of middle-class minorities reside. We see more diversity within racial groups and more mobility across racial groups (including upward mobility, socioeconomic diversity, and relocation to the suburbs among minority groups). Greater attention to these dynamics and how they intersect with racial status in an increasingly hostile anti-minority, anti-migrant climate, will bring our understanding of intergroup relation and its varied consequences into the twenty-first century.

The New South: New Minority Coalitions and White Retrenchment

The Nomination of Mr. Trump by the Republican Party will endure in the memory of Latinos in this country for generations to come. Our future historians will write about the Trump campaign and the nativist anger it unleashed with the same sense of hurt that African-Americans feel when they look back on the cruelties of Jim Crow, and that Asian-Americans experience as they contemplate the injustice of the Chinese Exclusion Act.

HÉCTOR TOBAR, journalist and writer

In October 2011, the Alabama NAACP joined the Alabama Coalition for Immigrant Justice (ACIJ) to collectively oppose the passage of Alabama's HB 56, which some African American leaders called a "Juan Crow Law." Now, they continue to work together to pressure the state to repeal HB 56 and restrictions on voters' rights. Wade Henderson, the African American president of the Leadership Conference on Civil and Human Rights, was among the first to denounce HB 56, noting that it was designed to "terrorize the state's Latino community."[1] Such efforts are indicative not only of a shift left on immigration by African American politicians in Alabama, but also of a broader shift toward greater support of immigrant rights throughout the region.[2] Black-brown coalitions are on the rise throughout the American Southeast.

Not only have local NAACP branches followed the national organization's lead in listing immigration as one of the core issues in its broader civil rights agenda,[3] but immigrant rights groups like ACIJ and the Mississippi Immigrant Rights Alliance (MIRA) have entered into formal partnerships with many longstanding Civil Rights Coalitions in North Carolina, Georgia, Alabama, Mississippi, Virginia, Tennessee, and elsewhere.[4] Organizers have marched together in Selma on the issue of voting rights and in DC in support of comprehensive immigration reform and the Dreamers movement. They have achieved collective victories in organizing low-wage workers in meatpacking plants, casinos, and the service industry. These sustained and, in many cases, successful efforts at coalition building and minority racial politics are both intentional and on the rise. The Southern Regional Council reports, "Enough collaboration between African Americans and Latinos has occurred to prompt Jennifer Gordon and Robin Lenhardt to say that 'the South has become something of a laboratory for such efforts.'"[5]

In focusing on local conditions in this book, I use Winston-Salem as an example of the importance of local context in shaping racial formation, race relations, and, under certain conditions, *minority linked fate*. However, in uncovering the mechanisms and practices at work in Winston, I reveal how they may also be shaping similar outcomes throughout the region. Certainly, the specifics of local context demonstrate that there is no single emergent color line; distinct constellations of class, race, and political relations lead to different racial schema. Still, the role of the South in influencing national-level change underscores the importance of theorizing the Southern context.

Our understandings and misunderstandings of how new Latinos are incorporated, build identities, relate to other groups, and ultimately develop a political consciousness are critical, as Latinos are already shaping political and social outcomes throughout the region. Latinos are expected to represent 40 percent of the growth in the American electorate by 2030, and the speed of such growth in the Southeast makes it a particularly good case study for understanding the political impact of demographic change. In this chapter, I consider the relationship between Winston and the region to the future of racial formation, race relations, and racial politics throughout the US.

✳

Many cite California as the nation's bellwether, a leader in demographic change and its attendant social and political change.[6] But where California has frequently served in our collective imaginations as a harbinger of the future, the Southeast has figured in as a representative of our collective past—historical, steeped in tradition, conservative, religious, and insular. Yet we forget that California was the epicenter of the restrictionist movement, ushering in such policies as proposition 187 (the Save our State Initiative) in 1994 and building a kind of exurban agenda of reactionist legislation that provides a direct contrast to the state's liberal coastal core.[7] Today, in the case of California and similar states, restrictionist movements are tempered by a plurality of white liberals who support a more progressive legislative agenda. Meanwhile, in the Southeast, an economic engine powered by the growth of black, Latino, and Asian populations is at work throughout the region. The New South, as it is known, is increasingly a locus of hyper-diversity, but without a substantial liberal white core standing in opposition to those who would double down on racial exclusion. As a result, while the path of California seems clear, the direction of the Southeast remains uncertain. Thus, while California may have led the US in shifting racial politics in much of the twentieth century (with notable exceptions, of course), we must look to the South in the twenty-first. Here, in Winston-Salem, I have uncovered indicators of new, divergent regional pathways in race relations and racial politics. Just as the South served as the core battleground for the civil rights agenda of the twentieth century, so too will it fight out the minority rights agenda in the twenty-first.

Backlash Politics

As this book shows, the experiences of Mexican migrants in the Winston-Salem area of North Carolina reveal that context matters greatly for shaping race and race relations. In Winston-Salem, a combination of an increasingly stifling regime of municipal and state immigration policies and Latino settlement into middle-class African American communities has deeply altered the ways in which Latino immigrants are incorporated relative to traditional receiving areas. In the South, where once-open and welcoming receptions were the norm, shifting economic and political factors have created institutional and social closure, changing the immigrant experiences of even those long-since settled. As a result, a rising context of closure is shaping and reshaping Latinos' racial identities and relationships, producing a sense of collective minority status that may have been unlikely in earlier decades.[8]

Not only is backlash to immigrant settlement widespread today, but so, too, are the conditions under which immigrants are likely to interpret this backlash as discriminatory and racializing. Evidence suggests that Latino identities and politics are changing. For example, the immigrant rights marches coordinated by local activists, unions, businesses, and other local leaders in 2006 were a response to concerted, national-level efforts to target immigrants—like the draconian measures in the Sensenbrenner bill that threatened entire communities for "aiding and abetting" undocumented immigrants—as well as similar local-level initiatives. Immigrant activism in 2018 was a direct reply to the Trumpist agenda, in which immigrants, particularly Mexicans and Central Americans (but also, not inconsequentially, Haitians and immigrants from Arab and Muslim dominant countries), were denigrated and targeted for raids, travel bans, increased border enforcement, and the rolling back of refugee programs, Temporary Protected Status (TPS), and Deferred Action for Childhood Arrivals (DACA).

At the same time, the core mechanisms that shaped integration pathways in Winston—resourced black communities, a low density of long-standing Latino communities, high levels of segregation and anti-immigrant sentiment and policy—are far from unique. Such conditions are present in various Southern cities and states with large black populations as the federal government rolls out more immigration enforcement programs. Under these conditions, the black leadership in these communities might also be expected to begin forming black-brown coalitions. We might expect these patterns in Georgia, for example, where there is also a large black middle-class, a low density of long-standing Latino communities, and high levels of segregation and anti-immigrant sentiment throughout the state.[9]

The Case of Georgia

In the PBS documentary *Latino Americans*, the filmmakers follow one family who settled in Dalton, Georgia, as part of a wave of immigrant workers arriving in the 1980s and 1990s. Like others, they had been recruited to work in the carpet business. Things took a sudden turn in the 2000s, when they found themselves subject to xenophobic and racist harassment and slurs. Unlike the largely accommodating context in Dalton described by Rubén Hernández-León and Victor Zúñiga in 2001, by mid-decade, the young citizen children of this family felt arbitrarily excluded from the city they had grown up in.[10] This experience and iterations of it across families throughout the state politicized first- and second-generation immigrants in unprecedented ways.

In 2006, the *Atlanta Journal Constitution* reported on the impact of such a rapid change in the state. The language the paper used bears striking similarities to what I saw in North Carolina. In 2006, a piece reports, Georgia passed SB 529, also known as the Georgia Security and Immigration Compliance Act, prohibiting undocumented immigrants from accessing some public benefits, requiring police to check the immigration status of those arrested for DUIs and felonies, and instituting sanctions for employers hiring undocumented immigrants. The bill and the sentiments behind it came as a surprise to many Latinos in the area. Mexican-born car dealer Lou Sobh, who had been living in the Atlanta area since 1990, noted, "Georgia has always been very welcoming, until 529."[11]

The article goes on to highlight comments from Sara Gonzales of the Georgia Hispanic Chamber of Commerce: "Immigrants are spooked, rumors are flying and people are misinformed. The rumor is, 'Oh', we are not wanted here. Oh, they are going to come and pick us up. Oh, I'm going to take the kids out of school . . . It's a panic. A huge can of worms has been opened."[12] Predictably, as in the case of Winston, these efforts were interpreted by Latino residents as largely anti-Latino and discriminatory. Arturo Adonay, a manager of a local business, was quoted as saying, "It's sad that this community will be affected, perhaps even in a racist way, by these new laws when really, they are here to work."[13] For immigrant Latinos in Georgia, as in North Carolina, 2006 marked a turning point. Once welcomed, Latinos were on the cusp of restriction, punishment, and exclusion.

At the state level, Georgia's crackdown on undocumented migrants was fierce and aggressive. Throughout the 2000s, the municipalities pursued several 287(g) policies, while the legislature passed laws banning undocumented immigrants from the University of Georgia system, passed laws requiring verification of legal status for many benefits and newly aggressive voter ID laws, and by 2012, adopted an aggressive omnibus bill, HB 87, inspired by Arizona and duplicated in South Carolina and Alabama, to restrict immigrant access to social services and representation. Fear, anger, sadness, and, in some cases, exit followed, but these political maneuvers also often had a long-term effect of increased pan-ethnic mobilization and minority identification. That is, the unintended consequence of backlash was politicization.

Immigrants in Georgia, like elsewhere, who invested years in the United States, building homes, families, and careers, could not simply accept social closure. In the case of Deferred Action for Childhood Arrivals, or DACA, activism among so-called Dreamers, those youth and young adults who arrived as children, consider themselves Americans, and hold social citizenship, demand access to education and relief from deportation, like their documented peers. The policy and social movement were originally part of an effort to push for immigration reform at the beginning of the 2000s; as those efforts stalled, states and municipalities began to aggressively exclude immigrants. Dreamers upped their protest. They continue to push for relief engaged in political action including civil disobedience, and were a major part of the 2006 marches and mobilization. Today, they press for a "Clean Dream Act" that would make DACA permanent, the expansion of citizenship, advocating for deportation relief for family members, and a pathway to citizenship for all. As of 2018, the future of DACA is uncertain, but activists continue to organize and make claims to social belonging and political rights.

These shifts in immigration politics demonstrate that, when minorities are backed into a corner, mobilization is often the only reasonable response. Rather than merely terrify immigrants and try to scare them out of town, a strategy known as "attrition through enforcement," legislative moves from the local to the federal level also motivated both newcomers and long-established immigrant claims to social and political rights and community inclusion. The 2016 election, with the rise of Trump and a newly visible anti-immigrant nationalist rhetoric, reportedly spurred record numbers of Latino immigrants to apply for citizenship and register to vote.[14] Thus, backlash in locales throughout the country, but certainly the South, as a region, is creating a generation of politically conscious Latinos who see their identities as shaped not primarily by the quest for upward mobility, but by efforts to truncate that rise through social and political exclusion of themselves and their families. In the case of Georgia, in response to these efforts at closure, Dreamers are engaged in constant and persistent protest, enrolling in Freedom University—a collective of artists, writers, and professors who collaborate and teach undocumented students in Georgia—and pressing the state to change its policies. Moreover, studies suggest that these efforts at closure are met with broad sympathy by African Americans in Georgia. Recent analysis by Irene Browne and colleagues comparing the mainstream press and the black press in Atlanta is indicative of a black counterdiscourse, in which immigrant Latinos are frequently framed in racialized ways, both as victims of discrimination and punitive behaviors by police, and in terms of linked fate and potential coalition partners. This is juxtaposed against the mainstream press, which more frequently criminalized Latino immigrants, advocating for punitive policies in the state.[15]

We are also beginning to see political coalitions develop in the state. For example, the Georgia Association of Elected Latino Officials and the Georgia NAACP joined with local residents to sue Gwinnett County (part of the broader Atlanta region) in 2016 over the commission and school board districts, which they claim are drawn in such a way to dilute the minority vote. Despite being a majority-minority district, no nonwhite has ever been elected to its commission or school board.[16] Throughout the region, it seems, Latinos in spaces with punitive policy efforts and anti-immigrant attitudes are beginning to understand their Latinoness as a function both of the experience of exclusion and of mobilized resistance.[17]

Becoming Latino

As Latinos are increasingly racialized, they learn what so many African Americans have long understood—there is no transcending race.[18] That is, despite a long-held belief in upward mobility, in whitening, and assimilation, "racelessness" is always out of reach. Richard Alba and others have long argued that many, if not most, Latinos would achieve a kind of whiteness, measured by their upward mobility and general acculturation into the mainstream.[19] To the extent that this has not yet occurred, Tomás Jiménez and others believe it is due to ethnic replenishment and other factors. I, however, argue that these scholars have failed to fully consider both sides of boundary work.[20]

Immigrants can be incorporated into the mainstream through slow but deliberate efforts at inclusion, as in the case of Eastern and Southern Europeans who were discriminated against and subject to ethnic slurs, but who were never, as David Roediger and Cybelle Fox and Thomas Guglielmo point out, barred from *eventual* inclusion.[21] Even some of the staunchest advocates of ethnic differentiation among European immigrants to the US argued that such populations would "become white" in three generations. Mexican Americans and others, however, have more often than not received the message they should return to their home countries, regardless of how many generations their families have resided in the US. Full inclusion was not on the table. In moments of fear and threat, these discriminatory attitudes were accompanied by concrete policy efforts to exclude—deportation orders, barring from access to social services, and criminalization.

In the United States, being Latino is no longer just a measure of country of origin, culture, or language. It is race. Latinos, as is reflected in the recommended (yet ultimately rejected, as of this writing) change to the 2020 census to make Latino a racial category, increasingly see themselves as a racial group. To many, discrimination and exclusion from whiteness as well as solidarity as Latinos are now part and parcel of American life. Among many of my respondents, the choice to talk about themselves and their co-ethnics as *Hispanos* or Latinos was a deliberate construction that reflected shared experiences of marginalization. On the census, the *ethnic* formulation of Hispanic or Latino was intended to capture the wide range of Latinos who self-identify racially as white or, in some significant, if fairly rare, cases, black. But the designation has become less useful over time as Latinos have been increasingly ascribed and denigrated as a racial group, regardless of phenotype. This is especially true in places like the Southeast where backlash politics and discourse dominate and are fought with explicitly racialized pro-immigrant language and civil rights advocacy.[22] As these kinds of political discourses get reproduced on a national scale, as in the 2016 election and Trumpist era, this shift is likely to spread.

In each census since Latinos were first counted in 1980, more and more Latinos have marked Latino as their ethnicity *and* written it in as their race. The data is consistent with opinion polls, in which more and more respondents are labeling themselves as racially Latino and reporting a sense of within-group commonality.[23] It's an important shift, since the Latino population in the US has vast diversity, particularly in terms of country of origin, and suggests that the "something else" people believe bonds them is race. This is best reflected in Pew Research Center data that shows that two trends rose together: the number of people claiming a Latino racial identity and the number of reporting discrimination due to their skin color more frequently than language or any other characteristic.[24] In 2015, Pew reported that 67 percent of Hispanic adults said that being Hispanic is a part of their racial background. This is true even among those whose primary language is Spanish, a good proxy for time in the US among newcomers (67 percent of Spanish dominant also reported that Hispanic is a racial background), suggesting that racialization can happen rapidly and is less determined by the length of time in the US than the quality of experiences while in the country.[25]

These changes reflect the reality of social experience and daily life, indicating that they are formative and likely to be long-lasting with regard to race, ethnicity, and identity into the second and third generation. In Karen Kaufmann's analysis of the 1990 Latino National Political Survey, she examines both pan-ethnic and interracial closeness well before the anti-immigrant turn in the post-9/11 era. Kaufmann shows that 75% percent of blacks reported a sense of commonality with Latinos, and 61% of blacks reported a commonality with whites, suggesting that African Americans have long been more likely to see Latinos as positioned similarly to themselves in the racial order. Latinos, she argued, have a strong sense of neither pan-ethnic nor racial identity; however, when there *is* a strong sense of pan-Latinoness, there is also a strong sense of closeness or affinity with blacks.[26] So, blacks see Latinos as similarly positioned minorities, and, to the extent that Latinos feel raced, they agree. This statistically significant relationship is a strong indicator of the importance of race as a relational and hierarchical category that shapes identity and the meaning of *minority linked fate*.[27] That is, the meaning of Latino as a racial identity is not constructed as an isolated phenomenon. Rather, it is constructed relationally, and understood as similar to blacks. This sense of *minority linked fate* is indicative of the racialization of the Latino experience. While this is national survey data, and thus glosses over many important distinctions in the Latino population and local context, it points to a far more complex, and perhaps shifting, picture of race relations than popular media would have us believe. *Minority linked fate* has been burgeoning between blacks and Latinos for decades, and efforts toward exclusionary policies and racial discrimination against those who appear to be Latino are likely to accelerate this trend, reinforcing blacks' and Latinos' sense that they are, together, maligned minorities similarly situated within a racial hierarchy.[28]

As early as the 2006 Latino National Political Survey, data on North Carolina showed that 58% of Latinos said that African Americans doing well matters some or a lot for Latinos doing well, and Latinos from all states reported having more in common with African Americans than with other groups.[29] Such findings suggest that national level changes in aggregate may be due in part to local or regional level dynamics—in the spaces in which Latinos are more likely to encounter African Americans *and* live under racialized conditions they may be more inclined to develop a sense of *minority linked fate*.

Indeed, these findings beg us to reconsider Kaufmann's discarded discrimination hypothesis, which states: "Latino/black affinity is rooted in perceived discrimination and shared outsider status" and therefore "Latinos who perceive high levels of anti-Latino discrimination, would also be the most likely to sense commonality with blacks."[30] This thesis appears far more accurate in the intensely hostile anti-immigrant context of the twenty-first century, particularly in the Southeast, than it did in the 1990s. Perceived discrimination and anti-Latino attitudes do, over time, appear to spark a sense strong Latino identity and shared experience. In turn, this triggers a sense of commonality and linked fate with blacks, especially where large populations of black residents are present.[31] For both Karen Kaufmann and Michael Dawson, this "symbolic glue" can bind or unite people despite differences, manifesting a sense of shared identity, trust, and mutual cooperation.[32] In the process of coming to see themselves as raced, Latinos look to other racialized groups to reinforce the meaning and significance they have attributed to their own collective experience.[33]

Despite these broader trends, I want to emphasize that identity shifts and racialization processes do not proceed in a uniform fashion. Rather, they are dynamic and context-specific. While I argue there that there are a few key mechanisms that matter in shaping racial formation and race relations (namely, racial status, economic status, and the conditions that shape those statuses—perceptions of resource competition, political incorporation, the level of segregation and existing race relations, demographic composition, anti-immigrant sentiment, and the "warmth of the welcome" at the local level), these conditions are contingent and vary widely across time and space, creating distinct dynamics in different locations. As a consequence, I argue that Latinos are, on balance, becoming racialized and building ties with African Americans, especially in the Southeast, yet I caution against defaulting to a color-line framework to make sense of emerging racial hierarchies.

Instead, I believe there is a patchwork of racial frameworks dependent on context, in which specific constellations of conditions shape hierarchies, meanings, and intergroup relations. While these mechanisms help us predict what color line might emerge under what conditions, color lines are multiple and mutable. No longer are national color lines useful, theoretically rich constructs. Instead, we must begin the work of constructing multiple models of racial system formations. While perhaps a more daunting task, in many ways, theorizing an absence of uniformity is not only more empirically accurate, but also more analytically rich, as we have more models to observe and investigate in order to more accurately predict change in racialization processes and race relations over time.

New Coalitions: Immigration and Civil Rights in the New South

A racialized Latinidad also changes how we think about politics. On the one hand, new civil rights coalitions and strategic alliances are emblematic of the kind of new minority politics resulting from anti-immigrant backlash across the South. On the other, sustained efforts to impose voting restrictions and punitive policies and an absence of discernable gains in representation suggest long-term political retrenchment may stymie change. These two political pathways operate in tandem, creating a dialectical political relationship worthy of careful consideration.

In Alabama for example, the institutionalization of HB 56 has galvanized a coalition of immigrant rights activists as part of a new civil rights coalition.[34] The ACIJ, as noted at the outset of this chapter, reorganized, led by a board of community activists and social justice advocates, including a number of the community's African American leaders. In 2012, the ACIJ became a lifetime member of the NAACP, and is a partner organization under the umbrella of the Birmingham Civil Rights Coalition. Its goal is not only to seek justice on immigration issues, but also to serve as coalition partners on a broad slate of minority rights issues. As a result, ACIJ has been a visible partner in the struggle to preserve the Voting Rights Act, marched alongside NAACP members to mark the anniversary of Selma, and is making a deliberate effort to brand itself as a partner in the struggle to obtain and preserve civil rights for all its black and Latino community members in Alabama. ACIJ organizers report that this reciprocal relationship is essential to their success, and that the vast majority of residents who participate in their events, collaborate in community meetings, and show up to support their efforts are Latino and African American.

In Mississippi, a similar coalition formed in 2000 and has seen remarkable success in reshaping immigration issues as part of a broader civil rights agenda. Using the exploitation of immigrant workers following Hurricane Katrina as a galvanizing moment for the articulation of a shared politics of social justice and labor rights, the Mississippi Immigrant Rights Alliance (MIRA) has become a model of multiracial progressive activism in the South. Their calls to reframe anti-immigrant policies as an attack on *all* minorities could not be more explicit, and are a key accomplishment of the movement. In response to one of the largest immigration raids in US history, which took place in Laurel, Mississippi, one African American MIRA board member and AFL-CIO staff member commented: "This raid is an effort to drive immigrants out of Mississippi. It is also an attempt to drive a wedge between immigrants, African Americans, white people and unions–all those who want political changed here." Patricia Ice, African American activist and immigration attorney for MIRA, commented, "This is political. They want a mass exodus of immigrants out of the state, the kind we've seen in Arizona and Oklahoma. The political establishment here is threatened by Mississippi's changing demographics and what they electorate might look like in 20 years."[35] Mississippi's multiracial coalition of advocates, civil rights activists, religious leaders, and labor organizers has successfully partnered with the black caucus to prevent any enforceable anti-immigrant bills from making it through the state legislature, despite nearly 300 efforts at restrictive legislation as of 2017.

One of the most surprising and important coalitional victories has been the unionization of the Smithfield Packing slaughterhouse in Tar Heel, North Carolina. Organized by the United Food and Commercial Workers, the union vote came from a nearly entirely black and Latino workforce in 2008. Fighting for the right to organize and vote by secret ballot after years of intimidation and litigation, the union won the election when "union organizers pushed for the cooperation of the plant's black and Hispanic workers. At lunchtime outspoken workers sometimes wore T-shirts saying 'Smithfield Justice' and gave speeches to hundreds of workers."[36] After a major 2006 raid on 1,500 Latino workers and the firing and intimidation of union supporters (as well as illegal activities undertaken by the Smithfield company, including spying, confiscating union materials, threatening to freeze wages, and threatening to shut the plant), successfully forming a union was no small achievement. As Steven Greenhouse wrote, "Lydia Victoria, who helps cut off hog tails at the plant, acknowledged, 'Many Hispanic workers were afraid of being seen as union supporters. Illegal immigrant workers are especially worried because they fear deportation.' 'A lot of Hispanic people,' Ms. Victoria said, 'were scared to support the union, sometimes because of the language, and sometimes because they feel they don't get the same treatment like the people who speak English.' 'But people came together,' she said. 'People wanted fair treatment. We fought so long to get this, and it finally happened.'"[37]

Even in the case of the most visible black social movement of this decade, Black Lives Matter, we see deep ties with Latino organizations and immigrant rights advocates. One of the founders of Black Lives Matter, Opal Tometi, is also the founder of the Black Association for Justice for Immigrants (BAJI). Her organization advocates for black immigrants, particularly undocumented immigrants who, like many Latinos, are targeted for deportation, are unlikely to receive judicial relief, and face an extremely difficult standard for legalization. This organization frequently partners with other immigrant rights organizations on marches, solidarity efforts, lobbying, and media campaigns. These organizational ties also link Black Lives Matter to the larger coalition of immigrant rights organizations, who are collaborating on efforts to put forth a shared agenda of decarceration and sanctuary for all.[38]

The public also seems to recognize ties between the issues facing blacks and Latinos: in 2015, in response to one of the first major civil disobedience efforts by the Black Lives Matter coalition in Chicago (a successful disruption of holiday shopping in the Magnificent Mile district over the Thanksgiving holiday weekend), Dante Franco, who was stuck with his family on Michigan Avenue, their minivan surrounded by protestors, told the media: "I'm good with this. I'm Hispanic and I feel like them."[39] In 2017, Black Lives Matter activists worked with immigration advocates to demand Birmingham declare itself a sanctuary city. The majority black city council agreed and voted in support of the declaration. And, in 2018, following a week of raids, undocumented Latino youth with Siembra NC–La Linea, worked with African American community members and Black Lives Matter Activists to clear post-tornado debris and make repairs to homes, public spaces, and a local domestic violence prevention center in an African American neighborhood in Greensboro, NC.

In the 2016 election cycle, Latinos registered to vote[40] and engaged in efforts to regularize their status and apply for citizenship in record numbers.[41] Latino youth became extraordinarily engaged in politics not only in terms of registering to vote, but also in undertaking public protest and issue campaigns.[42] And, Latinos, regardless of origin, began to strongly advocate for a Latino politics—a kind of linked fate that rejected anti-Mexican and anti-immigrant discourse as broadly anti-Latino—a crucial shift in shaping a broader minority agenda.

Certainly, there is precedent for these partnerships and coalitional efforts —think to the Black Panthers, the Young Lords, the Brown Berets, and others in the 1960s and 1970s—but we often fail to recognize these moments as important opportunities to theorize black-Latino relationships, identities, and politics. Instead, we return to the trope of conflict, explaining away coalitional efforts as anomalies rather than patterns of social change. I contend that Winston-Salem is not an isolated case, but emblematic of a set of context-specific practices that are becoming increasingly common across the South, and, in some cases, the nation. Indeed, in October 2008, the first national Black-Latino summit was held in Los Angeles, planting the seeds for a long-term national agenda.[43]

The case of Winston-Salem and coalitional efforts in neighboring states suggest that in the South, in particular, *minority linked fate* is being asserted and used as a platform for coalitional political work. That is, a sense of Latino identity and politics is embedded in a broader understanding of shared standing with other nonwhite minorities, and as a result, a shared politics with blacks. Should these patterns continue, it will have important consequences for an increasingly majority-minority region. We may see a viable progressive minority coalition emerge. However, these efforts are not emerging organically. Rather, they are developing in reaction to significant and intensive efforts to exclude, punish, and marginalize immigrants and nonwhite residents.

As states and municipalities strengthen their use of punitive policies toward immigrants, African Americans in leadership positions are intensifying their resistance. Still, the fact that such efforts have not materialized into major changes in electoral politics suggests that demography is not destiny, but a mobilizer and a threat. Demographics will continue to shape political change, but whether that will lead in the direction of new coalitions, white retrenchment, or both, remains to be seen.

A New Southern Strategy? White Retrenchment

In the early 1990s, George H. W. Bush successfully campaigned as a compassionate conservative, building a "points of light" platform that sought, in part, to appeal to Latino voters' religious attitudes. In the late 1990s, George W. Bush, too, sought to appeal to Latinos, running a number of campaign ads in Spanish and English and calling for comprehensive immigration reform, characterizing Latino immigrants as ideal Americans—patriotic, hard-working, family-oriented people of faith.[44]

Even in the post-9/11 era, in which securitization eclipsed efforts to reform immigration and the coalition for reform fell apart, it appeared in 2016 that the Republican party was renewing its efforts to include Latinos. The national party championed as its establishment candidates Marco Rubio and Jeb Bush, a Cuban American and a legacy candidate married to a Mexican woman, respectively. Arguably, this was with the understanding that the men could walk the fine line of integrating Latinos as Republican voters while remaining circumspect on immigration issues.

The party's base, it would appear, had other ideas. Intense anti-immigrant activism and successful passage of restrictionist policies at the municipal and state levels empowered and legitimated an anti-Latino agenda in which Latino immigrants, particularly Mexicans, were publicly pilloried not only as a threat to the economy, but as inherently criminal. This national-level discursive shift far eclipsed the negative rhetoric at the state level in the 2008 and 2012 campaigns.[45] As journalist Héctor Tobar reflects,

Back in 2000, when immigration reform seemed imminent, the Republican convention in Philadelphia offered a multicultural vision of a "kinder, gentler" America. I covered that gathering for the *Los Angeles Times,* and while walking the convention floor, I encountered Rosario Marín, a Mexican immigrant and a Republican city councilwoman from a Los Angeles. . . . As president, George W. Bush appointed Ms. Marín as treasurer of the United States. . . . Mrs. Marín has attended every Republican convention since 1996, but she told Fox News Latino that she would not attend [the 2016] gathering. "He's insulted me," she said of Mr. Trump, "the people I love, the community I represent." She also vowed never to vote for "the little orange man." "I'm in mourning," said Ms. Marín. "It's been very painful." Millions of Latino Americans, like Rosario Marín, will remember the affront of this moment in the voting booth. And they will remember it long afterward, when they send their children to school, telling them to study harder because of Mr. Trump and all that he represents.

Mirroring what Manuel Pastor, Justin Scoggins, and Sarah Treuhaft have called the *white/Latino generation gap* at the national level, many white Americans bought into a politics of fear (or a valorization of the past, as in, "Make America Great Again") that sought to protect a vision of America before large-scale social and demographic change.[46] Pastor and colleagues argue that this gap, between an increasingly browning generation of youth, and a shrinking, older white generation, goes a long way in explaining the kind of electoral conflict emerging throughout the United States. Arizona, for example, which has the largest age gap between whites and Latinos, appears to be emblematic of the kind of political conflict that emerged in the 2016 election. Increasingly, however, the brownest counties in the United States are in the South, suggesting that Southern states are likely to overtake Arizona in the age gap and we should prepare to see even more vitriolic calls for punitive immigration policies and the eradication of civil rights.

Indeed, if 2016 is any indication, the Republican Party has changed its approach, embracing what Marisa Abrajano and Zoltan Hajnal call, in *White Backlash,* a "less generous, more indignant politics that seeks to punish immigrants who violate US norms, and strives to cut off services and other public goods that could benefit them."[47] Likewise, Julie Weise writes that politics of resentment initiated at the local level appear to be driving a new, polarizing national political agenda.

This division was visible in the 2016 party platform agendas. While Trump certainly embodied the worst of the Republican Party's affront to Latinos, the party established a platform of further immigration restriction, new categories of deportation, and increased policing of the southern border, including the construction of a new border wall. Decried by the organization Immigration Impact as demonizing undocumented immigrants as threats to public safety, demonstrating a lack of understanding of the immigration process by admonishing immigrants to "get in line," and silent on the role of employers and the changing economy in shaping the flow of immigrants into the United States, adherence to the threat narrative as a policy platform was sanctioned at the national level.[48] Julianne Hing argues that the clear message "was that the safety of Americans (read white people) is directly threatened by the free movement of immigrants (namely Latinos), Muslims, and black people who assert their humanity."[49] With few exceptions, this agenda continued to dominate the Republican party as the Trump administration, in which Muslim bans, the punishment of sanctuary cities, and support of a border wall were some of its most popular goals, reshaped the Republican agenda.[50]

In the 1960s, Republicans had introduced the "Southern Strategy" as a way to wrest control of the Southern electorate from Democrats by essentially doubling down on racism. They sought to support "states' rights" and obstruct a broad-based civil rights agenda. By intervening in the Jim Crow South in an effort to promote desegregation and extend voting rights to all citizens, Democrats lost the region's white voters for a generation. In the 2010s, history appears to repeat itself, with retrenchment efforts to prevent further expansion of Democratic political power continuing within the region and throughout the country. Republicans flipped state after state legislature and governorship after governorship in 2010 and 2014, with many speculating it was a direct rebuke to the election and reelection of Barack Obama. In 2016, we saw major gaps between the popular vote and election results, including no substantive changes in congressional seats at the state and federal levels. In the Southeast, effective gerrymandering has made turnover of those seats all but impossible. Many white Southern Democrats had switched parties. The "Solid South" of the 1960s had reemerged by 2016. Republicans held 63 percent of seats in Southern legislatures and every governorship. Most seats not held by Republicans were in majority-minority districts, emphasizing the stark divide between minority and newcomer voters and the longstanding, largely white Republican majority in the region.[51] Moreover, the rollback of the Voting Rights Act led to numerous suits and complaints over voter suppression, new voter ID laws, and reduced availability of early voting options, especially in swing states and the Southeast. Black and Latino voters were purposefully intimidated into staying away from the polls as rumors of ICE oversight and police officers checking warrants at the ballot swirled. And where Republicans saw defeats, they fought the results. In North Carolina, the election of the sole Democratic governor in the region was met with accusations of voter fraud, expensive delays, and recount threats, and eventually a massive dilution of power by the state legislature before the governor was able to take office.[52]

In 2017, the *New York Times* queried whether North Carolina was the future of American politics—a state with a narrow partisan split, an effective Republican takeover, and a political shift toward the most conservative legislative record the country since 2011.[53] Despite optimism among Democrats and progressives,[54] because the political system in which we live in is not a direct, popular vote system, demographic change and minority coalition building cannot result in immediate political power. In fact, the *opposite* can result. Deep polarization appears to drive a "scorched earth strategy" to politics, in which compromise is replaced with voter suppression.[55]

The United States' federalism means that the increasingly divergent nature of state approaches to immigration policy, voting rights regimes, and other civil rights protections can either lead to empowerment or facilitate retrenchment in granular ways. A patchwork of policy opportunities and closures is available within a context of minimal federal guidance. There are also greater opportunities for retrenchment in the South, where a plurality of anti-minority Southern whites may place fundamental constraints on progressive multiracial coalitions' efforts to push forth political change. The kinds of shifts we saw in post-backlash California, for example, were facilitated in part by coalition partners in unions, nonprofits, and other left-leaning organizations allying with nonwhites to fundamentally shift the state's political direction into the foreseeable future. Such a straightforward shift is less likely across the South as a region, but it is not impossible on a state-by-state basis.

In looking toward the Southeast, then, there are two possible tracks forward. Each has important implications for national politics. In the first pathway, minority empowerment and mobilization among a coalition of minority and progressive voters will continue to grow in size and strength, and they will play a major role in shaping both local and national issues. In the second, retrenchment will see conservative whites disenfranchise minority voters, launch a stalwart voting block preventing change, and continually put forth policies to roll back civil rights reforms and propose punitive anti-immigrant legislation. Because the same mechanisms are at work in both mobilization and retrenchment, it is likely that these two pathways will happen simultaneously.

What this looks like in terms of outcomes will be shaped in large part by the growth of minority coalitions and the shifting power of progressive whites. States like North Carolina, Tennessee, and Georgia may be especially likely to change, not only due to their influx of Latinos, but also the reverse migration of blacks and progressive whites. Other states, however, may be shaped more intensely in the long term by retrenchment, though not without significant challenge. In these states, progressive successes at the local level or in blocking some anti–civil rights, anti-immigrant efforts will certainly be present alongside retrenchment. Progress along either path is likely to be bumpy and hard-fought, as the struggle over the direction of the country plays out.

In analyzing these distinct political strategies in the South and the dialectical relationship between them, as well as racialization and race relations processes, we gather insight into the mechanisms that may shift or maintain dynamics in other states. Moreover, to the extent that the Southeast is an important and influential region in terms of national politics and race relations, it has always had an outsized impact on social change. As such, the region may be the true gateway to political change in the twenty-first century.

Conclusion: Making Race: Conflict and Color Lines

Oppression only succeeds in knitting together the oppressed.
JOHN STEINBECK, *Grapes of Wrath*

In 2017, Winston-Salem's diverse municipal leaders had good reason to pat themselves on the back. Tracy, the longtime, African American leader of its Human Relations Commission, accepted the National League of Cities Award for promoting cultural diversity—specifically, for the Building Integrated Communities Newcomer Pipeline. In important ways, it seemed that Winston's minority leadership and its allies had actualized their vision of making Winston-Salem welcoming to newcomers. But in as much as this initiative was receiving accolades for its efforts at integration, so too were the ongoing processes of exclusion affecting the Latinos in the area. From the reverse incorporation spurred by, and demonstrated in, anti-immigrant rhetoric and policy, to the institutional closures facing Dreamers, to the rising sense of *minority linked fate* that spurred, and was driven, by black-Latino coalitions, Winston-Salem's racial relations had neither returned to my Latino respondents' memories of inclusion and welcome, nor become wholly and unceasingly hostile in the ways pundits may have expected with the new era of criminalization and stigma under the Trump administration.

In many ways, by 2018, Winston-Salem was working hard to build on the successes of its many initiatives to create positive interminority relations, provide information and services to Spanish-speakers, and eventually, beat back pressure from the county to participate in programs like 287(g) that allowed partnerships between localities and ICE (which local police officials uniformly opposed). In the process, it earned the distinction of a "welcoming city," awarded to "cities that develop creative and effective programs to improve and promote cultural diversity through a collaborative process with city officials, community leaders and residents." The Newcomer Pipeline program, initiated in 2014, worked to better coordinate agencies and organizations that serve newcomers, particularly Latinos.[1] This program, along with sustained efforts by community leaders to maintain dialogue among and between minority communities, created a pathway for local integration that had been closed in the mid to late 2000s.

The newcomer program and other efforts from city bureaucrats and service providers can seem like a stark contrast to the broader political climate, however, as the *state* of North Carolina continued to pursue punitive immigration policies, including the passage of a bill in 2015 banning sanctuary cities and targeting undocumented immigrants by limiting the forms of acceptable identification they could use,[2] as well as new proposals to further penalize sanctuary cities and allow judges to deny bail to undocumented immigrants charged with a driving offense, sex crime, or drug crime, or gang-related crime.[3] In 2015, the National Immigration Law Center concluded:

> North Carolina, much like the rest of our nation, is at a crossroads: We can continue to ostracize and criminalize vital members of our communities, or we can work together to come up with inclusive policies that make us all safer, healthier, and better able to use essential services when needed. We— along with those elected to represent us—must move past the hateful, anti-immigrant rhetoric that spurs legally questionable legislation and instead get to work on solutions that move our communities forward together.[4]

Indeed, the story of immigrant integration is, in North Carolina and elsewhere, once again, at a turning point in the American imagination. Coalitions of progressive and moderate Democrats across the region are working alongside racially diverse city leaders and bureaucrats, continuing the work that African American leaders embarked on several years ago. At the same time, retrenchment has only become more pronounced as North Carolina's mostly white, Republican leadership seeks to punish and exclude minority residents again even as black Democrats and their coalitional partners try to stop them. This visible opposition is most famously embodied in the Moral Mondays campaign initiated by Reverend Barber, a pastor and state-chapter president of the NAACP, in the Forward Together Movement. Moral Mondays bring together minority and progressive communities to fight voting restrictions, the rollback of civil rights and liberties, and attacks on the poor.[5] More importantly, the Forward Together Movement provides a platform through which activists can articulate and mobilize fusion politics and a moral argument for equal justice.

In many ways, the state of politics and the social location of Latino immigrants in 2018 shared many elements with the climate I first explored in 2008, amplified by larger populations and more entrenched political positions—

perhaps emblematic of the two political pathways of coalition building and retrenchment. Latinos face racialization and criminalization broadly, but receive local support from African Americans and other leaders, including progressive whites. Latino immigrants occupy a distinct position in the labor market and face obstacles to mobility, but do not, on balance, attribute these obstacles to their African American neighbors, whom they have come to see as allies and even mentors in the policy arena. Ultimately, the revocation of a certain community-level respect, warmth, and inclusion continued to produce the conditions for *minority linked fate* and an increasingly effective resistance. The kinds of changes that emerged in Winston in a decade of study have confirmed for me both the ways in which race and class continue to shape racial identities and intergroup relations, and the divergent paths of multiracial coalition building and white retrenchment that are shaping politics throughout the region. Such changes also highlight not only how context can change, but also how municipalities, counties, and states can be at odds in their approaches to immigration policy and integration measures, producing new formulations of identity and integration trajectories.

Immigrant Integration and Making Race

For new arrivals in the United States, like in generations past, how they will come to identify themselves and how they will be situated within the country's racial hierarchy are ongoing processes. The incorporation of immigrant newcomers has been a central issue of inquiry across the social sciences, engaging scholars of immigration and race, as well as researchers in the fields of politics, law, and urban studies. For my part, I have sought in this book to explain whether and how Mexicans in new, rather than traditional, immigrant destinations in the US, particularly in the American Southeast, would be racialized and how their presence would affect local and regional level race relations.

To answer this question, I have drawn from extensive fieldwork, interviews, and media analysis showing how the marginalization and racialization of new Latinos conditions them to think of themselves as minorities, developing both positive relationships and political ties with blacks. Specifically, I show that Latinos' new identity arises primarily from two related processes: a political backlash against Latino immigration that followed a substantial welcoming period—a process that I call *reverse incorporation*—and on-the-ground relations with native-born community members, whose attitudes and practices shape newcomers' ideas about race. A sense of *minority linked fate* becomes cemented through these Latinos' positive relations with blacks and negative relationships with whites. Together, the two processes not only undermine pervasive arguments that black-brown relations are always strained but also suggest how social and political conditions may be instigating a shift toward a powerful and sustainable multiracial coalition in the New South.

Drawing from my novel findings on Latino minority identity formation and interminority solidarity, this book has a number of implications for our understanding of immigration, race relations, and politics. Among these, I have worked to highlight three central findings. First, I show that in the post-9/11 era, Latinos are being racialized in new, long-lasting ways, shaping not only Latino immigrants' ideas about being Latino, but also their status in relation to other racial and ethnic groups. Moreover, Latinos are increasingly more likely to see themselves positioned as close to blacks and distant from whites. In Winston-Salem, a combination of an increasingly stifling regime of immigration policies and Latino settlement into middle-class minority communities has deeply altered the ways in which immigrants are incorporated. This context has helped shape Latino identities and race relations to produce a sense of collective minority status in ways that may have been unlikely in previous decades. In particular, this study provides new evidence of the impact of local immigration enforcement in creating a sense of discrimination and racialization among immigrants. The variations and complexities in local immigration enforcement and local context are, in fact, pivotal in structuring race and race relations.[6]

Overwhelmingly, the immigrant incorporation literature argues that newcomers develop racial identities by distancing themselves from blacks. But in the case of Mexicans and other Latinos facing increased social and legal discrimination, I find the opposite to be true. The processes I identify in *The Browning of the New South* do not suggest that incorporation and racialization are only the result of the (relatively) static conditions of legal status or phenotype. Rather, the conditions of incorporation can be highly local and volatile, forcing migrants to interpret changes in a manner that provokes the assertion of a *minority linked fate*.

This assertion of new identities is critical to our understanding of future social change. As the population of Latinos rises, social scientists, policy makers, and the press are considering the role or roles that Latinos will play in our newly diverse society. The racialization of Latinos as minorities suggests group consolidation and linked fate as well as context-specific repositioning, in which Latinidad is a distinctly minority identity. Despite these processes occurring as the result of volatility, racialization is quite durable; altering perceptions of group and self for a generation, as seen among Jessica Vasquez' respondents, who rely on memories of the Chicano movement and era-specific discrimination to articulate their identities and racialized views of Latinidad over three decades later.[7]

My second major finding is that the *minority linked fate* that Latinos of the New South express must revise our understanding of interminority relations. Where scholars and others have posited overwhelming conflict and competition between minority groups, in certain contexts, I demonstrate that minority alliances can emerge and find political recognition. This highlights the potential for a sense of shared racial status, intergroup closeness, and political coalitions. In this book, I have theorized the importance of racial and economic status in shaping both positive and negative relationships between racial groups, shedding new light on the relationship between immigration enforcement and race relations, and detailing the unintended political consequences of exclusion.

Specifically, in investigating settlement in a middle-class city, I have shown that minority status is not synonymous with the underclass. Integration into middle-class minority neighborhoods reduces the level of competition between nonwhite groups, who may unite under the umbrella of racialized status. Together, these groups are better able to build positive relationships, as higher economic and political status groups can advocate for those of lower economic and political status, and provide models of mobility and the acquisition of political power as Kathryn Neckerman, Prudence Carter, and Jennifer Lee have suggested.[8] Though the conditions I explored in Winston-Salem are specific, they are far from unique. The rapid spread of immigrants to new destinations suggests that incorporation into diverse middle-class neighborhoods with significant upwardly mobile minority populations is increasingly likely throughout the US, and some of the key conditions described in this book may help forecast future incorporation trends in new destinations, particularly the New South.

In a final focal area, I have worked to reveal how the experiences of Mexican migrants in Winston-Salem teach us that context critically shapes race and race relations and must be taken seriously when analyzing racial formation and intergroup relations. In *Browning of the New South*, I show that two key sets of mechanisms—class and race—operate within broader conditions of contextual change to shape racial formation and intergroup relations. In this case, Latino racialization and intergroup relations with African Americans are the result of conditions producing a sense of dissimilar socioeconomic status but similar racial status. When these conditions do not hold, alternative formulations, such as stronger identification and better relations with whites or competitive relations with blacks, can occur.[9]

The conditions of the labor market, the presence or absence of a stable mi-

nority middle-class (as understood through income, education, and occupation), and perceived access to education and social services by group all shape
class status. To the extent that community conditions promote dissimilar
class status, they can prevent perceptions of resource and labor market competition between minority groups.[10] Shared race status, on the other hand,
is in constant flux, given that the racial formation process is both an outcome and determinant of contextual conditions. Racial status is established
through contact, shaped by neighborhood composition, segregation, shared·
experiences of discrimination, intergroup attitudes, institutional receptivity,
and external threats. To the extent that there is an absence of a longstanding
Latino community, newcomers must look to other racial groups to interpret
their experiences; where Latinos find feelings of discrimination and hostility
from the white majority and support from blacks, a sense of shared racial status between the minority groups is likely to emerge. That is, despite distinct
histories, cultures, and phenotypes, minority groups can be brought together
to articulate individual and group identities through the lens of similar racial
status and marginalization.[11] Their position as minorities and the meaning
of that racial status is not only amplified, but also important in constructing
individual identity and intergroup relations.

The social-scientific literature has long established the importance of socioeconomic status in conditioning intergroup relations, but racial status has
not been adequately theorized as a concomitant process and mechanism that
is essential to shaping intergroup relationships. By racial status, I do not mean
membership in a particular racial group (although certainly, as I highlight in
chapters 3 and 4, these are related); instead, racial status refers to the status
of a population for whom social and economic opportunities may be limited
by the dominant group, resulting in conflict and stratification.[12] It is a form of
social stratification and group position that overlaps with, but is not identical to, economic status.[13] However, as pan-ethnicity scholars show, groupness
based on racialization and discrimination from the state and community can
produce a sense of group solidarity and shared interests among heretofore
disparate groups in a way that economic status rarely does.[14]

Racial groups form relationally, often in response to external treatment
constructing and reconstructing allies and adversaries while building group
consciousness, and through that process, racial status shapes intergroup relations. For the Latinos of Winston-Salem, ascription and identity formation
proceed relationally and dialectically,[15] and local context provides them the
raw materials through which such relations are built. To that end, in order
to make sense of not only racial identity, but also race relations, treating race
as malleable and shifting is necessary in order to understand race appropri-

ately.[16] Race is not merely group membership, but a set of meanings, practices, and identities that are constantly in formation. Moreover, race relations are not the function of dyadic interactions, as much of the literature suggests[17]; we must look not only at relations between multiple groups, but also at the ways in which an outside reference group affects intergroup relations, if we are to produce a more robust analysis of how race works.[18]

So much scholarship essentializes racial differences, assuming static social meanings and hierarchies and frequently treating race and racialized perspectives as uniform, rather than the products of ongoing struggle. In this sense, unpacking within-group variation over racial meanings, identities, and political views is a necessary component in "taking race seriously." For Latinos, whom scholars are often trying to locate in terms of identity, mobility outcomes, and position within broader racial hierarchies, these questions are especially consequential. In terms of black-Latino relations, the expectation is generally that distinct identities, perceptions of racial difference, and minority competition for scarce resources all produce conflict. I find, however, that within the context of Winston-Salem in the 2000s—Mexicans and Mexican Americans instead articulated a different experience and identity, in which they indicated strong positive social relations with blacks and saw themselves as similarly "raced" as Latinos. My respondents' sense of marginalization and discrimination was heightened as the labor market and economy tightened and as the context of reception became more and more "closed." As a result, many Latinos came to see these racialized experiences as a source of commonality, rather than competition, with African Americans in their communities. Their claims to similar status, then, are indicative of the ways in which race is developed and understood relationally, and they served as the basis for *minority linked fate*. Not unlike processes of pan-ethnic and boundary formation,[19] Mexican newcomers engaged in a process of shaping a broader group identity and politics in relation to the identity and politics of a reference racial group with which they were physically and socially close in Winston. Again, I am not making the case here that blacks and Latinos see themselves as part of the same bounded ethnoracial group, but that, in line with Blumer's theory of racial prejudice, both groups are reconceptualizing the relationship between their groups.[20] As discussed in chapter 4, despite distinct histories, cultures, and phenotypes, each recognized their shared, marginalized position within the racial hierarchy.[21] In this way, their position as minorities, and the meaning of that racial status, become not only amplified, but an important set of meanings and reconstructed identities through which they construct intergroup relations.

WINSTON AND BEYOND

The mechanisms at work in this study are broadly applicable and worthy of further exploration, beyond the case of Winston-Salem. In reflecting on previous research conducted in the Southeast, important insights are revealed. In the case of Helen Marrow's Latinos in rural eastern North Carolina,[22] for example, a context of reception perspective revealed hostilities between African Americans and Latinos. In her case, anti-immigration policies had not yet taken effect, demographic changes were less dramatic and less heavily Mexican-origin, and job competition for all Latinos and African Americans in those communities was very high. Moreover, because they were mostly poor and working-class, with little political power, African Americans lacked the community standing to play a role in ameliorating any tensions. In "Bedford" and "Wilcox" counties in 2004, the factors that could lead to shared minority consciousness were not present.

Indeed, various surveys and studies across the US have indicated a spectrum of relations between blacks and Latinos, from conflict and competition[23] to ambivalence,[24] civility and cooperation,[25] and, occasionally, political solidarity.[26] The variation, I argue, can be explained by the distinct constellation of context conditions and the resulting socioeconomic and racial status of the groups engaged intergroup relations. In other words, taking class and race seriously as mechanisms helps explain variation in minority groups' relationships, particularly since those categories are themselves the result of a patchwork of policies, status relations, and conditions that pattern intergroup relations in specific ways. For example, in Marrow,[27] Paula McClain et al.,[28] and others' work, intergroup competition prohibits the emergence of intergroup civility and cooperation. In some cases, these same factors of interminority competition appear to shore up positive relations between Latinos and *whites*. In the works of Rubén Hernández-León and Victor Zúñiga and Jaime Winders,[29] a lack of contact and general isolation from all out-groups spurs ambivalence between Latinos and others. By contrast, Jason Morin, Matt Barreto, and Gabriel Sánchez find that Latino friendships with blacks and high levels of African American density are mitigating factors in conflict, significantly decreasing perceptions of resource competition with blacks.[30]

In another North Carolina case, Vanesa Ribas finds that, at a meatpacking plant, Latin Americans of various national origins come together as Latinos through their shared subordination, but fail to see African Americans as sharing a similar status. Latinos in her study express feelings of competition and resentment toward an elevated status they believe African Americans possess, while African Americans largely see whites as their competitors and regard most Latinos with a range of views from ambivalence, to sympathy, to solidarity. In rejecting models of competitive threat as insufficiently complex to account for the ways in which racialized experiences, relational hierarchies, and linked fate shape intergroup relations, Ribas argues for greater analytical attention to the ways that race, particularly whiteness, works in developing theories of intergroup relations and structuring racial conditions on the factory floor.[31] Similarly, John D. Márquez rejects conflict narratives, arguing that they preserve white dominance and the colonial order. Such frameworks, he writes, fail to sufficiently account for both the ways in which white dominance structures interminority relations and the day-to-day realities of many communities, such as the Houston metro area he studied, in which blacks and Latinos live and work in shared neighborhoods and face similar forms of structural violence, such as police brutality, from the state. Márquez argues that the recognition of such conditions, rather than merely instigate conflict, can inspire black and Latino people to think and act collaboratively on the basis of their shared experiences in shared spaces.[32]

Collectively, these scholars show that attention to how race and class are shaped by community-level change is increasingly important to race and immigration research, as evidence suggests that immigrant incorporation is increasingly local and context specific.[33] In each of these studies, distinct contextual conditions shaped racial meanings and race relations, highlighting the divergence in racialized practices on the ground. I argue that because national patterns of immigrant incorporation have been supplanted by distinctly micro- and meso-level incorporation practices, racial formation, incorporation, and race relations may be best examined through an approach that allows for local variation in making sense of racial hierarchies.

In sum, this book questions assumptions frequently implicit in studies of immigrant incorporation: that blacks and Latinos are always in conflict; that blacks feel threatened by other minority groups; and that newcomers who seek upward mobility always avoid minority status, preferring association with whites. Instead, this study of local-level conditions in Winston-Salem allows us to untangle the factors that shape race and race relations to see how, in certain cases, a *minority linked fate* can emerge.

As was described in chapter 6, we also know that such processes matter not only in terms of identities and meanings, but in terms of the contours of local politics. Marginalized groups do cooperate, often with powerful political results, but the processes that lead to such collaborative frameworks are undertheorized. These alliances also matter because they can shape group identities and meaning, reinforcing the racialization process. This process of meaning-making is at the heart of *minority linked fate*. Intergroup relations, including contact with other racial groups, ascription through marginaliza-tion and discrimination, and a sense of position within the racial hierarchy in which one perceives unequal power dynamics and a sense of threat (or privi-lege), work together to shape one's sense of racial status. In this way, while the "group" that an individual belongs to may not change over time, the meaning of belonging can and frequently does. Minority status is then an additional scale of identity formation, in which similar mechanisms of discrimination and domination produce a sense of closeness with other groups. Race also plays a more complex role in immigrant incorporation than "obstacle" or "co-ethnic resource." Identity and identity strategies matter, too, for politicization, access to resources, political incorporation, and minority mobility strategies, as well as health and well-being. This shared sense of peoplehood is largely understood through a sense of shared interests and status, and therefore is both meaningful and instrumental, creating a position from which coalitions can emerge.

By this logic, race will likely persist as an essential category that structures social relations, but there is no reason to assume that the experiences and practices of groups will remain static over time. Nevertheless, the findings in this study, as well as national-level data, indicate that Latinos, particularly Mexicans and to a lesser extent Central Americans, are increasingly likely to experience and perceive discrimination in way that racializes them as minor-ities. As whites continue to decline demographically, the voices of those expe-riencing a sense of racial threat are likely to grow louder, undermining efforts to build positive relations between whites and racial minorities and provid-ing legitimate motivations for interminority coalitions. As in Winston-Salem, this process may contribute to a growing sense of widespread interminority cooperation and shared status, so long as resource competition remains low.

Because the factors that shape race and race relations are contingent, whether the findings in this study are generalizable or resilient is dependent on the stability of *context*—it is, after all, a study of contextual change spur-ring racial identity re-formation. Thus, while contemporary Latino migrants may have had their racial identities fixed, there is no reason to assume future generations will be shaped by similar experiences. In addition, while Mex-icans continue to dominate migration streams, birth rates, and the Latino population, differences in national origin, immigration status, and class can and do create divisions within the Latino community. In many traditional destinations, where populations may be more diverse along these axes, diver-sity may create long-term obstacles for pan-ethnic unity and political mobi-lization by undermining shared racial status and instigating perceptions of socioeconomic competition and threat.[34] Such variations across context and over time are worthy of theoretical attention and suggest that multiple patterns of racial formation and race relations are likely to unfold through future study.

Where immigrant groups other than Latinos fit into this paradigm is less clear, as they are a much smaller segment of the population, remain highly concentrated in traditional receiving areas, and are not yet key targets for anti-immigrant rhetoric and enforcement. Many nonwhite newcomers arrive either with documentation or as refugees (providing them some, but not complete, shelter from the increasingly racialized discourse of citizenship). Moreover, racial meanings imported from home countries and transnational relationships may create significant obstacles to pan-ethnic unity within the US. Looking toward longstanding special-status populations may provide more clues as to how these groups will become racialized, as well as how they might relate to one another.

Asians present a particularly sticky case, in part because there is such a wide variety of status and human capital within this group, and in part because longstanding international Asian conflicts have created complex inter-ethnic relationships. Pew reports from the 2012 Asian American Survey show that only 19 percent of Asian Americans describe themselves as such (14% describe themselves as American). These numbers rise only slightly among the second generation (to 22% who identify as Asian American and 28% who identify as American), suggesting that time in the US does not appear to be closely related to experiences of shared marginalization across immigrant groups.[35] Relatedly, scholars of pan-ethnicity have found Asian Americans to have relatively weak pan-ethnic ties, and these ties have only occasionally resulted in significant political coalitions.[36]

This is not true of all subgroups, however. Some national origin subgroups have seen their social status shift dramatically in a short period of time, particularly South Asians, who are often perceived in the US as Muslim. Rapid shifts in the political landscape for arguably upwardly mobile Asians such as the Japanese (in the 1940s and 1950s) and Arab Americans (in the 1990s and 2000s) quickly impacted subgroup identity, instigating a shift in favor of a pan-ethnic/racialized designation.

Broadly speaking, Pacific Islanders and Southeast Asians are more likely to be similar to Mexicans in terms of human capital, but are also likely to have protected status as refugees, and therefore may be shielded from some forms of ascription and discrimination. Pew reports that only one-fifth of

Asian Americans report having been treated unfairly in the past year, and just 13% of Asian Americans see discrimination against the group as a major problem.[37] As a group, Asians are highly likely to become upwardly mobile over time, suggesting that the structural and social obstacles they face may not be significant enough to trigger a strong sense of collective racialization. Due to these conditions, I speculate that Asian immigrants as a group are unlikely to develop a strong pan-ethnic identity or strong minority ties across ethnic divides.

Filipinos, however, may present an important exception to this pattern. The third largest origin group within the Asian immigrant population as of 2015, there are signs that Filipinos are more likely to identify as minorities and see minority status as a basis for political action than other Asian origin groups. Filipino organizations, for example, have been visible advocates against immigration enforcement in Los Angeles and are integrated into hip-hop communities in San Francisco.[38] Interestingly, rather than see Asian American as a potentially rich category from which they might build broader solidarity as a result of ascription and discrimination, some Filipinos, as Anthony Ocampo has found, reject Asian identity altogether; they choose to identify with Latinos, drawing on the history of Spanish colonialism to articulate these ties, circumventing the problems of Asian American consolidation and finding alternative ways to assert *minority linked fate*.[39] While Filipinos are highly likely to settle in traditional receiving destinations, their status and patterns of identification suggest that they might behave more like Mexicans in a similar context.

Although the black population in the US continues to diversify, Caribbean immigrants have long represented a key population that has failed to develop close relations with African Americans. As of 2013, 3.8 million or 8.7% of black Americans were foreign born (a number projected to reach 16.5% of the black American population by 2060).[40] To the extent that linked fate arises, it may hinge on the role of race in linking and shaping the experiences of black immigrants. Haitians may be an underexplored exception, particularly because their higher likelihood to be undocumented, increased experiences of discrimination, and lower levels of human capital make it likely that their experiences will be more similar to the Mexicans in this study. Indeed, some scholars have found that Haitians are highly likely to identify as minorities and with African Americans. In South Florida, Alex Stepick and Carol Dutton Stepick note that the context is positive for Cubans, less receptive for Nicaraguans and other Central Americans, and extremely negative at the local, regional, and federal levels for Haitians. As a result, some Haitians go "undercover," passing as African American.[41] In this context, racism pushes the two groups together to provide mutual support—creating a case in which assimilating into the native-born minority group has social, political, and economic advantages.[42] We also know from Waters and others that many distinctions or distancing practices fall away in the second generation, when marginalization due to blackness becomes the dominant frame among those born and raised in the US.[43]

Certainly, variation between groups and contexts is vast. I argue, however, that on-going, qualitative, community-level studies may be particularly well suited to reveal emergent patterns of intergroup relations, specifically among noncitizen populations whose views are not easily captured through political participation data such as voting and political representation.

PATCHWORKS OVER COLOR LINES: RACE IN THE TWENTY-FIRST CENTURY

Throughout the 1990s, scholars and journalists, reflecting on recent demographic trends, asserted that the United States was in the process of an important racial transformation. Herbert Gans entered into this debate in the late 1990s with his piece, "The Possibility of a New Racial Hierarchy in the Twenty-First Century United States," arguing that rather than focus on the new "face" of America, what the US was *really* witnessing was a reconfiguration of racial hierarchies. He wrote that the "the old white/nonwhite dichotomy" would be replaced by a new "black/nonblack" bimodal category, with a third reserve category for groups who do not yet fit into the racial dualism.[44] Gans asserted that while the rules would change slightly—though importantly, not for blacks, who would remain at the bottom—racial binaries would only become further entrenched.

In response to Gans' proposal, a variety of race scholars entered the debate by examining the history of US racial stratification as a historically black-white divide (defined as a white-nonwhite color line) and offering their prediction as to whether that paradigm can hold.[45] While each scholar makes an important contribution to our understanding of race by telling us where the color line will emerge within each of their studies' empirical context, color line theorizing does little to show us *how* the line will be drawn. Moreover, color line research may empirically examine local contexts, acknowledging local variation and distinct factors in producing racialization, but it often treats these as exceptional processes within a national system, rather than key to racialization itself.

I assert, instead, that new racial formation patterns will not be represented by national color lines, but by patchwork quilts of race relations determined by local conditions. These distinct local and regional racial hierarchies are formed, as Jose Antonio Padín writes, "As a result of these new immigration patterns, Latino population enclaves are forming in parts of the United States where 'race relations' have traditionally been defined in black and white. The newcomers are bound to strain, perhaps even precipitate a redefinition, of the dominant black-white axis of racial distinction. The context of immigrant reception along the moving frontier of Latino immigration will be shaped by processes that define the place of these newcomers *in relation to* whites and blacks."[46] Because the configuration of these new frontiers varies dramatically from place to place, I argue that we are better served by moving away from a national-level lens on racial cleavages, and that we should instead foreground the malleability and variation in race relations that shapes racial hierarchies at the local level. To understand the multiple, overlapping patterns at work in the US, research must turn away from the relatively thin framework of national color lines to a subnational or local-level approach, revealing the factors that drive distinct racial regimes rather than emphasizing outcomes alone. In building up from the local, closely examining local and regional patterns and shifts, we develop better theoretical tools for understanding and predicting how race and race relations may change across the US and across the twenty-first century.

Acknowledgments

Book writing is a difficult, long, laborious process, involving, if not blood and sweat, certainly plenty of tears. Of course, while the project belongs to you, it takes nothing short of an army for it to get to the light of day.

I was extremely lucky to have launched this book project while at the University of California, Berkeley. While at Berkeley, I had the great fortune to have numerous colleagues and mentors who have supported me and provided invaluable feedback, guidance, and mental and emotional support along the way. Colleagues Michael Burawoy, Laura Enriquez, and Raka Ray helped me to refine my thinking and develop my skills as a critical ethnographer. Irene Bloemraad and Michael Omi also provided excellent feedback and guidance throughout the data collection process, pushing me to dig deeper whenever I could not make sense of the patterns in front of me. Cybelle Fox was extraordinarily helpful in providing supportive and thoughtful feedback as the chapters of this book took shape. I also had the extraordinary opportunity to participate in the Afro-Latino Working Group, the Sociology Diversity Working Group, the Race Workshop, the Center for Race and Gender, the Center for Latin American Studies, and the Summer Institute for Preparing Future Faculty for the opportunity to workshop my research and move the manuscript into more theoretically rich directions.

I must extend a special thank you to my various writing and thinking partners over the years, especially Kemi Balogun, Hana Brown, Dawn Dow, Marcel Paret, and Petra Rivera-Rideau. Their time, friendship, and feedback have been invaluable. I'd also like to thank colleagues Ruha Benjamin, Nora Broege, Felipe Dias, Trevor Gardner, Shannon Gleeson, Juan Herrera, Margo Mahan, Sarah Anne Minkin, Shaun Ossei-Owusu, Heidy Sarabia, Tamera Stover, and Kara Young for their friendship and intellectual support. A special thank you goes to Hana Brown, Kimberly Hoang, Tianna Paschel, Jennifer Randles, and Leslie Wang, whose support improved not only my research but also preserved my sanity, supporting me not only by providing feedback but also through coffee, happy hours, writing retreats, weekly hikes, skype calls, and emails until the bitter end. They have collectively read draft after draft and memo after memo, and I am eternally grateful to their intellectual engagement over the years. I hope I have been as good a colleague and friend to them as they have been to me.

I owe a debt of quatitude for the development of this book to Sandra Smith, who helped me shepherd this book into being from beginning to end. Sandra showed me what true mentorship is, and provided a model for me to help my future students learn and grow. I cannot thank her enough for her patience, commitment, candor, and friendship. Even when I took one step forward, and then two steps back, Sandra stuck with me, talking me through puzzles at whiteboards, on scratch paper, and over many, many dinners, pushing me further than I thought I could go. I cannot imagine what this process would have been like without her, and I owe much of my success to her.

I also had the incredible fortune to have great colleagues in the sociology department at the Ohio State University, where I had the time and space to conceive of this project as a book and do much of the legwork to propel the manuscript forward. In particular, I benefited from the mentorship of Reanne Frank and Ruth Peterson, and the support of fellow postdoctoral fellows Cassi Pittman and Christi Smith, who were always willing to read drafts and talk shop.

The Browning of the New South really came into being at Notre Dame, where I received nothing but support for this book project. From the first day I set foot on campus and presented my work, Christian Smith offered enthusiastic support of the manuscript. Jessica Collett, Amy Langenkamp, Erin McDonnell, and Elizabeth McClintock invited me into a writing group and offered helpful feedback on chapter drafts, and various other colleagues, including Omar Lizardo, Terry McDonnell, Ricardo Ramirez, and Rory McVeigh, offered valuable feedback on the project at talks, through reading drafts or offering encouraging words of support throughout the book writing process. I also benefited from the extraordinary intellect of the students at Notre Dame. Mary Kate Blake, Eve Bjerre, Ceremontana Crowell, Nancy Diaz, Ethan Johnston, Caroline Sampson, Ryan Schaffler, and Yesenia Vargas, all provided essential support in archiving, coding, and analyzing the newspaper data, as well as reading drafts, searching for evidence, and all kinds of logistical support. I am eternally indebted to them. At the Institute for Latino Studies, I found champions in Luis Fraga and Timothy Matovina, who consistently offered support, the space to present drafts, and opportunities for me to solicit feedback on the manuscript in progress.

Luis Fraga, Tyrone Forman, Cecilia Menjívar, and David Fitzgerald helped me turn the draft into a book, reading the manuscript in its entirety, and providing exceptional detailed critical feedback chapter by chapter, as well useful guidance on developing the contribution of the book as a whole. I cannot thank them enough for their time and support.

I would be remiss to not also thank my wonderful colleagues at the University of Illinois at Chicago, who not only provided me with numerous opportunities to present portions of the manuscript in the Global Migration Working Group, the Latin American and Latino Studies Department, and the Race and Ethnicity Workshop, but also gave me time and space to revise the book in the Department of Latin American and Latino Studies, where I completed most of my manuscript revisions. In particular, I want to thank Xochitl Bada, Tyrone Forman, Amanda Lewis, Amalia Pallares, Andreas Feldmann, Lorena Garcia, and Patrisia Macias-Rojas for their feedback and guidance.

In addition to these wonderful colleagues, many other insightful sociologists have provided thoughtful feedback and conversation throughout the book-writing process, including, but not limited to, Julie Dowling, Hannah Gill, Laura López-Sanders, Helen Marrow, Dina Okamoto, Rashawn Ray, Michael Rodríguez-Muñiz, Wendy Roth, Jody Vallejo, Robert Vargas, and Simon Weffer. A special thank you to Sylvia Zamora and Celia Lacayo, who not only supported me throughout the writing process but inspired me to think differently and more critically about the project from our first conversations. Thank you for helping me to see the forest for the trees and joining me for a drink when I needed it most.

A special thank you also goes to the University of California Creative Connections Writing Retreat Program, organized by Tanya Golash-Boza and Zulema Valdez, who not only developed an extraordinary space for manuscript development, but also fellowship with extraordinary faculty whose support and insight I value tremendously. These include Alicia Cox, Caitlin Patler, Katie Hasson, Whitney Laster-Pirtle, Safiya Umoja Noble, Jemima Pierre, Lila Sharif, Vilna Bashi Treitler, Veronica Terriquez, and France Winddance Twine. I also want to express my gratitude to Kerry Ann Rocquemore, Ray Block, and the National Center for Faculty Development and Diversity for their coaching as I made my way through the manuscript drafting process. The support and motivation I received were essential as I made my final push to complete the book.

I am deeply indebted to my editor, Doug Mitchell, who reminded me first and foremost that I was an author, and supported the project from our first meeting. I was always delighted by Doug's charming notes and his company over lunch or drinks, and cannot thank him enough for embracing my vision for this book. Thanks also to the anonymous reviewers at the University of Chicago Press who carefully read through the entire draft manuscript and provided helpful feedback and support for revision. Thanks also to Letta Page, whose careful editorial feedback tremendously improved the clarity and impact of the manuscript.

I was inspired to write about issues of race, immigration, and politics very early on by my seventh grade history teacher Caitlin Bell, who took me aside one day and told me that she believed I could one day be a Supreme Court Justice if I wanted, and later by my Pomona College mentors and thesis advisors, Pierre Englebert, Phyllis Jackson, Sidney Lemelle, and Heather Williams, who encouraged me to consider an academic career. They may not realize it, but by offering me a summer research position to work on their newest book projects, Eric Klinenberg and Mary Pattillo at Northwestern University introduced me to sociology and changed my life by encouraging me to pursue the questions that motivated me.

I could not have completed this project without the support of graduate and research funding. Special thanks to the National Science Foundation, the UC Center for New Racial Studies, the Berkeley Department of Sociology Lynnea Stephens Memorial Research Grant Program, the University of California Diversity Initiative for Graduate Study in the Social Sciences (UC DIGSSS) Faculty Mentored Research Award Program, the Department of Sociology Research Grant Program, the Center for Race and Gender, and the Abigail Hodgen Publication Award program for their support. Many thanks also to the Wake Forest University Sociology Department, who hosted me as a Visiting Scholar during the field work for this book. Special thanks to Joan Habib, Catherine Harris, and Ian Taplin for their hospitality during my tenure. I am incredibly grateful for the resources provided by the department to conduct my research, as well as the opportunity to present work in progress.

I am very lucky to have a network of support well beyond my academic colleagues. Friends and loved ones have been there for me in the most important ways throughout my academic career. Dear friends Euna Chi, Leah Drew, Lea Mosena, and Katherine Sklarsky, have been rocks of support throughout my life and buoyed me through their confidence in my ability to get this book done. I would be remiss to not also extend a special thank you to Robert Littwin, whose kindness and home-cooked dinners saw me through the end.

I'd like to thank my parents, Patricia Lasley and Keith Jones, grandparents Anna and William Lasley, and sister, Pamela Jones, who, over the years, have helped me with money and moves, listened to my lamenting about progress and getting pale in the library, encouraged me through writing blocks, bragged about me to their friends and acquaintances, fed me dinner, and always treated my efforts as worthwhile, if not downright heroic. I'd also like to express my deep gratitude to my parents for investing in my education, even when we had very little. My mother especially committed to making sure that I had access to the people and institutions that would allow me to flourish, even at great sacrifice. I see now how much easier it would have been to do otherwise, and I am certain I would not have had the same success without those opportunities. My sister has also been a special source of support, never wavering in her belief that I would accomplish all I set out to and expressing real interest and curiosity in the various intellectual rabbit-holes and pathways I often found myself lost in. I am also grateful for the gently prodding questions and steadfast support from family members Richard Lasley, David Lasley, Gloria Lasley, Linda Lasley, Billy Lasley, Virgil Jones, Christina Jones, and Istvan Fekete, who kept me on my toes, invited themselves to mythical future appearances on the Daily Show, and swore me to provide them with signed copies of the book, while also chiding me to make sure it wasn't too boring because they planned to read it. I hope I've met their expectations.

I want to acknowledge the women in my family, who not only have been pillars of strength and caring but also have led by example through a commitment to achievement and independence. In particular, my grandmother, Anna Lasley, throughout her life has been a woman ahead of her time, undeterred by the many doors closed to her and always willing to see things from a new perspective. She has born the brunt of life's challenges with calm and a smile and is generous with her gifts to a fault. I feel especially blessed to be able to be a source of pride and vindication for her.

Finally, this project is, in part, about the ways in which Mexican migrants' experience of immigration enforcement, exclusion, and discrimination terrorizes, inspires fear, and ultimately, changes the way they think about themselves and others. I am eternally grateful to the many men and women who shared their time and their stories with me, both in Mexico and in North Carolina, trusting both that I would relate their stories honestly and carefully and that they would be safe from retribution. Given the difficulties many of them faced in their daily lives, this was no small thing. I hope I have done them justice. Many thanks also to the community members and gatekeepers in my study, who helped me understand the lay of the land, introduced me to the right people, and helped me to see the big picture. This project would not have been possible without them. Through the crafting of this book, I am reminded of the many sacrifices that many people continue to make, and the barriers they face, just to provide their families with food, shelter, and safety. I thank all of those, seen and unseen, who have helped me get here, and hope that my work can play a small role in improving their lives by documenting the costs and unintended consequences of the social and political choices we make every day.

Appendix A. Methodological Note: Race Work and Positionality

So, tell me, where are you from?

B L A N C A , Winston-Salem resident

Social scientists, especially those of us who do qualitative work, must take positionality seriously. How do *we* shape the interactions we seek to observe and the observations we seek to interpret? After all, in his long-lauded treatise on the sociological imagination, C. Wright Mills outlined for us the invisible forces of social membership acting on and within everything, from our structural location to our day-to-day interactions. None of us can be immune, none of us can be objective.[1]

As a person from a mixed-race family, I constantly observe and marvel at my relatives' different experiences of the social world. We share a background, but the hue of our skin affects so much of our actual lives. As Patricia Hill Collins theorizes, women of color like me navigate white and male spaces in which we are acutely aware of outsiderness, of the kinds of practices, behaviors, or code switches needed to signal belonging, or at least, comfort, to those of different backgrounds than ourselves.[2] I often make choices about how I should present myself and whether such shifts are necessary. Is this a person that I need to use a certain kind of language around? Do I need to explain my background differently? Or is this a person who "gets it"— around whom I can be myself? Or do I *choose* to be myself, even when it might make others uncomfortable, because, well, why should I always be the one to adjust? Everyone does this in small ways on a regular basis—we curate our social media presence, we "dress for the job we want" in an interview, we "fake it until we make it." These social practices shape not only our role in the social interaction, but everyone's role. It is a truth of social life that there is no "neutral" interaction. And yet, we desire, as social scientists, to get to some thoughtful, maybe even generalizable understanding of how society works. If we hope to fulfill that desire, we have to take account of our position, use it as a base of knowledge and a lens of understanding, while also still pointing to the broader truths within.

In my research, in which I study race, immigration, politics, and identity through everyday practice, my attention to these issues must be especially acute. In some ways, I attempt to manage this through detailed and rigorous observation and recording. I constantly make notes of race making and race observing that go beyond presumed group membership—including, but not limited to, skin color, language, comfort level, and identity talk. I do this in public settings, where I am just one observer among many, and in small settings and interviews, where the subjects and I are responding to each other directly or in dialogue. I also attempt to triangulate my understanding and analysis through broader and ostensibly more neutral means—using archival research, reports, and newspaper data to understand broad trends and practices of a community over time and space.

However, my position in this study, I believe, surely shaped my findings in, perhaps, unexpected ways. I am a light-skinned African American woman with curly hair. I speak Spanish without a strong national or regional accent, but English is my primary language. My immediate family presents similarly (though I am the only one who speaks Spanish). The result of this bodily presentation is that I am often misread. Frequently, in the US, others assume that I am Puerto Rican, Dominican, or Mexican. On occasion, I have been approached by Spanish-speakers seeking directions or assistance. When I travel, people often conclude that I am an urban resident of whatever country I happen to be in. Often it takes me awhile to perceive this misrecognition because it mostly goes unstated. Most people don't make it a habit of asking you where you are from immediately (though it does happen)—they just draw conclusions based on context. In North Carolina, at the time of my study, few new non-Latinos spoke Spanish. So, many of my Latino respondents presumed I was Latina. Occasionally, people would ask me at the end of an interview, or after several interactions at a church or at various meetings around town, where I was from. Offering "Chicago" as a response was generally unsatisfying; it usually spurred follow-up questions about my parents (being from a diverse major city apparently yields no useful clues). It was only at that point that my respondents expressed surprise that I was African American of mixed ancestry, telling me that they thought I was Mexican, or Dominican, or Puerto Rican. Second generation, perhaps. This occurred more often than not.

These questions came up less often with my African American respondents. Some correctly presumed my racial identity, others weren't sure, and a third group began our interaction under one assumption, then became confused, whether by my interest in immigration or my facility with Spanish, and later arrived at another assumption. Such confusion often led to queries or long explanation about the source of their racial puzzlement. Generally, though, between African Americans and Latinos, each group presumed I was a member of *their* group. White Americans expressed puzzlement, too, but they generally just asked, presuming that I was African American or Latina, but certainly not white.

While I in no way attempted to "pass" or hide my parentage or belonging, code switch or change my attire, alter my accent, or present or hide information that would misinform my respondents, the confusion was a regular occurrence. I can only presume that it impacted my research. In retrospect, I think my positionality in this study was often of that an insider-outsider-insider. That is, I often *believed* myself to be an outsider, not merely due to race, but also citizenship status, and as a Northerner. But to many of my respondents, I was an *insider*, at least as far as race was concerned. To the extent that my race mattered for understanding race relations, I can only surmise that it meant my subjects performed minimal "shielding." That is, respondents, in thinking that I shared *their* racial status, had very little incentive to change their language or hide their views in the ways they might if they thought I was from a different race.

This kind of interaction is not terribly unusual. It is well documented among multiracials and members of mixed race families, who often find themselves in conversations that disparage Asians or African Americans, for example, because it is unknown to the group that they have Asian or African American family members or are of Asian or African American heritage themselves.[3] It is less well understood to what extent this positionality shapes qualitative research. I can say that I believe it, in some ways, lends more reliability and credibility to my observations. In other ways, however, I believe the impossibility of a neutral interaction suggests that this study merely adds another layer to our body of knowledge of how race is formed relationally and what qualitative research, including the positionality of the researchers, can tell us about that process.

Appendix B: Interview Questions

Interview Topics for Mexican Respondents and Other Migrants or Latinos

I am going to begin by asking you a series of questions about your background and your experience with migration.

1. Where are you from originally (country, state, town)?
2. When and how did you come to the United States? Winston-Salem?
3. How did you choose to migrate to Winston-Salem?
4. How long have you lived in the US? In Winston-Salem?
5. Do you have concerns about your documentation status?
6. Have you had any negative or positive experiences as a result of your documentation status?
7. If you do not have documentation, do you plan to obtain documentation, return to Mexico, or migrate elsewhere?
8. Are you married? If so, where is your partner from?
9. Do you have children? If so, were they born in the US?
10. Do you have other family in the US?
11. Do you attend church here in Winston-Salem? Can you describe your church?
12. What race do you belong to in the US? Have you heard of a group of Afro-descendant Mexicans here?

EMPLOYMENT/EDUCATION

Now I am going to ask you a series of questions about your job or school and experiences in the workplace and school.

13. What is your job/profession? Where do you work, or where did you most recently work?

14. How would you describe your experience at your place of work?

15. How would you describe race relations at your place of work?

16. What other jobs have you had since you arrived in the US? Can you describe these work experiences?

17. Can you describe how you got these jobs? Describe the steps.

18. How has the economy impacted you?

19. How do you think race affects you on the job? How do you think it affects your interactions with your employer and coworkers?

20. How do you feel your immigration status impacts your ability to get work? To succeed in the workplace?

21. How do you think Latinos are treated generally on the job? Mexicans? Afro-Mexicans?

22. How do you think Latinos are treated compared to African Americans? Whites?

23. Can you describe what you think employers think of Latino workers?

24. Can you describe what you think African American and/or white workers think of Latino employers?

25. How do you think the work ethic of Latinos compares to African Americans? Compared to whites?

26. What is your education level?

27. Did you attend school in the US? What years? What schools?

28. How do you think race impacted your experience or your children's experience in school, if at all?

29. Are you satisfied with your education level? Why or why not?

30. How do you think Latinos are treated generally in the schools here? Mexicanos? Afro-Mexicanos? Afro-Americanos?

31. How do you think race has impacted your access to opportunity in school or at work?

32. How do you think Latinos are faring in school and the labor market?

33. What do you think about the level of opportunity available to Latinos in Winston-Salem?

34. What do you think about the opportunities available to Latinos here compared to your home town? Compared to other parts of the United States?

COMMUNITY VIEWS

Now I am going to ask you a series of questions about your views and experiences in your community.

35. What neighborhood do you live in and how did you come to live there?

36. What do you think of your neighborhood?

37. Who lives there? (Ages, racial/ethnic groups, types of families)

38. How has the community changed since you arrived, if at all? Why do you think these changes have occurred?

39. Is there anything about your neighborhood or Winston-Salem generally that reminds you of home?

40. How close do you feel toward your neighbors?

41. What conflicts have emerged that you are aware of? Please describe them.

42. How safe do you feel in your neighborhood?

43. Do you feel as though you live in a close community? Please describe why you think that is.

44. If you could move to another neighborhood in Winston-Salem, where would that be? Why?

45. Would you prefer to leave Winston-Salem? Leave North Carolina? Why or why not?

46. I asked you about your church earlier. How does your church or other churches play a role in how Latino immigrants are treated in Winston-Salem, if at all?

RACE QUESTIONS

Now I am going to ask you a series of questions about your views on your own race and identity.

47. How has living in the US and Winston-Salem affected your view of your own racial identity?

48. Do you think that people identify more by their state or nationally by their home country, or as Latinos/Hispanics? Why or why not?

49. What do others (blacks, whites, other Latinos) consider you? Why do they say this? Can you give examples of these experiences?

50. Do people ever misrecognize you or assume you are from a different racial group? Can you give an example of this experience? What do you do in those circumstances?

51. How do you think your family impacts your views about race and race relations?

52. How do you think your gender impacts your views about race and race relations?

53. How do you think African Americans perceive you?

54. How do you think whites perceive you?

55. How do you think Latinos perceive you?

Now I will ask you some questions about your experiences and relationships with other races and ethnicities.

56. How close do you feel to African Americans generally in Winston-Salem?

57. How close do you feel to whites generally in Winston-Salem?

58. How close do you feel to Latinos generally in Winston-Salem?

59. How would you describe your personal relationships with African Americans? Whites? Other Latinos? Afro-Mexicans?

60. How close do you feel generally to whites, Afro-Americans, and other Latinos? To Afro-Mexicans?

61. How would you describe the relationship between whites, African Americans, and Latinos? Examples?

62. Do you feel you have more in common with whites or African Americans? Why?

63. What similarities, if any, exist between African Americans and Afro-Mexicans? How would you describe them? In your opinion, why do these similarities exist?

64. What similarities, if any, exist between African Americans, and Latinos? How would you describe them? In your opinion, why do these similarities exist?

65. How would you describe relations between African Americans and Afro-Mexicans? Can you give me any examples? Afro-Americans and Latinos generally?

66. Under what circumstances do you come into contact with African Americans? Can you describe these interactions?

67. Describe any conflict that you have experienced with African Americans personally, or you have heard of between African Americans and Latinos from friends or relatives.

68. Under what circumstances do you come into contact with whites? Can you describe these interactions?

69. Describe any conflict that you have experienced with whites personally, or you have heard of between whites and Latinos from friends or relatives.

70. Describe any or the most recent experience of discrimination or stereotypes (if any) from African Americans.

71. Describe any or the most recent experience of discrimination or stereotypes (if any) from whites.

72. Describe any or the most recent experience of discrimination or stereotypes (if any) from Latinos.

73. What group do you believe discriminates against you the most? Can you explain why you believe this is the case?

74. Describe any efforts (if any) at mobilization or action for a common cause from African Americans that you have experienced or know of. Any action between whites and Latinos?

75. Describe any efforts at mobilization or action on behalf of Latinos or immigrants from African Americans that you experienced or know of. Any action by whites on behalf of Latinos?

76. How accepted do you feel by other existing racial or ethnic groups other than Latino? Please describe why you feel that way.

77. How would you describe the generational differences in how different races interact?

78. Do you see any interracial dating or marriage? Does it happen often? Between who? How do others in the Afro-Mexican or Latino community respond to interracial dating or marriage?

79. Typically, in the past, people have described race relations in Winston-Salem as whites on top and blacks on the bottom. Do you think that migration has changed the way racial groups are ordered in Winston? How do Latinos fit in? How do Afro-Mexicans fit in?

80. Do you believe that African Americans and Latinos are treated similarly? Please explain why or why not.

81. How do you think race relations in Winston-Salem have changed, if at all?

82. How do you think the level of segregation in Winston-Salem has changed, if at all?

LATINOS AND IMMIGRATION

Now I will ask you a series of questions about Latinos and race relations among Latinos.

83. How would you describe the divisions, if any, in the Latino community? Please describe between whom and give examples.

84. How would you describe the level of closeness in the Latino community?

85. Do you think there are generational differences in how Latinos think about race and race relations? Please explain.

86. How do you think your experience of race is different than other Latinos in the community, if at all?

87. Please describe the differences between Afro-Mexicans and other Latinos.

88. Please describe the similarities and differences between Afro-Mexicans and Dominicans, Puerto Ricans, and Cubans.

89. Are there conflicts between Afro-Mexicans, Dominicans, Puerto Ricans, or Cubans? If so, between who and why?

90. Do you see Latinos as a group becoming more or less politically active? Why do you believe this?

91. How do you think the larger Winston-Salem community views Latino migrants?

92. What differences do you see in how people view Afro-Mexicans compared to other Latino migrants?

Now I will ask you a series of questions about immigration.

93. How do you view new migrants to the community? Are they different than previous migrants or other groups?

94. Why do you think new migrants are coming?

95. How do you feel about the issue of immigration and the changes to the laws here in North Carolina?

96. What, if any, are the divisions in the Latino community around the issue of immigration?

97. Have you had any experiences with ICE or know anyone whose had experiences with ICE? What happened? How do you feel about ICE?

98. How do you feel the change in laws and the issue of immigration impacts your daily life? Please describe.

Now I will ask you a few questions about the local government and institutions here.

99. What are your feelings about the local government and services here? Do you feel you are treated fairly?

100. Do you believe that whites, African Americans, and Latinos are treated equally by the local government?

101. Do you think what happens to African Americans in this country has something to do with what happens in your life?

102. Do you think what happens to whites in this country has something to do with what happens in your life?

103. How do you feel about the state government?

104. Do you believe that whites, African Americans, and Latinos are treated equally by the state government?

105. What do you think of the state government's way of dealing with the immigration issue?

106. How do you feel about the federal government? Has it changed because of the new president?

107. What do you think of the federal government's treatment of Latinos? Its way of dealing with the immigration issue?

108. Do you believe that whites, African Americans, and Latinos are treated equally by the federal government?

109. What do you think WS will look like 5–10 years from now? How will things be for Latinos?

Those are all my questions. Is there anything else you feel I need to know about your experience or the Winston-Salem community?

Interview Topics for Native-Born Community Members, Employers, and Officials

I will begin by asking you some information about your background.

1. What is your educational attainment/occupation?

2. How do you feel about race relations at your place of work?

3. How do you identify racially/ethnically?
4. What do others consider you to be racially? Do people ever misrecognize you?
5. Do you feel closer to certain racial groups than others?
6. How would you describe race relations in Winston-Salem?
7. How do you feel about the community in which you live? Do you feel it has changed in the last 10–15 years due to migration?
8. How do you feel about the schools your children/other family members attend? Do you feel it has changed in the last 10–15 years due to migration?
9. Do you attend a church in Winston-Salem? Do you feel that churches play a role in how Latinos are integrated into the community? Do you feel your church has changed in the last 10–15 years due to migration?
10. Do you see generational differences in how people are identifying racially and interacting with other groups?
11. Do you think your opinions are affected by being a man (woman), or married (single)?
12. What are the major reasons, in your opinion, for conflict or social closeness between racial groups in Winston-Salem?

Now I will ask you some questions about immigration generally.

13. How do you view new migrants to the community? Are they different than previous migrants or other groups?
14. Why do you think they are coming? How do you think they get here?
15. How would you classify them racially?
16. Do you see Latinos as competition or positive contribution in the labor market? Explain.
17. Do you see Latinos as a burden or positive contribution in schools and other institutions? Explain.
18. Are you concerned with immigration? How do you feel about migrants who do not have citizenship?
19. Have you had any interactions with migrants? What are some examples?
20. Do you feel that that community has changed as a result of migration?
21. How do you think whites in Winston-Salem perceive Latinos? African Americans?
22. How do you think the local government treats Latinos? African Americans?
23. Do you think see Latinos as problematic or positive contributors to the community? What do you think of the changes to state law regarding immigrants (access to licenses, community colleges, 287[g])? ICE? What changes do you think need to happen regarding immigration at the local, state, and national level?

Now I will ask you some questions about race and the Winston-Salem community.

24. Do you see differences within the Latino community? Divides? Please describe.
25. Are you aware of the Afro-descendant Mexican community? Do you have a sense of how they are different or similar to other Latinos?
26. Have your views on Latinos/blacks/whites changed as a result of the rise in migration?
27. Do you think having more Latinos affects what people think about their own identity? Racial group?
28. How do you think others (blacks or whites) view migrants?
29. How do you think employers (teachers, health care providers) view migrants?
30. Have you heard of Latino immigrants experiencing discrimination or stereotypes?
31. Have you experienced discrimination or stereotyping from migrants/Latinos? Whites? African Americans?
32. Have you ever heard of or you yourself misrecognized someone thinking they were Latino or not, or a migrant or not? Describe the experience.
33. How do race and ethnic relations in the community impact you in your interpersonal experiences?
34. How do race and ethnic relations impact you in your interactions with employers and coworkers?
35. How do race and ethnic relations impact you in your interactions with schools, government, or other institutions?
36. How do race and ethnic relations impact you at church or in your neighborhood?
37. Do you think what happens to Latinos in this country will have something to do with what happens in your life?
38. Do you feel you have more in common with whites, African Americans, or Latinos? [choose the two other groups]
39. Do you see benefits to being black/white/Latino/other group?
40. How close do you feel to Latinos? African Americans? Whites?
41. How close do you think Latinos are to blacks? Whites?
42. How close do you think Afro-Latinos are to blacks? Whites?
43. Do you see much interracial dating or marriage? Between what groups? Why you think this is (or isn't) occurring?
44. Describe the relationship between Hispanics and blacks; Hispanics and whites; Afro-descendants and blacks; Afro-descendants and whites.
45. Do you think that the three racial groups have been reordered in terms of status here in Winston? How do you think Afro-Mexicans fit in?

Now I will ask you some questions about your work and the community.

46. Can you tell me a little bit about what your organization (business, etc.) does?
47. How do you think immigration has changed your organization?
48. What do you think Winston-Salem will look like 5–10 years from now? For Latinos? For others?

Those are all my questions. Is there anything else you feel I need to know about your experience or the Winston-Salem community?

Appendix C: Key Terms, Organizations, and Policies

American Civil Liberties Union (ACLU): Founded in the early 1920s, the ACLU is a national organization with local chapters that aims to defend and preserve the individual rights and liberties that the Constitution and laws of the United States guarantee. They have several topic areas, including an active immigrant rights program.

The Border Protection, Anti-terrorism, and Illegal Immigration Control Act of 2005 (HR 4437, also known as the Sensenbrenner Bill): The Sensenbrenner Bill was introduced by Representative Jim Sensenbrenner (R-WI) in 2005, and passed the House, but did not pass the Senate. Widely considered the catalyst for the immigration reform protests of 2006, the bill would have built new fences along the border, would have increased border surveillance, and would have made illegal entry a crime, smuggling a federal offense, and knowingly aiding undocumented entry a crime; it included various other forms of border control and enforcement. Some of the more extreme provisions of the bill included a $3000 fine for voluntary removals and a minimum sentence of 10 years for fraudulent documents; also, it would have made it a crime to assist anyone who lacks authority to reside in the US.

Criminal Alien Program (CAP): A program through which ICE agents screen noncitizens who are currently incarcerated in federal and state prisons and local jails for immigration status to determine which noncitizens should be taken into immigration custody for removability. It is the oldest and most extensive enforcement program managed by ICE.[1] CAP was created in response to IRCA. IRCA required the Attorney General, "in the case of an alien who is convicted of an offense which makes the alien subject to deportation . . . [to] begin any deportation proceeding as expeditiously as possible after the date of the conviction." In 1988, the Alien Criminal Apprehension Program (ACAP) and the Institutional Removal Program (IRP) were created. In 2006, ICE consolidated ACAP and IRP into CAP.[2]

Deferred Action for Childhood Arrivals (DACA) Program: An executive order instituted by the Obama administration and rescinded by the Trump administration in 2017, DACA allowed some individuals who arrived in the United States as minors to receive temporary work permits, social security numbers, and driver's licenses, and to receive relief from deportation on a temporary basis that would be eligible for renewal. Qualifications for the program included a birthdate on or after June 16, 1981, and arrival in the country before the age of 16; enrolled in school, completed a GED or high school, or an honorably discharged veteran;

resided in the US continually since 2007; a clean criminal record, and unlawful status in the United States. Estimates indicated that at the time of announcement, 1.7 million residents were eligible and approximately 800,000 DACA permits were granted as of 2016. As of 2018, the legality of ending the DACA by executive order was being challenged in the courts.

Development, Relief and Education of Alien Minors Act (DREAM Act): The DREAM Act is a bipartisan-sponsored bill first introduced in 2001 by Senator Orrin Hatch, but more recently championed by Senator Richard Durbin. The DREAM Act would provide conditional permanent residency for persons between the ages of 12 and 35 who have lived in the US for five consecutive years, and either attended a US high school, completed a GED, or have been accepted to an institution of higher education. Once a person applies and is accepted, they must enroll in a higher degree program or the military, and complete two years either in the military or degree program within six years of the application date. Once 5.5 years have passed, the individual can then apply for legal permanent residency. Passage of the DREAM Act would provide a pathway to legal residency for youth, particularly those who were brought to the US as minors. Advocates of a "clean" DREAM, independent of any other provisions, pushed for passage again in 2018 following the termination of DACA under the Trump administration.

Department of Homeland Security (DHS): The Department of Homeland Security was instituted in 2002 under the Homeland Security Act. In 2003, the agency combined 22 different government agencies, including the Immigration and Naturalization Service (INS), which was renamed and reorganized as Immigration and Customs Enforcement (ICE). The department's official aims are to coordinate agencies in order to prevent terrorism and enhance security, secure and manage US borders, enforce and administer immigration laws, safeguard and secure cyberspace, and ensure resilience to disasters.

Department of Justice (DOJ): Led by the Attorney General, the mission of the Department of Justice is "to enforce the law and defend the interests of the United States according to the law; to ensure public safety against threats foreign and domestic; to provide federal leadership in preventing and controlling crime; to seek just punishment for those guilty of unlawful behavior; and to ensure fair and impartial administration of justice for all Americans." The Department of Justice directs federal criminal prosecutions, including immigration enforcement, through advice provided by the Office of Legal Counsel.

Immigration Act of 1917 (Also known as the Asiatic Barred Zones Act): Extended the Chinese Exclusion Act over President Wilson's veto to exclude immigrants from the continent of Asia. It also excluded the poor, gays and lesbians, those with mental and physical handicaps, and various other "undesirable" persons. A literacy test and medical evaluation was also imposed as a part of this Act.

Immigration Reform and Control Act of 1986 (IRCA) (also known as the Simpson-Mazzoli Act): IRCA amended the Immigration and Nationality Act to improve enforcement and made it illegal to knowingly hire undocumented workers, as well as offered amnesty to continuously residing undocumented immigrants who arrived in the United States before 1982.

Immigration and Customs Enforcement (ICE): Immigration and Customs Enforcement (ICE) is the principal investigative arm of the US Department of Homeland Security (DHS) and the second largest investigative agency in the federal government. Created in 2003 through a merger of the investigative and interior enforcement elements of the US Customs Service and the Immigration and Naturalization Service, it is the federal government's primary immigration enforcement agency.

Immigration and Nationality Act (INA): The INA contains the code governing immigration matters and delegates authority to enforce immigration law. Before 1952, there were various
statutes and codes that governed immigration law, but they were not organized into a single
text. The statute originally passed in 1952 (also known as the McCarran-Walter Act). The
1952 act abolished racial restrictions, but retained national origin quotas and other excludable categories. Since 1953, the INA has been amended several times. The most notable shift
in the INA was in 1965 (also known as the Hart-Cellar Act), which abolished the national
quota system in favor of a family and skills-based system.

Immigration and Naturalization Service (INS): The INS was created in 1933 to manage United
States immigration and naturalization policy. The INS was disbanded in 2003 and most of
its functions were transferred to ICE in 2003.

The Illegal Immigration Reform and Immigrant Responsibility Act of 1996 (IIRIRA): IIRIRA reorganized several provisions for increased border patrols and enforcement and changed
the procedure for deportation, including new rules pertaining to terrorism and national
security. 287(g) was one such provision included in IIRIRA and aimed to address high-level
criminals, particularly human and drug trafficking.

Immigration Reform Protests of 2006: In response to the Sensenbrenner bill and a general lack of
federal response to the call for immigration reform, millions of people across the country,
including significant numbers of undocumented immigrants, particularly Latinos, participated in coordinated demonstrations from March through May 2006 in a peaceful call for
comprehensive immigration form.

Johnson and Reed Act of 1924 (also known as the Immigration Act of 1924): Changed immigration statutes to set quotas for entry for immigrants from various countries who were not
in a non-quota category (the non-quota categories included wives and unmarried children
of US citizens under 18, academics, students under 15, and residents of the Western Hemisphere). Asians continued to be barred, and all nonwhite persons continued to be ineligible
for naturalization under the Naturalization Act of 1790 (the Naturalization Act of 1870 extended citizenship to African Americans, and the 1952 Naturalization Act finally prohibited
gender and racial discrimination). The Act limited the annual number of immigrants from
any country not in the Western Hemisphere to 2% of the number of foreign-born people
already living in the US from that country. The Act was intended to restrict immigration of
Southern and Eastern Europeans. It also effectively restricted Africans and banned Arabs
entirely, alongside existing Asian bans.

Memorandum of Agreement (MOA) under the 287(g) program: An official agreement negoti-
ated by ICE with state or local authorities that delineates the powers and responsibilities of
the latter under the 287(g) program. The Assistant Secretary for Immigration and Customs
Enforcement and certain state or local elected officials in participating jurisdictions (e.g.,
governors, county supervisors, or mayors) must sign the agreements.[3]

North American Free Trade Agreement (NAFTA): A free trade agreement between Canada, the
United States and Mexico, signed on January 1, 1994. All restrictions and duties were phased
out gradually, and were completely phased out by 2008. In 2010, the combined NAFTA
partners of Mexico and Canada purchased over 31 billion dollars in agricultural exports
from the United States. Studies have shown that the policy, while generally good for Mexican economic growth, has been a major source of displacement for small-scale Mexican
farmers who can no longer compete with American grain prices, and contributed signifi-

cantly to growth in migration numbers to the United States in the 1990s, largely from states where migration had previously been uncommon practice.[4]

Proposition 187 (also known as the Save Our State Initiative): Proposition 187 was a voter initiative passed by the voters of California in 1994. This initiative would have barred or restricted immigrant access to a variety of state institutions, including public schools and health care. Virtually all of the provisions of proposition 187 were determined to be unconstitutional, and were never put into force. Many argue that the proposition was intended as a deterrent to immigrants and to register dissatisfaction with the economic pressure on California.

Real ID Act: Enacted in 2005, Real ID (proposed by Representative Sensenbrenner) changed the federal standards for driver's licenses and state-issued identification cards to be accepted by any federal agency. It also had some provisions for asylum and border enforcement. In addition to certain standards for what ID cards must contain, it required that ID applicants show evidence of legal status and social security number. This process makes it illegal for undocumented persons to obtain federally compliant identification and difficult for many visa holders, as well as those who do not already hold government identification. Before Real ID, each state set its own criteria regarding both the issuance of ID cards and what information they contained. Initially set to be effective as of 2008, all 50 states filed for extension, and many states have expressed opposition, including passing legislation against the mandate, with support from organizations such as the ACLU. The federal requirement that states issue driver's licenses only to those who possess a social security number and can demonstrate evidence of legal status was extended to 2013, though a small number of states complied voluntarily shortly after the passage of the law, and have taken a very pro–Real ID stance, including North Carolina. Other states have begun issuing alternative forms of ID and driving permits that are not for federal ID purposes. Department of Homeland Security extended compliance on various aspects of its measures until 2020.

Section 287(g): Section 287(g) is a provision from the IIRIRA that authorizes the federal government to enter into partnerships with state and local law enforcement agencies, which enable the latter to perform certain immigration enforcement standards.[5]

Secure Communities: A program through which ICE uses federal databases to screen the status and previous immigration violations of inmates in state prisons and local jails. Screening is integrated into existing procedures for checking arrestees' fingerprint data against FBI databases for the commission of other federal and state crimes. In participating jurisdictions, prints are automatically forwarded to ICE, and ICE officers notify state and local officials if inmates may be subject to removal.[6]

2002 Department of Justice Memo: In 2002, the Department of Justice issued a memo that affirmed the provisions set forth in 1996 through the 287(g) provision, stating that state and local agents have the authority to arrest undocumented immigrants in violation of federal law. The memo was written by the Office of Legal Counsel and issued by Jay S. Baybee, who also wrote several controversial memos regarding the interrogation of terrorism suspects. This memo has been cited as a roadblock for lawsuits filed by the Department of Justice over the 2010 Arizona legislation, particularly since the Obama administration did not withdraw the memo. In general, the memo is considered an important legal opinion in support of municipal level immigration enforcement.

Notes

Chapter One

1. Toni Morrison, "On the Backs of Blacks," *Time*, December 2, 1993.

2. David R. Roediger, *Working toward Whiteness: How America's Immigrants Became White: The Strange Journey from Ellis Island to the Suburbs* (New York: Basic, 2005); Mary C. Waters, "Ethnic and Racial Identities of Second-Generation Black Immigrants in New York City," *International Migration Review* Special Issue: The New Second Generation. 28, no. 4 (2010): 795–820; Mary C. Waters, Philip Kasinitz, and Asad L. Asad, "Immigrants and African Americans," *Annual Review of Sociology* 40 (2014): 369–90.

3. David Smiley, "McDuffie Riots: Revisiting, Retelling Story—35 Years Later," *Miami Herald*, May 16, 2015, http://www.miamiherald.com/news/local/community/miami-dade/article 21178995.html

4. Isabel Wilkerson, "In Florida, a Death Foretold," *New York Times*, March 31, 2012, http://www.nytimes.com/2012/04/01/opinion/sunday/a-native-caste-society.html

5. Paula D. McClain et al., "Black Americans and Latino Immigrants in a Southern City: Friendly Neighbors or Economic Competitors?" *DuBois Review* 4, no. 1 (2007): 97–117; Helen B. Marrow, "Hispanic Immigration, Black Population Size, and Intergroup Relations in the Rural and Small-Town South," in *New Faces in New Places: The Changing Geography of American Immigration*, ed. Douglas Massey (New York: Russell Sage Foundation Publications, 2008).

6. Samuel Huntington, "The Hispanic Challenge," *Foreign Policy*, October 28, 2009. See also Ari Berman, "The Man behind Trump's Voter-Fraud Obsession," *New York Times*, June 13, 2017, https://www.nytimes.com/2017/06/13/magazine/the-man-behind-trumps-voter-fraud -obsession.html

7. William H. Frey, *Diversity Explosion: How New Racial Demographics Are Remaking America* (Washington, DC: Brookings Institution Press, 2014).

8. Frey, *Diversity Explosion*, 2–4.

9. Leo Ralph Chavez, *The Latino Threat: Constructing Immigrants, Citizens, and the Nation* (Stanford, CA: Stanford University Press, 2008); Otto Santa Ana, *Brown Tide Rising: Metaphors of Latinos in Contemporary American Public Discourse* (Austin: University of Texas Press, 2002).

10. It is also worth noting that significant numbers of Asians and Asian Americans are also settling in the Southeast, further diversifying the Southern population. Frey, *Diversity Explosion*.

11. Eduardo Bonilla-Silva, "From Bi-racial to Tri-racial: Towards a New System of Racial Stratification in the USA," *Ethnic and Racial Studies* 27, no. 6 (2004): 931–50.

12. For more information about the racialization of black Mexicans, see Jennifer Anne Meri Jones, "'Mexicans Will Take the Jobs That Even Blacks Won't Do': An Analysis of Blackness, Regionalism and Invisibility in Contemporary Mexico," *Ethnic and Racial Studies* 36, no. 10 (2013): 1564–81.

13. Brian D. Behnken, "African-American and Latino Activism(s) and Relations: An Introduction," in *Civil Rights and Beyond: African American and Latino/a Activism in the Twentieth-Century United States*, ed. Brian Behnken (Athens: University of Georgia Press, 2016), 1–19; Hannah Gill, "Southern Solidarities: U.S. Civil Rights and Latin American Social Movements in the Nuevo South," in *Civil Rights and Beyond*, 241–62 .

14. Behnken, "African-American and Latino Activism(s) and Relations."

15. It is important to note that I did track observed skin color of my interview respondents to account for correlations in behavior using a skin color scale of 1–10 that approximated the NIS color scale, which uses hands to approximate a range of skin tones from light to dark, developed by Doug Massey et al. While I did observe significant variation in skin color, I did not note significant differences by skin color in terms of racial language, whether or not an individual indicated high levels of closeness to African Americans, or whether they identified as Latino. The one exception to this was that those who were darker skinned and Afro-descendant were more likely make additional claims to familiarity and shared culture with African Americans, though not exclusively. White or light-skinned individuals, however, were no more or less likely to claim high levels of affinity with and similarity to African Americans relative to other Latinos.

16. See Desiree Evans, "The Hands behind the Turkey," The Institute for Southern Studies, November 25, 2008, http://www.southernstudies.org/2008/11/the-hands-behind-the-turkey .html

17. The 287(g) program, one of the initiatives of the US Immigration and Customs Enforcement (ICE) activated under the 1996 immigration reforms, allows a state and local law enforcement entity to enter into a partnership with ICE, under a joint Memorandum of Agreement (MOA). The state or local entity receives delegated authority for immigration enforcement within their jurisdictions.

18. HB 56, or the Beason-Hammon Alabama Taxpayer and Citizen Protection Act, was passed in 2011 and earned the distinction of the strictest anti-immigrant bill in the country, modeled after Arizona's SB1070 law.

19. Geena Jackson, "Congressional Members to Join Civil Rights Groups in Fight Against Alabama's 'Juan Crow' Law," ImmigrationImpact.com, accessed November 3, 2011, http:// immigrationimpact.com/2011/11/03/congressional-members-to-join-civil-rights-groups-in -fight-against-alabama%E2%80%99s-%E2%80%9Cjuan-crow%E2%80%9D-law/

20. See, for example, Helen B. Marrow, "New Immigrant Destinations and the American Colour Line," *Ethnic and Racial Studies* 32 (2009): 1037–57; Marrow, "Hispanic Immigration, Black Population Size, and Intergroup Relations in the Rural and Small-Town South"; McClain et al., "Black Americans and Latino Immigrants in a Southern City"; Paula D. McClain, "Racial Intergroup Relations in a Set of Cities: A Twenty-Year Perspective," *Journal of Politics* 68, no. 4 (2006): 757–70; Nick Corona Vaca, *The Presumed Alliance: The Unspoken Conflict between Latinos and Blacks and What It Means for America* (New York: Rayo, 2004).

21. Moon-Kie Jung, "The Racial Unconscious of Assimilation Theory," *Du Bois Review* 6, no. 2 (2009): 375–95.

22. Zandria F. Robinson, *This Ain't Chicago: Race, Class, and Regional Identity in the Post-Soul South* (Chapel Hill: University of North Carolina Press, 2014).

23. Robinson, *This Ain't Chicago*, 31.

24. Moon-Kie Jung, *Reworking Race: The Making of Hawaii's Interracial Labor Movement* (New York: Columbia University Press, 2010), 3.

25. Jung, "The Racial Unconscious of Assimilation Theory," 375.

26. Victoria Hattam, *In the Shadow of Race: Jews, Latinos, and Immigrant Politics in the United States* (Chicago: University of Chicago Press, 2007).

27. Hana Brown and Jennifer A. Jones, "Rethinking Panethnicity and the Race-Immigration Divide," *Sociology of Race and Ethnicity* 1, no. 1 (2015): 181–91.

28. Milton Myron Gordon, *Assimilation in American Life: The Role of Race, Religion, and National Origins* (New York: Oxford University Press, 1964); Robert Ezra Park, *Race and Culture* (Glencoe, IL: Free Press, 1950).

29. For a review of the assimilation and incorporation literature, see Rafæl Alarcón, Luis Escala, Olga Odgers, and Roger Waldinger, *Making Los Angeles Home: The Integration of Mexican Immigrants in the United States*, trans. Dick Cluster (Oakland: University of California Press, 2016), 34–57.

30. James Barrett and David Roediger, "In-Between Peoples: Race, Nationality, and the 'New Immigrant' Working Class," *Journal of American Ethnic History* 25, no. 2/3 (1997): 33–47; Karen Brodkin Sacks, *How Jews Became White Folks and What That Says about Race in America* (New Brunswick, NJ: Rutgers University Press, 1998); Matthew Frye Jacobson, *Whiteness of a Different Color: European Immigrants and the Alchemy of Race* (Cambridge, MA: Harvard University Press, 1998); Noel Ignatiev, *How the Irish Became White* (New York: Routledge, 1995); Peter Kolchin, "Whiteness Studies: The New History of Race in America," *Journal of American History* 89 (2002): 154–73; David R. Roediger, *The Wages of Whiteness: Race and the Making of the American Working Class* (London: Verso, 1991); Roediger, *Working toward Whiteness*.

31. Marrow, "New Immigrant Destinations and the American Colour Line"; Alejandro Portes and Min Zhou, "The New Second Generation: Segmented Assimilation and Its Variants," *Annals of the American Academy of Political and Social Science* 530 (1993): 74–96; Rubén G. Rumbaut, "The Crucible Within: Ethnic Identity, Self-Esteem and Segmented Assimilation among Children of Immigrants," *International Migration Review* 28 (1994): 748–94; Mary C. Waters, *Black Identities: West Indian Immigrant Dreams and American Realities* (Cambridge, MA: Harvard University Press, 1999).

32. But see Vilna Treitler, who conceives of these practices as ethnic projects, with varying degrees of success. Vilna Bashi Treitler, *The Ethnic Project: Transforming Racial Fiction into Ethnic Factions* (Stanford, CA: Stanford University Press, 2013).

33. Portes and Zhou, "The New Second Generation"; Rumbaut, "The Crucible Within"; Scott J. South, Kyle Crowder, and Erick Chavez, "Migration and Spatial Assimilation among U.S. Latinos: Classical versus Segmented Trajectories," *Demography* 42, no. 3 (2005): 497–521; Waters, *Black Identities*; Min Zhou, "Segmented Assimilation: Issues, Controversies, and Recent Research on the New Second Generation," *International Migration Review* 31, no. 4 (1997): 975–1008.

34. Portes and Zhou, "The New Second Generation"; Zhou, "Segmented Assimilation."

35. Portes and Zhou, "The New Second Generation," 82.

36. Waters, *Black Identities*; Philip Kasinitz, *Caribbean New York: Black Immigrants and the Politics of Race* (Ithaca: Cornell University Press, 1992).

37. Waters, *Black Identities*; Roy Simon Bryce-Laporte, "Black Immigrants: The Experience of Invisibility and Inequality," *Journal of Black Studies* 3, no. 1 (1972): 29–56.

38. Treitler, *The Ethnic Project*. Importantly, Treitler argues that ethnic formation is a func-

tion of racialization. That is, all ethnic groups are initially racialized. Because racialization cannot be avoided, she argues, groups must collectively engage it. "In their response to ethnoracialization—a process that has most new ethnic groups enter at the bottom of the hierarchy—a group likely chooses to recreate their ethnicity in a way that can serve as a counterweight to the severely limiting racial characterizations they are assigned." Treitler, *The Ethnic Project*, 10.

39. Alejandro Portes and Rubén Rumbaut, *Immigrant America: A Portrait* (Berkeley: University of California Press, 1996); Alejandro Portes and Alex Stepick, *City on the Edge: The Transformation of Miami* (Berkeley: University of California Press, 1993).

40. Milton Vickerman, *Crosscurrents: West Indian Immigrants and Race* (New York: Oxford University Press, 1999); Kasinitz, *Caribbean New York*; Constance Sutton and Susan Makiesky-Barrow, "Migration and West Indian Racial and Ethnic Consciousness," in *Migration and Development: Implications for Ethnic Identity and Political Conflict*, ed. H. Safa and B. du Toit (Paris: Mouton, 1975), 113–44.

41. Alex Stepick and Carol Dutton Stepick, "Diverse Contexts of Reception and Feelings of Belonging," *Forum: Qualitative Social Research* 10, no. 3 (2009): 13.

42. Philip Kasinitz, John Mollenkopf, Mary C. Waters, and Jennifer Holdaway, *Inheriting the City: The Children of Immigrants Come of Age* (New York: Russell Sage Foundation, 2008).

43. Kathryn M. Neckerman, Prudence Carter, and Jennifer Lee, "Segmented Assimilation and Minority Cultures of Mobility," *Ethnic and Racial Studies* 22, no. 6 (1999): 945–65.

44. Neckerman, Carter, and Lee, "Segmented Assimilation and Minority Cultures of Mobility," 949.

45. Joel Perlmann and Roger Waldinger, "Second Generation Decline? Children of Immigrants, Past and Present- A Reconsideration," *International Migration Review* 31, no. 4 (1997): 893–922.

46. Robert Courtney Smith, "Black Mexicans, Conjunctural Ethnicity, and Operating Identities: Long-Term Ethnographic Analysis," *American Sociological Review* 79, no. 3 (2014): 517–48.

47. Smith, "Black Mexicans, Conjunctural Ethnicity, and Operating Identities"; Perlmann and Waldinger, "Second Generation Decline?"

48. Julie A. Dowling, *Mexican Americans and the Question of Race* (Austin: University of Texas Press, 2014).

49. Dowling, *Mexican Americans and the Question of Race*, 26.

50. Dowling, *Mexican Americans and the Question of Race*, 23.

51. G. Cristina Mora, "Cross-Field Effects and Ethnic Classification: The Institutionalization of Hispanic Panethnicity, 1965 to 1990," *American Sociological Review* 79, no. 2 (2014): 183–210.

52. Neil Foley, *Quest for Equality: The Failed Promise of Black-Brown Solidarity* (Cambridge, MA: Harvard University Press, 2010); Edward Eric Telles and Vilma Ortiz, *Generations of Exclusion: Mexican Americans, Assimilation, and Race* (New York: Russell Sage Foundation, 2008).

53. Dowling, *Mexican Americans and the Question of Race*.

54. Foley, *Quest for Equality*.

55. See Tomás Almaguer, *Racial Fault Lines: The Historical Origins of White Supremacy in California* (Berkeley: University of California Press, 2008 [1994]); Dowling, *Mexican Americans and the Question of Race*; Martha Menchaca, *Recovering History, Constructing Race: The Indian, Black, and White Roots of Mexican Americans* (Austin: University of Texas Press, 2001).

56. Treitler, *The Ethnic Project*.

57. Carleen Basler, "White Dreams and Red Votes: Mexican Americans and the Lure of Inclusion in the Republican Party," *Ethnic and Racial Studies* 31, no. 1 (2008): 123–66; William A.

Darity Jr., Jason Dietrich, and Darrick Hamilton, "Bleach in the Rainbow: Latin Ethnicity and Preference for Whiteness," *Transforming Anthropology* 13, no. 2 (2005): 103–9; Reanne Frank, Ilana Redstone Akresh, and Bo Lu, "Latino Immigrants and the U.S. Racial Order," *American Sociological Review* 75, no. 3 (2010): 378–401; Herbert J. Gans, "The Possibility of a New Racial Hierarchy in the Twenty-First Century United States," in *The Cultural Territories of Race: Black and White Boundaries,* ed. Michelle Lamont (Chicago: University of Chicago Press, 1999), 371–79; Marrow, "Hispanic Immigration, Black Population Size, and Intergroup Relations in the Rural and Small-Town South."

58. Nate Cohen, "More Hispanics Declaring Themselves White," *New York Times,* May 21, 2014. Importantly, however, few studies have examined exactly what it means to identify as white on the census. See Dowling, *Mexican Americans and the Question of Race,* for an in-depth analysis of this question.

59. Similar questions have also been raised regarding Asian Americans, although their relatively small proportion of the population limits the broad reach of such discourse. See Yen Le Espiritu, *Asian American Panethnicity: Bridging Institutions and Identities* (Philadelphia: Temple University Press, 1992); and Dina G. Okamoto, *Redefining Race: Asian American Panethnicity and Shifting Ethnic Boundaries* (New York: Russell Sage Foundation, 2014), for a discussion of pan-ethnic formation and group identity among Asian Americans.

60. Basler, "White Dreams and Red Votes."

61. Frank et al., "Latino Immigrants and the U.S. Racial Order."

62. Gans, "The Possibility of a New Racial Hierarchy in the Twenty-First Century United States"; Jennifer Lee and Frank D. Bean, "Redrawing the Color Line?" *City & Community* 6 (2007): 49–62.

63. Frank et al., "Latino Immigrants and the U.S. Racial Order."

64. Néstor Rodríguez, "New Southern Neighbors: Latino Immigration and Prospects for Intergroup Relations between African-Americans and Latinos in the South," *Latino Studies* 10, no. 1–2 (2012): 18–40.

65. Audrey Singer, *The New Geography of United States Immigration,* Brookings Immigration Series, vol. 3 (Washington, DC: Brookings Institution, 2009).

66. Jeffrey S. Passel and D'Vera Cohn, *Unauthorized Immigrant Population: National and State Trends, 2010* (Washington, DC: Pew Hispanic Center, 2011). The number of unauthorized migrants declined only 8% from 2007 to 2011 despite massive immigration enforcement efforts and a nationwide recession (Passel and Cohn, *Unauthorized Immigrant Population*). More surprisingly, the number of unauthorized Mexicans declined only slightly to 6.5 million in 2010, a much smaller reduction than anticipated despite a doubling of removals and significant shrinking of the economy.

67. As of 2000, 54% of Latinos resided in the suburbs, a 71% increase in the number of Latinos living there. See Roberto Suro, Audrey Singer, Brookings Institution, Center on Urban and Metropolitan Policy, and Pew Hispanic Center, "Latino Growth in Metropolitan America: Changing Patterns, New Locations" (Washington, DC: Brookings Institution, Center on Urban and Metropolitan Policy in collaboration with the Pew Hispanic Center, 2002). In 2007, just 34% of the foreign-born resided in the primary cities of the top 100 metropolitan areas, indicating a massive change in the lifestyles of immigrant Latinos in the United States. See Singer, *The New Geography of United States Immigration.*

68. William H. Frey, *Analysis of US Census Bureau Population Estimates* (Washington, DC: Brookings Institution Press, June 2013).

69. Waters et al., "Immigrants and African Americans," 376.

70. Rakesh Kochhar, Roberto Suro, and Sonya Tafoya, "The New Latino South: The Context and Consequences of Rapid Population Growth," Pew Research Center (Washington, DC: Pew Research Center, 2005).

71. Kochhar, Suro, and Tafoya, "The New Latino South," iii.

72. Suro et al., *Latino Growth in Metropolitan America.*

73. While approximately 40% of Latinos in the state are authorized or citizens, that number is skewed toward children, who represent a much more significant share of the legal resident and citizen population.

74. Passel and Cohn, *Unauthorized Immigrant Population.*

75. Kochhar, Suro, and Tafoya, "The New Latino South"; Ivan Light, "Coming Soon to Your Community: Why Mexican Immigrants Now Seek the American Heartland," *Applied Research in Economic Development* 5 (May 2008): 15–22.

76. Marrow, "New Immigrant Destinations and the American Colour Line"; Marrow, "Hispanic Immigration, Black Population Size, and Intergroup Relations in the Rural and Small-Town South"; McClain et al., "Black Americans and Latino Immigrants in a Southern City"; McClain, "Racial Intergroup Relations in a Set of Cities"; Nick Corona Vaca, *The Presumed Alliance: The Unspoken Conflict between Latinos and Blacks and What it Means for America* (New York: Rayo, 2004).

77. National Conference of State Legislatures, "Immigration," accessed July 27, 2014, http://www.ncsl.org/research/immigration.aspx

78. Jamie Winders, "Re-Placing Southern Geographies: The Role of Latino Migration in Transforming the South, Its Identities, and Its Study," *Southeastern Geographer* 51, no. 2 (2011): 342–58.

79. In Mississippi, the black legislative caucus has been very successful in blocking over 285 punitive bills targeting immigrants in the state. With the exception of an e-verify bill that went unfunded, no efforts at excluding immigrants have been successful in the state. See Hana Brown, Jennifer Jones, and Taylor Dow, "Unity in the Struggle: Immigration and the South's Emerging Civil Rights Consensus," *Law and Contemporary Problems* 79 (2016): 5–27.

80. Waters et al., "Immigrants and African Americans."

81. Arthur D. Murphy, Colleen Blanchard, and Jennifer A. Hill, *Latino Workers in the Contemporary South* (Athens: University of Georgia Press, 2001); Heather Smith and Owen Furuseth, *Latinos in the New South: Transformations of Place* (Burlington: Ashgate, 2006); Leon Fink and Alvis E. Dunn, *The Maya of Morganton: Work and Community in the Nuevo New South* (Chapel Hill: University of North Carolina Press, 2003); Víctor Zúñiga and Rubén Hernández-León, eds., *New Destinations: Mexican Immigration in the United States* (New York: Russell Sage Foundation, 2005).

82. Rodríguez in particular points to the importance of immigration patterns, workplace dynamics, enforcement strategies, and residential segregation in local context in shaping interminority relations. See Rodríguez, "New Southern Neighbors."

83. Marrow, "Hispanic Immigration, Black Population Size, and Intergroup Relations in the Rural and Small-Town South"; Mary E. Odem and Elaine Cantrell Lacy, eds., *Latino Immigrants and the Transformation of the U.S. South* (Athens: University of Georgia Press, 2009).

84. Cameron D. Lippard and Charles A. Gallagher, *Being Brown in Dixie: Race, Ethnicity, and Latino Immigration in the New South* (Boulder, CO: First Forum, 2011); Roberto Lovato, "Juan Crow in Georgia: Immigrant Latinos Live under a Matrix of Oppressive Laws, Customs

and Institutions," *Nation*, May 8, 2008, http://www.thenation.com/doc/20080526/lovato/; Odem and Lacy, *Latino Immigrants and the Transformation of the U.S. South.*

85. See also Tatcho Mindola Jr., Yolanda Flores Niemann, and Néstor-Rodríguez, *Black-Brown Relations and Stereotypes* (Austin: University of Texas Press, 2003), which examines black-brown relations and the potential for conflict and cooperation in the case of Houston in the 1990s, a Southern, though not Southeastern, city that experienced massive growth in the Latino population in the 1980s and 1990s (Latinos outnumbered African Americans for the first time in 2000), ahead of other metro areas in the region.

86. Angela C. Stuesse, "Race, Migration, and Labor Control: Neoliberal Challenges to Organizing Mississippi's Poultry Workers," in *Latino Immigrants and the Transformation of the U.S. South*, ed. Mary E. Odem and Elaine Cantrell Lacy (Athens: University of Georgia Press, 2009); Angela Stuesse, *Scratching Out a Living: Latinos, Race, and Work in the Deep South* (Oakland: University of California Press, 2016).

87. Despite this assertion by African Americans, Stuesse argues that whites' provisional acceptance of some Latinos and positioning of Latino immigrants as hard workers locates them in an intermediary position between black and white. See Stuesse, *Scratching Out a Living*, 116–19.

88. Vanesa Ribas, *On the Line: Slaughterhouse Lives and the Making of the New South* (Oakland: University of California Press, 2016).

89. Natalia Deeb-Sossa, *Doing Good: Racial Tensions and Workplace Inequalities at a Community Clinic in El Nuevo South* (Tucson: University of Arizona Press, 2013).

90. Raymond A. Mohl, "Globalization, Latinization, and the Nuevo New South," *Journal of American Ethnic History* 22, no. 4 (2003): 31–66; Zúñiga and Hernández-León, *New Destinations*. There is a long history of stirring up racial animosity between working-class whites and nonwhites through the labor market throughout the United States, where, especially in manufacturing centers, immigrants and African Americans were brought in to undercut labor costs or break strikes.

91. Jamie Winders, *Nashville in the New Millennium: Immigrant Settlement, Urban Transformation, and Social Belonging* (New York: Russell Sage Foundation, 2013).

92. Charlie LeDuff, "At a Slaughterhouse, Some Things Never Die," *New York Times*, June 16, 2000, http://www.nytimes.com/2000/06/16/us/slaughterhouse-some-things-never-die-who-kills-who-cuts-who-bosses-can-depend.html; Mohl, "Globalization, Latinization, and the Nuevo New South."

93. Elaine C. Lacy, "Integrating into New Communities: The Latino Perspective," in *Being Brown in Dixie: Race, Ethnicity and Latino Immigration in the New South*, ed. Cameron D. Lippard and Charles A. Gallagher (Boulder, CO: First Forum, 2011), 115–32.

94. Brian L. Rich and Marta Miranda, "The Sociopolitical Dynamics of Mexican Immigration in Lexington, Kentucky, 1997 to 2002: An Ambivalent Community Responds," in *New Destinations: Mexican Immigration in the United States*, ed. Victor Zúñiga and Rubén Hernández-León (New York: Russell Sage Foundation, 2005), 187–219.

95. Laura López-Sanders, "Trapped at the Bottom: Racialized and Gendered Labor Queues in New Immigrant Destinations," unpublished manuscript, 2009.

96. Helen B. Marrow, *New Destination Dreaming: Immigration, Race, and Legal Status in the Rural American South* (Stanford, CA: Stanford University Press, 2011).

97. Although quantitative analyses do not seem to show this competition, finding instead few negative economic consequences of Latino migration for non-Latinos. Waters et al., "Immigrants and African Americans," 380.

98. But see John Hagan, Carla Shedd, and Monique Payne, "Race, Ethnicity, and Youth Perceptions of Criminal Injustice," *American Sociological Review* 70 (2005): 381–407; Alejandro Portes, "The Economics of Immigration," *Contemporary Sociology* 19 (November 1990): 853–55; Michael Jones-Correa and Diana Hernàndez, "Commonalities, Competition and Linked Fate: On Latino Immigrants in New and Traditional Receiving Areas," paper presented to American Sociological Association Annual Meeting, New York, New York, August 11–14, 2007.

99. Dowling, *Mexican Americans and the Question of Race.*

100. A brief definitional note: Throughout the book, I refer to both Latinos and Mexicans. It is generally the case that most Latinos in Winston-Salem, though not all, are of Mexican origin. However, it is also the case that this group overwhelmingly understands and refers to itself as Latinos. They use this term in addition to the national origin label of Mexican and Mexican American to describe their identities and experiences in the US as racialized and pan-ethnic. Throughout the text, I follow their lead, using both terms according to the loose and yet overlapping distinctions made by my respondents.

101. While workplaces are often excellent sites for studying intergroup dynamics, I declined to observe workplaces largely because blacks and Latinos did not frequently work together, with the exception of construction fields. In addition, this would provide little class variation, and would overwhelmingly bias subjects to socioeconomic competition. At the time of study, workplaces were also highly volatile settings for immigrants, as workplaces are also key sites for immigration raids and policing.

102. It is also worth noting that both churches and unions share (in the contemporary moment) a kind of multiracial logic that is built into the ethos of the space, particularly in terms of coalition building and political organizing. At the same time, both institutional spaces have had a long history of division and racial acrimony, often undermining their larger social goals. Such positioning makes churches a potentially useful alternative space to examine interracial relations in the absence of unions and the presence of high levels of workplace fear.

103. 84 percent of Latinos are Catholic, Protestant, or other Christian, compared to 85 percent of blacks. Blacks are the most likely to report a formal religious affiliation, followed by Latinos. See Pew Survey Center, "U.S. Religious Landscape Study: Religious Affiliation Diverse and Dynamic" (Washington, DC: Pew Forum on Religious and Public Life, February 2008).

104. While workplaces and other institutions are also potentially important places for interaction and organizing, focusing on them exclusively can overemphasize the role of resource distribution in shaping relations.

105. It is important to note that in many new immigrant destinations, the Mexican immigrant population also includes significant proportions of indigenous migrants, many of whom speak no Spanish. This was not my observation in Winston-Salem, but nevertheless points to the heterogeneity of the Latino population, even when hailing from the same national or even regional background.

106. Recent research indicates that skin color impacts Latinos' affinities with blacks and whites, with darker-skinned Mexicans in particular identifying more closely to blacks. (See Wilkerson, "In Florida, a Death Foretold.") Mexicans in this study represented a wide range of skin tone (as observed by the author), but no differences in reporting affinities by skin tone were detected.

107. While Mexican immigrants and Mexican Americans show significant educational mobility in the United States, they enter the US at a significant disadvantage. According to Organization for Economic Cooperation and Development (OECD) statistics, in 2012 only 37% of

Mexican adults have completed schooling beyond the 10th grade. See Grace Kao and Jennifer S. Thompson, "Racial and Ethnic Stratification in Educational Achievement and Attainment," *Annual Review of Sociology* 29, no. 1 (2003): 417–42; Jennifer Lee and Min Zhou, *The Asian American Achievement Paradox* (New York: Russell Sage Foundation, 2015); OECD, *Education at a Glance 2014: OECD Indicators* (Paris: OECD, 2014), http://dx.doi.org/10.1787/eag-2014-en

108. Studies indicate that approximately 42 percent of Latinos in North Carolina lack legal status. See Hannah Gill, *The Latino Migration Experience in North Carolina: New Roots in the Old North State* (Chapel Hill: University of North Carolina Press, 2010).

109. After dropping irrelevant articles, the archive of *Winston-Salem Journal* articles totaled 2554.

Chapter Two

1. Langdon Oppermann, *Winston-Salem's African-American Neighborhoods: 1870–1950* (Winston-Salem, NC: Architectural and Planning Report, 1994), 19.

2. Robinson, *This Ain't Chicago*, 95.

3. This included the recruitment not only of Mexicans, but also of Chinese and Italian immigrants, especially in the Mississippi Delta. Most workers did not stay, however, unwilling to tolerate the abusive working conditions of agricultural labor through the turn of the twentieth century. Julie M. Weise, *Corazón de Dixie: Mexicanos in the U.S. South since 1910* (Chapel Hill: University of North Carolina Press, 2015); James W. Loewen, *The Mississippi Chinese: Between Black and White*, 2nd ed. (Long Grove, IL: Waveland, 1988).

4. Importantly, the Bracero program not only outlined minimum wages and living conditions, but exempted Braceros from racial discrimination, such as formal segregation practices.

5. Douglas S. Massey, *New Faces in New Places: The Changing Geography of American Immigration* (New York: Russell Sage Foundation, 2008); Audrey Singer, Susan Wiley Hardwick, and Caroline B. Brettell, *Twenty-First-Century Gateways: Immigrant Incorporation in Suburban America* (Washington, DC: Brookings Institution Press, 2009).

6. Kochhar, Suro, and Tafoya, "The New Latino South," i.

7. Kochhar, Suro, and Tafoya, "The New Latino South," i.

8. Kochhar, Suro, and Tafoya, "The New Latino South," i.

9. This is an increase of about 30,000 since the 2000 census, due in large part to suburban annexation. The mayor believes that this still is an undercount, and estimates the population at around 225,000.

10. The top cities in population are Charlotte, Raleigh, Greensboro, and Durham. Fayetteville is the only other city in North Carolina with a population above 100,000.

11. It should be noted that *bucolic* has been a reviled descriptor in Winston-Salem due to F. Ross Johnston's description of Winston-Salem as "bucolic" and therefore inadequately urban for the young professionals that worked at his company, RJ Reynolds-Nabisco. Johnston moved the company's headquarters to Atlanta soon after.

12. For a discussion of the importance of analyzing local contexts and moving beyond methodological nationalism in evaluating immigration politics, see Mark Ellis, "Unsettling Immigrant Geographies: US Immigration and the Politics of Scale," *Tijdschrift Voor Economische En Sociale Geografie* 97, no. 1 (2006): 49–58.

13. US Census Bureau, "Money Income in the United States: 2000," Current Population Reports (Washington, DC: US Census Bureau, 2000).

14. According to the 2000 census, approximately 21.2% of Hispanic households were below the poverty line. J. Dalaker, US Census Bureau, Current Population Reports, Series P60-214, *Poverty in the United States: 2000* (Washington, DC: US Government Printing Office, 2001).

15. The Council for Community and Economic Research, "Cost of Living Index, Annual Average 2010," C2ER (Arlington, VA: ACCRA, 2010), accessed December 1, 2017, https://www2 .census.gov/library/publications/2011/compendia/statab/131ed/tables/12s0728.xls; United States Census Bureau, "Cost of Living Index—Selected Metropolitan Areas: Fourth Quarter 2005" (Washington, DC: US Census Bureau, 2005), accessed December 1, 2017, https://www.census .gov/search-results.html?page=1&stateGeo=&searchtype=web&cssp=&q=cost+of+living +index+2005&search.x=0&search.y=0&search=submit

16. Moravians are a small but mainline denomination of Protestants, affiliated in the United States with the Evangelical Lutheran Church of America. They were one of the first denominations to engage in missionary work. They also favored a communal style of living and work, favoring prayer and simplicity, and thus garnering comparisons to the Quakers.

17. Oppermann, *Winston-Salem's African-American Neighborhoods*, 11.

18. Frank V. Tursi, *Winston-Salem: A History* (Winston-Salem: John F. Blair, 1994).

19. Salem College website, accessed December 1, 2017, http://www.salem.edu/about/our -history

20. Cheryl Streeter Harry, *Winston-Salem's African American Legacy* (Charleston: Arcadia, 2012).

21. This was followed shortly thereafter by the establishment of the North Carolina School of the Arts in 1963.

22. Robert Rodgers Korstad, *Civil Rights Unionism: Tobacco Workers and the Struggle for Democracy in the Mid-Twentieth-Century South* (Chapel Hill: University of North Carolina Press, 2003), 2.

23. Korstad, *Civil Rights Unionism*, 2.

24. Tursi, *Winston-Salem*.

25. Tursi, *Winston-Salem*.

26. Korstad, *Civil Rights Unionism*.

27. Korstad, *Civil Rights Unionism*, 414.

28. Korstad, *Civil Rights Unionism*, 9.

29. Adelaide Lisetta Fries, *Forsyth County* (Winston, NC: Stewarts' Print. House, 1898), http://archive.org/details/forsythcounty00frie

30. Oppermann, *Winston-Salem's African-American Neighborhoods*, 17–18.

31. In addition, deregulation in 1984 forced Piedmont Aviation (formerly Camel City Flying Service) to close its plant in the area, and in 1989 USAir merged with Piedmont Aviation and changed its employment center, while at the same time all of Winston-Salem trucking industries collapsed.

32. Tursi, *Winston-Salem*.

33. Tursi, *Winston-Salem*.

34. Tursi, *Winston-Salem*.

35. Kochhar, Suro, and Tafoya, "The New Latino South," 18.

36. Kochhar, Suro, and Tafoya, "The New Latino South," 20.

37. Altha J. Cravey and Gabriela Valdivia, "Carolina Del Norte: An Introduction," *Southeastern Geographer* 51, no. 2 (2011): 213–26; Krista M. Perreira, "Mexican Families in North Carolina: The Socio-historical Contexts of Exit and Settlement," *Southeastern Geographer* 51, no. 2 (2011): 260–86.

38. For more on the impact of NAFTA on the Mexican economy and outmigration to North Carolina, see Perreira, "Mexican Families in North Carolina."

39. Perreira, "Mexican Families in North Carolina."

40. Perreira, "Mexican Families in North Carolina," 262.

41. Perreira, "Mexican Families in North Carolina."

42. These economic shifts and changes in the opportunity structure in Mexico have resulted in a move toward necessary migration among the able-bodied adult men in many of these communities. As they settle in the US for extended periods, they frequently send for their wives and later children to join them in the US.

43. While there certainly was diversity in the Latino population across the state and the broader metropolitan region, according to 2010 census data, the vast majority of Latino residents in Winston-Salem were of Mexican origin. Mexican-origin Latinos were 10.2 percent of the population (or 70 percent of the Latino population), followed most closely by Central Americans at 1.6 percent and Puerto Ricans at 0.9 percent. Latinos represented approximately 14.7 percent of the total population in 2010, suggesting that Latinos in Winston-Salem were more heavily Mexican than the national average. See US Census Bureau, US Census Bureau, 2010 Census, Summary File 1, Hispanic or Latino by Type, Winston-Salem, NC (Washington DC: US Census Bureau, 2016), accessed October 20, 2016, http://factfinder.census.gov/faces/tableservices/jsf/pages/productview.xhtml?src=CF

44. David C. Griffith, "Rural Industry and Mexican Immigration and Settlement in North Carolina," in *New Destinations: Mexican Immigration in the United States*, ed. Zúñiga and Hernández-León (New York: Russell Sage Foundation, 2005), 50–77; Kochhar, Suro, and Tafoya, "The New Latino South."

45. John D. Kasarda and James H. Johnson, *The Economic Impact of the Hispanic Population on the State of North Carolina* (Chapel Hill, NC: Frank Hawkins Kenan Institute of Private Enterprise, 2006), 5.

46. Heather A. Smith and Owen J. Furuseth, "The 'Nuevo South': Latino Place Making and Community Building in the Middle-Ring Suburbs of Charlotte," in *Twenty-First Century Gateways*, ed. Audrey Singer, Susan W. Hardwick, and Caroline B. Brettell (Washington, DC: Brookings Institution Press 2008), 281–308.

47. The only visible union force in Winston-Salem is the Farm Labor Organizing Committee (FLOC), which has successfully organized some agricultural workers and undertaken an ongoing campaign to pressure R. J. Reynolds to improve working condition standards at its contracted tobacco farms.

48. In 2009, however, black and Latino meatpackers at the Smithfield meatpacking plant successfully organized a union. Organizers' efforts to build a multiracial coalition are credited for this unprecedented success.

49. Kasarda and Johnson, *The Economic Impact of the Hispanic Population on the State of North Carolina*, 5; Massey, *New Faces in New Places*.

50. Douglas S. Massey, Jorge Durand, and Nolan J. Malone, *Beyond Smoke and Mirrors: Mexican Immigration in an Era of Economic Integration* (New York: Russell Sage Foundation, 2003).

51. Griffith, "Rural Industry and Mexican Immigration and Settlement in North Carolina," 50–75.

52. Rubén Hernández-León and Víctor Zúñiga, "Mexican Immigrant Communities in the South and Social Capital: The Case of Dalton, Georgia," *Southern Rural Sociology* 19, no. 1 (2002): 20–45.

53. Jorge Durand, Douglas S. Massey, and Rene M. Zenteno, "Mexican Immigration to the United States: Continuities and Changes," *Latin American Research Review* 36, no. 1 (2001): 107–27.

54. Durand, Massey, and Zenteno, "Mexican Immigration to the United States," 111.

55. Steven Zahniser and William Coyle, "U.S.-Mexico Corn Trade during the NAFTA Era: New Twists to an Old Story," USDA electronic report, *Economic Research Service* (2004): 1–20.

56. For more on the role of neoliberal economic relations in restructuring the North Carolina and Mexican economies and its role in shaping immigration flows, see Jeff Popke, "Latino Migration and Neoliberalism in the U.S. South: Notes toward a Rural Cosmopolitanism," *Southeastern Geographer* 51, no. 2 (2011): 242–59.

57. This community is also one of Mexico's most evidently Afro-descendant communities, and the site of its sole Afro-Mexican Museum. As small-scale farmers largely cut off from state resources, many Afro-descendant Mexicans alongside mestizos, indigenous, were motivated to migrate, decimating local towns. Familiarity with the US meant that for many migrants, blackness as a culturally and socially meaningful category was available to them in ways that it was not for other Mexicans. The region's increasingly strong ties to the US and sense of marginalization and abandonment from the metropole, both structurally and ideologically, meant that many Mexicans here were open to adopting a racialized identity that embraced blackness. This was true even as they faced systemic discrimination and invisibility in Mexico's larger urban centers, like Veracruz, further incentivizing migration. See Christina Sue, *Land of the Cosmic Race: Race Mixture, Racism, and Blackness in Mexico* (Oxford: Oxford University Press, 2013).

58. Gill, *The Latino Migration Experience in North Carolina*.

59. Kasarda and Johnson, *The Economic Impact of the Hispanic Population on the State of North Carolina*, 2.

60. Kitty Calavita, "New Politics of Immigration: Balanced-Budget Conservatism and the Symbolism of Proposition 187," *Social Problems* 43 (1996): 284.

61. Scholars also show that poultry-processing, meatpacking, construction, and manufacturing firms recruited migrant workers directly. See Gill, *The Latino Migration Experience in North Carolina*, 71–73.

62. Suro et al., *Latino Growth in Metropolitan America*.

63. Migration Policy Institute, "State Immigration Data Profiles," Migration Policy Institute (Washington, DC: Migration Policy Institute, 2015), accessed December 26, 2017, https://www.migrationpolicy.org/data/state-profiles/state/demographics/NC/

64. Passel and Cohn, *Unauthorized Immigrant Population*.

65. Between 65% and 75% of these migrants are Mexican. Still, of the 4.658 million workers in the state, only 250,000 are unauthorized, representing a mere 5.4% of the state work force, just slightly above the national average of unauthorized immigrant workers. Passel and Cohn, *Unauthorized Immigrant Population*.

66. Suro et al., *Latino Growth in Metropolitan America*, 12.

67. Migration Policy Institute, "State Immigration Data Profiles"; US Census Bureau, "Winston-Salem, NC Population Estimates: 2008," Current Population Reports (Washington, DC: US Census Bureau, 2008).

68. US Census Bureau, "Winston-Salem, NC Population Estimates: 2008."

69. To this day, a popular community organization dedicated to issues facing minority communities is called "Crossing 52."

70. Such racialized settlement was common in North Carolina, though less so in the

Nashville and Atlanta metro regions. See Jamie Winders and Barbara Ellen Smith, "Excepting/Accepting the South: New Geographies of Latino Migration, New Directions in Latino Studies," *Latino Studies* 10, no. 1–2 (2012): 220–45.

71. Weise, *Corazón de Dixie*; Rudy P. Guevarra Jr., *Becoming Mexipino: Multiethnic Identities and Communities in San Diego* (New Brunswick, NJ: Rutgers University Press, 2012).

72. Mary Giunca, "Stymied: Dashed Plan No Victory in Southside," *Winston-Salem Journal*, January 30, 2003.

73. The key exception would be schools, which have experienced significant growing pains due to the massive increase of Latino school children, not only increasing the number of students served, but also requiring special accommodations such as an increased need for ESL courses and bilingual teachers and staff.

74. Cravey and Valdivia, "Carolina Del Norte."

75. Marrow, *New Destination Dreaming*.

76. Cybelle Fox, *Three Worlds of Relief: Race, Immigration, and the American Welfare State from the Progressive Era to the New Deal* (Princeton: Princeton University Press, 2012).

77. For more on bureaucratic incorporation in the 1990s and early 2000s, see also Marrow, *New Destination Dreaming*; Jamie Winders, "Seeing Immigrants: Institutional Visibility and Immigrant Incorporation in New Immigrant Destinations," *Annals of the American Academy of Political and Social Science* 641 (2012): 58–78.

78. This is not to suggest the region was free from racism in this period. While agricultural areas of Georgia, for example, were largely welcoming, Mexicans experienced open hostility and violence from the Klan in majority white factory towns (Weise, *Corazón de Dixie*, 132). Still, this kind of public sentiment was the exception rather than commonplace. For example, Weise argues that it was not until the twenty-first century that the South's exurban residents, who had fled integration in the 1970s, 1980s, and 1990s to new exurban developments, took their lead from similar movements on the West Coast to mount the first anti-immigrant movement targeting Latinos in the Southeast (184).

79. Gill, *The Latino Migration Experience in North Carolina*, 8.

80. Popke, "Latino Migration and Neoliberalism in the U.S. South."

81. Shannon Buggs, Angela Paik, and Jay Price, "The Land of Full Employment," *News and Observer*, July 26, 1998, A1.

82. In this metro area, African Americans have been particularly upwardly mobile due to significant economic opportunities open to blacks first in well-paid blue-collar jobs in tobacco factories and education at the local historically black college, and later through the growth of research, medical, and corporate industries headquartered in the area.

83. Buggs, Paik, and Price, "The Land of Full Employment."

84. Richard Craver, "Bank Gives Gift to Center; Money Goes toward Forsyth Tech's Goal," *Winston-Salem Journal*, November 14, 2006, D1.

85. Jeanne Sturiale, "Opening Doors: Southern Community Bank Makes It Its Business to Pull In Hispanic Customers," *Winston-Salem Journal*, November 24, 2002, D1.

86. Sturiale, "Opening Doors."

87. John Railey, "Changed World: Americans Search for Hope as Events Bring Uncertainty," *Winston-Salem Journal*, January 1, 2002, A1.

88. Richard Craver, "Safety and Numbers: Hispanics Caught between Risks of Carrying Cash and Banking It," *Winston-Salem Journal*, January 22, 2003, D1.

89. Craver, "Safety and Numbers."

90. Amy Frazier and Michelle Johnson, "Hispanics Hit Hard by Downturn: Many Work in State's Struggling Industries, Such as Manufacturing," *Winston-Salem Journal*, January 24, 2002.

91. Amy Frazier and Jim Sparks, "Work for Pay: Mexican Immigrants Welcome the Chance to Earn a Living and Have a Reliable Source of Income That Is Not Available to Them Back Home," *Winston-Salem Journal*, January 6, 2002, A1.

92. David B. Grusky and Kim A. Weeden, "Does the Sociological Approach to Studying Mobility Have a Future?" in *Mobility and Inequality: Frontiers of Research in Sociology and Economics*, ed. Stephen L. Morgan, David B. Grusky, and Gary S. Fields (Stanford, CA: Stanford University Press, 2006), 85–108.

93. Kasarda and Johnson, *The Economic Impact of the Hispanic Population on the State of North Carolina*.

94. The Piedmont Triad area refers to the municipalities of Greensboro, Winston-Salem, and High-Point. These three communities are geographically adjacent.

95. Lorraine Ahear, "Latino Community Coming into Focus," *News and Record*, July 4, 1995, A1.

96. Hans P. Johnson, "Movin' Out: Domestic Migration to and from California in the 1990s," *California Counts: Population Trends and Profiles* 2, no. 1 (San Francisco: Public Policy Institute of California, August 2000); Jeffrey Passel and Wendy Zimmerman, "Are Immigrants Leaving California? Settlement Patterns of Immigrants in the Late 1990s" (Washington, DC: Urban Institute, 2001).

97. Felix Büchel and Joachim R. Frick, "Immigrants' Economic Performance across Europe—Does Immigration Policy Matter?" *Population Research and Policy Review* 24 (2005): 175–212.

98. The year 1993 also saw coverage in excess of 100 articles at 158, after just 45 articles in 1992 and 21 in 1994.

99. Andrea Ball, "UNCG Welcomes Immigrants; UNCG Holds Family Day to Introduce Immigrants to College Life," *News and Record*, June 27,1998, B2.

100. Ball, "UNCG Welcomes Immigrants."

101. Amy Frazier, "Two Together as One: Rise in Yadkin Hispanic Population Is Inspiration for New Church for Parishes," *Winston-Salem Journal*, January 22, 2002.

102. Glenna Musante, "Immigrant Success Story Lends a Hand to Newcomers," *News and Observer*, August 9, 1998, B1.

103. Angier is a small town in the greater Raleigh-Durham area, approximately 20 miles south of Raleigh.

104. Musante, "Immigrant Success Story Lends a Hand to Newcomers."

105. "Traffic Questions and Answers," *Winston-Salem Journal*, January 4, 2002, A10.

106. "N.C. County Leaders to Travel to Mexico," *Winston-Salem Journal*, February 28, 2002, B5.

107. Carey Hamilton, "Local Leaders to Visit Mexico: Purpose Is Firmer Grasp on Culture," *Winston-Salem Journal*, March 1, 2002.

108. "Trip to Mexico," *Winston-Salem Journal*, May 15, 2002, A10.

109. Lisa Hoppenjans, "Spanish-Language Phone Service Serves 5 Counties: United Way Organizations Hope to Help Growing Hispanic Population Find Assistance," *Winston-Salem Journal*, January 17, 2004, B1.

110. Carey Hamilton, "More Riders Wanted on Buses: Campaign Intends to Reach Hispanics," *Winston-Salem Journal*, April 28, 2002, B1.

111. Wesley Young, "Mexican Consulate Promotes ID Program," *Winston-Salem Journal*, May 30, 2002, 1.

112. Jeanne Sturiale, "Media Right Agency Specializes in Animation and Art Projects,". *Winston-Salem Journal*, January 26, 2003, D9.

113. "Milestones," *Winston-Salem Journal*, January 6, 2003, B2.

114. Weise, *Corazón de Dixie*, 186.

115. This is not to suggest that anti-immigrant sentiment was entirely absent. In 2002, there was one letter to the editor that decried the use of state department (and therefore taxpayer funds) for the Winston-Salem delegation trip to Mexico, considering it a form of political correctness and buying votes; there was also a letter responding to reporting that crimes against Latinos were less likely to be solved because police were not bilingual and relied on temporary interpreters with the suggestion that the US be made English only. However, these types of letters were considerably less frequent than responses to articles on African Americans, and considerably less frequent than at mid-decade. See chapter 3 for an extensive discussion of the backlash toward Latino immigrants.

116. Fran Daniel, "Hispanics Growing as Furniture Buyers Group Vital to Sales, Expert Says," *Winston-Salem Journal*, February 9, 2002, D1.

117. Fran Daniel, "An American Dream: Jesus Ruiz's Hard Work Has Made Mi Pueblo Restaurants Succeed," *Winston-Salem Journal*, March 9, 2002, D1.

118. Richard D. Alba, *Ethnic Identity: The Transformation of White America* (New Haven, CT: Yale University Press, 1990); Mary C. Waters, *Ethnic Options: Choosing identities in America* (Berkeley: University of California Press, 1990).

119. Amy Frazier, "Immigrant Dies at 29; He Bridged Gaps between Hispanics, Others," *Winston-Salem Journal*, April 27, 2002, B2.

120. Patrick Wilson,"For Moms: Hispanic Youth Group Sings the Praises of Mothers," *Winston-Salem Journal*, May 12, 2002, B1.

121. "Changing Face of America," *Winston-Salem Journal*, January 27, 2003, A8.

122. Kasarda and Johnson, *The Economic Impact of the Hispanic Population on the State of North Carolina*.

123. Ivan Light, *Deflecting Immigration: Networks, Markets, and Regulation in Los Angeles* (New York: Russell Sage, 2006).

124. John Sparks, "Area Residents Also Encountering Long DMV Waits; Examiner Shortage, Rush to Beat New ID Rules Are Causing Delays," *Winston-Salem Journal*, January 22, 2004, B1.

Chapter Three

1. "Gangs, Fraud and Sexual Predators: Struggling with the Consequences of Illegal Immigration." Hearing before the Subcommittee on Criminal Justice, Drug Policy, and Human Resources of the Committee on Government Reform, US House of Representatives, One Hundred Ninth Congress Second Session, April 12, 2006. http://www.gpo.gov/fdsys/pkg/CHRG-109hhrg30529/html/CHRG-109hhrg30529.htm

2. While a higher proportion of Latinos in the Southeast are foreign born than in other parts of the country, and a significant proportion of the Latino American–origin foreign-born are undocumented, it is important to note that a significant number of Latinos, especially youth, in North Carolina and throughout the region are native-born Latinos. Racial lumping, however, means that most Latinos are perceived as foreign born and unauthorized. Moreover, since there few longstanding Latino communities in the region, options for incorporation—say into middle class Latino neighborhoods—are limited.

3. Gill, *The Latino Migration Experience in North Carolina*, 8.

4. Angela S. García, "Hidden in Plain Sight: How Unauthorized Migrants Strategically Assimilate in Restrictive Localities," *Journal of Ethnic and Migration Studies* 40, no. 12 (2014): 1895–914; Cecilia Menjívar and Leisy J. Abrego, "Legal Violence: Immigration Law and the Lives of Central American Immigrants," *American Journal of Sociology* 117, no. 5 (2012):1380–421.

5. Such shifts indicate that contextual level changes, particularly at the institutional level, can play an important role in shaping access to resources that transmits across generations. See Leisy Janet Abrego, "'I Can't Go to College Because I Don't Have Papers': Incorporation Patterns of Latino Unauthorized Youth," *Latino Studies* 4 (2006): 212–31; Leisy Janet Abrego and Roberto G. Gonzales, "Blocked Paths, Uncertain Futures: The Postsecondary Education and Labor Market Prospects of Undocumented Latino Youth," *Journal of Education for Students Placed at Risk* 15, no. 1–2 (2010): 144–57; Joanna Dreby, *Everyday Illegal: When Policies Undermine Immigrant Families* (Oakland: University of California Press, 2015); Menjívar and Abrego, "Legal Violence."

6. Roberto G. Gonzales, "Learning to Be Illegal: Undocumented Youth and Shifting Legal Contexts in the Transition to Adulthood," *American Sociological Review* 76, no. 4 (2011): 602–19; Menjívar and Abrego, "Legal Violence."

7. Abrego, "'I Can't Go to College Because I Don't Have Papers'"; Abrego and Gonzales, "Blocked Paths, Uncertain Futures"; Dreby, *Everyday Illegal*; Menjívar and Abrego, "Legal Violence."

8. Gonzales, "Learning to Be Illegal."

9. Alarcón et al., *Making Los Angeles Home*, xxi.

10. Tomás R. Jiménez, *Replenished Ethnicity: Mexican Americans, Immigration, and Identity* (Berkeley: University of California Press, 2010).

11. Jiménez acknowledges this limitation, noting that his interviews and data collection preceded the ramp-up in immigration debates in 2006, highlighting that nativism tended to be episodic rather than continual (Jiménez, *Replenished Ethnicity*, 147).

12. Jiménez, *Replenished Ethnicity*, 141.

13. Michael Lipsky, *Street-Level Bureaucracy: Dilemmas of the Individual in Public Services* (New York: Russell Sage Foundation, 2010 [1980]).

14. But see Cecilia Menjívar and Daniel Kanstroom, "Introduction—Immigrant 'Illegality': Constructions and Critiques," in *Constructing Immigrant "Illegality": Critiques, Experiences, and Responses*, ed. Cecilia Menjívar and Daniel Kanstroom (Cambridge: Cambridge University Press, 2014); Mae M. Ngai, *Impossible Subjects: Illegal Aliens and the Making of Modern America* (Princeton, NJ: Princeton University Press, 2004).

15. David Scott FitzGerald and David Cook-Martín, *Culling the Masses: The Democratic Origins of Racist Immigration Policy in the Americas* (Cambridge, MA: Harvard University Press, 2014).

16. Ngai, *Impossible Subjects*, 59. From 1882 to 1907 only a few hundred immigrants were deported per year, and from 1908 to 1920, this number went up to two to three thousand, though mostly from hospitals, asylums, and jails. Prior to 1917, entry without medical inspection was not a reason to exclude migrants (only when an immigrant failed inspection, something that Mexican laborers were uniquely targeted for). Moreover, after five years, immigrants were considered assimilated and settled, creating a de facto statute of limitation on deportations. Ngai, *Impossible Subjects*.

17. Ngai, *Impossible Subjects*, 60.

18. Ngai, *Impossible Subjects*, 3.

19. Ngai, *Impossible Subjects*, 247.

20. Abrego, "'I Can't Go to College Because I Don't Have Papers,'" 215.

21. Though such sentiments were not altogether absent, as, for example, David Duke organized an anti-immigrant rally in North Carolina as early as 2000 (Gill, *The Latino Migration Experience in North Carolina*, 8).

22. See chapter 2 for a greater elaboration on the push and pull of Mexican immigration in the 1990s.

23. Amada Armenta, "From Sheriff's Deputies to Immigration Officers: Screening Immigrant Status in a Tennessee Jail," *Law and Policy* 34, no. 2 (2012): 191–210; Mary Bauer and Sarah Reynolds, *Under Siege: Life for Low-Income Latinos in the South* (Montgomery, AL: Southern Poverty Law Center, 2009); Mathew Coleman, "The 'Local' Migration State: The Site-Specific Devolution of Immigration Enforcement in the U.S. South," *Law & Policy* 34, no. 2 (2012): 159–90; Mark Lopez, Rich Morin, and Paul Taylor, "Illegal Immigration Backlash Worries, Divides Latinos" (Washington, DC: Pew Hispanic Center, October 28, 2010); Douglas S. Massey and Magaly Sánchez, *Brokered Boundaries: Creating Immigrant Identity in Anti-immigrant Times* (New York: Russell Sage Foundation, 2010). It is unclear exactly why the increase in restrictive immigration policy occurred when it did. It is likely that economic changes, including globalization, regional partnerships like NAFTA, and regional economic decline in the US, contributed to changes in the treatment and perception of immigrants beginning in the 1990s. At the same time, the 1990s marked a political shift away from Cold War era politics to a focus on terrorism. Together, these changes likely spurred an incremental shift at the political level that increased dramatically after the September 11th terrorist attacks. However, the concrete causal links between these processes remain unclear.

24. Richard Alba and Victor Nee, "Rethinking Assimilation Theory for a New Era of Immigration," *International Migration Review* 31, no. 4 (1997): 826–874.

25. David Manuel Hernández, "Pursuant to Deportation: Latinos and Immigrant Detention," *Latino Studies* 6, no. 1–2 (2008): 39. Drawing from Rumbaut and Ewing, Hernández notes that Latino criminality is largely a myth, as incarceration rates are lowest for immigrants regardless of ethnic group and education level. This holds true for Mexicans and other Latinos that make up the bulk of the immigrant population (Hernández, "Pursuant to Deportation").

26. Latinos, especially Mexicans but occasionally others (such as Puerto Ricans, Central Americans), have long been framed as threats to American society. See, for example, Natalia Molina, *How Race Is Made in America: Immigration, Citizenship, and the Historical Power of Racial Scripts* (Berkeley: University of California Press, 2014).

27. Carrie Arnold, "Racial Profiling in Immigration Enforcement: State and Local Agreements to Enforce Federal Immigration Law," *Arizona Law Review* 49, no. 113 (2007): 113–42.

28. 287(g) is a clause of the 1996 Illegal Immigration Reform and Immigrant Responsibility Act (IIRIRA) that allowed state and local law enforcement to enter into partnerships with Immigration and Customs Enforcement (ICE) to receive delegated authority for immigration enforcement within their jurisdictions. These agreements were not employed until 2002 and not widely used until 2006. See Richard Skinner, *Department of Homeland Security Office of Inspector General: The Performance of 287(g) Agreements* (Washington, DC: Department of of Homeland Security, 2010).

287(g) was intended to address terrorism and human trafficking. Under the agreement, state, county and city law enforcement in partnerships with ICE can receive training and act as deputized ICE agents within their local jurisdictions. The program consists of three different models. One is jail-based, in which arrested individuals are also processed for immigration violations, and one is task force–based, in which street patrols are authorized to act as ICE agents in the field. A third version combines the first two models.

29. In 2008, ICE began piloting its Secure Communities program, which took the same form as the jail-based 287(g) program and which eventually became federal mandate. Many North Carolina counties volunteered as pilot sites for the program, but others sued for the right to decline participation. In the interim years, Secure Communities came to replace 287(g) as the key federal-local partnership strategy. At the time of this writing, the Secure Communities program was discontinued in favor of a new Priority Enforcement Program or PEP, in which an individual must be convicted of a priority offense to be transferred into custody. A more highly regulated 287(g) program remains on the books.

30. US Department of Homeland Security, *Fact Sheet: Delegation of Immigration Authority Section 287(g) Immigration and Nationality Act* (Washington, DC: DHS, Office of Public Affairs, 2009).

31. Arnold, "Racial Profiling in Immigration Enforcement."

32. Michael W. McCann, *Rights at Work: Pay Equity Reform and the Politics of Legal Mobilization* (Chicago: University of Chicago Press, 1994), 8–9.

33. Others, however, especially states with longstanding powerful immigrant populations such as New York, California, and Illinois, took the opposite approach, expanding access to state and municipal resources, declaring noncooperation with federal agencies, and suing for the right to integrate immigrants on their own terms.

34. Sensenbrenner also introduced The Patriot Act in 2001, and was the main sponsor of HR 44337 in 2005, which introduced criminal penalties for aiding illegal immigration, a highly controversial bill that failed in the senate, and is widely considered as a major catalyst for the 2006 immigrant protests around the country.

35. Seventeen states passed legislation rejecting this mandate; many expressed concerns that it placed undue burden on citizens to prove their status (National Immigration Law Center, "The Real ID Act: Questions and Answers," National Immigration Law Center, last updated January 2016, https://www.nilc.org/wp-content/uploads/2015/11/REAL-ID-Act-Q-and-A.pdf). North Carolina quickly passed the Technical Corrections Act in 2005 to comply.

36. Armenta, "From Sheriff's Deputies to Immigration Officers"; Coleman, "The 'Local' Migration State."

37. Randy Capps, Marc R. Rosenblum, Cristina Rodríguez, and Muzaffar Chishti, *Delegation and Divergence: A Study of 287(g) State and Local Immigration Enforcement* (Washington, DC: Migration Policy Institute, January 2011); Mark Lopez and Susan Minushkin, "2008 Survey of Latinos: Hispanics See Their Situation in U.S. Deteriorating; Oppose Key Immigration Enforcement Measures" (Washington, DC: Pew Hispanic Center, September 2008); Daniel J. Hopkins, "Politicized Places: Explaining Where and When Immigrants Provoke Local Opposition," *American Political Science Review* 104 (2010): 40–60; S. Karthick Ramakrishnan and Tom Wong, "Partisanship, not Spanish: Explaining Municipal Ordinances Affecting Undocumented Immigrants," in *Taking Local Control: Immigration Policy Activism in U.S. Cities and States*, ed. Monica Varsanyi (Stanford, CA: Stanford University Press, 2010), 73–96.

38. Leo Chavez, "The Condition of Illegality," *International Migration* 45, no. 3 (2007): 192–95; Leo Ralph Chavez, *The Latino Threat*; Marrow, *New Destination Dreaming*.

39. Lipsky, *Street-Level Bureaucracy*, xi.

40. Abrego, "'I Can't Go to College Because I Don't Have Papers'"; Gonzales, "Learning to Be Illegal"; Menjívar and Abrego, "Legal Violence."

41. To my knowledge, while immigrants were heavily recruited to North Carolina through efforts by the business lobby, their most significant role in shaping immigration legislation has been their opposition to any comprehensive e-verify bill. Their influence appears less evident regarding policy proposals that would limit immigrant access to education, for example, though it is often difficult to discern what kinds of agreements are reached behind closed doors. While the business lobby have been vocally supportive of comprehensive immigration reform and wary of punitive omnibus bills in North Carolina, it also does not appear they attempted to influence many of the piecemeal forms of legislation proposed in the state, nor did they attempt to improve the general climate for immigrants in the state. Unions have lobbied against punitive immigration bills since the 1990s but have limited influence in North Carolina and throughout the South.

42. Capps, Rosenblum, Rodríguez, and Chishti, *Delegation and Divergence*; Gill, *The Latino Migration Experience in North Carolina*; Singer et al., *Twenty-First Century Gateways*.

43. Coleman, "The 'Local' Migration State"; Gill, *The Latino Migration Experience in North Carolina*; Marrow, *New Destination Dreaming*; Kochhar, Suro, and Tafoya, "The New Latino South"; Weise, *Corazón de Dixie*; Jamie Winders, "Changing Politics of Race and Region: Latino Migration to the US South," *Progress in Human Geography* 29, no. 6 (2005): 683–99.

Certainly, we can speculate that these shifts were due at least in part to demographic change, though they lagged major influxes by several years. Nor had the community reached a saturation point, muddling exactly how demographic changes shaped institutional closure. Economic factors might have also played a role, but Winston-Salem experienced a minor downturn in the early 2000s, and then not again until 2008, indicative of another puzzling time issue in terms of causal mechanisms. Political mechanisms also do not appear to provide much insight, as the Senate and House were under Democratic control until 2010, suggesting that that party politics did not play a direct role. Indeed, the causal mechanisms are much more likely to be the result of the interaction between local and regional shifts, empowering key actors to promote more hostile approaches to managing immigrant populations in their communities.

44. Rick Martinez, "Immigration Hits 'Critical Mass' in NC: Rapid Influxes of Hispanics, Most of Them Illegal, Creating Tensions," *Carolina Journal News Reports*, December 12, 2005, http://www.carolinajournal.com/articles/display_story.html?id=2983

45. Not all states accepted this mandate. Seventeen states passed legislation rejecting this mandate, and many have expressed concerns that it places undue burden on citizens to prove their status, particularly the elderly and disabled (National Immigration Law Center, "The Real ID Act"). North Carolina is not one of those states. It quickly passed the Technical Corrections Act in 2005 to comply with the national Real ID Act, despite the fact that the federal deadline to meet Real ID standards was extended to 2020.

46. Marrow, *New Destination Dreaming*, 215–21.

47. See also Julie Stewart, "Fiction over Facts: How Competing Narrative Forms Explain Policy in a New Immigration Destination," *Sociological Forum* 27, no. 3 (2012): 591–616.

48. Gill, *The Latino Migration Experience in North Carolina*, 41.

49. Adie Tomer, Elizabeth Kneebone, Robert Puentes, and Alan Berube, "Missed Opportunity: Transit and Jobs in Metropolitan America," Metropolitan Infrastructure Initiative Series and Metropolitan Opportunity Series: Brookings Institute (Washington, DC: Brookings Institute, 2011).

50. Similar effects were observed in Arizona. For more on these effects, see Cecilia Menjívar, "The Power of the Law: Central Americans' Legality and Everyday Life in Phoenix, Arizona,"

Latino Studies 9, no. 4 (2011): 377–95; Doris Marie Provine and Gabriella Sanchez, "Suspecting Immigrants: Exploring Links between Racialised Anxieties and Expanded Police Powers in Arizona," *Policing and Society* 21, no. 4 (December 2011): 468–79, https://doi.org/10.1080/10439463.2011.614098

51. Gill, *The Latino Migration Experience in North Carolina*; Marrow, *New Destination Dreaming*, 221–25.

52. According to WRAL.com, former Mecklenberg county sheriff Jim Pendergraph was the first to launch the 287(g) program in North Carolina, and became a major advocate for the program. Shortly thereafter, he was hired by ICE as executive director for state and local coordination at ICE. He became the regional coordinator for 287(g) programs under ICE. During this period, every southeast county agreement was designed to be a universal (not targeted) jail-based program, similar to Mecklenberg County's agreement. He stepped down in 2008 just before the November election, perhaps in part due to complaints that the southeast region was responsible for the majority of detainers issued for misdemeanors and traffic violations. See Capps, Rosenblum, Rodríguez, and Chishti, *Delegation and Divergence*.

53. Capps, Rosenblum, Rodríguez, and Chishti, *Delegation and Divergence*.

54. Gill, *The Latino Migration Experience in North Carolina*, 40.

55. American Civil Liberties Union (ACLU) of North Carolina Legal Foundation and Immigration & Human Rights Policy Clinic of University of North Carolina (UNC) at Chapel Hill, *The Policies and Politics of Local Immigration Enforcement Laws 287(g) Program in North Carolina* (Chapel Hill: UNC School of Law, 2009), 46.

56. 287(g) programs account for 10% of people identified for potential removal annually, totaling approximately 186,000 from October 2005 to October 2010; 100,000 of these were in the past two years (Capps, Rosenblum, Rodríguez, and Chishti, *Delegation and Divergence*, 18). There are three types, jail-based, hybrid, and task force models. They can also be enforced as targeted or universal operations and have provisions for checks at various stages of the process (for example, Los Angeles County had a post-conviction check only program). Programs that are universal and jail based have the lowest levels of oversight and are most likely to detain high numbers of level 3 offenders—those who are believed to have committed misdemeanors—and are the lowest priority of ICE. Over 50% of such ICE detainers nationally are level 3, traffic violations, or no offense at all (Capps, Rosenblum, Rodríguez, and Chishti, *Delegation and Divergence*).

57. Elizabeth DeOrnellas, "$76,000 for New Position is Questioned: Sheriff Says He Didn't Request Money for Immigration Job," *Winston-Salem Journal*, June 2, 2008, B1; Laura Giovanelli, "Protests Smaller This Year; 60–70 People Gather for Pro Immigration Rally in Winston-Salem," *Winston-Salem Journal*, May 3, 2007, B1.

58. Kasarda and Johnson, *The Economic Impact of the Hispanic Population on the State of North Carolina*.

59. In Coleman's work on Durham and Wake counties in North Carolina, he finds that interest from the North Carolina Sheriffs' Association (NCSA) in 2006, alongside Sheriff Pendergraph's (of Mecklenburg County) successful application for a 287(g) agreement that year, spurred the interest of many peer counties in the program. In 2007, Pendergraph was then hired to head up ICE's office of State and Local Coordination to oversee the program, which he then promoted to many of his peers in North Carolina; Coleman, "The 'Local' Migration State."

60. American Civil Liberties Union (ACLU) of North Carolina Legal Foundation and Immigration & Human Rights Policy Clinic of University of North Carolina (UNC) at Chapel

Hill, *The Policies and Politics of Local Immigration Enforcement Laws 287(g) Program in North Carolina*, 46.

61. Jessica M. Vaughan and James R. Edwards, "The 287(g) Program: Protecting Home Towns and Homeland" (Washington, DC: Center for Immigration Studies, 2009).

62. Joanne Lin, Mónica Ramírez, and Reginald Shuford, "Written Statement for a Hearing on Examining 287(g): The Role of State and Local Enforcement in Immigration Law Submitted to the U.S. House of Representatives Committee on Homeland Security" (Washington, DC: American Civil Liberties Union, March 4, 2009), 6.

63. Peter St. Onge, "He Is the Man Who Sends the Illegal Immigrants Home," *Charlotte Observer*, December 10, 2006.

64. As of 2017, 38 law enforcement agencies had formal 287(g) agreements with ICE. In January of that year, however, President Trump signed an executive order to ramp up the program. https://www.theatlantic.com/politics/archive/2017/02/trump-immigration-enforcement/517071/

65. ICE Secure Communities, Activated Jurisdiction Report.

66. Full national compliance was completed in 2013.

67. National Council of State Legislatures.

68. American Association of State Colleges and Universities.

69. Marrow, *New Destination Dreaming*, 191–95.

70. Lipsky, *Street-Level Bureaucracy*.

71. Lipsky, *Street-Level Bureaucracy*.

72. See also Gill, *The Latino Migration Experience in North Carolina*; Marrow, *New Destination Dreaming*.

73. Gill, *The Latino Migration Experience in North Carolina*, 142.

74. Gill, *The Latino Migration Experience in North Carolina*, 143.

75. Diego is likely referring to the well-publicized raids on the Smithfield meatpacking plant in Tar Heel North Carolina in January 2007, as well as a subsequent raid on area homes later that year. These raids were particularly contentious because they followed efforts to unionize by black and Latino workers at the plant. In 1998, a handful of immigrants were held by then INS (Immigration and Naturalization Service) in the area who were employed at the Sara Lee plant, but the presence of ICE did not become common in the state until the mid-2000s.

76. American Civil Liberties Union (ACLU) of North Carolina Legal Foundation and Immigration & Human Rights Policy Clinic of University of North Carolina (UNC) at Chapel Hill, *The Policies and Politics of Local Immigration Enforcement Laws: 287(g) Program in North Carolina*, 20, http://www.law.unc.edu/documents/clinicalprograms/287gpolicyreview.pdf

77. Dan Galindo, "Immigration Study Casts Doubt on Law: Partnership Unfair to Immigrants, Critics Say," *Winston-Salem Journal*, February 19, 2009.

78. A second representative is reportedly of Latin American descent but does not identify as Latino. He is also a Republican.

79. Gill, *The Latino Migration Experience in North Carolina*, 144.

80. Gill, *The Latino Migration Experience in North Carolina*, 142.

81. Virginia Foxx, "Congresswoman Virginia Foxx: Immigration," accessed February 22, 2011, http://foxx.house.gov/index.cfm?sectionid=37

82. Scott Sexton, "Immigration Debate Strays from Ideas to Ideologies," *Winston-Salem Journal*, April 13, 2006, Metro Edition, B1.

83. Wesley Young, "Forsyth's New Face; Cultural Character of Country Is in Flux; Census

Estimate Shift Is Youngest in Age Groups," *Winston-Salem Journal*, August 15, 2007, Metro Edition, A1.

84. Deborah Weissman, "Written Statement for a Joint Hearing on the "Public Safety and Civil Rights Implications of State and Local Enforcement of Federal Immigration Laws" (Washington, DC: US House of Representatives, April 2, 2009),14.

85. Lin et al., "Written Statement for a Hearing on Examining 287(g)," 7.

86. Bauer and Reynolds, *Under Siege*.

87. Lopez et al., "Illegal Immigration Backlash Worries, Divides Latinos."

88. Lopez et al., "Illegal Immigration Backlash Worries, Divides Latinos."

89. Ramiro Martínez Jr., Jacob I. Stowell, and Matthew T. Lee, "Immigration and Crime in an Era of Transformation: A Longitudinal Analysis of Homicides in San Diego Neighborhoods," *Criminology* 48 (2010): 797–829; Robert J. Sampson, "Rethinking Crime and Immigration," *Contexts* (Winter 2008): 28–33; Maria B. Vélez, "Contextualizing the Immigration and Crime Effect: An Analysis of Homicide in Chicago Neighborhoods," *Homicide Studies* 13, no. 3 (2009): 325–35.

90. Royce Bernstein Murray and Mary Giovagnoli, *DHS Progress Report: The Challenge of Reform* (Washington, DC: Immigration Policy Center, 2010).

91. Khalil Gibran Muhammad, *The Condemnation of Blackness: Race, Crime, and the Making of Modern Urban America* (Cambridge, MA: Harvard University Press, 2011).

92. Hernández, "Pursuant to Deportation"; Douglas S. Massey, *Categorically Unequal: The American Stratification System* (New York: Russell Sage Foundation, 2007); Ngai, *Impossible Subjects*.

93. Monte Mitchell, "Man Charged with Second-Degree Murder in Wreck; He Had Also Been Charged with Driving while Impaired; One Man Killed," *Winston-Salem Journal*, November 28, 2007, B1.

94. "Boonville Textile Plant Damaged in Fire," *Winston-Salem Journal*, September 20, 2007, A2.

95. Kasarda and Johnson, *The Economic Impact of the Hispanic Population on the State of North Carolina*.

96. "Census Shows Shift in Status; Whites Are Now the Minority in 10 Percent of Counties in the U.S.," *Winston-Salem Journal*, August 9, 2007, A1; Young, "Forsyth's New Face."

97. Laura Giovanelli, "Poll: Immigrants Are Burden to N.C.; Negative Opinion Is Up by 12 Percent since April," *Winston-Salem Journal*, November 21, 2006, Metro Edition, B2.

98. Michael Hewlett, "Hispanic Students a Pressure on Schools? Two Commissioners Raise Issue as Board Grapples with System's Needs," *Winston-Salem Journal*, November 11, 2005, Metro Edition, B1.

99. For an analysis of similar racializing practices in another context, see Celia Olivia Lacayo, "Perpetual Inferiority: Whites' Racial Ideology toward Latinos," *Sociology of Race and Ethnicity* 3, no. 4 (October 1, 2017): 566–79, https://doi.org/10.1177/2332649217698165

100. Richard Craver, "Spotlight on Hiring; Two Watchdog Groups Moving into the Triad Will Go After Employers of Illegal Immigrants," *Winston-Salem Journal*, September 10, 2006, Metro Edition, D1.

101. Weise, *Corazón de Dixie*,184.

102. Weise, *Corazón de Dixie*.

103. Weise, *Corazón de Dixie*, 200.

104. Importantly, Weise also notes that in Charlotte, efforts to push an anti-immigrant coalition onto Democrats failed, as African American commissioners in particular declined to join the anti-immigrant movement. Weise, *Corazón de Dixie*, 204–6.

105. Blair Goldstein, "Flaws in Forsyth's Data Cited; Study Gauged Services to Illegal Hispanic Immigrants," *Winston-Salem Journal*, December 30, 2007, A1.

106. National Academies of Sciences, Engineering, and Medicine, *The Integration of Immigrants into American Society* (Washington, DC: National Academies Press, 2015), 9–10.

107. National Academies of Sciences, Engineering, and Medicine, *The Integration of Immigrants into American Society*, 9–10.

108. Gordon, *Assimilation in American Life*.

109. Cassie Miller and Alexandra Wener-Winslow, "Ten Days After: Harassment and Intimidation in the Aftermath of the Election," *Southern Poverty Law Center*, November 29, 2016, https://www.splcenter.org/20161129/ten-days-after-harassment-and-intimidation-aftermath-election

110. Young, "Forsyth's New Face."

111. Menjívar and Abrego, "Legal Violence," 1381.

112. See also Hopkins, "Politicized Places." Many scholars contend that unwelcome contexts result from economic stagnation and demographic change; see Ted Brader, Nicholas A. Valentino, and Elizabeth Suhay, "What Triggers Public Opposition to Immigration? Anxiety, Group Cues, and Immigration Threat," *American Journal of Political Science* 52, no. 4 (2008): 959–78; Massey and Sánchez, *Brokered Boundaries*. Though the recession undoubtedly harmed immigrants, it intensified an ongoing process of closure already in process before 2008. Similarly, closure in this case happens out of sync with moments of major demographic change, suggesting that no singular mechanism explains how macro-level shifts shape local-level contextual change.

113. Shea Riggsbee Denning, "The Impact of North Carolina Driver's License Requirements and the REAL ID Act of 2005 on Unauthorized Immigrants," *Popular Government* 74, no. 3 (2009) Spring/Summer Online Supplement.

114. Grusky and Weeden, "Does the Sociological Approach to Studying Mobility Have a Future?"

115. Coleman, "The 'Local' Migration State"; Jamie Winders, "Bringing Back the (B)order: Post-9/11 Politics of Immigration, Borders, and Belonging in the Contemporary US South," *Antipode* 39, no. 5 (November 1, 2007): 920–42.

116. Kochhar, Suro, and Tafoya, "The New Latino South."

117. There is huge debate about whether caseworkers can do this. Legally, citizen children are eligible for programs like these but many states base all eligibility determinations on the parent (which is also legal to do).

118. Sheldon Danzinger, Koji Chavez, and Erin Cumberworth, *Poverty and the Great Recession* (Stanford, CA: Stanford Center on Poverty and Inequality, 2012); Rakesh Kochhar, Richard Fry, and Paul Taylor, "Wealth Gaps Rise to Record Highs between Whites, Blacks, Hispanics: Twenty to One," Pew Research Center Social & Demographic Trends website (Washington, DC: Pew Research Center, 2011).

119. Unfortunately, there is very little opinion poll data to corroborate shifting attitudes. Few opinion polls on immigration issues or Latinos had samples from the South of more than 15 respondents. However, in response to the immigrant marches, a Public Policy Polling poll in 2006 indicated that 81% of voters in the state of North Carolina would back a candidate who prefers tighter immigration controls.

120. Cravey and Valdivia, "Carolina Del Norte"; Gill, *The Latino Migration Experience in North Carolina*; Marrow, *New Destination Dreaming*; Smith and Furuseth, "The 'Nuevo South.'"

121. Cravey and Valdivia, "Carolina Del Norte."

122. Keith Barber, "Winston-Salem Residents Voice Concerns about Police Checkpoints,"

Yes! Weekly, December 14, 2011, http://yesweekly.com/article-13249-winston-salem-residents-voice-concerns-about-police-checkpoints.html

123. Kristin Collins, "Road Checkpoints Alarm Hispanics; Drunks, not Hispanics Are the Targets," *News and Observer*, August 8, 2008, B3.

124. Douglas S. Massey, "Racial Formation in Theory and Practice: The Case of Mexicans in the United States," *Race and Social Problems* 1, no. 1 (2009): 12–26; Portes and Rumbaut, *Immigrant America*; Gabriel R. Sánchez and Natalie Masuoka, "Brown-Utility Heuristic? The Presence and Contributing Factors of Latino Linked Fate," *Hispanic Journal of Behavioral Sciences* 32, no. 4 (2010): 519–31; Michael Jones-Correa, "Commonalities, Competition, and Linked Fate," in *Just Neighbors? Research on African American and Latino Relations in the United States*, ed. Edward E. Telles, Mark Q. Sawyer, and Gaspar Rivera-Salgado (New York: Russell Sage Foundation, 2011), 63–95.

125. Dina Okamoto and Kim Ebert, "Beyond the Ballot: Immigrant Collective Action in Gateways and New Destinations in the United States," *Social Problems* 57, no. 4 (2010): 529–58.

126. Massey and Sánchez, *Brokered Boundaries*; Portes and Rumbaut, *Immigrant America*; Portes and Stepick, *City on the Edge*.

127. Capps, Rosenblum, Rodríguez, and Chishti, *Delegation and Divergence*, 43.

128. Amalia Pallares and Nilda Flores-Gonzales, *Marcha: Latino Chicago and the Immigrant Rights Movement* (Champaign-Urbana: University of Illinois Press, 2010).

129. Aarti Kohli, Peter L. Markowitz, and Lisa Chavez, "Research Report: Secure Communities by the Numbers: An Analysis of Demographics and Due Process" (Berkeley: The Chief Justice Earl Warren Institute on Law and Social Policy at the University of California, Berkeley Law School, October 2011).

130. Brown and Jones, "Rethinking Panethnicity and the Race-Immigration Divide."

131. Helen B. Marrow, "Immigrant Bureaucratic Incorporation: The Dual Roles of Professional Missions and Government Policies," *American Sociological Review* 74 (2009): 756–76.

132. Kathryn Freeman Anderson and Jessie K. Finch, "Racially Charged Legislation and Latino Health Disparities: The Case of Arizona's S.B. 1070," *Sociological Spectrum* 34, no. 6 (2014): 526–48; Kathryn Freeman Anderson and Jessie K. Finch, "The Role of Racial Microaggressions, Stress, and Acculturation in Understanding Latino Health Outcomes in the USA," *Race and Social Problems* 9, no. 3 (2017): 218–33.

133. Ortiz, Vilma and Edward Telles. "Third Generation Disadvantage among Mexican Americans." *Sociology of Race and Ethnicity* 3, no. 4 (2017): 441–457.

134. Monica W. Varsanyi, Paul G. Lewis, Doris Marie Provine, and Scott Decker, "A Multilayered Jurisdictional Patchwork: Immigration Federalism in the United States," *Law & Policy* 34, no. 2 (2012): 138–58.

135. Douglas S. Massey and Karen A. Pren, "Origins of the New Latino Underclass," *Race and Social Problems* 4, no. 1 (2012): 5–17; Paul Taylor, Rakesh Kochhar, Richard Fry, Gabriel Velasco, and Seth Motel, "Twenty to One: Wealth Gaps Rise to Record Highs between Whites, Blacks, and Hispanics," *Pew Hispanic Center Research Report* 145 (Washington, DC: Pew Hispanic Center, 2011).

136. David Bell and David Blanchflower, "Young People and the Great Recession," *Oxford Review of Economic Policy* 27, no. 2 (2011): 241–67; Paola Giuliano and Antonio Spilimbergo, "Growing Up in a Recession: Beliefs and the Macroeconomy," NBER Working Paper 15321, issued September 2009, retrieved May 16, 2015, http://www.nber.org/papers/w15321

137. Carola Suárez-Orozco and Marcelo M. Suárez-Orozco, *Children of Immigration* (Cambridge, MA: Harvard University Press, 2001).

138. Frank D. Bean, Jennifer Lee, and James D. Bachmeier, "Immigration and the Color Line at the Beginning of the 21st Century," *Daedalus* 142, no. 3 (2013): 123–40.

139. Rubén G. Rumbaut and Alejandro Portes, *Ethnicities: Children of Immigrants in America* (Berkeley: University of California Press, 2001).

Chapter Four

1. Although some Afro-Mexican residents referred to themselves as Latino and black.

2. This shared status or *minority linked fate* between Latinos and African Americans in not unique to Winston-Salem in the early 2000s. Such shared frameworks (often resulting in political coalitions) have emerged at various points and locations throughout US history. In the wake of the civil rights movement, for example, Latinos in New York and Chicago built alliances with African Americans on the grounds of shared marginalization and exclusion in their communities.

3. Menjívar and Abrego, "Legal Violence."

4. Clare Jean Kim, "The Racial Triangulation of Asian Americans," *Politics & Society* 27, no. 1 (1999): 105–38.

5. Dowling, *Mexican Americans and the Question of Race*; Tanya Golash-Boza and William Darity, "Latino Racial Choices: The Effects of Skin Colour and Discrimination on Latinos' and Latinas' Racial Self-Identifications," *Ethnic and Racial Studies* 31, no. 5 (2008): 899–934; George Yancey, *Who Is White?* (Boulder, CO: Lynne Reiner, 2003).

6. Neil Foley, "Straddling the Color Line: The Legal Construction of Hispanic Identity in Texas," in *Not Just Black and White: Historical and Contemporary Perspectives on Immigration, Race, and Ethnicity in the United States*, ed. Nancy Foner and George M. Fredrickson (New York: Russell Sage Foundation, 2004), 341–57; Lani Guinier and Gerald Torres, *The Miner's Canary: Enlisting Race, Resisting Power, Transforming Democracy* (Cambridge, MA: Harvard University Press, 2002); David Montejano, *Chicano Politics and Society in the Late Twentieth Century* (Austin: University of Texas Press, 1999).

7. Rumbaut and Portes, *Ethnicities*; Portes and Stepick, *City on the Edge*; Reuel. R. Rogers, "Race-Based Coalitions among Minority Groups: Afro-Caribbean Immigrants and African Americans in New York City," *Urban Affairs Review* 39, no. 3 (2004): 283–317.

8. Vickerman, *Crosscurrents*; Kasinitz, *Caribbean New York*; Sutton and Makiesky-Barrow, "Migration and West Indian Racial and Ethnic Consciousness."

9. Rogers, *Afro-Caribbean Immigrants and the Politics of Incorporation*.

10. Rogers, *Afro-Caribbean Immigrants and the Politics of Incorporation*.

11. Hattam, *In the Shadow of Race*.

12. Dowling, *Mexican Americans and the Question of Race*; Gilda L. Ochoa, *Becoming Neighbors in a Mexican American Community: Power, Conflict, and Solidarity* (Austin: University of Texas Press, 2004); G. Cristina Mora, *Making Hispanics: How Activists, Bureaucrats, and Media Constructed a New American* (Chicago: University of Chicago Press, 2014).

13. Paul S. Taylor, *An American-Mexican Frontier* (Chapel Hill: University of North Carolina Press, 2011 [1934]), 37–38.

14. Taylor, *An American-Mexican Frontier*, 38.

15. Taylor, *An American-Mexican Frontier*, 254.

16. Taylor, *An American-Mexican Frontier*, 255.

17. Taylor, *An American-Mexican Frontier*, 267.

18. Taylor, *An American-Mexican Frontier*, 296.

19. Almaguer, *Racial Fault Lines*, xi.

20. Almaguer, *Racial Fault Lines*.

21. Almaguer, *Racial Fault Lines*.

22. Almaguer, *Racial Fault Lines*, 9.

23. Almaguer, *Racial Fault Lines*. Nevertheless, it was the Chinese, not Mexicans, who were most associated with blackness in the California context at the turn of the century. Longstanding practices of Chinese exclusion and the perception of Chinese as dirty and unscrupulous laborers located them, if temporarily, at the bottom of the racial hierarchy.

24. Molina, *How Race Is Made in America*.

25. Dowling, *Mexican Americans and the Question of Race*.

26. Ian F. Haney López, *Racism on Trial: The Chicano Fight for Justice* (Cambridge, MA: Harvard University Press, 2009).

27. Gloria Anzaldúa, *Borderlands/La Frontera: The New Mestiza* (San Francisco: Spinsters/ Aunt Lute Books, 1987); Haney López, *Racism on Trial*; Rafael Pérez-Torres, *Mestizaje: Critical Uses of Race in Chicano Culture* (Minneapolis: University of Minnesota Press, 2006); Victor Valle and Rodolfo D. Torres, "The Idea of Mestizaje and the 'Race' Problematic: Racialized Media Discourse in a Post-Fordist Landscape," in *Culture and Difference: Critical Perspectives on the Bicultural Experience in the United States* (Westport, CT: Bergin & Garvey, 1995), 139–50.

28. G. Cristina Mora and Michael Rodríguez-Muñiz, "Latinos, Race, and the American Future: A Response to Richard Alba's 'The Likely Persistence of a White Majority,'" *New Labor Forum* 26, no. 2 (2017): 45.

29. Winders and Smith, "Excepting/Accepting the South."

30. Gonzales, "Learning to Be Illegal"; Jessica M. Vasquez, *Mexican Americans across Generations: Immigrant Families, Racial Realities* (New York: New York University Press, 2011); John A. Garcia, Gabriel R. Sánchez, Shannon Sanchez-Youngman, Edward D. Vargas, and Vickie D.Ybarra, "Race as Lived Experience," *DuBois Review* 12, no. 2 (2015): 349–73; Rodolfo Espino and Michael M. Franz, "Latino Phenotypic Discrimination Revisited: The Impact of Skin Color on Occupational Status," *Journal of Social Psychology* 83, no. 2 (2002): 25–33.

31. Neckerman, Carter, and Lee, "Segmented Assimilation and Minority Cultures of Mobility"; Tomás R. Jiménez and Adam L. Horowitz, "When White Is Just Alright: How Immigrants Redefine Achievement and Reconfigure the Ethnoracial Hierarchy," *American Sociological Review* 78, no. 5 (2013): 849–71; Okamoto and Ebert, "Beyond the Ballot"; Natalie Masuoka, "Together They Become One: Examining the Predictors of Panethnic Group Consciousness among Asian Americans and Latinos," *Social Science Quarterly* 87, no.1 (2006): 993–1011.

32. Espiritu, *Asian American Panethnicity*.

33. Edward D. Vargas, Gabriel R. Sánchez, and Juan A. Valdez, "Immigration Policies and Group Identity: How Immigrant Laws Affect Linked Fate among U.S. Latino Populations," *Journal of Race, Ethnicity and Politics* 2, no. 1 (2017): 35–62.

34. Brown and Jones, "Rethinking Panethnicity and the Race-Immigration Divide."

35. Muhammad, *The Condemnation of Blackness*.

36. Sylvia Zamora, "Mexican Illegality, Black Citizenship, and White Power: Immigrant Perceptions of the U.S. Sociracial Hierarchy," *Journal of Ethnic and Migration Studies* (2017): 1–18.

37. http://www.pewhispanic.org/2008/11/05/the-hispanic-vote-in-the-2008-election/

38. NALEO, "Latino Decisions/NALEO/ImpreMedia National Post-Election Survey— Nov 2008," accessed December 4, 2017, http://www.latinodecisions.com/files/2913/3749/5067/ NALEO.Nov08.pdf

39. Latino Decisions, "Latino Decisions: Tracking Poll Week 10," last updated November 1, 2010, http://www.latinodecisions.com/files/4413/4697/5947/tracking_nov1.pdf.

Gallup reported similarly high ratings among Latinos throughout Obama's tenure. The year 2009 began with 74% approval among Latinos, spiked to 82% around the 100-day mark; 2010 began with 70% approval among Latinos, with a fairly steady drop throughout the year. The year 2011 began with 60% approval among Latinos, dipping slightly but staying relatively constant throughout the year; 2012 began with 55% approval among Latinos. This jumped to 75% at the end of 2012, and dipped slightly to 71% in the first few months of 2013. See Frank Newport, "Hispanics' Approval of Obama Down since '12," last updated September 26, 2014, http://www.gallup .com/poll/177404/hispanics-approval-obama-down.aspx for greater detail.

40. Lawrence Bobo and Vincent L. Hutchings, "Perceptions of Racial Group Competition: Extending Blumer's Theory of Group Position to a Multiracial Social Context," *American Sociological Review* 61, no. 6 (1996): 951–72; Michael C. Thornton and Yuko Mizuno, "Economic Well-Being and Black Adult Feelings toward Immigrants and Whites, 1984," *Journal of Black Studies* 30, no. 1 (1999): 15–44.

41. Dowling, *Mexican Americans and the Question of Race*, 2.

42. Dowling, *Mexican Americans and the Question of Race*, 73.

43. The "honorary white" thesis, popularized by Eduardo Bonilla-Silva and others, argues that in a shifting racial landscape, rather than become racial minorities, whites will instead absorb some minority groups, particularly certain Asian and Latino groups, as honorary whites. As such, while they may not be phenotypically white, they will acquire some of the social and structural privileges associated with whiteness.

44. For more discussion on racial triangulation, see Kim, "The Racial Triangulation of Asian Americans."

45. Tanya Golash-Boza, "Dropping the Hyphen? Becoming Latino(a)-American through Racialized Assimilation," *Social Forces* 85, no. 1 (September 2006): 28.

46. Ngai, *Impossible Subjects*.

47. Douglas S. Massey, "The Racialization of Mexicans in the United States? Racial Stratification in Theory and Practice, *Migracion y Desarrollo* 10, First Semester (2008): 59–85.

48. Fredrik Barth, *Ethnic Groups and Boundaries: The Social Organization of Culture Difference* (Long Grove, IL: Waveland, 1998).

49. Massey, *New Faces in New Places*, 64.

50. Devah Pager and Hana Shepherd, "The Sociology of Discrimination: Racial Discrimination in Employment, Housing, Credit, and Consumer Markets," *Annual Review of Sociology* 34 (2008): 181–209.

51. Margey Austin Turner, Rob Santos, Diane K. Levy, Doug Wissoker, Claudia Aranda, Rob Pitingolo, and the Urban Institute, *Housing Discrimination against Racial and Ethnic Minorities: Executive Summary* (Washington DC: US Department of Housing and Urban Development, 2013).

52. Telles and Ortiz, *Generations of Exclusion*.

53. Telles and Ortiz, *Generations of Exclusion*, 15.

54. Vasquez, *Mexican Americans across Generations*.

55. Golash-Boza, "Dropping the Hyphen?"

56. Many respondents mentioned Martin Luther King Jr. specifically, and appear to have learned about him from various sources—Martin Luther King Day celebrations, marches, and prayer breakfasts, newspaper coverage in the Spanish-language press, schools, and native-born friends and colleagues.

57. Gabriel R. Sánchez, "Latino Group Consciousness and Perceptions of Commonality with African Americans," *Social Science Quarterly* 89, no. 2 (2008): 428–44.

58. José Antonio Padín, "The Normative Mulattoes: The Press, Latinos, and the Racial Climate on the Moving Immigration Frontier," *Sociological Perspectives* 48, no. 1 (2005): 54.

59. Alejandro Portes and Rubén G. Rumbaut, *Legacies: The Story of the Immigrant Second Generation* (Berkeley: University of California Press, 2001), 189.

60. Even beyond the Southern context, recent scholarship indeed finds that those Latinos who do assert a pan-ethnic identity and who report discrimination are more likely to report closeness to African Americans. See Karen M. Kaufmann, "Cracks in the Rainbow: Group Commonality as a Basis for Latino and African American Political Coalitions," *Political Research Quarterly* 56, no. 2 (2003): 199–210; McClain, "Racial Intergroup Relations in a Set of Cities"; Sánchez, "Latino Group Consciousness and Perceptions of Commonality with African Americans."

61. Sánchez and Masuoka, "Brown-Utility Heuristic?"

62. Michael C. Dawson, *Behind the Mule: Race and Class in African-American Politics* (Princeton, NJ: Princeton University Press, 1994), 76.

63. Dawson, *Behind the Mule*, 77.

64. Pei-te Lien, *The Making of Asian America through Political Participation* (Philadelphia: Temple University Press, 2001); Pei-te Lien, M. Margaret Conway, and Janelle Wong, *The Politics of Asian Americans: Diversity and Community* (New York: Routledge, 2004); Masuoka, "Together They Become One"; Eric J. Oliver and Janelle Wong, "Intergroup Prejudice in Multiethnic Settings," *American Journal of Political Science* 47, no. 4 (2003): 567–82; Atiya Kai Stokes, "Latino Group Consciousness and Political Participation," *American Politics Research* 31, no. 4 (2003): 361–78.

65. Darity, Dietrich, and Hamilton, "Bleach in the Rainbow"; Golash-Boza, "Dropping the Hyphen?"; Paula D. McClain, Jessica D. Johnson Carew, Eugene Walton, and Candis S. Watts, "Group Membership, Group Identity, and Group Consciousness: Measures of Racial Identity in American Politics?" *Annual Review of Political Science* 12, no. 1 (2009): 471–85; Clara E. Rodríguez, *Changing Race: Latinos, the Census, and the History of Ethnicity in the United States* (New York: NYU Press, 2000).

66. Massey and Sánchez, *Brokered Boundaries*; Rodríguez, *Changing Race*. Possible—at least among the overwhelmingly Mexican population in Winston-Salem. While the demographics of the city are similar to many other communities in the region, in 2000, Central Americans numbered 1,101 compared to 11,908 Mexicans, and in 2010, Central Americans numbered 3,757, compared to 23,427 Mexicans residing in Winston-Salem (American Community Survey, US Census Data 2000 and 2010).

67. Lisa García Bedolla, "The Identity Paradox: Latino Language, Politics and Selective Dissociation," *Latino Studies* 1, no. 2 (2003): 264–83.

68. Kaufmann, "Cracks in the Rainbow."

69. Regina Freer and Claudia Sandoval Lopez, "Black, Brown, Young, and Together," in *Just Neighbors? Research on African American and Latino Relations in the United States*, ed. Edward E. Telles, Mark Q. Sawyer, and Gaspar Rivera-Salgado (New York: Russell Sage Foundation, 2011), 267–98; Jones-Correa and Hernàndez, "Commonalities, Competition and Linked Fate," 1–24; Karen M. Kaufmann, "Black and Latino Voters in Denver: Responses to Each Other's Political Leadership," *Political Science Quarterly* 118, no. 1 (2003): 107–26.

70. Dawson, *Behind the Mule*; Okamoto and Ebert, "Beyond the Ballot; Michael Rodríguez-Muñiz, "Grappling with Latinidad: Puerto Rican Activism in Chicago's Pro-Immigrant Rights

Movement," in *¡Marcha! Latino Chicago and the Immigrant Rights Movement* , ed. N. Flores-González and A. Pallares (Champaign-Urbana: University of Illinois Press, 2010), 237–58.

71. Sanchez and Masuoka, "Brown-Utility Heuristic?"

72. Chris Zepeda-Millán and Sophia J. Wallace, "Racialization in Times of Contention: How Social Movements Influence Latino Racial Identity," *Politics, Groups and Identities* 1, no. 4 (2013): 510–27.

73. Dawson, *Behind the Mule*, 76.

Chapter Five

1. Elizabeth Fussell, "Warmth of the Welcome: Attitudes toward Immigrants and Immigration Policy in the United States," *Annual Review of Sociology* 40, no. 1 (2014): 479–98; James H. Johnson and Melvin L. Oliver, "Interethnic Minority Conflict in Urban America: The Effects of Economic and Social Dislocations," *Urban Geography* 10, no. 5 (1989): 449–63; Paula D. McClain et al., "Racial Distancing in a Southern City: Latino Immigrants' Views of Black Americans," *Journal of Politics* 68, no. 3 (2006): 571–84; McClain et al., "Black Americans and Latino Immigrants in a Southern City."

2. The bulk of the intergroup relations literature emphasizes the problems that emerge from intergroup relations. That is, what we care about as social scientists is, more often than not, conflict. Certainly, this is a logical emphasis, as intergroup conflict has been shown to result in all sorts of problematic outcomes, undermining community trust, and suppressing social and political cooperation. See Cybelle Fox, "The Changing Color of Welfare? How Whites' Attitudes toward Latinos Influence Support for Welfare," *American Journal of Sociology* 110, no. 3 (2004): 580–625; Jennifer L. Hochschild and Reuel R. Rogers, "Race Relations in a Diversifying Nation," in *New Directions: African Americans in a Diversifying Nation*, ed. James S. Jackson (Washington, DC: National Policy Association, 2000), 45–85. But without an understanding of what happens when groups engage in civil or cooperative relations and the conditions under which positive relations emerge, we only have one part of the story, can say very little about intergroup relations in general, and have few tools to make sense of the kind of positive race relations and black-Latino relations we observe in Winston-Salem and elsewhere.

3. See Claudine Gay, "Seeing Difference: The Effect of Economic Disparity on Black Attitudes toward Latinos," *American Journal of Political Science* 50, no. 4 (2006): 982–97; Hochschild and Rogers, "Race Relations in a Diversifying Nation"; Earl Ofari Hutchinson, *The Latino Challenge to Black America* (Los Angeles: Middle Passage, 2007); Kaufmann, "Cracks in the Rainbow"; Vaca, *The Presumed Alliance*; Wilkerson, "In Florida, a Death Foretold," for examples of conflict; for examples of literature that reviews this emphasis, see Edward E. Telles, Mark Q. Sawyer, and Gaspar Rivera-Salgado, *Just Neighbors? Research on African American and Latino Relations in the United States* (New York: Russell Sage Foundation, 2011).

4. The populations of two of the four main states of origin of Mexicans in Winston-Salem (Guerrero and Veracruz) are known for having high levels of African ancestry, including significant numbers of Afro-Mexicans. See Laura A. Lewis, "Blacks, Black Indians, Afromexicans: The Dynamics of Race, Nation, and Identity in a Mexican Moreno Community (Guerrero)," *American Ethnologist* 27, no. 4 (November 2000): 898–926; Sue, *Land of the Cosmic Race*.

5. Ramón's labeling of whites as "Americans" was not uncommon in my study. Many of my respondents referred to whites as Americans, while specifying Moreno, Negro, Afro-Americano, black American, or African American for US-born black Americans. This discursive move is consistent with much of the language I observed when doing preliminary research in Mexico as well.

6. Guinier and Torres, *The Miner's Canary*, 4.

7. See Barth, *Ethnic Groups and Boundaries*; Andreas Wimmer, "The Making and Unmaking of Ethnic Boundaries: A Multilevel Process Theory," *American Journal of Sociology* 113, no. 4 (2008): 970–1022.

8. Guinier and Torres, *The Miner's Canary*, 10.

9. Guinier and Torres, *The Miner's Canary*, 10.

10. Guinier and Torres, *The Miner's Canary*, 17.

11. Luis R. Fraga, John A. Garcia, Rodney E. Hero, Michael Jones-Correa, Valerie Martinez-Ebers, and Gary M. Segura, *Latinos in the New Millennium: An Almanac of Opinion, Behavior, and Policy Preferences* (New York: Cambridge University Press, 2011), 168–69.

12. David Lopez and Yen Le Espiritu, "Panethnicity in the United States: A Theoretical Framework," *Ethnic and Racial Studies* 13, no. 2 (1990): 198–224; Joane Nagel, "American Indian Ethnic Renewal: Politics and the Resurgence of Identity," *American Sociological Review* 60, no. 6 (1995): 947–65; Mora, "Cross-Field Effects and Ethnic Classification."

13. Brown and Jones, "Rethinking Panethnicity and the Race-Immigration Divide."

14. Lopez and Espiritu, "Panethnicity in the United States"; Nagel, "American Indian Ethnic Renewal."

15. Lopez and Espiritu, "Panethnicity in the United States"; Mora, *Making Hispanics*; Rodríguez-Muñiz, "Grappling with Latinidad."

16. See Brown and Jones, "Rethinking Panethnicity and the Race-Immigration Divide"; Matt A. Barreto, Benjamin F. Gonzalez, and Gabriel R. Sánchez, "Rainbow Coalition in the Golden State? Exposing Myths, Uncovering New Realities in Latino Attitudes towards Blacks," in *Black and Brown Los Angeles: A Contemporary Reader*, ed. Laura Pulido and Josh Kun (Berkeley: University of California Press, 2010), 203–32; Sánchez and Masuoka, "Brown-Utility Heuristic?"

17. Brown and Jones, "Rethinking Panethnicity and the Race-Immigration Divide."

18. I posit that interracial relations are a function of both socioeconomic and racial status, but that in much of the scholarship on intergroup relations, race and class are conflated, inadequately accounting for circumstances where socioeconomic status does not breed competition, and that racial status is characterized by *minority linked fate*. Resource competition emerges between minority groups of perceived equal socioeconomic status who engage in zero-sum analysis of their access to institutional resources and the labor market. There are cases, however, in which racial status changes intergroup perceptions of equal economic status so that they are believed to be not a basis for competition, but a basis for solidarity. In these cases, racial status, especially shared external threat, is especially robust, and zero-sum thinking is not employed. See Michael Clemmons, "Beyond the Barriers: Toward a Durable African-American-Latino Political Coalition," *Journal of Latino/Latin American Studies* 5, no. 1 (2013): 40–56; Jennifer Gordon and R. A. Lenhardt, "Rethinking Work and Citizenship," *UCLA Law Review* 55, no. 1161 (2008): 1162–238; John D. Márquez, *Black-Brown Solidarity: Racial Politics in the New Gulf South* (Austin: University of Texas Press, 2014); George Priestly, "Ethnicity, Class, and Race in the United States: Prospects for African-American/Latino Alliances," *Latin American Perspectives* 34, no. 1 (2007): 53–63.

In this study, I accept the theoretical and methodological assumptions of conflict theory that shared socioeconomic status can breed conflict, but not the common assumption that minority groups are at the bottom of the socioeconomic ladder; see Karyn R. Lacy, *Blue-Chip Black: Race, Class, and Status in the New Black Middle Class* (Berkeley: University of California Press, 2007); Neckerman, Carter, and Lee, "Segmented Assimilation and Minority Cultures of Mobility"; Mary Pattillo-McCoy, *Black Picket Fences: Privilege and Peril among the Black Middle Class* (Chicago: University of Chicago Press, 1999); Perlmann and Waldinger, "Second Generation Decline?" As theorized under contact theory, under conditions where economic competition is absent, sociable contact between equal status groups reduces racial animus by fostering positive encounters between groups with similar tastes, values, and behaviors; therefore, creating a sense of collectivity. See Gordon W. Allport, *The Nature of Prejudice: 25th Anniversary Edition* (New York: Basic, 1979 [1954]); Stuart W. Cook, "Experimenting on Social Issues: The Case of School Desegregation," *American Psychologist* 40, no. 4 (1985): 452–60; Samuel L. Gaertner, Mary C. Rust, John F. Dovidio, Betty A. Bachman, and Phyllis A. Anastasio, "The Contact Hypothesis: The Role of a Common Ingroup Identity on Reducing Intergroup Bias," *Small Group Research* 25, no. 2 (1994): 224–49; Lee Sigelman and Susan Welch, "The Contact Hypothesis Revisited: Black-White Interaction and Positive Racial Attitudes," *Social Forces* 71, no. 3 (1993): 781–95.

Under the contact thesis then, rather than necessarily breed conflict, proximity can have the opposite effect, reducing intergroup animus by breaking down group boundaries. However, positive contact—amicable, intimate, and regular—is more likely to emerge when groups inhabit, or believe they inhabit, *distinct socioeconomic* statuses. Otherwise, when both groups' socioeconomic status is low, contact may fuel feelings of threat and competition, as suggested under conflict theory, or remain neutral when both groups' socioeconomic status is high. This is an important intervention, because while threat and competition research frequently assumes minorities occupy positions of low socioeconomic status, I argue that we must recognize socioeconomic diversity among minority communities while emphasizing that socioeconomic status is not sufficient in understanding how status shapes intergroup relations. In this way, a sense of shared racial status as minorities, or *minority linked fate*, alongside a failure to perceive shared and, therefore, competitive socioeconomic status, fosters social ties that produce feelings of closeness rather than conflict. Unlike extant theories of intergroup relations, I show how race, as relationally constructed and experienced, shapes how groups perceive and interact with one another. Moreover, I suggest that while class and race are not identical forms of status, they interact to inform and shape intergroup relations. While socioeconomic status can serve an exclusionary function, racial status can foster unity. Whether or not groups share these statuses and how they interact plays an important role in producing intergroup relations.

19. In Winston 40 percent of blacks lived in owner-occupied dwellings as of 2000, compared to 76 percent of whites, and 15 percent of Latinos. See US Census Bureau, "Money Income in the United States: 2000."

20. Middle-class minorities are more likely to live alongside lower-middle or working-class neighbors (Pattillo-McCoy, *Black Picket Fences*).

21. See Waters et al., "Immigrants and African Americans."

22. It should be noted that not all cities that have undergone racial and ethnic change have appeared to experience this same level of tension. For example, the settling of significant Mexican and Central American populations in Oakland, and Puerto Rican, Dominican, and Caribbean origin populations in Harlem/Spanish Harlem, have not resulted in overt conflict.

23. In the larger context of this interview, "they" refers to a conventional wisdom understanding of conflict. During this period, there were no reports of black-Latino conflict in the local media.

24. It might be posed that high-quality contact leading to solidarity is a circular argument—the thinking being that solidarity may actually produce high-quality contact rather than the other way around. Certainly, I would argue that there is a dialectical relationship between high-

quality contact and solidarity, in that as solidarity increases, high-quality contact is also likely to increase. Likewise, as high-quality contact increases, solidarity is more likely to occur. However, I would argue in terms of causal relations, high-quality contact is needed for solidarity to occur. This sense of shared relations and commonality is needed to establish the conditions for solidarity work.

25. Analysis of 2011–2015 American Community Survey census data indicate that 16% of Winston-Salem metro area newlyweds are intermarried, but the sample size was too small to disaggregate race or ethnicity by category. Pew Research Center, "Intermarriage across the U.S. by Metro Area," Pew Research Center's Social & Demographic Trends Project (blog), May 18, 2017, http://www.pewsocialtrends.org/interactives/intermarriage-across-the-u-s-by-metro-area/

26. Camille Zubrinksy Charles, *Won't You Be My Neighbor? Race, Class, and Residence in Los Angeles* (New York: Russell Sage Foundation, 2006).

27. Virginia Foxx was the US representative to the 5th district of North Carolina (R), and was known for her strict anti-immigrant stance, particularly in the 2008 election cycle.

28. In 2011, the ACLU filed a formal inquiry in response to hundreds of complaints that police checkpoints unfairly targeted black and Latino residents. See Bertrand Gutierrez, "ACLU Reviewing City Checkpoints," *Winston-Salem Journal*, September 16, 2011, http://www.journalnow.com/news/local/aclu-reviewing-city-police-checkpoints/article_2d5572b9-7f90-587a-a10a-674997e83702.html

29. Wendy Brown, "Wounded Attachments," *Political Theory* 21, no. 3 (1993): 390–410; Espiritu, *Asian American Panethnicity*; Jennifer A. Jones, "Who Are We? Producing Group Identity through Everyday Practices of Conflict and Discourse," *Sociological Perspectives* 54, no. 2 (2011): 139–62.

30. Fraga et al., *Latinos in the New Millennium*, 16.

31. Fraga et al., *Latinos in the New Millennium*, 148.

32. See also Kim M. Williams, "Black Political Interests on Immigrant Rights: Evidence from Black Newspapers, 2000–2013." *Journal of African American Studies* 20, no. 3–4 (December 1, 2016): 248–71.

33. In general, however, Hispanic issues were infrequently raised in council meetings, largely by community members in attendance who raised issues regarding resource access and services for Latinos in the community. Between 2006 and 2010, 2008 had the highest proportion of discussions on Latino issues, with 12.5% of the meetings including some discussion of Latinos. Topics included a need for more city services and fair treatment in the city for all minorities.

34. City Council Meeting Minutes, April 21, 2008.

35. The Winston police chief from 2004–2008 was a black woman, replaced in 2008 by a white man who pledged to maintain the policy of declining to participate in immigration enforcement.

36. Fraga et al., *Latinos in the New Millennium*, 158.

37. Other signatories included the Mexican American Legal Defense and Educational Fund, the National Council of La Raza, the NAACP, and the Center for Asian American Justice. http://leyesdeimigracion.blogspot.com/2009/; http://www.univision.com/noticias/reforma-migratoria/mas-de-520-organizaciones-pidieron-a-obama-cancelar-programa-antiinmigrante; http://www.univision.com/content/content.jhtml?chid=3&schid=278&secid=12134&cid=2067613&pagenum=3

38. Mary M. Shaffrey, "Caucus Lists Steps for Reform; Blacks' Immigration Ideas like Democrats," *Winston-Salem Journal*, August 6, 2006, A1.

39. Dan Galindo, "Blacks, Hispanics Begin a Dialogue: NAACP, City Agency Sponsor Meeting to Explore Ways to Remove Barriers," *Winston-Salem Journal*, June 24, 2005, B1.

40. Human Relations Commission archives, video recording.

41. I presume here she is referring broadly to the communities of color, particularly Latinos, that she engages with in her organizing work.

42. It is worth noting that Winston-Salem city leadership is quite stable and operates under a council manager system, in which the city council determines city policies, which are implemented and overseen by a city manager, hired by the council. The city manager is responsible for hiring most city employees, who in turn report directly to the city manager or assistant city managers. Since 2006, Lee Garrity has served as Winston's City Manager and has worked for the city in a variety of administrative positions since 1990. Mayor Allen Joines was elected in 2001, and as of this writing, continues to serve in that position. See http://www.cityofws.org/departments/city-manager/more-about-city-managers-office

43. These events were largely organized by city and church leaders rather than community organizers. However, it is important to note that in Winston-Salem, while there was a large base of nonprofit organizations and service agencies in the city, few community activist organizations existed outside of the church.

44. The police chief took over from an African American woman chief in 2008.

45. Lewis A. Coser, *Functions of Social Conflict* (New York: Simon and Schuster, 1956), but see Kaufmann, "Cracks in the Rainbow."

46. Bernice Powell Johnson, "Civil Rights Journal: Teaching Children Survival Skills," *Winston-Salem Chronicle*, November 7, 1997, A10.

47. Courtney Gaillard, "Black Rep Reaches Out by Adding Hispanic Wing," *Winston-Salem Chronicle*, August 8, 2002, A9.

48. Paul Collins, "Cross-Cultural: Quality Schools Celebrate American Latin American Culture Day," *Winston-Salem Chronicle*, June 5, 2003, C1–2.

49. Weise, *Corazón de Dixie*, 187–88.

50. Courtney Galliard, "Hispanic, Black Ministers PowWow," *Winston-Salem Chronicle*, May 26, 2005, A1.

51. Fraga et al., *Latinos in the New Millennium*, 77.

52. Mindola et al., *Black-Brown Relations and Stereotypes*, 40.

53. It should be noted here that because this study focuses on community leadership from the viewpoint of Latinos, there is asymmetry in the interviews conducted with black residents. While I also draw from newspaper and community observations, such limitations raise the question—is there a difference in the black population between leaders and locals? It is certainly the case that the black leadership was unified in its pro-Latino, pro-immigrant politics. While these views were widespread in the broader community and consistent with national data (see Waters et al., "Immigrants and African Americans") that shows greater levels of support and a sense of shared status among blacks that other groups, there was nevertheless a minority of locals who expressed more competitive or conflictual views. While they failed to derail efforts by leaders or sway Latino attitudes, the mechanisms that produced these less hospitable views are explored later in the chapter.

54. Molina, *How Race Is Made in America*, 125. See also Weise's discussion of black politicians in North Carolina who constantly sought to stymie anti-Latino sentiment with an eye toward long-term coalition building. Weise, *Corazón de Dixie*, 206.

55. Waters et al., "Immigrants and African Americans."

56. Thomas F. Pettigrew, "Intergroup Contact Theory," *Annual Review of Psychology* 49 (1998): 65–85.

57. The Darryl Hunt case refers to the conviction and eventual exoneration of a young black man of 19 of the rape and murder of a white woman in the 1984. DNA results proved his innocence in 1994, but he was not exonerated until 2004. Eventually, another man whose DNA matched the profile on the scene, confessed to the murder. Hunt received over a million dollars in a settlement against Winston-Salem in 2007. Hunt's case served as a lightning rod for race relations in Winston-Salem for decades. See Innocence Project, "Darryl Hunt Time Served: 19 Years," accessed July 5, 2016, http://www.innocenceproject.org/cases/darryl-hunt/

58. US House of Representatives, "Gangs, Fraud and Sexual Predators."

59. Weise, *Corazón de Dixie*, 200.

60. Michael W. Giles and Arthur Evans, "External Threat, Perceived Threat, and Group Identity," *Social Science Quarterly* 66, no. 1 (1985): 50; Hank Rothgerber, "External Intergroup Threat as an Antecedent to Perceptions in In-Group and Out-Group Homogeneity," *Journal of Personality and Social Psychology* 73, no. 6 (1997): 1206–12; Sanchez and Masuoka, "Brown-Utility Heuristic?"

61. Darity, Dietrich, and Hamilton, "Bleach in the Rainbow"; Golash-Boza and Darity, "Latino Racial Choices"; Marrow, *New Destination Dreaming*.

62. Jennifer Lee and Frank D. Bean, "Reinventing the Color Line: Immigration and America's New Racial/Ethnic Divide," *Social Forces* 86, no. 2 (2007): 561–86.

63. It is relevant to note here that unions play a very minimal role in shaping race relations and immigration discourse in Winston-Salem. Although North Carolina, like most states in the region, is a right-to-work state, other communities have seen significant progress in union activism, including notable alliances between black and Latino workers to unionize Smithfield meatpacking plants as well as other efforts to advocate for workers' rights throughout the state. Union pressure in the Winston-Salem metro area, however, is especially low. In Winston-Salem and neighboring areas, high wages and union-busting efforts throughout the twentieth century prevented unions from gaining much traction despite the long history of manufacturing in the region.

64. The free paper is widely available, and printed in three city editions.

65. Weise, *Corazón de Dixie*, 202–4.

66. It is important to reiterate here that the majority of the interviews I conducted with African Americans were with community leaders. Consequently, the voices of the general public may be somewhat muted relative to that of the leadership. However, this study is also embedded in a yearlong ethnography and examination of newspaper records that provided significant additional context and insight into the views and practices of community members regardless of social status.

67. Herbert Blumer, "Race Prejudice as a Sense of Group Position," *Pacific Sociological Review* 1, no. 1 (1958): 3–7.

68. Bobo and Hutchings, "Perceptions of Racial Group Competition."

69. But see Lawrence D. Bobo, "Prejudice as Group Position: Microfoundations of a Sociological Approach to Racism and Race Relations," *Journal of Social Issues* 55, no. 3 (1999): 445–72; Laura López-Sanders, "Embedded and External Brokers: The Distinct Roles of Intermediaries in Workplace Inequality," *American Behavioral Scientist* 58, no. 2 (2014): 331–46.

70. Robert M. Adelman, Cameron Lippard, Charles Jaret, and Lesley Williams Reid, "Jobs, Poverty, and Earnings in American Metropolises: Do Immigrants Really Hurt the Economic

Outcomes of Blacks?" *Sociological Focus* 38, no. 4 (2005): 261–85; Bobo and Hutchings, "Perceptions of Racial Group Competition"; Mindola et al., *Black-Brown Relations and Stereotypes*; Frank Morris and James G. Gimpel, *Immigration, Intergroup Conflict, and the Erosion of African American Political Power in the 21st Century* (Washington, DC: Center for Immigration Studies, 2007).

71. George J. Borjas, *Friends or Strangers: The Impact of Immigrants on the U.S. Economy* (New York: Basic, 1990); Morris and Gimpel, *Immigration, Intergroup Conflict, and the Erosion of African American Political Power in the 21st Century*; Hutchinson, *The Latino Challenge to Black America*; Johnson and Oliver, "Interethnic Minority Conflict in Urban America"; Thornton and Mizuno, "Economic Well-Being and Black Adult Feelings toward Immigrants and Whites, 1984."

72. Kaufmann, "Black and Latino Voters in Denver"; Rene R. Rocha, "Black-Brown Coalitions in Local School Board Elections," *Political Research Quarterly* 60, no. 2 (2007): 315–27.

73. Kaufmann, "Cracks in the Rainbow"; Paula D. McClain and Albert K. Karnig, "Black and Hispanic Socioeconomic and Political Competition," *American Political Science Review* 84, no. 2 (1990): 535–45; Kent L. Tedin and Richard W. Murray, "Support for Biracial Political Coalitions among Blacks and Hispanics," *Social Science Quarterly* 75, no. 4 (1994): 772–89.

74. Altha J. Cravey, "The Changing South Latino Labor and Poultry Production in Rural North Carolina," *Southeastern Geographer* 37, no. 2 (1997): 295–300; William A. Kandel and Emilio Parrado, "Hispanic Population Growth and Public School Response in Two New South Immigrant Destinations," in *Latinos in the New South: Transformations of Place*, ed. Heather A. Smith and Owen J. Furuseth (Burlington: Ashgate, 2006), 111–34; Ann V. Millard and Jorge Chapa, *Apple Pie & Enchiladas: Latino Newcomers in the Rural Midwest* (Austin: University of Texas Press, 2004).

75. But see Gay, "Seeing Difference"; Monica McDermott, "Black Attitudes and Hispanic Immigrants in South Carolina," in *Just Neighbors? Research on African American and Latino Relations in the United States*, ed. Edward Telles, Mark Q. Sawyer, and Gaspar Rivera-Salgado (New York: Russell Sage Foundation, 2011), 242–66.

76. But see Adelman et al. (2005), who find that while there is competition between blacks and Latinos of a low socioeconomic status in the labor market, middle-class blacks benefit from the presence of immigrant newcomers.

77. John Iceland, *Where We Live Now: Immigration and Race in the United States* (Berkeley: University of California Press, 2009); Neckerman, Carter, and Lee, "Segmented Assimilation and Minority Cultures of Mobility"; Odem and Lacy, *Latino Immigrants and the Transformation of the U.S. South.*

78. US Census Bureau, "B19001B [for each census tract]: Household Income in the Past 12 Months (in 2010 Inflation-Adjusted Dollars) (Black or African American Alone Householder), American Community Survey 5-Year Estimates, 2010," American Fact Finder website (Washington, DC: US Census Bureau), retrieved January 2, 2015, http://factfinder2.census.gov ·

79. Pattillo-McCoy, *Black Picket Fences.*

80. But see Frank D. Bean, James D. Bachmeier, Susan K. Brown, and Rosaura Tafoya-Estrada, "Immigration and Labor Market Dynamics," in *Just Neighbors? Research on African American and Latino Relations in the United States*, ed. Edward E. Telles, Mark Q. Sawyer, and Gaspar Rivera-Salgado (New York: Russell Sage Foundation, 2011), 37–60.

81. See Waters et al., "Immigrants and African Americans," 379, for a discussion of divergence in studies and the importance of both racial and class composition in shaping divergent empirical outcomes at the community level.

82. Rodney E. Hero, "Multiracial Coalitions in City Elections Involving Minority Candidates: Some Evidence from Denver," *Urban Affairs Quarterly* 25, no. 2 (1989); Kenneth J. Meier, Paula D. McClain, J. L. Polinard, and Robert D. Wrinkle, "Divided or Together? Conflict and Cooperation between African Americans and Latinos," *Political Research Quarterly* 57, no. 3 (2004): 399–409; McClain et al., "Black Americans and Latino Immigrants in a Southern City."

83. Shang Ha, "The Consequences of Multiracial Contexts on Public Attitudes Toward Immigration," paper presented at the American Political Science Association, Philadelphia, Pennsylvania, August 31–September 3, 2006; Kaufmann, "Black and Latino Voters in Denver"; Gary M. Segura and Helena Alves Rodrigues, "Comparative Ethnic Politics in the United States: Beyond Black and White," *Annual Review of Political Science* 9 (2006): 375–95.

84. López-Sanders, "Embedded and External Brokers"; Ribas, *On the Line.*

85. Yen Le Espiritu, "Asian American Panethnicity: Contemporary National and Transnational Possibilities," in *Not Just Black and White: Historical and Contemporary Perspectives on Immigration, Race, and Ethnicity in the United States,* ed. Nancy Foner and George M. Fredrickson (New York: Russell Sage Foundation, 2005), 217–34; Jean Junn, "From Coolie to Model Minority: U.S. Immigration Policy and the Construction of Racial Identity, *DuBois Review* 4, no. 2 (2007): 355–73.

86. Amy Foerster, "Race, Identity, and Belonging: 'Blackness' and the Struggle for Solidarity in a Multiethnic Labor Union," *Social Problems* 51, no. 3 (2004): 386–409, https://doi.org/10.1525/sp.2004.51.3.386; Nancy Foner, "Introduction. West Indian Migration to New York: An Overview," in *Islands in the City: West Indian Migration to New York,* edited by N. Foner (Berkeley: University of California Press, 2001), 1–22; Michael Jones-Correa, Sophia J. Wallace, and Chris Zepeda-Millán, "The Impact of Large-Scale Collective Action on Latino Perceptions of Commonality and Competition with African-Americans," *Social Science Quarterly* 97, no. 2 (2015): 458–75.

87. López-Sanders, "Embedded and External Brokers."

88. Stuesse, *Scratching Out a Living,* 114–16.

89. Stuesse, *Scratching Out a Living,* 221.

90. Richard Alba, Rubén G. Rumbaut, and Karen Marotz, "A Distorted Nation: Perceptions of Racial/Ethnic Group Sizes and Attitudes toward Immigrants and Other Minorities," *Social Forces* 4, no. 2 (2006): 899–917; Bobo and Hutchings, "Perceptions of Racial Group Competition"; Susan Olzak and Joane Nagel, *Competitive Ethnic Relations* (Orlando: Academic, 1986); Muzafer Sherif, *Groups in Harmony and Tension: An Integration of Studies on Intergroup Relations* (New York: Harper, 1953); Muzafer Sherif, O. J. Harvey, B. Jack White, William R. Hood, Carolyn W. Sherif, *Intergroup Conflict and Cooperation: The Robbers Cave Experiment* (Norman, OK: University Book Exchange, 1961); Pierre L. Van den Berghe, *Race and Racism: A Comparative Perspective* (New York: Wiley, 1967); Donald R. Kinder and Nicholas Winter, "Exploring the Racial Divide: Blacks, Whites, and Opinion on National Policy," *American Journal of Political Science* 45, no. 2 (2001): 439–56.

91. It is worth noting that in Blumer's (1958) race prejudice thesis, he argues that race prejudice stems not from feelings toward the outgroup, but a sense of group position, including both a sense of belonging to the in-group and difference from the outgroup, but much of the work on threat misstates the centrality of conflict to his argument, theorizing proximity as the primary mechanism shaping intergroup prejudice. Blumer's argument is subtler, theorizing that the process of acquiring a sense of prejudice is as much a process of defining and giving meaning to the in-group as an orientation to the outgroup as a result of interaction between groups

in the public arena. In Blumer's formulation then, group position is not fixed, but shaped by an ongoing process of intergroup interactions and communications, in which the dominant group defines and redefines both the subordinate group and relations between them. In this process the subordinate group can shift.

92. Rogers Brubaker, *Ethnicity without Groups* (Cambridge, MA: Harvard University Press, 2004).

93. Fraga et al., *Latinos in the New Millennium*.

94. Although a full range of perceptions was experienced in both cases.

95. It is also relevant for the purposes of understanding intergroup relations, that many immigrant respondents also reported hostilities within the Latino group. Some suggested that access to citizenship divided Latinos and prevented true solidarity. Others suggested that a stronger sense of Americanness among Puerto Ricans, in particular, distanced them from immigrants' issues. While many others also argued that there was true solidarity among Latinos, it is important to keep in mind that both intra- and intergroup relations are complex and varied. As race is a socially constructed group, there is reason to assume that solidarity is natural, just as there is no reason to presume that intergroup relations are necessarily conflictual.

96. It is important to note that among the Mexican immigrants I interviewed, there were varying interpretations of African American and civil rights history in the United States. In part due to varying levels of education and a lack of experience with US history, many immigrants held incorrect assumptions about US history. Some reported that Martin Luther King freed the slaves, while others argued that African Americans arrived as immigrants. On occasion, these misinterpretations shaped their ideas about race and race relations between blacks and Latinos.

97. This is consistent with a classical model of prejudice, which emphasizes the "social learning of cultural ideas and affective responses to particular groups." Bobo and Hutchings, "Perceptions of Racial Group Competition," 954.

98. Mindola et al., *Black-Brown Relations and Stereotypes*.

99. Ted Brader, Nicholas A. Valentino, Ashley E. Jardina, and Timothy J. Ryan, "The Racial Divide on Immigration Opinion: Why Blacks Are Less Threatened by Immigrants," SSRN Scholarly Paper (Rochester, NY: Social Science Research Network, 2010).

100. Brown and Jones, "Rethinking Panethnicity and the Race-Immigration Divide."

101. Brubaker, *Ethnicity without Groups*; Celina Su, "We Call Ourselves by Many Names: Storytelling and Interminority-Coalition Building," *Community Development Journal* 45, no. 4 (2010): 439–57.

102. Foerster, "Race, Identity, and Belonging"; Su, "We Call Ourselves by Many Names."

103. Jennifer A. Jones, "Blacks May Be Second Class, but They Can't Make Them Leave: Mexican Racial Formation and Immigrant Status in Winston-Salem," *Latino Studies* 10, no. 1 (2012): 60–80.

104. Chris Zepeda-Millán, *Latino Mass Mobilization: Immigration, Racialization, and Activism* (Cambridge: Cambridge University Press, 2017), 15.

105. Zepeda-Millán, *Latino Mass Mobilization*, 16–17.

106. John Bentacur and Douglas Gills, "The African American and Latino Coalition Experience in Chicago under Mayor Harold Washington," in *The Collaborative City: Opportunities and Struggles for Blacks and Latinos in U.S. Cities*, ed. John Bentacur and Douglas Gills (New York: Routledge, 2000), 59–88; Steven Greenhouse, "After 15 Years, North Carolina Plant Unionizes," *New York Times*, December 12, 2008, A10; Jennifer Lee, *Civility in the City: Blacks, Jews, and Koreans in Urban America* (Cambridge, MA: Harvard University Press, 2002); Jeffrey Ogbar,

"Puerto Rico en mi Corazon: The Young Lords, Black Power and Puerto Rican Nationalism in the U.S. 1966–1972," *Centro Journal* 18, no. 1 (2006): 148–69.

107. See also Behnken, *Civil Rights and Beyond*, for a discussion regarding the complicated and multifaced relations between blacks and Latinos in the twentieth century.

108. Neckerman, Carter, and Lee, "Segmented Assimilation and Minority Cultures of Mobility"; see also Dawson, *Behind the Mule*; Foerster, "Race, Identity, and Belonging"; Reuel Rogers, "Black Like Who? Afro-Caribbean Immigrants, African Americans, and the Politics of Group Identity," in *Islands in the City: West Indian Migration to New York*, ed. N. Foner (Berkeley: University of California Press, 2001), 163–92.

109. In 2014, only one state lawmaker, Tom Apodara, self-identified as Latino (R-Henderson), despite Latinos making up 8.4% of the state population at the time. Blacks, who were 22% of the state, were 18% of the legislature in 2013. Throughout the region, Latinos are rarely present in public office. In 2014, with the exception of Florida and Texas, only 6 Latinos served in Congress, statewide offices, or state legislatures throughout the South (http://www.naleo.org/at_a_glance).

110. http://www.wral.com/few-women-latinos-in-general-assembly/13784129/; http://www.naleo.org/appointments

111. Jackson, "Congressional Members to Join Civil Rights Groups in Fight against Alabama's 'Juan Crow' Law"; Krissah Thompson, "Immigrant Groups Reach Out to Blacks," *Washington Post*, March 20, 2010, A3.

112. Gill, "Southern Solidarities."

113. By racial alienation, I refer to the concept of group position as defined by Bobo and Hutchins, based on Blumer's model of group-position, in which perceptions of both in-group identity and belonging and resources access and opportunity shape one's views toward the out-group (p. 95). Importantly, then, in their analysis, racial alienation is primarily, but not entirely, a function of race. Class position also plays an important role in shaping their sense of alienation.

Chapter Six

1. Jackson, "Congressional Members to Join Civil Rights Groups in Fight against Alabama's 'Juan Crow' Law."

2. Kim M. Williams, "Black Political Interests on Immigrant Rights: Evidence from Black Newspapers, 2000–2013," *Journal of African American Studies* 20, no. 3–4 (December 1, 2016): 248–71; Kim M. Williams and Lonnie Hannon, "Immigrant Rights in A Deep South City: The Effects of Anti-Immigrant Legislation on Black Elite Opinion in Birmingham, Alabama," *Du Bois Review* 13, no. 1 (2016): 139–57, https://doi.org/10.1017/S1742058X16000060.

3. NAACP, "Immigration Factsheet and Talking Points," accessed October 27, 2017, https://www.naacp.org/wp-content/uploads/2016/04/Immig%20Factsheet%20Tlkng%20Pts%20Final%20July%202011.pdf

4. See Gill, "Southern Solidarities."

5. Joel Alvarado and Charles Jaret, *Building Black-Brown Coalitions in the Southeast: Four Case Studies of African American-Latino Collaborations* (Atlanta, GA: Southern Regional Council, 2009), 8; Jennifer Gordon and Robin A. Lenhardt, *Conflict and Solidarity between African American and Latino Immigrant Workers*, a report prepared for the University of California, Berkeley's Chief Justice Earl Warren Institute on Race, Ethnicity and Diversity, 2007.

6. See Peter Schrag, *California: America's High-Stakes Experiment* (Berkeley: University of California Press, 2007).

7. See Celia Lacayo, "Latinos Need to Stay in Their Place: Differential Segregation in a Multiethnic Suburb," *Societies* 6, no. 3 (August 15, 2016): 25; Weise, *Corazón de Dixie*.

8. Importantly, these conditions are quite distinct from many of our traditional receiving areas like Texas and California, where people of Mexican origin are the majority in many municipalities, where the question of legality is not so easily assigned, and the white-nonwhite dichotomy may be less clear. In these places, as scholars like Julie Dowling and Rafael Alarcon demonstrate, racial identities and politics may vary widely. Alarcón et al., *Making Los Angeles Home*; Dowling, *Mexican Americans and the Question of Race*.

9. Beth Tarasawa, "New Patterns of Segregation: Latino and African-American Students in Metro Atlanta High Schools," *Southern Spaces*, January 19, 2009, https://southernspaces .org/2009/new-patterns-segregation-latino-and-african-american-students-metro-atlanta-high -schools

10. Rubén Hernández-León and Victor Zúñiga, "Appalachia Meets Aztlan: Mexican Immigration and Intergroup Relations in Dalton, Georgia," in *New Destinations: Mexican Immigration in the United States*, ed. V. Zúñiga and R. Hernández-León (New York: Russell Sage Foundation, 2005), 244–73.

11. Mary Lou Pickel, "Response from Hispanics in Georgia Muted," *Atlanta Journal-Constitution*, March 28, 2006.

12. Pickel, "Response from Hispanics in Georgia Muted."

13. Pickel, "Response from Hispanics in Georgia Muted."

14. Gustavo Lopéz and Renee Stepler, "Latinos in the 2016 Election: North Carolina," Pew Hispanic Center, last updated January 19, 2016, http://www.pewhispanic.org/fact-sheet/latinos -in-the-2016-election-north-carolina/

15. Irene Browne, Natalie Delia Deckard, and Cassaundra Rodriguez, "Different Game, Different Frame? Black Counterdiscourses and Depictions of Immigration in Atlanta's African-American and Mainstream Press," *Sociological Quarterly* 57, no. 3 (August 1, 2016): 520–43.

16. Tyler Estep, "Attorney: Gwinnett Has Spent More than $1M Fighting Voting Rights Suit," *Atlanta-Georgia Constitution*, March 28, 2018, https://www.myajc.com/news/local-govt -politics/attorney-gwinnett-has-spent-more-than-fighting-voting-rights-suit/bvKyfxc5QzJy HQX7wxkK0L/

17. Some might argue that this process is happening at the national level as much as it is at the local level through national media and political discourse. This is likely true, but only to the extent that national media shape and reflect daily life in local context. For example, in 2001, the immediate discursive backlash against Latino immigrants lacked impact, especially as immigration reform remained on the table. In both 2006 and 2016, however, when punitive policies were proposed that would alternately build a wall, deport, or otherwise criminalize immigrants and their families, politicization and racialization occurred.

18. Greg Howard, "Why 'Transcending Race' Is a Lie," *New York Times Magazine*, June 17, 2016.

19. Alba and Nee, "Rethinking Assimilation Theory for a New Era of Immigration"; Richard Alba and Victor Nee, *Remaking the American Mainstream: Assimilation and Contemporary Immigration* (Cambridge, MA: Harvard University Press, 2009).

20. Jiménez, *Replenished Ethnicity*. But see Edward Murguia and Tyrone Forman, "Shades of Whiteness: The Mexican American Experience in Relation to Anglos and Blacks," in *White Out: The Continuing Significance of Racism*, ed. Ashley Doane and Eduardo Bonilla-Silva (New York: Routledge, 2003).

21. Cybelle Fox and Thomas A. Guglielmo, "Defining America's Racial Boundaries: Blacks, Mexicans, and European Immigrants, 1890–1945," *American Journal of Sociology* 118, no. 2 (2012): 327–79; Roediger, *The Wages of Whiteness*.

22. Hana Brown, Jennifer Jones, and Andrea Becker, "The Racialization of Latinos in New Immigrant Destinations: Criminality, Ascription, and Counter-Mobilization," unpublished manuscript.

23. Roberto Suro, Gabriel Escobar, and Pew Hispanic Center, *2006 National Survey of Latinos: The Immigration Debate* (Washington, DC: Pew Hispanic Center, 2006).

24. Lopez and Minushkin, "Hispanics See Their Situation in U.S. Deteriorating."

25. Ana Gonzales-Barrera and Mark Hugo Lopez, "Is Being Hispanic a Matter of Race, Ethnicity, or Both?" *Pew Hispanic Center: Think Tank*, June 15, 2015.

26. Kaufmann, "Cracks in the Rainbow."

27. Kaufmann, "Cracks in the Rainbow."

28. Suro et al., *2006 National Survey of Latinos*.

29. Jones-Correa and Hernàndez, "Commonalities, Competition and Linked Fate."

30. Kaufmann, "Cracks in the Rainbow," 202.

31. Alvarado and Jaret, *Building Black-Brown Coalitions in the Southeast*, 21.

32. Alvarado and Jaret, *Building Black-Brown Coalitions in the Southeast*, 21; Dawson, *Behind the Mule*; Kaufmann, "Cracks in the Rainbow."

33. Anecdotal evidence also indicates that the criminalization of both groups may play a role in highlighting connections between African Americans and Latinos. Certainly, we see evidence of this in many of the coalitional efforts among more youth-oriented organizations, who are collaborating on anti-deportation and anti-"school to prison" pipeline initiatives as part of a shared analysis of the racism embedded in the criminal justice system aimed at both Latinos and African Americans.

34. Brown, Jones, and Dow, "Unity in the Struggle."

35. Both quotes from MIRA newsletter, 2008, A7.

36. Greenhouse, "After 15 Years, North Carolina Plant Unionizes."

37. Greenhouse, "After 15 Years, North Carolina Plant Unionizes."

38. Notimore, "Declaración Sobre el Alzamiento en Baltimore," April 28, 2015, http://www.notonemoredeportation.com/2015/04/28/7631/

39. Mark Guarino, "Protestors Shut Down Chicago's 'Magnificent Mile' in Demonstrations over Police Slaying of Laquan McDonald," *Washington Post*, November 27, 2015.

40. Phillip Bump, "Hispanic Voter Registration Is Climbing in Some States: Is It Because of Donald Trump?" *Washington Post*, May 9, 2016, https://www.washingtonpost.com/news/the-fix/wp/2016/05/09/hispanic-registration-is-up-in-at-least-three-states-but-not-only-because-of-donald-trump/?utm_term=.6fd30222c8f1

41. Such shifts in the electorate are critical, and indicative of important changes in the coming decades. Due to the young age and immigration status of the Latino population, political representation greatly lags the share of the population, especially in new destinations and swing states. Efforts to register and naturalize in significant numbers may accelerate this process. See Frey, *Diversity Explosion*.

42. At the time of this writing, much has been written about the high turnout of Latino voters for Trump in the 2016 election. Estimates indicate that Latino turnout was the highest on record, but that somewhere between 28 and 18 percent of Latinos voted for Trump. Political scientists Gabriel Sánchez and Matt Barreto of *Latino Decisions* offered the lower-bound estimate based on their Latino polling data, also indicating that this gap in political preference is

the highest in history as well, suggesting that despite news media accounts, Latinos are voting increasingly as a Democratic block. See Gabriel Sánchez and Matt Barreto, "In Record Numbers, Latino Voters Voted Overwhelmingly against Trump. We Did the Research," *Washington Post*, Monkey Cage, November 11, 2016.

43. Alvarado and Jaret, *Building Black-Brown Coalitions in the Southeast*, 7.

44. Arlene Dávila, *Latino Spin: Public Image and the Whitewashing of Race* (New York: New York University Press, 2008).

45. Marisa Abrajano and Zoltan L. Hajnal, *White Backlash: Immigration, Race, and American Politics* (Princeton: Princeton University Press, 2015).

46. Manuel Pastor, Justin Scoggins, and Sarah Treuhaft, "Bridging the Racial Generation Gap Is the Key to America's Economic Future," *Policy Link*, University of Southern California, September 2017, http://nationalequityatlas.org/sites/default/files/RacialGenGap_%20final.pdf

47. Abrajano and Hajnal, *White Backlash*, 27.

48. Walter Ewing, "Republican Party Platform Shows Little Understanding of Immigration Policy," American Immigration Council, accessed July 30, 2016, http://immigrationimpact.com/2016/07/19/republican-party-platform-immigration-policy/

49. Julianne Hing, "The Republican Worldview Is One of Racist False Binaries," *Nation*, July 19, 2016.

50. Rob Suls, "Most Americans Continue to Oppose U.S. Border Wall, Doubt Mexico Would Pay for It," Pew Research Center, February 24, 2017, http://www.pewresearch.org/fact-tank/2017/02/24/most-americans-continue-to-oppose-u-s-border-wall-doubt-mexico-would-pay-for-it/; Pew Research Center, "In First Month, Views of Trump Are Already Strongly Felt, Deeply Polarized; Views of Trump's Executive Order on Travel Restrictions" (Washington, DC: Pew Research Center, February 16, 2017), http://www.people-press.org/2017/02/16/2-views-of-trumps-executive-order-on-travel-restrictions/

51. Christopher Jones-Cruise, "Republicans Have Gained Strength in State Legislatures and Governorships," Republican State Leadership Committee blog, October 4, 2016, http://rslc.gop/blog/2016/10/04/republicans-have-gained-stength-in-state-legislatures-and-governorships/

52. Trip Gabriel, "North Carolina G.O.P. Moves to Limit Power of New Democratic Governor," *New York Times*, December 14, 2016.

53. Jason Zengerele, "Is North Carolina the Future of American Politics?" *New York Times Magazine*, June 20, 2017, https://nyti.ms/2sKLLp1

54. Zengerele, "Is North Carolina the Future of American Politics?"

55. Frey notes that in 2012 "overly stringent voter identification legislation, proposed in some states, was intended to prevent uniformed minorities from registering to vote. Furthermore, there were accusations that voting opportunities and poll stations were deliberately restricted in some minority-populated areas." While these accusations increased in 2016, resulting in several lawsuits, Frey argues that "over the long haul, the effects of any such attempts to suppress voters will pale in comparison with the larger demographic sweep of minority groups that will shape the nation's civic decision making." Frey, *Diversity Explosion*, 217.

Chapter Seven

1. Yes! Weekly, "Winston-Salem Wins National League of Cities Cultural Diversity Award," YES! Weekly (blog), last modified April 3, 2017, http://yesweekly.com/winston-salem-wins-national-league-of-cities-cultural-diversity-award/

2. Elise Foley, "North Carolina Governor Signs Bill Targeting 'Sanctuary Cities,' Undocu-

mented Immigrants," Huffington Post, last modified October 28, 2015, sec. Politics. https://www
.huffingtonpost.com/entry/north-carolina-immigration-law_us_56311d41e4b06317991094e7

3. Colin Campbell, "NC House Panel Debates Tougher Immigration Laws, Penalties for
Sanctuary Cities," *News and Observer*, February 21, 2017, http://www.newsobserver.com/news/
politics-government/state-politics/article134094579.html

4. Adela De la Torre, "North Carolina Anti-immigrant Bill Becomes Law," National Immigration Law Center (blog), October 28, 2015, https://www.nilc.org/2015/10/28/north-carolina
-anti-immigrant-bill-becomes-law/

5. Jedediah Purdy, "North Carolina's Long Moral March and Its Lessons for the Trump Resistance," *New Yorker*, February 17, 2017, https://www.newyorker.com/news/news-desk/north
-carolinas-long-moral-march-and-its-lessons-for-the-trump-resistance

6. It is important to note that there is significant variation across the types of observa-
tional sites emphasized in the growing body of New South studies. While this study emphasizes
churches, but also triangulates across additional sites to develop a community-level analysis, as
well as draws from extensive interview and newspaper data, other ethnographic studies take
more traditional approaches, focusing on the workplace, bureaucratic or social service institutions, or encounters in public spaces. Each of these distinct types of locales may produce
observations that are more or less likely to lean toward conflict. For example, in the workplace
or in welfare administration offices, perceptions of competition or conflict may be more likely
to occur than in public spaces or town hall meetings. While I have attempted to triangulate
across sites in order to account for variation as much as possible in this study, it should be noted
that variation in site may determine relation quality as well, suggesting that even in sites where
researchers have found cooperation or conflict, mixed or alternate relationships may exist in the
same community.

7. Vasquez, *Mexican Americans across Generations*.

8. Neckerman, Carter, and Lee, "Segmented Assimilation and Minority Cultures of Mobility."

9. Though it is important to note that shared racial status can depress a sense of economic
threat even among those of similar economic status and position in the labor market, such as in
unionization efforts.

10. It is important to note that there are some caveats here. It is possible for solidarity to
emerge even when groups occupy a similar class status if the perception of competition is
avoided, and shared racial status prevails. For a broader discussion of these kinds of coalitions,
see Alvarado and Jaret, *Building Black-Brown Coalitions in the Southeast*.

11. Jennifer Anne Meri Jones, "'Mexicans Will Take the Jobs That Even Blacks Won't Do.'"

12. Max Weber, *Economy and Society* (Berkeley: University of California Press, 1922).

13. Blumer, "Race Prejudice as a Sense of Group Position."

14. Lopez and Espiritu, "Panethnicity in the United States"; Nagel, "American Indian Ethnic
Renewal." There are, of course, exceptions. However, economic solidarity is generally combined
with other shared grievances, such as racial exploitation, or general critiques of capitalism and
labor exploitation; see Craig Calhoun, "Occupy Wall Street in Perspective," *British Journal of
Sociology* 64, no. 1 (2011): 26–38.

15. Brown and Jones, "Rethinking Panethnicity and the Race-Immigration Divide."

16. Brubaker, *Ethnicity without Groups*; Su, "We Call Ourselves by Many Names."

17. But see Ribas, *On the Line*.

18. For additional works that examine race from the perspective of multiple groups, see
Almaguer, *Racial Fault Lines*; Loewen, *The Mississippi Chinese*; Kim, "The Racial Triangulation
of Asian Americans."

19. Dina G. Okamoto, "Institutional Panethnicity: Boundary Formation in Asian-American Organizing." *Social Forces* 85, no. 1 (2006): 1–25; Mehdi Bozorgmehr, Paul Ong, and Sarah Tosh, "Panethnicity Revisited: Contested Group Boundaries in the Post-9/11 Era," *Ethnic and Racial Studies* 39, no. 5 (2016): 727–45; Natalie Masuoka, "Defining the Group: Latino Identity and Political Participation," *American Politics Research* 36, no. 1 (2007): 33–61.

20. Blumer, "Race Prejudice as a Sense of Group Position."

21. Jones, "Blacks May Be Second Class, but They Can't Make Them Leave."

22. Marrow, *New Destination Dreaming.*

23. Marrow, "Hispanic Immigration, Black Population Size, and Intergroup Relations in the Rural and Small-Town South"; Marrow, *New Destination Dreaming*; McClain et al., "Black Americans and Latino Immigrants in a Southern City"; McDermott, "Black Attitudes and Hispanic Immigrants in South Carolina"; Rich and Miranda, "The Sociopolitical Dynamics of Mexican Immigration in Lexington, Kentucky, 1997–2002"; Stuesse, "Race, Migration, and Labor Control."

24. Hernández-León and Zúñiga, "Mexican Immigrant Communities in the South and Social Capital"; Jamie Winders, "Nashville's New Sonido: Latino Migration and the Changing Politics of Race," in *New Faces in New Places: The Changing Geography of American Immigration*, ed. Douglas Massey (New York: Russell Sage Foundation, 2008), 249–73.

25. McDermott, "Black Attitudes and Hispanic Immigrants in South Carolina."

26. Greenhouse, "After 15 Years, North Carolina Plant Unionizes."

27. Marrow, "Hispanic Immigration, Black Population Size, and Intergroup Relations in the Rural and Small-Town South"; Marrow, *New Destination Dreaming.*

28. McClain et al., "Black Americans and Latino Immigrants in a Southern City."

29. Hernández-León and Zúñiga, "Mexican Immigrant Communities in the South and Social Capital"; Winders, "Nashville's New Sonido."

30. Jason Morin, Gabriel R. Sánchez, and Matt A. Barreto, "Perceptions of Competition," in *Just Neighbors? Research on African American and Latino Relations in the United States*, ed. Edward E. Telles, Mark Q. Sawyer, and Gaspar Rivera-Salgado (New York: Russell Sage Foundation, 2011), 96–124.

31. Ribas, *On the Line.*

32. Márquez, *Black-Brown Solidarity.*

33. Alejandro Portes, "Immigration Theory for a New Century: Some Problems and Opportunities," *International Migration Review* 31, no. 4 (1997): 799–825.

34. It is important to note that when considering Latinos broadly, there is significant diversity within the population, not only in terms of national origin, but also race, class, and documentation status. In the case of the Winston-Salem metro area, this is also true, although the vast majority of the Latino population is of Mexican origin. As of 2010, Mexican origin residents accounted for approximately 69.4% of the Latino population, followed most closely by Puerto Ricans at 5.8% and Salvadorans, also at 5.8%. These numbers more closely mirror national demographics, and are similar to those elsewhere in the region. Nevertheless, rapidly shifting migration patterns, both internally and externally, should caution us to consider how increasing diversity may complicate or contest these categories and meanings. US Census Bureau, "Results. Winston-Salem city, North Carolina," American FactFinder website, accessed October 30, 2017. https://factfinder.census.gov/faces/tableservices/jsf/pages/productview.xhtml?src=CF

35. Pew Research Center, "The Rise of Asian Americans," Washington, DC: Pew Research Center, April 4, 2013, http://www.pewsocialtrends.org/2012/06/19/the-rise-of-asian-americans/

36. Espiritu, *Asian American Panethnicity*; Taeku Lee, "From Shared Demographic Catego-

ries to Common Political Destinies," *DuBois Review: Social Science Research on Race* 4, no. 2 (2008): 433–56.

37. Pew Research Center, "The Rise of Asian Americans."

38. Oliver Wang, *Legions of Boom: Filipino American Mobile DJ Crews in the San Francisco Bay Area* (Durham: Duke University Press, 2015); Deutche Welle, "Undocumented Filipino Migrants in the US Anxious as Deportation Looms," *Deutche Welle*, accessed December 1, 2017, http://www.dw.com/en/undocumented-filipino-migrants-in-the-us-anxious-as-deportation -looms/a-38228440; Alyssa Aquino, "Undocumented Filipinos Are Living a Special Nightmare in Trump's America," Foreign Policy in Focus, March 10, 2017, http://fpif.org/undocumented -filipinos-are-living-a-special-nightmare-in-trumps-america/

39. Anthony Ocampo, "Are Second Generation Filipinos Becoming Asian American or Latino? Historical Colonialism, Culture, and Panethnic Identity," *Ethnic and Racial Studies* 37, no. 4 (2013): 425–45.

40. Monica Anderson, "A Rising Share of the U.S. Black Population is Foreign Born," Pew Research Center, Washington, DC: Pew Research Center, April 9, 2015, http://www .pewsocialtrends.org/2015/04/09/a-rising-share-of-the-u-s-black-population-is-foreign-born/

41. Stepick and Stepick, "Diverse Contexts of Reception and Feelings of Belonging," 13.

42. Stepick and Stepick, "Diverse Contexts of Reception and Feelings of Belonging," 13.

43. Waters, *Black Identities*.

44. Gans, "The Possibility of a New Racial Hierarchy in the Twenty-First Century United States," 371.

45. Eduardo Bonilla-Silva and David G. Embrick, "Black, Honorary White, White: The Future of Race in the United States?" in *Mixed Messages: Doing Race in the Color-Blind Era*, ed. David Brunsma (Boulder, CO: Lynne Rienner, 2006), 33–48; Lee and Bean, "Redrawing the Color Line?"; Tyrone A. Forman, Carla Goar, and Amanda E. Lewis, "Neither Black nor White? An Empirical Test of the Latin Americanization Thesis," *Race and Society* 5, no. 1 (2002): 65–84; Jennifer Lee and Frank D. Bean, *The Diversity Paradox: Immigration and the Color Line in Twenty-First Century America* (New York: Russell Sage Foundation, 2010); Marrow, "New Immigrant Destinations and the American Colour Line."

46. Padín, "The Normative Mulattoes, 50.

Appendix A

1. C. Wright Mills, *The Sociological Imagination* (Oxford: Oxford University Press, 2000).

2. Patricia Hill Collins, "Learning from the Outsider Within: The Sociological Significance of Black Feminist Thought," *Social Problems* 33, no. 6 (December 1, 1986): 14–32.

3. Ann Phoenix and Barbara Tizard, *Black, White or Mixed Race? Race and Racism in the Lives of Young People of Mixed Parentage* (London: Routledge, 2002 [1993]).

Appendix C

1. Capps, Rosenblum, Rodríguez, and Chishti, *Delegation and Divergence*, 60.

2. American Immigration Council, "The Criminal Alien Program: Immigration Enforcement in Prisons and Jails," (Washington, DC: American Immigration Council, 2013), 7, updated August 2013, https://www.americanimmigrationcouncil.org/sites/default/files/research/cap_fact _sheet_8–1_fin_0.pdf

3. Capps, Rosenblum, Rodriguez, and Chishti, *Delegation and Divergence*, 61.

4. http://www.ustr.gov/trade-agreements/free-trade-agreements/north-american-free-trade-agreement-nafta

5. http://www.ustr.gov/trade-agreements/free-trade-agreements/north-american-free-trade-agreement-nafta

6. http://www.ustr.gov/trade-agreements/free-trade-agreements/north-american-free-trade-agreement-nafta

References

Abrajano, Marisa, and Zoltan L. Hajnal. *White Backlash: Immigration, Race, and American Politics.* Princeton: Princeton University Press, 2015.

Abrego, Leisy Janet. "'I Can't Go to College Because I Don't Have Papers': Incorporation Patterns of Latino Unauthorized Youth." *Latino Studies* 4 (2006): 212–31.

Abrego, Leisy Janet, and Roberto G. Gonzales. "Blocked Paths, Uncertain Futures: The Postsecondary Education and Labor Market Prospects of Undocumented Latino Youth." *Journal of Education for Students Placed at Risk* 15, no.1–2 (2010): 144–57.

Adelman, Robert M., Cameron Lippard, Charles Jaret, and Lesley Williams Reid. "Jobs, Poverty, and Earnings in American Metropolises: Do Immigrants Really Hurt the Economic Outcomes of Blacks?" *Sociological Focus* 38, no. 4 (2005): 261–85.

Ahear, Lorraine. "Latino Community Coming into Focus." *News and Record*, July 4, 1995, A1.

Alarcón, Rafael, Luis Escala, Olga Odgers, and Roger Waldinger. *Making Los Angeles Home: The Integration of Mexican Immigrants in the United States.* Translated by Dick Cluster. Oakland: University of California Press, 2016.

Alba, Richard D. *Ethnic Identity: The Transformation of White America.* New Haven, CT: Yale University Press, 1990.

Alba, Richard, and Victor Nee. *Remaking the American Mainstream: Assimilation and Contemporary Immigration.* Cambridge, MA: Harvard University Press, 2009.

Alba, Richard, and Victor Nee. "Rethinking Assimilation Theory for a New Era of Immigration." *International Migration Review* 31, no. 4 (1997): 826–74.

Alba, Richard, Rubén G. Rumbaut, and Karen Marotz. "A Distorted Nation: Perceptions of Racial/Ethnic Group Sizes and Attitudes toward Immigrants and Other Minorities." *Social Forces* 4, no. 2 (2006): 899–917.

Allport, Gordon W. *The Nature of Prejudice: 25th Anniversary Edition.* Unabridged. New York: Basic, 1979 [1954].

Almaguer, Tomás. *Racial Fault Lines: The Historical Origins of White Supremacy in California.* Berkeley: University of California Press, 2008 [1994].

Alvarado, Joel, and Charles Jaret. *Building Black-Brown Coalitions in the Southeast: Four Case Studies of African American-Latino Collaborations.* Atlanta, GA: Southern Regional Council, 2009.

American Civil Liberties Union (ACLU) of North Carolina Legal Foundation and Immigration & Human Rights Policy Clinic of University of North Carolina (UNC) at Chapel Hill. *The Policies and Politics of Local Immigration Enforcement Laws 287(g) Program in North Carolina*. Chapel Hill, NC: UNC School of Law, 2009.

Anderson, Kathryn Freeman, and Jessie K. Finch. "Racially Charged Legislation and Latino Health Disparities: The Case of Arizona's S.B. 1070." *Sociological Spectrum* 34, no. 6 (2014): 526–48.

Anderson, Kathryn Freeman, and Jessie K. Finch. "The Role of Racial Microaggressions, Stress, and Acculturation in Understanding Latino Health Outcomes in the USA." *Race and Social Problems* 9, no. 3 (2017): 218–33.

Anderson, Monica. "A Rising Share of the U.S. Black Population Is Foreign Born." Pew Research Center. Washington, DC: Pew Research Center, April 9, 2015. http://www.pewsocialtrends .org/2015/04/09/a-rising-share-of-the-u-s-black-population-is-foreign-born/

Anzaldúa, Gloria. *Borderlands/La Frontera: The New Mestiza*. San Francisco: Spinsters/Aunt Lute Books, 1987.

Aquino, Alyssa. "Undocumented Filipinos Are Living a Special Nightmare in Trump's America." Foreign Policy in Focus. March 10, 2017. http://fpif.org/undocumented-filipinos-are-living -a-special-nightmare-in-trumps-america/

Armenta, Amada. "From Sheriff's Deputies to Immigration Officers: Screening Immigrant Status in a Tennessee Jail." *Law and Policy* 34, no. 2 (2012): 191–210.

Arnold, Carrie. "Racial Profiling in Immigration Enforcement: State and Local Agreements to Enforce Federal Immigration Law." *Arizona Law Review* 49, no. 113 (2007): 113–42.

Ball, Andrea. "UNCG Welcomes Immigrants; UNCG Holds Family Day to Introduce Immigrants to College Life." *News and Record*, June 27,1998, B2.

Barber, Keith. "Winston-Salem Residents Voice Concerns about Police Checkpoints." *Yes! Weekly*, December 14, 2011. http://yesweekly.com/article-13249-winston-salem-residents -voice-concerns-about-police-checkpoints.html

Barreto, Matt A., Benjamin F. Gonzalez, and Gabriel R. Sánchez. "Rainbow Coalition in the Golden State? Exposing Myths, Uncovering New Realities in Latino Attitudes towards Blacks." In *Black and Brown Los Angeles: A Contemporary Reader*, edited by Laura Pulido and Josh Kun, 203–32. Berkeley: University of California Press, 2010.

Barrett, James, and David Roediger. "In-Between Peoples: Race, Nationality, and the 'New Immigrant' Working Class." *Journal of American Ethnic History* 25, no. 2/3 (1997): 33–47.

Barth, Fredrik. *Ethnic Groups and Boundaries: The Social Organization of Culture Difference*. Long Grove, IL: Waveland, 1998.

Basler, Carleen. "White Dreams and Red Votes: Mexican Americans and the Lure of Inclusion in the Republican Party." *Ethnic and Racial Studies* 31, no.1 (2008): 123–66.

Bauer, Mary, and Sarah Reynolds. *Under Siege: Life for Low-Income Latinos in the South*. Montgomery, AL: Southern Poverty Law Center, 2009.

Bean, Frank D., James D. Bachmeier, Susan K. Brown, and Rosaura Tafoya-Estrada. "Immigration and Labor Market Dynamics." In *Just Neighbors? Research on African American and Latino Relations in the United States*, edited by Edward E. Telles, Mark Q. Sawyer, and Gaspar Rivera-Salgado, 37–60. New York: Russell Sage Foundation, 2011.

Bean, Frank D., Jennifer Lee, and James D. Bachmeier. "Immigration and the Color Line at the Beginning of the 21st Century." *Daedalus* 142, no. 3 (2013): 123–40.

Behnken, Brian D. "African-American and Latino Activism(s) and Relations: An Introduction." In *Civil Rights and Beyond: African American and Latino/a Activism in the Twentieth-*

Century United States, edited by Brian Behnken, 1–19. Athens: University of Georgia Press, 2016.

Bedolla, Lisa García. "The Identity Paradox: Latino Language, Politics and Selective Dissociation." *Latino Studies* 1, no. 2 (2003): 264–83.

Bell, David, and David Blanchflower. "Young People and the Great Recession." *Oxford Review of Economic Policy* 27, no. 2 (2011): 241–67.

Bentacur, John, and Douglas Gills. "The African American and Latino Coalition Experience in Chicago under Mayor Harold Washington." In *The Collaborative City: Opportunities and Struggles for Blacks and Latinos in U.S. Cities*, edited by John Bentacur and Douglas Gills, 59–88. New York: Routledge, 2000.

Berman, Ari. "The Man behind Trump's Voter-Fraud Obsession." *New York Times*, June 13, 2017. https://www.nytimes.com/2017/06/13/magazine/the-man-behind-trumps-voter-fraud -obsession.html

Blumer, Herbert. "Race Prejudice as a Sense of Group Position." *Pacific Sociological Review* 1, no. 1 (1958): 3–7.

Bobo, Lawrence D. "Prejudice as Group Position: Microfoundations of a Sociological Approach to Racism and Race Relations." *Journal of Social Issues* 55, no. 3 (1999): 445–72.

Bobo, Lawrence, and Vincent L. Hutchings. "Perceptions of Racial Group Competition: Extending Blumer's Theory of Group Position to a Multiracial Social Context." *American Sociological Review* 61, no. 6 (1996): 951–72.

Bonilla-Silva, Eduardo. "From Bi-racial to Tri-racial: Towards a New System of Racial Stratification in the USA." *Ethnic and Racial Studies* 27, no. 6 (2004): 931–50.

Bonilla-Silva, Eduardo, and David G. Embrick. "Black, Honorary White, White: The Future of Race in the United States?" In *Mixed Messages: Doing Race in the Color-Blind Era*, edited by David Brunsma, 33–48. Boulder, CO: Lynne Rienner, 2006.

"Boonville Textile Plant Damaged in Fire." *Winston-Salem Journal*, September 20, 2007, A2.

Borjas, George J. *Friends or Strangers: The Impact of Immigrants on the U.S. Economy*. New York: Basic, 1990.

Bozorgmehr, Mehdi, Paul Ong, and Sarah Tosh. "Panethnicity Revisited: Contested Group Boundaries in the Post-9/11 Era." *Ethnic and Racial Studies* 39, no. 5 (2016): 727–45.

Brader, Ted, Nicholas A. Valentino, Ashley E. Jardina, and Timothy J. Ryan. "The Racial Divide on Immigration Opinion: Why Blacks Are Less Threatened by Immigrants." SSRN Scholarly Paper. Rochester, NY: Social Science Research Network, 2010.

Brader, Ted, Nicholas A. Valentino, and Elizabeth Suhay. "What Triggers Public Opposition to Immigration? Anxiety, Group Cues, and Immigration Threat." *American Journal of Political Science* 52, no. 4 (2008): 959–78.

Brodkin Sacks, Karen. *How Jews Became White Folks and What That Says about Race in America*. New Brunswick, NJ: Rutgers University Press, 1998.

Brown, Hana, and Jennifer A. Jones. "Rethinking Panethnicity and the Race-Immigration Divide." *Sociology of Race and Ethnicity* 1, no. 1 (2015): 181–91.

Brown, Hana, Jennifer Jones, and Andrea Becker. "The Racialization of Latinos in New Immigrant Destinations: Criminality, Ascription, and Counter-Mobilization." Unpublished manuscript.

Brown, Hana, Jennifer Jones, and Taylor Dow. "Unity in the Struggle: Immigration and the South's Emerging Civil Rights Consensus." *Law and Contemporary Problems* 79 (2016): 5–27.

Brown, Wendy. "Wounded Attachments." *Political Theory* 21, no. 3 (1993): 390–410.

Browne, Irene, Natalie Delia Deckard, and Cassaundra Rodriguez. "Different Game, Different Frame? Black Counterdiscourses and Depictions of Immigration in Atlanta's African-American and Mainstream Press." *Sociological Quarterly* 57, no. 3 (August 1, 2016): 520–43.

Brubaker, Rogers. *Ethnicity without Groups*. Cambridge, MA: Harvard University Press, 2004.

Bryce-Laporte, Roy Simon. "Black Immigrants: The Experience of Invisibility and Inequality." *Journal of Black Studies* 3, no.1 (1972): 29–56.

Büchel, Felix, and Joachim R. Frick. "Immigrants' Economic Performance across Europe—Does Immigration Policy Matter?" *Population Research and Policy Review* 24 (2005): 175–212.

Buggs, Shannon, Angela Paik, and Jay Price. "The Land of Full Employment." *News and Observer*, July 26, 1998, A1–A2.

Bump, Phillip. "Hispanic Voter Registration Is Climbing in Some States: Is It Because of Donald Trump?" *Washington Post*, May 9, 2016. https://www.washingtonpost.com/news/the-fix/wp/2016/05/09/hispanic-registration-is-up-in-at-least-three-states-but-not-only-because-of-donald-trump/?utm_term=.6fd30222c8f1

Calavita, Kitty. "New Politics of Immigration: Balanced-Budget Conservatism and the Symbolism of Proposition 187." *Social Problems* 43 (1996): 284.

Calhoun, Craig. "Occupy Wall Street in Perspective." *British Journal of Sociology* 64, no.1 (2011): 26–38.

Campbell, Colin. "NC House Panel Debates Tougher Immigration Laws, Penalties for Sanctuary Cities." *News and Observer*, February 21, 2017. http://www.newsobserver.com/news/politics-government/state-politics/article134094579.html

Capps, Randy, Marc R. Rosenblum, Cristina Rodriguez, and Muzaffar Chishti. *Delegation and Divergence: A Study of 287(g) State and Local Immigration Enforcement*. Washington, DC: Migration Policy Institute, January 2011.

"Census Shows Shift in Status; Whites Are Now the Minority in 10 Percent of Counties in the U.S." *Winston-Salem Journal*, August 9, 2007, A1.

"Changing Face of America." *Winston-Salem Journal*, January 27, 2003, A8.

Charles, Camille Zubrinksy. *Won't You Be My Neighbor? Race, Class, and Residence in Los Angeles*. New York: Russell Sage Foundation, 2006.

Chavez, Leo. "The Condition of Illegality." *International Migration* 45, no. 3 (2007): 192–95.

Chavez, Leo Ralph. *The Latino Threat: Constructing Immigrants, Citizens, and the Nation*. Stanford, CA: Stanford University Press, 2008.

Clemmons, Michael. "Beyond the Barriers: Toward a Durable African-American-Latino Political Coalition." *Journal of Latino/Latin American Studies* 5, no. 1 (2013): 40–56.

Cohen, Nate. "More Hispanics Declaring Themselves White." *New York Times*, May 21, 2014.

Coleman, Mathew. "The 'Local' Migration State: The Site-Specific Devolution of Immigration Enforcement in the U.S. South." *Law & Policy* 34, no. 2 (2012): 159–90.

Collins, Kristin. "Road Checkpoints Alarm Hispanics; Drunks, not Hispanics Are the Targets." *News and Observer*, August 8, 2008, B3.

Collins, Patricia Hill. "Learning from the Outsider Within: The Sociological Significance of Black Feminist Thought." *Social Problems* 33, no. 6 (December 1, 1986): 14–32.

Collins, Paul. "Cross-Cultural: Quality Schools Celebrate American Latin American Culture Day." *Winston-Salem Chronicle*, June 5, 2003, C1–2.

Cook, Stuart W. "Experimenting on Social Issues: The Case of School Desegregation." *American Psychologist* 40, no. 4 (1985): 452–60.

Coser, Lewis A. *Functions of Social Conflict*. New York: Simon and Schuster, 1956.

Craver, Richard. "Bank Gives Gift to Center; Money Goes toward Forsyth Tech's Goal." *Winston-Salem Journal*, November 14, 2006, D1.

Craver, Richard. "Safety and Numbers: Hispanics Caught between Risks of Carrying Cash and Banking It." *Winston-Salem Journal*, January 22, 2003, D1.

Craver, Richard. "Spotlight on Hiring; Two Watchdog Groups Moving into the Triad Will Go After Employers of Illegal Immigrants." *Winston-Salem Journal*, September 10, 2006, Metro Edition, D1.

Cravey, Altha J. "Latino Labor and Poultry Production in Rural North Carolina." *Southeastern Geographer* 37, no. 2 (1997): 295–300.

Cravey, Altha J., and Gabriela Valdivia. "Carolina del Norte: An Introduction." *Southeastern Geographer* 51, no. 2 (2011): 213–26.

Dalaker, J., US Census Bureau, Current Population Reports, Series P60-214. *Poverty in the United States: 2000*. Washington, DC: US Government Printing Office, 2001.

Daniel, Fran. "An American Dream: Jesus Ruiz's Hard Work Has Made Mi Pueblo Restaurants Succeed." *Winston-Salem Journal*, March 9, 2002, D1.

Daniel, Fran. "Hispanics Growing as Furniture Buyers Group Vital to Sales, Expert Says." *Winston-Salem Journal*, February 9, 2002, D1.

Danzinger, Sheldon, Koji Chavez, and Erin Cumberworth. *Poverty and the Great Recession*. Stanford, CA: Stanford Center on Poverty and Inequality, 2012.

Darity, William A., Jr., Jason Dietrich, and Darrick Hamilton. "Bleach in the Rainbow: Latin Ethnicity and Preference for Whiteness." *Transforming Anthropology* 13, no. 2 (2005): 103–9.

Dávila, Arlene. *Latino Spin: Public Image and the Whitewashing of Race*. New York: New York University Press, 2008.

Dawson, Michael C. *Behind the Mule: Race and Class in African-American Politics*. Princeton, NJ: Princeton University Press, 1994.

Deeb-Sossa, Natalia. *Doing Good: Racial Tensions and Workplace Inequalities at a Community Clinic in El Nuevo South*. Tucson: University of Arizona Press, 2013.

De la Torre, Adela. "North Carolina Anti-immigrant Bill Becomes Law." National Immigration Law Center (blog). October 28, 2015. https://www.nilc.org/2015/10/28/north-carolina-anti-immigrant-bill-becomes-law/

Denning, Shea Riggsbee. "The Impact of North Carolina Driver's License Requirements and the Real ID Act of 2005 on Unauthorized Immigrants." *Popular Government* 74, no. 3 (2009) Spring/Summer Online Supplement.

DeOrnellas, Elizabeth. "$76,000 for New Position Is Questioned: Sheriff Says He Didn't Request Money for Immigration Job." *Winston-Salem Journal*, June 2, 2008, B1.

Deutsche Welle. "Undocumented Filipino Migrants in the US Anxious as Deportation Looms." *Deutsche Welle*. Accessed December 1, 2017. http://www.dw.com/en/undocumented-filipino-migrants-in-the-us-anxious-as-deportationlooms/a-38228440

Dowling, Julie A. *Mexican Americans and the Question of Race*. Austin: University of Texas Press, 2014.

Dreby, Joanna. *Everyday Illegal: When Policies Undermine Immigrant Families*. Oakland: University of California Press, 2015.

Durand, Jorge, Douglas S. Massey, and Rene M. Zenteno. "Mexican Immigration to the United States: Continuities and Changes." *Latin American Research Review* 36, no.1 (2001): 107–27.

Ellis, Mark. "Unsettling Immigrant Geographies: US Immigration and the Politics of Scale." *Tijdschrift Voor Economische En Sociale Geografie* 97, no. 1 (2006): 49–58.

Espino, Rodolfo, and Michael M. Franz. "Latino Phenotypic Discrimination Revisited: The Impact of Skin Color on Occupational Status." *Journal of Social Psychology* 83, no. 2 (2002): 25–33.

Espiritu, Yen Le. *Asian American Panethnicity: Bridging Institutions and Identities.* Philadelphia: Temple University Press, 1992.

Espiritu, Yen Le. "Asian American Panethnicity: Contemporary National and Transnational Possibilities." In *Not Just Black and White: Historical and Contemporary Perspectives on Immigration, Race, and Ethnicity in the United States*, edited by Nancy Foner and George M. Fredrickson, 217–34. New York: Russell Sage Foundation, 2004.

Estep, Tyler. "Attorney: Gwinnett Has Spent More than $1M Fighting Voting Rights Suit," *Atlanta-Georgia Constitution*, March 28, 2018. https://www.myajc.com/news/local-govt-politics/attorney-gwinnett-has-spent-more-than-fighting-voting-rights-suit/bvKyfxc5QzJy HQX7wxkK0L/

Evans, Desiree. "The Hands behind the Turkey." November 25, 2008. The Institute for Southern Studies. https://www.facingsouth.org/2008/11/the-hands-behind-the-turkey.html

Ewing, Walter. "Republican Party Platform Shows Little Understanding of Immigration Policy." American Immigration Council. Accessed July 30, 2016. http://immigrationimpact.com/2016/07/19/republican-party-platform-immigration-policy/

Fink, Leon, and Alvis E. Dunn. *The Maya of Morganton: Work and Community in the Nuevo New South.* Chapel Hill: University of North Carolina Press, 2003.

FitzGerald, David Scott, and David Cook-Martín. *Culling the Masses: The Democratic Origins of Racist Immigration Policy in the Americas.* Cambridge, MA: Harvard University Press, 2014.

Foerster, Amy. "Race, Identity, and Belonging: 'Blackness' and the Struggle for Solidarity in a Multiethnic Labor Union." *Social Problems* 51, no. 3 (2004): 386–409. https://doi.org/10.1525/sp.2004.51.3.386

Foley, Elise. "North Carolina Governor Signs Bill Targeting 'Sanctuary Cities,' Undocumented Immigrants." Huffington Post, last modified October 28, 2015, sec. Politics. https://www.huffingtonpost.com/entry/north-carolina-immigration-law_us_56311d41e4b06317 991094e7

Foley, Neil. *Quest for Equality: The Failed Promise of Black-Brown Solidarity.* Vol. 8. Cambridge, MA: Harvard University Press, 2010.

Foley, Neil. "Straddling the Color Line: The Legal Construction of Hispanic Identity in Texas." In *Not Just Black and White: Historical and Contemporary Perspectives on Immigration, Race, and Ethnicity in the United States*, edited by Nancy Foner and George M. Fredrickson, 341–57. New York: Russell Sage Foundation, 2004.

Foner, Nancy, ed. *Islands in the City: West Indian Migration to New York.* Berkeley: University of California Press, 2001.

Forman, Tyrone A., Carla Goar, and Amanda E. Lewis. "Neither Black nor White? An Empirical Test of the Latin Americanization Thesis." *Race and Society* 5, no. 1 (2002): 65–84.

Fox, Cybelle. "The Changing Color of Welfare? How Whites' Attitudes toward Latinos Influence Support for Welfare." *American Journal of Sociology* 110, no. 3 (2004): 580–625.

Fox, Cybelle. *Three Worlds of Relief: Race, Immigration, and the American Welfare State from the Progressive Era to the New Deal.* Princeton, NJ: Princeton University Press, 2012.

Fox, Cybelle, and Thomas A. Guglielmo. "Defining America's Racial Boundaries: Blacks, Mexicans, and European Immigrants, 1890–1945." *American Journal of Sociology* 118, no. 2 (2012): 327–79.

Foxx, Virginia. "Congresswoman Virginia Foxx: Immigration." Accessed February 22, 2011. http://foxx.house.gov/index.cfm?sectionid=37

Fraga, Luis R., John A. Garcia, Rodney E. Hero, Michael Jones-Correa, Valerie Martinez-Ebers, and Gary M. Segura. *Latinos in the New Millennium: An Almanac of Opinion, Behavior, and Policy Preferences*. New York: Cambridge University Press, 2011.

Frazier, Amy. "Immigrant Dies At 29; He Bridged Gaps between Hispanics, Others." *Winston-Salem Journal*, April 27, 2002, B2.

Frazier, Amy. "Two Together as One: Rise in Yadkin Hispanic Population Is Inspiration for New Church for Parishes." *Winston-Salem Journal*, January 22, 2002.

Frazier, Amy, and Michelle Johnson. "Hispanics Hit Hard by Downturn: Many Work in State's Struggling Industries, Such as Manufacturing." *Winston-Salem Journal*, January 24, 2002.

Frazier, Amy, and Jim Sparks. "Work for Pay: Mexican Immigrants Welcome the Chance to Earn a Living and Have a Reliable Source of Income That Is Not Available to Them Back Home." *Winston-Salem Journal*, January 6, 2002, A1.

Frank, Reanne, Ilana Redstone Akresh, and Bo Lu. "Latino Immigrants and the U.S. Racial Order." *American Sociological Review* 75, no. 3 (2010): 378–401.

Freer, Regina, and Claudia Sandoval Lopez. "Black, Brown, Young, and Together." In *Just Neighbors? Research on African American and Latino Relations in the United States*, edited by Edward E. Telles, Mark Q. Sawyer, and Gaspar Rivera-Salgado, 267–98. New York: Russell Sage Foundation, 2011.

Frey, William H. *Analysis of US Census Bureau Population Estimates*. Washington, DC: Brookings Institution Press, June 2013.

Frey, William H. *Diversity Explosion: How New Racial Demographics Are Remaking America*. Washington, DC: Brookings Institution Press, 2014.

Fries, Adelaide Lisetta. *Forsyth County*. Winston, NC: Stewarts' Print. House, 1898. http://archive.org/details/forsythcounty00frie

Fussell, Elizabeth. "Warmth of the Welcome: Attitudes toward Immigrants and Immigration Policy in the United States." *Annual Review of Sociology* 40, no. 1 (2014): 479–98.

Gabriel, Trip. "North Carolina G.O.P. Moves to Limit Power of New Democratic Governor." *New York Times*, December 14, 2016.

Gaertner, Samuel L., Mary C. Rust, John F. Dovidio, Betty A. Bachman, and Phyllis A. Anastasio. "The Contact Hypothesis: The Role of a Common Ingroup Identity on Reducing Intergroup Bias." *Small Group Research* 25, no. 2 (1994): 224–49.

Gaillard, Courtney. "Black Rep Reaches Out by Adding Hispanic Wing." *Winston-Salem Chronicle*, August 8, 2002, A9.

Galliard, Courtney. "Hispanic, Black Ministers PowWow." *Winston-Salem Chronicle*, May 26, 2005, A1.

Galindo, Dan. "Blacks, Hispanics Begin a Dialogue: NAACP, City Agency Sponsor Meeting to Explore Ways to Remove Barriers." *Winston-Salem Journal*, June 24, 2005, B1.

Galindo, Dan. "Immigration Study Casts Doubt on Law: Partnership Unfair to Immigrants, Critics Say." *Winston-Salem Journal*, February 19, 2009

Gans, Herbert J. "The Possibility of a New Racial Hierarchy in the Twenty-First Century United States." In *The Cultural Territories of Race: Black and White Boundaries*, edited by Michelle Lamont, 371–79. Chicago: University of Chicago Press, 1999.

García, Angela S. "Hidden in Plain Sight: How Unauthorized Migrants Strategically Assimilate in Restrictive Localities." *Journal of Ethnic and Migration Studies* 40, no. 12 (2014): 1895–914.

Garcia, John A., Gabriel R. Sánchez, Shannon Sanchez-Youngman, Edward D. Vargas, and Vickie D. Ybarra. "Race as Lived Experience." *Du Bois Review* 12, no. 2 (2015): 349–73.

Gay, Claudine. "Seeing Difference: The Effect of Economic Disparity on Black Attitudes toward Latinos." *American Journal of Political Science* 50, no. 4 (2006): 982–97.

Giles, Michael W., and Arthur Evans. "External Threat, Perceived Threat, and Group Identity." *Social Science Quarterly* 66, no.1 (1985): 50.

Gill, Hannah. *The Latino Migration Experience in North Carolina: New Roots in the Old North State*. Chapel Hill: University of North Carolina Press, 2010.

Gill, Hannah. "Southern Solidarities: U.S. Civil Rights and Latin American Social Movements in the Nuevo South." In *Civil Rights and Beyond: African American and Latino/a Activism in the Twentieth-Century United States*, edited by Brian Behnken, 241–62. Athens: University of Georgia Press, 2016.

Giovanelli, Laura. "Poll: Immigrants Are Burden to N.C.; Negative Opinion Is Up by 12 Percent since April." *Winston-Salem Journal*, November 21, 2006, Metro Edition, B2.

Giovanelli, Laura. "Protests Smaller This Year; 60–70 People Gather for Pro Immigration Rally in Winston-Salem." *Winston-Salem Journal*, May 3, 2007, B1.

Giuliano, Paola, and Antonio Spilimbergo. "Growing Up in a Recession: Beliefs and the Macroeconomy." NBER Working Paper 15321. Issued September 2009. Retrieved May 16, 2015. http://www.nber.org/papers/w15321

Giunca, Mary. "Stymied: Dashed Plan No Victory in Southside." *Winston-Salem Journal*, January 30, 2003.

Golash-Boza, Tanya. "Dropping the Hyphen? Becoming Latino(a)-American through Racialized Assimilation." *Social Forces* 85, no. 1 (September 2006): 27–55.

Golash-Boza, Tanya, and William Darity. "Latino Racial Choices: The Effects of Skin Colour and Discrimination on Latinos' and Latinas' Racial Self-Identifications." *Ethnic and Racial Studies* 31, no. 5 (2008): 899–934.

Goldstein, Blair. "Flaws in Forsyth's Data Cited; Study Gauged Services to Illegal Hispanic Immigrants." *Winston-Salem Journal*, December 30, 2007, A1.

Gonzales, Roberto G. "Learning to Be Illegal: Undocumented Youth and Shifting Legal Contexts in the Transition to Adulthood." *American Sociological Review* 76, no. 4 (2011): 602–19.

Gonzales-Barrera, Ana, and Mark Hugo Lopez. "Is Being Hispanic a Matter of Race, Ethnicity, or Both?" *Pew Hispanic Center: Think Tank*, June 15, 2015. Washington, DC: Pew Hispanic Center.

Gordon, Jennifer, and Robin A. Lenhardt. *Conflict and Solidarity between African American and Latino Immigrant Workers*. A report prepared for the University of California, Berkeley's Chief Justice Earl Warren Institute on Race, Ethnicity and Diversity, 2007.

Gordon, Jennifer, and Robin A. Lenhardt. "Rethinking Work and Citizenship." *UCLA Law Review* 55, no. 1161 (2008): 1162–238.

Gordon, Milton Myron. *Assimilation in American Life: The Role of Race, Religion, and National Origins*. New York: Oxford University Press, 1964.

Greenhouse, Steven. "After 15 Years, North Carolina Plant Unionizes." *New York Times*, December 12, 2008, A10.

Griffith, David C. "Rural Industry and Mexican Immigration and Settlement in North Carolina." In *New Destinations: Mexican Immigration in the United States*, edited by Victor Zúñiga and Rubén Hernández-León, 50–77. New York: Russell Sage Foundation, 2005.

Grusky, David B., and Kim A. Weeden. "Does the Sociological Approach to Studying Mobility Have a Future?" In *Mobility and Inequality: Frontiers of Research in Sociology and Economics*, edited by Stephen L. Morgan, David B. Grusky, and Gary S. Fields, 85–108. Stanford, CA: Stanford University Press, 2006.

Guarino, Mark. "Protestors Shut Down Chicago's 'Magnificent Mile' in Demonstrations over Police Slaying of Laquan McDonald." *Washington Post*, November 27, 2015.

Guevarra, Rudy P., Jr. *Becoming Mexipino: Multiethnic Identities and Communities in San Diego.* New Brunswick, NJ: Rutgers University Press, 2012.

Guinier, Lani, and Gerald Torres. *The Miner's Canary: Enlisting Race, Resisting Power, Transforming Democracy.* Cambridge, MA: Harvard University Press, 2002.

Gutierrez, Bertrand. "ACLU Reviewing City Checkpoints." *Winston-Salem Journal*, September 16, 2011. http://www.journalnow.com/news/local/aclu-reviewing-city-police-check points/article_2d5572b9-7f90-587a-a10a674997e83702.html

Ha, Shang. "The Consequences of Multiracial Contexts on Public Attitudes toward Immigration." Paper presented at the American Political Science Association, Philadelphia, Pennsylvania, August 31–September 3, 2006.

Hagan, John, Carla Shedd, and Monique Payne. "Race, Ethnicity, and Youth Perceptions of Criminal Injustice." *American Sociological Review* 70 (2005): 381–407.

Hamilton, Carey. "Local Leaders to Visit Mexico: Purpose Is Firmer Grasp on Culture." *Winston-Salem Journal*, March 1, 2002.

Hamilton, Carey. "More Riders Wanted on Buses: Campaign Intends to Reach Hispanics." *Winston-Salem Journal*, April 28, 2002, B1.

Haney López, Ian F. *Racism on Trial: The Chicano Fight for Justice.* Cambridge, MA: Harvard University Press, 2009.

Hattam, Victoria. *In the Shadow of Race: Jews, Latinos, and Immigrant Politics in the United States.* Chicago: University of Chicago Press, 2007.

Hernández, David Manuel. "Pursuant to Deportation: Latinos and Immigrant Detention." *Latino Studies* 6, no. 1–2 (2008): 35–63.

Hernández-León, Rubén, and Victor Zúñiga. "Appalachia Meets Aztlan: Mexican Immigration and Intergroup Relations in Dalton, Georgia." In *New Destinations: Mexican Immigration in the United States*, edited by V. Zúñiga and R. Hernández-León, 244–73. New York: Russell Sage Foundation, 2005.

Hernández-León, Rubén, and Víctor Zúñiga. "Mexican Immigrant Communities in the South and Social Capital: The Case of Dalton, Georgia." *Southern Rural Sociology* 19, no. 1 (2002): 20–45.

Hero, Rodney E. "Multiracial Coalitions in City Elections Involving Minority Candidates: Some Evidence from Denver." *Urban Affairs Quarterly* 25, no. 2 (1989).

Hewlett, Michael. "Hispanic Students a Pressure on Schools? Two Commissioners Raise Issue as Board Grapples with System's Needs." *Winston-Salem Journal*, November 11, 2005, Metro Edition, B1.

Hing, Julianne. "The Republican Worldview Is One of Racist False Binaries." *Nation*, July 19, 2016.

Hochschild, Jennifer L., and Reuel R. Rogers. "Race Relations in a Diversifying Nation." In *New Directions: African Americans in a Diversifying Nation*, edited by James S. Jackson, 45–85. NPA report no. 297. Washington, DC: National Policy Association, 2000.

Hopkins, Daniel J. "Politicized Places: Explaining Where and When Immigrants Provoke Local Opposition." *American Political Science Review* 104 (2010): 40–60.

Hoppenjans, Lisa. "Spanish-Language Phone Service Serves 5 Counties: United Way Organizations Hope to Help Growing Hispanic Population Find Assistance." *Winston-Salem Journal*, January 17, 2004, B1.

Howard, Greg. "Why 'Transcending Race' Is a Lie." *New York Times Magazine*, June 17, 2016.

Huntington, Samuel. "The Hispanic Challenge." *Foreign Policy*, October 28, 2009.

Hutchinson, Earl Ofari. *The Latino Challenge to Black America.* Los Angeles: Middle Passage, 2007.

Iceland, John. *Where We Live Now: Immigration and Race in the United States.* Berkeley: University of California Press, 2009.

Ignatiev, Noel. *How the Irish Became White.* New York: Routledge, 1995.

Innocence Project. "Darryl Hunt Time Served: 19 Years." Accessed July 5, 2016. http://www
.innocenceproject.org/cases/darryl-hunt/

Jackson, Geena. "Congressional Members to Join Civil Rights Groups in Fight against Alabama's 'Juan Crow' Law." ImmigrationImpact.com. Accessed November 3, 2011. http://
immigrationimpact.com/2011/11/03/congressional-members-to-join-civil-rights-groups-in
-fight-against-alabama%E2%80%99s-%E2%80%9Cjuan-crow%E2%80%9D-law/

Jacobson, Matthew Frye. *Whiteness of a Different Color: European Immigrants and the Alchemy of Race.* Cambridge, MA: Harvard University Press, 1998.

Jiménez, Tomás R. *Replenished Ethnicity: Mexican Americans, Immigration, and Identity.* Berkeley: University of California Press, 2010.

Jiménez, Tomás R., and Adam L. Horowitz. "When White Is Just Alright: How Immigrants Redefine Achievement and Reconfigure the Ethnoracial Hierarchy." *American Sociological Review* 78, no. 5 (2013): 849–71.

Johnson, Hans P. *Movin' Out: Domestic Migration to and from California in the 1990s.* California Counts: Population Trends and Profiles 2, no. 1. San Francisco: Public Policy Institute of California, August 2000.

Johnson, James H., and Melvin L. Oliver. "Interethnic Minority Conflict in Urban America: The Effects of Economic and Social Dislocations." *Urban Geography* 10, no. 5 (1989): 449–63.

Jones, Jennifer A. "Blacks May Be Second Class, but They Can't Make Them Leave: Mexican Racial Formation and Immigrant Status in Winston-Salem." *Latino Studies* 10, no. 1 (2012): 60–80.

Jones, Jennifer A. "Who Are We? Producing Group Identity through Everyday Practices of Conflict and Discourse." *Sociological Perspectives* 54, no. 2 (2011): 139–62.

Jones, Jennifer Anne Meri. "'Mexicans Will Take the Jobs That Even Blacks Won't Do': An Analysis of Blackness, Regionalism and Invisibility in Contemporary Mexico." *Ethnic and Racial Studies* 36, no. 10 (2013): 1564–81.

Jones-Correa, Michael. "Commonalities, Competition, and Linked Fate." In *Just Neighbors? Research on African American and Latino Relations in the United States,* edited by Edward E. Telles, Mark Q. Sawyer, and Gaspar Rivera-Salgado, 63–95. New York: Russell Sage Foundation, 2011.

Jones-Correa, Michael, and Diana Hernàndez. "Commonalities, Competition and Linked Fate: On Latino Immigrants in New and Traditional Receiving Areas." Paper presented to American Sociological Association Annual Meeting, New York, New York, August 11–14, 2007.

Jones-Correa, Michael, Sophia J. Wallace, and Chris Zepeda-Millán. "The Impact of Large-Scale Collective Action on Latino Perceptions of Commonality and Competition with African-Americans." *Social Science Quarterly* 97, no. 2 (2015): 458–75.

Jones-Cruise, Christopher. "Republicans Have Gained Strength in State Legislatures and Governorships." Republican State Leadership Committee blog. October 4, 2016. http://rslc.gop/blog/
2016/10/04/republicans-have-gained-stength-in-state-legislatures-and-governorships/

Jung, Moon-Kie. "The Racial Unconscious of Assimilation Theory." *Du Bois Review* 6, no. 2 (2009): 375–95.

Jung, Moon-Kie. *Reworking Race: The Making of Hawaii's Interracial Labor Movement.* New York: Columbia University Press, 2010.

Junn, Jean. "From Coolie to Model Minority: U.S. Immigration Policy and the Construction of Racial Identity. *DuBois Review* 4, no. 2 (2007): 355–73.

Kandel, William A., and Emilio Parrado. "Hispanic Population Growth and Public School Response in Two New South Immigrant Destinations." In *Latinos in the New South: Transformations of Place*, edited by Heather A. Smith and Owen J. Furuseth, 111–34. Aldershot, England: Ashgate, 2006.

Kao, Grace, and Jennifer S. Thompson. "Racial and Ethnic Stratification in Educational Achievement and Attainment." *Annual Review of Sociology* 29, no. 1 (2003): 417–42.

Kasarda, John D., and James H. Johnson. *The Economic Impact of the Hispanic Population on the State of North Carolina*. Chapel Hill, NC: Frank Hawkins Kenan Institute of Private Enterprise, 2006.

Kasinitz, Philip. *Caribbean New York: Black Immigrants and the Politics of Race*. Ithaca: Cornell University Press, 1992.

Kasinitz, Philip, John H. Mollenkopf, Mary C. Waters, and Jennifer Holdaway. *Inheriting the City: The Children of Immigrants Come of Age*. New York: Russell Sage Foundation, 2008.

Kaufmann, Karen M. "Black and Latino Voters in Denver: Responses to Each Other's Political Leadership." *Political Science Quarterly* 118, no. 1 (2003): 107–26.

Kaufmann, Karen M. "Cracks in the Rainbow: Group Commonality as a Basis for Latino and African-American Political Coalitions." *Political Research Quarterly* 56, no. 2 (2003): 199–210.

Kim, Clare Jean. "The Racial Triangulation of Asian Americans." *Politics & Society* 27, no. 1 (1999): 105–38.

Kinder, Donald R., and Nicholas Winter. "Exploring the Racial Divide: Blacks, Whites, and Opinion on National Policy." *American Journal of Political Science* 45, no. 2 (2001): 439–56.

Kochhar, Rakesh, Richard Fry, and Paul Taylor. "Wealth Gaps Rise to Record Highs between Whites, Blacks, Hispanics: Twenty to One." Pew Research Center Social & Demographic Trends website. Washington, DC: Pew Research Center, 2011.

Kochhar, Rakesh, Roberto Suro, and Sonya Tafoya. "The New Latino South: The Context and Consequences of Rapid Population Growth." Pew Research Center. Washington, DC: Pew Research Center, 2005.

Kohli, Aarti, Peter L. Markowitz, and Lisa Chavez. "Research Report: Secure Communities by the Numbers: An Analysis of Demographics and Due Process." Berkeley: The Chief Justice Earl Warren Institute on Law and Social Policy at the University of California, Berkeley Law School, October 2011.

Kolchin, Peter. "Whiteness Studies: The New History of Race in America." *Journal of American History* 89 (2002): 154–73.

Korstad, Robert Rodgers. *Civil Rights Unionism: Tobacco Workers and the Struggle for Democracy in the Mid-Twentieth-Century South*. Chapel Hill: University of North Carolina Press, 2003.

Lacayo, Celia. "Latinos Need to Stay in Their Place: Differential Segregation in a Multi-ethnic Suburb." *Societies* 6, no. 3 (August 15, 2016): 25.

Lacayo, Celia Olivia. "Perpetual Inferiority: Whites' Racial Ideology toward Latinos." *Sociology of Race and Ethnicity* 3, no. 4 (October 1, 2017): 566–79. https://doi.org/10.1177/2332649217698165.

Lacy, Elaine C. "Integrating into New Communities: The Latino Perspective." In *Being Brown in Dixie: Race, Ethnicity and Latino Immigration in the New South*, edited by Cameron D. Lippard and Charles A. Gallagher, 115–32. Boulder, CO: First Forum, 2011.

Lacy, Karyn R. *Blue-Chip Black: Race, Class, and Status in the New Black Middle Class.* Berkeley: University of California Press, 2007.

Latino Decisions. "Latino Decisions: Tracking Poll Week 10." Last updated November 1, 2010. http://www.latinodecisions.com/files/4413/4697/5947/tracking_nov1.pdf

LeDuff, Charlie. "At a Slaughterhouse, Some Things Never Die." *New York Times*, June 16, 2000. http://www.nytimes.com/2000/06/16/us/slaughterhouse-some-things-never-die-who-kills -who-cuts-who-bosses-can-depend.html

Lee, Jennifer. *Civility in the City: Blacks, Jews, and Koreans in Urban America.* Cambridge, MA: Harvard University Press, 2002.

Lee, Jennifer, and Frank D. Bean. *The Diversity Paradox: Immigration and the Color Line in Twenty-First Century America.* New York: Russell Sage Foundation, 2010.

Lee, Jennifer, and Frank D. Bean. "Redrawing the Color Line?" *City & Community* 6 (2007): 49–62.

Lee, Jennifer, and Frank D. Bean. "Reinventing the Color Line: Immigration and America's New Racial/Ethnic Divide." *Social Forces* 86, no. 2 (2007): 561–86.

Lee, Jennifer, and Min Zhou. *The Asian American Achievement Paradox.* New York: Russell Sage Foundation, 2015.

Lee, Taeku. "From Shared Demographic Categories to Common Political Destinies." *DuBois Review* 4, no. 2 (2008): 433–56.

Lewis, Laura A. "Blacks, Black Indians, Afromexicans: The Dynamics of Race, Nation, and Identity in a Mexican Moreno Community (Guerrero)." *American Ethnologist* 27, no. 4 (November 2000): 898–926.

Lien, Pei-te. *The Making of Asian America through Political Participation.* Philadelphia: Temple University Press, 2001.

Lien, Pei-te, M. Margaret Conway, and Janelle Wong. *The Politics of Asian Americans: Diversity and Community.* New York: Routledge, 2004.

Light, Ivan. "Coming Soon to Your Community: Why Mexican Immigrants Now Seek the American Heartland." *Applied Research in Economic Development* 5 (May 2008): 15–22.

Light, Ivan. *Deflecting Immigration: Networks, Markets, and Regulation in Los Angeles.* New York: Russell Sage, 2006.

Lin, Joanne, Mónica Ramírez, and Reginald Shuford. "Written Statement for a Hearing on Examining 287(g): The Role of State and Local Enforcement in Immigration Law Submitted to the U.S. House of Representatives Committee on Homeland Security." Washington, DC: The American Civil Liberties Union, March 4, 2009.

Lippard, Cameron D., and Charles A. Gallagher. *Being Brown in Dixie: Race, Ethnicity, and Latino Immigration in the New South.* Boulder, CO: First Forum, 2011.

Lipsky, Michael. *Street-Level Bureaucracy: Dilemmas of the Individual in Public Services.* New York: Russell Sage Foundation, 2010 [1980].

Loewen, James W. *The Mississippi Chinese: Between Black and White.* 2nd ed. Long Grove, IL: Waveland, 1988.

Lopez, David, and Yen Le Espiritu. "Panethnicity in the United States: A Theoretical Framework." *Ethnic and Racial Studies* 13, no. 2 (1990): 198–224.

López, Gustavo, and Renee Stepler. "Latinos in the 2016 Election: North Carolina." Pew Hispanic Center. Last updated January, 19, 2016. http://www.pewhispanic.org/fact-sheet/latinos-in -the-2016-election-north-carolina/

Lopez, Mark H., and Susan Minushkin. "Hispanics See Their Situation in U.S. Deteriorating;

Oppose Key Immigration Enforcement Measures." Pew Research Center, Hispanic Trends. Washington, DC: Pew Research Center, 2008.

Lopez, Mark, Rich Morin, and Paul Taylor. "Illegal Immigration Backlash Worries, Divides Latinos." Washington, DC: Pew Hispanic Center, October 28, 2010.

López-Sanders, Laura. "Embedded and External Brokers: The Distinct Roles of Intermediaries in Workplace Inequality." *American Behavioral Scientist* 58, no. 2 (2014): 331–46.

López-Sanders, Laura. "Trapped at the Bottom: Racialized and Gendered Labor Queues in New Immigrant Destinations." Unpublished manuscript, 2009.

Lovato, Roberto. "Juan Crow in Georgia: Immigrant Latinos Live under a Matrix of Oppressive Laws, Customs and Institutions." *Nation*, May 8, 2008. http://www.thenation.com/doc/20080526/lovato/

Márquez, John D. *Black-Brown Solidarity: Racial Politics in the New Gulf South*. Austin: University of Texas Press, 2014.

Marrow, Helen B. "Hispanic Immigration, Black Population Size, and Intergroup Relations in the Rural and Small-Town South." In *New Faces in New Places: The Changing Geography of American Immigration*, edited by Douglas Massey. New York: Russell Sage Foundation, 2008.

Marrow, Helen. "Immigrant Bureaucratic Incorporation: The Dual Roles of Professional Missions and Government Policies." *American Sociological Review* 74 (2009): 756–76.

Marrow, Helen B. *New Destination Dreaming: Immigration, Race, and Legal Status in the Rural American South*. Stanford, CA: Stanford University Press, 2011.

Marrow, Helen B. "New Immigrant Destinations and the American Colour Line." *Ethnic and Racial Studies* 32 (2009): 1037–57.

Martínez, Ramiro, Jr., Jacob I. Stowell, and Matthew T. Lee. "Immigration and Crime in an Era of Transformation: A Longitudinal Analysis of Homicides in San Diego Neighborhoods." *Criminology* 48 (2010): 797–829.

Martinez, Rick. "Immigration Hits 'Critical Mass' in NC: Rapid Influxes of Hispanics, Most of Them Illegal, Creating Tensions." *Carolina Journal News Reports*, December 12, 2005. http://www.carolinajournal.com/articles/display_story.html?id=2983

Massey, Douglas S. *Categorically Unequal: The American Stratification System*. New York: Russell Sage Foundation, 2007.

Massey, Douglas S. *New Faces in New Places: The Changing Geography of American Immigration*. New York: Russell Sage Foundation, 2008.

Massey, Douglas S. "Racial Formation in Theory and Practice: The Case of Mexicans in the United States." *Race and Social Problems* 1, no. 1 (2009): 12–26.

Massey, Douglas. "The Racialization of Mexicans in the United States? Racial Stratification in Theory and Practice." *Migracion y Desarrollo* 10, First Semester (2008): 59–85.

Massey, Douglas S., Jorge Durand, and Nolan J. Malone. *Beyond Smoke and Mirrors: Mexican Immigration in an Era of Economic Integration*. New York: Russell Sage Foundation, 2003.

Massey, Douglas S., and Karen A. Pren. "Origins of the New Latino Underclass." *Race and Social Problems* 4, no. 1 (2012): 5–17.

Massey, Douglas S., and Magaly Sánchez. *Brokered Boundaries: Creating Immigrant Identity in Anti-immigrant Times*. New York: Russell Sage Foundation, 2010.

Masuoka, Natalie. "Defining the Group: Latino Identity and Political Participation." *American Politics Research* 36, no.1 (2007): 33–61.

Masuoka, Natalie. "Together They Become One: Examining the Predictors of Panethnic Group

Consciousness among Asian Americans and Latinos." *Social Science Quarterly* 87, no.1 (2006): 993–1011.

McCann, Michael W. *Rights at Work: Pay Equity Reform and the Politics of Legal Mobilization.* Chicago: University of Chicago Press, 1994.

McClain, Paula D. "Racial Intergroup Relations in a Set of Cities: A Twenty-Year Perspective." *Journal of Politics* 68, no. 4 (2006): 757–70.

McClain, Paula D., Niambi M. Carter, Victoria M. DeFrancesco Soto, Monique L. Lyle, Jeffrey D. Grynaviski, Shayla C. Nunnally, Thomas J. Scotto, J. Alan Kendrick, Gerald F. Lackey, and Kendra Davenport Cotton. "Racial Distancing in a Southern City: Latino Immigrants' Views of Black Americans." *Journal of Politics* 68, no. 3 (2006): 571–84.

McClain, Paula D., Jessica D. Johnson Carew, Eugene Walton, and Candis S. Watts. "Group Membership, Group Identity, and Group Consciousness: Measures of Racial Identity in American Politics?" *Annual Review of Political Science* 12, no. 1 (2009): 471–85.

McClain, Paula D., Monique L. Lyle, Niambi M. Carter, Victoria M. DeFrancesco Soto, Gerald F. Lackey, Kendra Davenport Cotton, Shayla C. Nunnally, Thomas J. Scotto, Jeffrey D. Grynaviski, and J. Alan Kendrick. "Black Americans and Latino Immigrants in a Southern City: Friendly Neighbors or Economic Competitors?" *Du Bois Review* 4, no. 1 (2007): 97–117.

McDermott, Monica. "Black Attitudes and Hispanic Immigrants in South Carolina." In *Just Neighbors? Research on African American and Latino Relations in the United States*, edited by Edward E. Telles, Mark Q. Sawyer, and Gaspar Rivera-Salgado, 242–66. New York: Russell Sage Foundation, 2011.

Meier, Kenneth J., Paula D. McClain, J. L. Polinard, and Robert D. Wrinkle. "Divided or Together? Conflict and Cooperation between African Americans and Latinos." *Political Research Quarterly* 57, no. 3 (2004): 399–409.

Menchaca, Martha. *Recovering History, Constructing Race: The Indian, Black, and White Roots of Mexican Americans.* Austin: University of Texas Press, 2001.

Menjívar, Cecilia. "The Power of the Law: Central Americans' Legality and Everyday Life in Phoenix, Arizona." *Latino Studies* 9, no. 4 (2011): 377–95.

Menjívar, Cecilia, and Leisy J. Abrego. "Legal Violence: Immigration Law and the Lives of Central American Immigrants." *American Journal of Sociology* 117, no. 5 (2012): 1380–421.

Menjívar, Cecilia, and Daniel Kanstroom. "Introduction—Immigrant 'Illegality': Constructions and Critiques." In *Constructing Immigrant "Illegality": Critiques, Experiences, and Responses*, edited by Cecilia Menjívar and Daniel Kanstroom. New York: Cambridge University Press, 2014.

Migration Policy Institute. "State Immigration Data Profiles." Migration Policy Institute. Washington, DC: Migration Policy Institute, 2015. https://www.migrationpolicy.org/data/state -profiles/state/demographics/NC//

"Milestones." *Winston-Salem Journal,* January 6, 2003, B2.

Millard, Ann V., and Jorge Chapa. *Apple Pie & Enchiladas: Latino Newcomers in the Rural Midwest.* Austin: University of Texas Press, 2004.

Miller, Cassie, and Alexandra Wener-Winslow. "Ten Days After: Harassment and Intimidation in the Aftermath of the Election." *Southern Poverty Law Center*, November 29, 2016. https:// www.splcenter.org/20161129/ten-days-after-harassment-and-intimidation-aftermath -election

Mills, C. Wright. *The Sociological Imagination.* Oxford: Oxford University Press, 2000.

Mindola, Tatcho, Jr., Yolanda Flores Niemann, and Nestor Rodriguez. *Black-Brown Relations and Stereotypes*. Austin: University of Texas Press, 2003.

Mississippi Immigrant Rights Alliance. MIRA newsletter, 2008, A7.

Mitchell, Monte. "Man Charged with Second-Degree Murder in Wreck; He Had Also Been Charged with Driving while Impaired; One Man Killed." *Winston-Salem Journal*, November 28, 2007, B1.

Mohl, Raymond A. "Globalization, Latinization, and the Nuevo New South." *Journal of American Ethnic History* 22, no.4 (2003): 31–66.

Molina, Natalia. *How Race Is Made in America: Immigration, Citizenship, and the Historical Power of Racial Scripts*. Berkeley: University of California Press, 2014.

Montejano, David. *Chicano Politics and Society in the Late Twentieth Century*. Austin: University of Texas Press, 1999.

Mora, G. Cristina. "Cross-Field Effects and Ethnic Classification: The Institutionalization of Hispanic Panethnicity, 1965 to 1990." *American Sociological Review* 79, no. 2 (2014): 183–210.

Mora, G. Christina. *Making Hispanics: How Activists, Bureaucrats, and Media Constructed a New American*. Chicago: University of Chicago Press, 2014.

Mora, G. Cristina, and Michael Rodríguez-Muñiz. "Latinos, Race, and the American Future: A Response to Richard Alba's 'The Likely Persistence of a White Majority.'" *New Labor Forum* 26, no. 2 (2017): 45.

Morin, Jason, Gabriel R. Sánchez, and Matt A. Barreto. "Perceptions of Competition." In *Just Neighbors? Research on African American and Latino Relations in the United States*, edited by Edward E. Telles, Mark Q. Sawyer, and Gaspar Rivera-Salgado, 96–124. New York: Russell Sage Foundation, 2011.

Morris, Frank, and James G. Gimpel. *Immigration, Intergroup Conflict, and the Erosion of African American Political Power in the 21st Century*. Washington, DC: Center for Immigration Studies, 2007.

Morrison, Toni. "On the Backs of Blacks." *Time*, December 2, 1993.

Muhammad, Khalil Gibran. *The Condemnation of Blackness: Race, Crime, and the Making of Modern Urban America*. Cambridge, MA: Harvard University Press, 2011.

Murguia, Edward, and Tyrone Forman. "Shades of Whiteness: The Mexican American Experience in Relation to Anglos and Blacks." In *White Out: The Continuing Significance of Racism*, edited by Ashley Doane and Eduardo Bonilla-Silva. New York: Routledge, 2003.

Murphy, Arthur D., Colleen Blanchard, and Jennifer A. Hill. *Latino Workers in the Contemporary South*. Athens: University of Georgia Press, 2001.

Murray, Royce Bernstein, and Mary Giovagnoli. *DHS Progress Report: The Challenge of Reform*. Washington, DC: Immigration Policy Center, 2010.

Musante, Glenna. "Immigrant Success Story Lends a Hand to Newcomers." *News and Observer*, August 9, 1998, B1.

NAACP. "Immigration Factsheet and Talking Points." Accessed October 27, 2017. https://www.naacp.org/wp-content/uploads/2016/04/Immig%20Factsheet%20Tlkng%20Pts%20Final%20July%202011.pdf

Nagel, Joane. "American Indian Ethnic Renewal: Politics and the Resurgence of Identity." *American Sociological Review* 60, no. 6 (1995): 947–65.

NALEO. 2017. "Latino Decisions/NALEO/ImpreMedia National Post-Election Survey—Nov 2008." Accessed December 4, 2017. http://www.latinodecisions.com/files/2913/3749/5067/NALEO.Nov08.pdf

National Academies of Sciences, Engineering, and Medicine. *The Integration of Immigrants into American Society*. Washington, DC: National Academies Press, 2015.

National Conference of State Legislatures. "Immigration." Accessed July 27, 2014. http://www .ncsl.org/research/immigration.aspx

National Immigration Law Center. "The Real ID Act: Questions and Answers." National Immigration Law Center. Last updated January 2016. https://www.nilc.org/wp-content/uploads/ 2015/11/REAL-ID-Act-Q-and-A.pdf

"N.C. County Leaders to Travel to Mexico." *Winston-Salem Journal*, February 28, 2002, B5.

Neckerman, Kathryn M., Prudence Carter, and Jennifer Lee. "Segmented Assimilation and Minority Cultures of Mobility." *Ethnic and Racial Studies* 22, no. 6 (1999): 945–65.

Newport, Frank. "Hispanics' Approval of Obama Down since '12." Last updated September 26, 2014. http://www.gallup.com/poll/177404/hispanics-approval-obama-down.aspx

Ngai, Mae M. *Impossible Subjects: Illegal Aliens and the Making of Modern America*. Princeton, NJ: Princeton University Press, 2004.

Not One More Deportation. Participant Email. Accessed July 31, 2016. http://www.notonemore deportation.com/2015/04/28/7631/

Not1more. "Declaración Sobre el Alzamiento en Baltimore." April 28, 2015. Not One More Deportation. http://www.notonemoredeportation.com/2015/04/28/7631/

Ocampo, Anthony. "Are Second Generation Filipinos Becoming Asian American or Latino? Historical Colonialism, Culture, and Panethnic Identity." *Ethnic and Racial Studies* 37, no. 4 (2013): 425–45.

Ochoa, Gilda L. *Becoming Neighbors in a Mexican American Community: Power, Conflict, and Solidarity*. Austin: University of Texas Press, 2004.

Odem, Mary E., and Elaine Cantrell Lacy, eds. *Latino Immigrants and the Transformation of the U.S. South*. Athens: University of Georgia Press, 2009.

OECD. *Education at a Glance 2014: OECD Indicators*. Paris: OECD, 2014. http://dx.doi.org/10 .1787/eag-2014-en

Ogbar, Jeffrey. "Puerto Rico en mi Corazon: The Young Lords, Black Power and Puerto Rican Nationalism in the U.S. 1966–1972." *Centro Journal* 18, no. 1 (2006): 148–69.

Okamoto, Dina G. "Institutional Panethnicity: Boundary Formation in Asian-American Organizing." *Social Forces* 85, no. 1 (2006): 1–25.

Okamoto, Dina G. *Redefining Race: Asian American Panethnicity and Shifting Ethnic Boundaries*. New York: Russell Sage Foundation, 2014.

Okamoto, Dina G., and Kim Ebert. "Beyond the Ballot: Immigrant Collective Action in Gateways and New Destinations in the United States." *Social Problems* 57, no. 4 (2010): 529–58.

Oliver, Eric J., and Janelle Wong. "Intergroup Prejudice in Multiethnic Settings." *American Journal of Political Science* 47, no. 4 (2003): 567–82.

Olzak, Susan, and Joane Nagel. *Competitive Ethnic Relations*. Orlando: Academic, 1986.

Oppermann, Langdon. *Winston-Salem's African-American Neighborhoods: 1870–1950*. Winston-Salem, NC: Architectural and Planning Report, 1994.

Padín, José Antonio. "The Normative Mulattoes: The Press, Latinos, and the Racial Climate on the Moving Immigration Frontier." *Sociological Perspectives* 48, no. 1 (2005): 49–75.

Pager, Devah, and Hana Shepherd. "The Sociology of Discrimination: Racial Discrimination in Employment, Housing, Credit, and Consumer Markets." *Annual Review of Sociology* 34 (2008): 181–209.

Pallares, Amalia, and Nilda Flores-Gonzales. *Marcha: Latino Chicago and the Immigrant Rights Movement*. Champaign-Urbana: University of Illinois Press, 2010.

Park, Robert Ezra. *Race and Culture.* Glencoe, IL: Free Press, 1950.

Passel, Jeffrey S., and D'Vera Cohn. *Unauthorized Immigrant Population: National and State Trends, 2010.* Washington, DC: Pew Hispanic Center, 2011.

Passel, Jeffrey, and Wendy Zimmerman. "Are Immigrants Leaving California? Settlement Patterns of Immigrants in the Late 1990s." Washington, DC: Urban Institute, 2001.

Pastor, Manuel, Justin Scoggins, and Sarah Treuhaft. "Bridging the Racial Generation Gap Is the Key to America's Economic Future." *Policy Link.* University of Southern California, September 2017. http://nationalequityatlas.org/sites/default/files/RacialGenGap_%20final .pdf

Pattillo-McCoy, Mary. *Black Picket Fences: Privilege and Peril among the Black Middle Class.* Chicago: University of Chicago Press, 1999.

Pérez-Torres, Rafael. *Mestizaje: Critical Uses of Race in Chicano Culture.* Minneapolis: University of Minnesota Press, 2006.

Perlmann, Joel, and Roger Waldinger. "Second Generation Decline? Children of Immigrants, Past and Present—A Reconsideration." *International Migration Review* 31, no. 4 (1997): 893–922.

Perreira, Krista M. "Mexican Families in North Carolina: The Socio-historical Contexts of Exit and Settlement." *Southeastern Geographer* 51, no. 2 (2011): 260–86.

Pettigrew, Thomas F. "Intergroup Contact Theory." *Annual Review of Psychology.* 49 (1998): 65–85.

Pew Research Center. "'Borders First': A Dividing Line in the Immigration Debate." Pew Research Center/USA Today Poll. Washington, DC: Pew Research Center, June 23, 2013. http:// www.people-press.org/2013/06/23/section-2-view-of-undocumented-immigrants-impact -of-legalization/

Pew Research Center. "In First Month, Views of Trump Are Already Strongly Felt, Deeply Polarized; Views of Trump's Executive Order on Travel Restrictions." Washington, DC: Pew Research Center, February 16, 2017. http://www.people-press.org/2017/02/16/2-views-of -trumps-executive-order-on-travel-restrictions/

Pew Research Center. "Intermarriage across the U.S. by Metro Area." Pew Research Center's Social & Demographic Trends Project (blog), May 18, 2017. http://www.pewsocialtrends.org/ interactives/intermarriage-across-the-u-s-by-metro-area/

Pew Research Center. "The Rise of Asian Americans." Washington, DC: Pew Research Center, April 4, 2013. http://www.pewsocialtrends.org/2012/06/19/the-rise-of-asian-americans/

Pew Survey Center. "U.S. Religious Landscape Study: Religious Affiliation Diverse and Dynamic." Washington, DC: Pew Forum on Religious and Public Life, February 2008. Accessed September 15, 2017. http://www.pewforum.org/files/2013/05/report-religious-landscape-study -full.pdf

Phoenix, Ann, and Barbara Tizard. *Black, White or Mixed Race? Race and Racism in the Lives of Young People of Mixed Parentage.* London: Routledge, 2002 [1993].

Pickel, Mary Lou. "Response from Hispanics in Georgia Muted." *Atlanta Journal-Constitution,* March 28, 2006.

Popke, Jeff. "Latino Migration and Neoliberalism in the U.S. South: Notes toward a Rural Cosmopolitanism." *Southeastern Geographer* 51, no. 2 (2011): 242–59.

Portes, Alejandro. "The Economics of Immigration." *Contemporary Sociology* 19 (November 1990): 853–55.

Portes, Alejandro. "Immigration Theory for a New Century: Some Problems and Opportunities." *International Migration Review* 31, no. 4 (1997): 799–825.

Portes, Alejandro, and Rubén Rumbaut. *Immigrant America: A Portrait*. Berkeley: University of California Press, 1996.

Portes, Alejandro, and Rubén G. Rumbaut. *Legacies: The Story of the Immigrant Second Generation*. Berkeley: University of California Press, 2001.

Portes, Alejandro, and Alex Stepick. *City on the Edge: The Transformation of Miami*. Berkeley: University of California Press, 1993.

Portes, Alejandro, and Min Zhou. "The New Second Generation: Segmented Assimilation and Its Variants." *Annals of the American Academy of Political and Social Science* 530 (1993): 74–96.

Powell Johnson, Bernice. "Civil Rights Journal: Teaching Children Survival Skills." *Winston-Salem Chronicle*, November 7, 1997, A10.

Priestly, George. "Ethnicity, Class, and Race in the United States: Prospects for African-American/Latino Alliances." *Latin American Perspectives* 34, no. 1 (2007): 53–63.

Provine, Doris Marie, and Gabriella Sanchez. "Suspecting Immigrants: Exploring Links between Racialised Anxieties and Expanded Police Powers in Arizona." *Policing and Society* 21, no. 4 (December 2011): 468–79. https://doi.org/10.1080/10439463.2011.614098

Purdy, Jedediah. "North Carolina's Long Moral March and Its Lessons for the Trump Resistance." *New Yorker*, February 17, 2017. https://www.newyorker.com/news/news-desk/north-carolinas-long-moral-march-and-its-lessons-for-the-trump-resistance

Railey, John. "Changed World: Americans Search for Hope as Events Bring Uncertainty." *Winston-Salem Journal*, January 1, 2002, A1.

Ramakrishnan, S. Karthick, and Tom Wong. "Partisanship, not Spanish: Explaining Municipal Ordinances Affecting Undocumented Immigrants." In *Taking Local Control: Immigration Policy Activism in U.S. Cities and States*, edited by Monica Varsanyi, 73–96. Stanford, CA: Stanford University Press, 2010.

Ribas, Vanesa. *On the Line: Slaughterhouse Lives and the Making of the New South*. Oakland: University of California Press, 2016.

Rich, Brian L., and Marta Miranda. "The Sociopolitical Dynamics of Mexican Immigration in Lexington, Kentucky, 1997 to 2002: An Ambivalent Community Responds." In *New Destinations: Mexican Immigration in the United States*, edited by Victor Zúñiga and Rubén Hernández-León, 187–219. New York: Russell Sage Foundation, 2005.

Robinson, Zandria F. *This Ain't Chicago: Race, Class, and Regional Identity in the Post-Soul South*. Chapel Hill: University of North Carolina Press, 2014.

Rocha, Rene R. "Black-Brown Coalitions in Local School Board Elections." *Political Research Quarterly* 60, no. 2 (2007): 315–27.

Rodríguez, Clara E. *Changing Race: Latinos, the Census, and the History of Ethnicity in the United States*. New York: NYU Press, 2000.

Rodríguez, Néstor. "New Southern Neighbors: Latino Immigration and Prospects for Intergroup Relations between African-Americans and Latinos in the South." *Latino Studies* 10, no. 1–2 (2012): 18–40.

Rodríguez-Muñiz, Michael. "Grappling with Latinidad: Puerto Rican Activism in Chicago's Immigrant Rights Movement." In *¡Marcha!: Latino Chicago and the Immigrant Rights Movement*, edited by N. Flores-González and A. Pallares, 237–58. Chicago: University of Illinois Press, 2010.

Roediger, David R. *The Wages of Whiteness: Race and the Making of the American Working Class*. London: Verso, 1991.

Roediger, David R. *Working toward Whiteness: How America's Immigrants Became White: The Strange Journey from Ellis Island to the Suburbs.* New York: Basic, 2005.

Rogers, Reuel. "Black like Who? Afro-Caribbean Immigrants, African Americans, and the Politics of Group Identity." In *Islands in the City: West Indian Migration to New York*, edited by N. Foner, 163–92. Berkeley: University of California Press, 2001.

Rogers, Reuel R. "Race-Based Coalitions among Minority Groups: Afro-Caribbean Immigrants and African Americans in New York City." *Urban Affairs Review* 39, no. 3 (2004): 283–317.

Rothgerber, Hank. "External Intergroup Threat as an Antecedent to Perceptions in In-Group and Out-Group Homogeneity." *Journal of Personality and Social Psychology* 73, no. 6 (1997): 1206–12.

Rumbaut, Rubén G. "The Crucible Within: Ethnic Identity, Self-Esteem and Segmented Assimilation among Children of Immigrants." *International Migration Review* 28 (1994): 748–94.

Rumbaut, Rubén G., and Alejandro Portes. *Ethnicities: Children of Immigrants in America.* Berkeley: University of California Press, 2001.

Sampson, Robert J. "Rethinking Crime and Immigration." *Contexts* (Winter 2008): 28–33.

Sánchez, Gabriel R. "Latino Group Consciousness and Perceptions of Commonality with African Americans." *Social Science Quarterly* 89, no. 2 (2008): 428–44.

Sánchez, Gabriel, and Matt Barreto. "In Record Numbers, Latino Voters Voted Overwhelmingly against Trump. We Did the Research." *Washington Post*, Monkey Cage, November 11, 2016.

Sánchez, Gabriel R., and Natalie Masuoka. "Brown-Utility Heuristic? The Presence and Contributing Factors of Latino Linked Fate." *Hispanic Journal of Behavioral Sciences* 32, no. 4 (2010): 519–31.

Santa Ana, Otto. *Brown Tide Rising: Metaphors of Latinos in Contemporary American Public Discourse.* Austin: University of Texas Press, 2002.

Schrag, Peter. *California: America's High-Stakes Experiment.* Berkeley: University of California Press, 2007.

Segura, Gary M., and Helena Alves Rodrigues. "Comparative Ethnic Politics in the United States: Beyond Black and White." *Annual Review of Political Science* 9 (2006): 375–95.

Sexton, Scott. "Immigration Debate Strays from Ideas to Ideologies." *Winston-Salem Journal*, April 13, 2006, Metro Edition, B1.

Shaffrey, Mary M. "Caucus Lists Steps for Reform; Blacks' Immigration Ideas like Democrats'." *Winston-Salem Journal*, August 6, 2006, A1.

Sherif, Muzafer. *Groups in Harmony and Tension: An Integration of Studies on Intergroup Relations.* New York: Harper, 1953.

Sherif, Muzafer, O. J. Harvey, B. Jack White, William R. Hood, and Carolyn W. Sherif. *Intergroup Conflict and Cooperation: The Robbers Cave Experiment.* Norman, OK: University Book Exchange, 1961.

Sigelman, Lee, and Susan Welch. "The Contact Hypothesis Revisited: Black-White Interaction and Positive Racial Attitudes." *Social Forces* 71, no. 3 (1993): 781–95.

Singer, Audrey. *The New Geography of United States Immigration.* Brookings Immigration Series, vol. 3. Washington, DC: Brookings Institution, 2009.

Singer, Audrey, Susan W. Hardwick, and Caroline B. Brettell, eds. *Twenty-First Century Gateways: Immigrant Incorporation in Suburban America.* Washington, DC: Brookings Institution Press, 2008.

Skinner, Richard. *Department of Homeland Security Office of Inspector General: The Performance of 287(g) Agreements.* Washington, DC: Department of Homeland Security, 2010.

Smiley, David. "McDuffie Riots: Revisiting, Retelling Story—35 Years Later." *Miami Herald*, May 16, 2015. http://www.miamiherald.com/news/local/community/miami-dade/article 21178995.html

Smith, Heather, and Owen Furuseth. *Latinos in the New South: Transformations of Place*. Burlington: Ashgate, 2006.

Smith, Heather A., and Owen J. Furuseth. "The 'Nuevo South': Latino Place Making and Community Building in the Middle-Ring Suburbs of Charlotte." In *Twenty-First Century Gateways: Immigrant Incorporation in Suburban America*, edited by Audrey Singer, Susan Hardwick, and Caroline Brettell, 281–308. Washington, DC: Brookings Institution Press, 2008.

Smith, Robert Courtney. "Black Mexicans, Conjunctural Ethnicity, and Operating Identities: Long-Term Ethnographic Analysis." *American Sociological Review* 79, no. 3 (2014): 517–48.

South, Scott J., Kyle Crowder, and Erick Chavez. "Migration and Spatial Assimilation among U.S. Latinos: Classical versus Segmented Trajectories." *Demography* 42, no. 3 (2005): 497–521.

Sparks, John. "Area Residents Also Encountering Long DMV Waits; Examiner Shortage, Rush to Beat New ID Rules Are Causing Delays." *Winston-Salem Journal*, January 22, 2004, B1.

Stepick, Alex, and Carol Dutton Stepick. "Diverse Contexts of Reception and Feelings of Belonging." *Forum: Qualitative Social Research* 10, no. 3 (2009): 13.

Stewart, Julie. "Fiction over Facts: How Competing Narrative Forms Explain Policy in a New Immigration Destination." *Sociological Forum* 27, no. 3 (2012): 591–616.

Stokes, Atiya Kai. "Latino Group Consciousness and Political Participation." *American Politics Research* 31, no. 4 (2003): 361–78.

St. Onge, Peter. "He Is the Man Who Sends the Illegal Immigrants Home." *Charlotte Observer*, December 10, 2006.

Streeter Harry, Cheryl. *Winston-Salem's African American Legacy*. Charleston: Arcadia, 2012.

Stuesse, Angela C. "Race, Migration, and Labor Control: Neoliberal Challenges to Organizing Mississippi's Poultry Workers." In *Latino Immigrants and the Transformation of the U.S. South*, edited by Mary E. Odem and Elaine Cantrell Lacy. Athens: University of Georgia Press, 2009.

Stuesse, Angela. *Scratching Out a Living: Latinos, Race, and Work in the Deep South*. Oakland: University of California Press, 2016.

Sturiale, Jeanne. "Media Right Agency Specializes in Animation and Art Projects." *Winston-Salem Journal*, January 26, 2003, D9.

Sturiale, Jeanne. "Opening Doors: Southern Community Bank Makes It Its Business to Pull In Hispanic Customers." *Winston-Salem Journal*, November 24, 2002, D1.

Su, Celina. "We Call Ourselves by Many Names: Storytelling and Interminority-Coalition Building." *Community Development Journal* 45, no. 4 (2010): 439–57.

Suárez-Orozco, Carola, and Marcelo M. Suárez-Orozco. *Children of Immigration*. Cambridge, MA: Harvard University Press, 2001.

Sue, Christina. *Land of the Cosmic Race: Race Mixture, Racism, and Blackness in Mexico*. Oxford: Oxford University Press, 2013.

Suls, Rob. "Most Americans Continue to Oppose U.S. Border Wall, Doubt Mexico Would Pay for It." Pew Research Center. February, 24, 2017. http://www.pewresearch.org/fact-tank/2017/02/24/most-americans-continue-to-oppose-u-s-border-wall-doubt-mexico-would-pay-for-it/

Suro, Roberto, Gabriel Escobar, and Pew Hispanic Center. *2006 National Survey of Latinos: The Immigration Debate*. Washington, DC: Pew Hispanic Center, 2006.

Suro, Roberto, Audrey Singer, Brookings Institution, Center on Urban and Metropolitan Policy, and Pew Hispanic Center. *Latino Growth in Metropolitan America: Changing Patterns, New Locations.* Washington, DC: Brookings Institution, Center on Urban and Metropolitan Policy in collaboration with the Pew Hispanic Center, 2002.

Sutton, Constance, and Susan Makiesky-Barrow. "Migration and West Indian Racial and Ethnic Consciousness." In *Migration and Development: Implications for Ethnic Identity and Development,* edited by H. Safa and B. du Toit, 113–44. Paris: Mouton, 1975.

Tarasawa, Beth. "New Patterns of Segregation: Latino and African-American Students in Metro Atlanta High Schools." Southern Spaces, January 19, 2009. https://southernspaces.org/2009/new-patterns-segregation-latino-and-african-american-students-metro-atlanta-high -schools

Taylor, Paul S. *An American-Mexican Frontier.* Chapel Hill: University of North Carolina Press, 2011 [1934].

Taylor, Paul, Rakesh Kochhar, Richard Fry, Gabriel Velasco, and Seth Motel. "Twenty to One: Wealth Gaps Rise to Record Highs between Whites, Blacks, and Hispanics." *Pew Hispanic Center Research Report* 145. Washington, DC: Pew Hispanic Center, 2011.

Tedin, Kent L., and Richard W. Murray. "Support for Biracial Political Coalitions among Blacks and Hispanics." *Social Science Quarterly* 75, no. 4 (1994): 772–89.

Telles, Edward Eric, and Vilma Ortiz. *Generations of Exclusion: Mexican Americans, Assimilation, and Race.* New York: Russell Sage Foundation, 2008.

Telles, Edward E., Mark Q. Sawyer, and Gaspar Rivera-Salgado. *Just Neighbors? Research on African American and Latino Relations in the United States.* New York: Russell Sage Foundation, 2011.

Thompson, Krissah. "Immigrant Groups Reach Out to Blacks." *Washington Post,* March 20, 2010, A3.

Thornton, Michael C., and Yuko Mizuno. "Economic Well-Being and Black Adult Feelings toward Immigrants and Whites, 1984." *Journal of Black Studies* 30, no. 1 (1999): 15–44.

Tomer, Adie, Elizabeth Kneebone, Robert Puentes, and Alan Berube. "Missed Opportunity: Transit and Jobs in Metropolitan America." Metropolitan Infrastructure Initiative Series and Metropolitan Opportunity Series: Brookings Institute. Washington, DC: Brookings Institute, 2011.

"Traffic Questions and Answers." *Winston-Salem Journal,* January 4, 2002, A10.

Treitler, Vilna Bashi. *The Ethnic Project: Transforming Racial Fiction into Ethnic Factions.* Stanford, CA: Stanford University Press, 2013.

"Trip to Mexico." *Winston-Salem Journal,* May 15, 2002, A10.

Turner, Margey Austin, Rob Santos, Diane K. Levy, Doug Wissoker, Claudia Aranda, Rob Pitingolo, and the Urban Institute. *Housing Discrimination against Racial and Ethnic Minorities: Executive Summary.* Washington, DC: US Department of Housing and Urban Development, June 2013.

Tursi, Frank V. *Winston-Salem: A History.* Winston-Salem: John F. Blair, 1994.

US Census Bureau. "B19001B [for each census tract]: Household Income in the Past 12 Months (in 2010 Inflation-Adjusted Dollars) (Black or African American Alone Householder), American Community Survey 5-Year Estimates, 2010." American FactFinder website. Washington, DC: US Census Bureau. Retrieved January 2, 2015. http://factfinder2.census.gov.

US Census Bureau. "Money Income in the United States: 2000." Current Population Reports. Washington, DC: US Census Bureau, 2000.

US Census Bureau. "Results. Winston-Salem city, North Carolina." American FactFinder website. Accessed October 30, 2017. https://factfinder.census.gov/faces/tableservices/jsf/pages/productview.xhtml?src=CF.

US Census Bureau. US Census Bureau, 2010 Census. Summary File 1, Hispanic or Latino by Type, Winston-Salem, NC. Washington DC: US Census Bureau. Accessed October 20, 2016. http://factfinder.census.gov/faces/tableservices/jsf/pages/productview.xhtml?src=CF

US Census Bureau. "Winston-Salem, NC Population Estimates: 2008." Current Population Reports. Washington, DC: US Census Bureau, 2008.

US Department of Homeland Security. *Fact Sheet: Delegation of Immigration Authority Section 287(g) Immigration and Nationality Act*. Washington, DC: DHS, Office of Public Affairs, 2009.

US House of Representatives. "Gangs, Fraud and Sexual Predators: Struggling with the Consequences of Illegal Immigration." US House of Representatives Hearing. April 12, 2006. Washington, DC: US Government Printing Office. http://www.gpo.gov/fdsys/pkg/CHRG109hhrg30529/html/CHRG-109hhrg30529.htm

Vaca, Nick Corona. *The Presumed Alliance: The Unspoken Conflict between Latinos and Blacks and What It Means for America*. New York: Rayo, 2004.

Valle, Victor, and Rodolfo D. Torres. "The Idea of Mestizaje and the 'Race' Problematic: Racialized Media Discourse in a Post-Fordist Landscape." In *Culture and Difference: Critical Perspectives on the Bicultural Experience in the United States*, 139–50. Westport, CT: Bergin & Garvey, 1995.

Van den Berghe, Pierre L. *Race and Racism: A Comparative Perspective*. New York: Wiley, 1967.

Vargas, Edward D., Gabriel R. Sánchez, and Juan A. Valdez. "Immigration Policies and Group Identity: How Immigrant Laws Affect Linked Fate among U.S. Latino Populations." *Journal of Race, Ethnicity and Politics* 2, no. 1 (2017): 35–62.

Varsanyi, Monica W., Paul G. Lewis, Doris Marie Provine, and Scott Decker. "A Multilayered Jurisdictional Patchwork: Immigration Federalism in the United States." *Law & Policy* 34, no. 2 (2012): 138–58.

Vasquez, Jessica M. *Mexican Americans across Generations: Immigrant Families, Racial Realities*. New York: New York University Press, 2011.

Vaughan, Jessica M., and James R. Edwards. "The 287(g) Program: Protecting Home Towns and Homeland." Washington, DC: Center for Immigration Studies, 2009.

Vélez, Maria B. "Contextualizing the Immigration and Crime Effect: An Analysis of Homicide in Chicago Neighborhoods." *Homicide Studies* 13, no. 3 (2009): 325–35.

Vickerman, Milton. *Crosscurrents: West Indian Immigrants and Race*. New York: Oxford University Press, 1999.

Wang, Oliver. *Legions of Boom: Filipino American Mobile DJ Crews in the San Francisco Bay Area*. Durham: Duke University Press, 2015.

Waters, Mary C. *Black Identities: West Indian Immigrant Dreams and American Realities*. Cambridge, MA: Harvard University Press, 1999.

Waters, Mary C. "Ethnic and Racial Identities of Second-Generation Black Immigrants in New York City." *International Migration Review* Special Issue: The New Second Generation. 28, no. 4 (2010): 795–820.

Waters, Mary C. *Ethnic Options: Choosing Identities in America*. Berkeley: University of California Press, 1990.

Waters, Mary C., Philip Kasinitz, and Asad L. Asad. "Immigrants and African Americans." *Annual Review of Sociology* 40 (2014): 369–90.

Weber, Max. *Economy and Society*. Berkeley: University of California Press, 1922.

Weise, Julie M. *Corazón de Dixie: Mexicanos in the U.S. South since 1910*. Chapel Hill: University of North Carolina Press, 2015.

Weissman, Deborah. "Written Statement for a Joint Hearing on the 'Public Safety and Civil Rights Implications of State and Local Enforcement of Federal Immigration Laws.'" Washington, DC: US House of Representatives, April 2, 2009.

Wilkerson, Isabel. "In Florida, a Death Foretold." *New York Times*, March 31, 2012. http://www.nytimes.com/2012/04/01/opinion/sunday/a-native-caste-society.html

Williams, Kim M. "Black Political Interests on Immigrant Rights: Evidence from Black Newspapers, 2000–2013." *Journal of African American Studies* 20, no. 3–4 (December 1, 2016): 248–71.

Williams, Kim M., and Lonnie Hannon. "Immigrant Rights in a Deep South City: The Effects of Anti-Immigrant Legislation on Black Elite Opinion in Birmingham, Alabama." *Du Bois Review* 13, no. 1 (2016): 139–57.

Wilson, Patrick. "For Moms: Hispanic Youth Group Sings the Praises of Mothers." *Winston-Salem Journal*, May 12, 2002, B1.

Wimmer, Andreas. "The Making and Unmaking of Ethnic Boundaries: A Multilevel Process Theory." *American Journal of Sociology* 113, no. 4 (2008): 970–1022.

Winders, Jamie. "Bringing Back the (B)order: Post-9/11 Politics of Immigration, Borders, and Belonging in the Contemporary US South." *Antipode* 39, no. 5 (November 1, 2007): 920–42.

Winders, Jamie. "Changing Politics of Race and Region: Latino Migration to the US South." *Progress in Human Geography* 29, no. 6 (2005): 683–99.

Winders, Jamie. *Nashville in the New Millennium: Immigrant Settlement, Urban Transformation, and Social Belonging*. New York: Russell Sage Foundation, 2013.

Winders, Jamie. "Nashville's New Sonido: Latino Migration and the Changing Politics of Race." In *New Faces in New Places: The Changing Geography of American Immigration*, edited by Douglas Massey, 249–73. New York: Russell Sage Foundation, 2008.

Winders, Jamie. "Re-Placing Southern Geographies: The Role of Latino Migration in Transforming the South, Its Identities, and Its Study." *Southeastern Geographer* 51, no. 2 (2011): 342–58.

Winders, Jamie. "Seeing Immigrants: Institutional Visibility and Immigrant Incorporation in New Immigrant Destinations." *Annals of the American Academy of Political and Social Science* 641 (2012): 58–78.

Winders, Jamie, and Barbara Ellen Smith. "Excepting/Accepting the South: New Geographies of Latino Migration, New Directions in Latino Studies." *Latino Studies* 10, no. 1–2 (2012): 220–45.

Yancey, George. *Who Is White?* Boulder, CO: Lynne Reiner, 2003.

Yes! Weekly. "Winston-Salem Wins National League of Cities Cultural Diversity Award." YES! Weekly (blog). Last modified April 3, 2017. http://yesweekly.com/winston-salem-wins-national-league-of-cities-cultural-diversity-award/

Young, Wesley. "Forsyth's New Face; Cultural Character of County Is in Flux; Census Estimate Shift Is in Youngest Age Groups." *Winston-Salem Journal*, August 15, 2007, A1.

Young, Wesley. "Mexican Consulate Promotes ID Program." *Winston-Salem Journal*, May 30, 2002, 1.

Zahniser, Steven, and William Coyle. "U.S.-Mexico Corn Trade during the NAFTA Era: New Twists to an Old Story." USDA electronic report. *Economic Research Service* (2004): 1–20.

Zamora, Sylvia. "Mexican Illegality, Black Citizenship, and White Power: Immigrant Perceptions of the U.S. Sociocial Hierarchy." *Journal of Ethnic and Migration Studies* (2017): 1–18.

Zengerele, Jason. "Is North Carolina the Future of American Politics?" *New York Times Magazine*, June 20, 2017. https://nyti.ms/2sKLLp1

Zepeda-Millán, Chris. *Latino Mass Mobilization: Immigration, Racialization, and Activism.* Cambridge: Cambridge University Press, 2017.

Zepeda-Millán, Chris, and Sophia J. Wallace. "Racialization in Times of Contention: How Social Movements Influence Latino Racial Identity." *Politics, Groups and Identities* 1, no. 4 (2013): 510–27.

Zhou, Min. "Segmented Assimilation: Issues, Controversies, and Recent Research on the New Second Generation." *International Migration Review* 31, no. 4 (1997): 975–1008.

Zúñiga, Víctor, and Rubén Hernández-León, eds. *New Destinations: Mexican Immigration in the United States.* New York: Russell Sage Foundation, 2005.

Index

Note: page numbers followed by "f" and "n" refer to figures and endnotes, respectively.